ATLAS OF MEDIEVAL EUROPE

The *Atlas of Medieval Europe* covers the period from the fall of the Roman Empire through to the beginnings of the Renaissance, spreading from the Atlantic coast to the Russian steppes. Each map approaches a separate issue or series of events in medieval history, and a commentary locates it in its broader context.

The maps provide a vivid representation of the development of nations, peoples and social structures. As well as charting political and military events, they illustrate the fluctuation of frontiers and patterns of settlement. They show the lands at the fringes of Christendom, the development of religious beliefs and practices, and the crusades, pogroms and persecutions that occurred across the continent. Individual maps take a detailed look at a variety of key areas including language and literature; the development of trade, art and architecture; and the great cities and lives of historical figures. This second edition has over forty new maps covering a variety of topics including the Moravian Empire, environmental change, the travels and correspondence of Froissart and travellers in the east, and the layout of great castles and palaces. Thorough coverage is also given to geographically peripheral areas such as Portugal, Poland, Scandinavia and Ireland.

The *Atlas of Medieval Europe* brings the complex and colourful history of the Middle Ages to life. With over 180 maps, expert commentaries and an extensive bibliography, this is the essential reference guide to medieval Europe.

David Ditchburn is Senior Lecturer in History at the University of Aberdeen. His publications include *Scotland and Europe: The Medieval Kingdom and its Contacts with Christendom, c. 1215–1545* (2001). **Simon MacLean** is Lecturer in Mediaeval History at the University of St Andrews. His publications include *Kingship and Politics in the Late Ninth Century: Charles the Fat and the End of the Carolingian Empire* (2003). **Angus MacKay** was Professor of Medieval History at the University of Edinburgh. His publications include *Spain in the Middle Ages: From Frontier to Empire, 1000–1500* (1977).

ATLAS
of
MEDIEVAL EUROPE

2nd Edition

EDITED BY DAVID DITCHBURN, SIMON MACLEAN
AND ANGUS MACKAY

Routledge
Taylor & Francis Group

LONDON AND NEW YORK

First published 2007
by Routledge
2 Park Square, Milton Park, Abingdon, Oxon OX14 4RN

Simultaneously published in the USA and Canada
by Routledge
270 Madison Ave, New York NY 10016

First published in paperback 1997
Reprinted 1998, 1999, 2000, 2002, 2003, 2005
Second edition published 2007

Routledge is an imprint of the Taylor & Francis Group, an informa business

Typeset in Garamond by
RefineCatch Limited, Bungay, Suffolk
Printed and bound in Great Britain by
TJ International Ltd, Padstow, Cornwall

British Library Cataloguing in Publication Data
A catalogue record for this book is available from the British Library

Library of Congress Cataloging in Publication Data
A catalog record for this book has been requested

ISBN10: 0–415–34454–9 (hbk)
ISBN10: 0–415–38302–1 (pbk)

ISBN13: 978–0–415–34454–8 (hbk)
ISBN13: 978–0–415–38302–8 (pbk)

CONTENTS

THE CENTRAL MIDDLE AGES, c. 1100–c. 1300

War and politics

Government, society and economy

Religion and culture

PREFACE TO THE SECOND EDITION

In the original preface to this volume Angus MacKay began by noting that the preparation of an atlas of medieval Europe presents numerous problems. One of the most difficult which we have faced in its revision has been in deciding what, exactly, to revise. In the event we have taken the opportunity to tidy up the prose, correct some errors and revise the bibliography, which within a decade (thanks perhaps to the UK's Research Assessment Exercise) is radically different to that published in the first edition. We might have left it there. But as one reviewer of the first edition commented, 'we all want more maps'. The temptation (within limits indulged by our publisher) was to fiddle, both with the order and with the content. While the three chronological sections of the first edition have been retained, the themes within each section have been reorganized. The sections on religion and culture have been merged since, especially in the earlier period, the two are so closely linked. Some maps and texts have also switched section. Indeed, several topics could be appropriately located in more than one section. We should make it clear that pragmatism has been the guiding principle in determining the ordering of themes. We are not suggesting that religion and culture are any less important than war and politics, or that the latter determine what follows.

Aside from reordering, some maps included in the first edition have disappeared. Many others have been revised. In addition, there are over forty new contributions. Much of the new material relates to what some may still regard as Europe's peripheries. There is more extensive treatment of Poland, in particular, but also of other parts of eastern Europe, as well as of Portugal, Ireland, the Low Countries and Scandinavia. We are acutely aware that gaps remain but we have tried to fill many of those noted in the (generous) reviews which were published of the first edition. In any case, despite the gaps, we hope that the geographical, chronological and thematic range makes for an effective introduction to medieval Europe as well as a useful reference tool.

It is not an easy task to supervise over fifty contributors. We owe particular thanks to those who met the deadline, even if only just. Barbara McGillivray, a veritable superwoman at the keyboard, retyped the first edition quickly and accurately, ensuring that it once again became a working document which could be easily revised. Andrew Johnstone provided sound advice on Dufay. At Taylor & Francis Eve Setch ensured that the project has not fallen too far behind schedule. Proofreading was undertaken efficiently by Susan Dunsmore.

Finally, we would like to note that although Angus MacKay was not directly involved in revising the volume, it remains very much a monument to his own wideranging research and teaching.

David Ditchburn
Department of History
University of Aberdeen
and
Simon MacLean
Department of Mediaeval History
University of St Andrews

PREFACE

The preparation of an atlas of the history of Europe during the Middle Ages presents numerous and complex difficulties. In the first place the period to be covered stretches from the late fourth century to the late fifteenth (or even early sixteenth) century. In addition, however, an atlas of this kind evidently cannot be confined to western Europe: Byzantium and eastern Europe have to be included, as indeed do such important matters as the exploits of crusading Europeans overseas, the impact of Muslims or Mongols, travel abroad, and the early voyages of discovery. In term of social groupings equally formidable problems present themselves. Obviously the main political events from the fall of the Roman Empire down to the battles and treaties of the Hundred Years War have to be included, but so too do the activities of other protagonists; for example, popes and antipopes, those who attended and participated in the great Church Councils or in parliamentary assemblies, Italian and Hanseatic merchants, tax collectors, women, colonists, peasants, shepherds (and their sheep), Jews and New Christians, heretics, writers and translators, troubadours, and architects and artists. Despite the difficulties inherent in such a task, however, the inclusion of such varied facets offers some positive advantages. For in addition to the emperors, kings, princes and great nobles, the artisans and peasants who participated in the French Jacquerie or the English revolt of 1381 left their mark on the period, as indeed did the humble Béguines and Beghards.

An atlas is an essential tool for the study of medieval history. This has long been recognized, but I believe that no adequate solution, specifically designed for this purpose, exists. When I was a student, which was admittedly a long time ago, we were advised to use a German atlas which was incredibly detailed and well nigh incomprehensible. The present volume does not aim at minute detail compressed into a few cluttered maps. On the contrary, the main objective has been clarity, and each map is accompanied by an explanatory text.

Using nearly 140 maps, the atlas spans the entire medieval period. The actual selection of maps to be included was primarily determined by the years of undergraduate teaching experienced by the editor and contributors.

I am extremely grateful to all those colleagues who have helped in preparing this volume. Those who have contributed the maps, the accompanying texts and suggestions for further reading (contained in the bibliography) have suffered from my incessant demands, requests for clarification and advice, and all the delays inevitable in bringing such a co-operative enterprise to its conclusion. I owe a special debt to David Ditchburn whose efficiency and versatile talents have frequently made me ashamed of my own shortcomings.

It was Richard Stoneman who originally conceived of the project, and his constant encouragement and exemplary patience have been much appreciated. His successive assistants – Anita Roy, Jackie Dias, Kate Morrall and particularly Victoria Peters – have all displayed charitable forbearance when dealing with my absent-mindedness.

Finally, special thanks are due to the cartographer, Jayne Lewin, for her skill in converting rough drafts or even mere sketches into clear maps, dealing patiently with late changes, and in resolving contradictions implicit in some of the difficult instructions sent in by contributors.

I hope that university undergraduates, senior school pupils and professional historians will find the atlas useful and rewarding. I also imagine that enlightened tourists interested in the history and culture of the countries they are visiting may benefit from the maps and commentaries provided by the expert contributors.

Angus MacKay
Department of History
University of Edinburgh

CONTRIBUTORS

Frances Andrews, University of St Andrews
Michael J. Angold, Edinburgh
Malcolm C. Barber, Reading
Robert J. Bartlett, University of St Andrews
Ian Beavan, University of Aberdeen
Philip E. Bennett, University of Edinburgh
Louise M. Bourdua, University of Aberdeen
Thomas S. Brown, University of Edinburgh
Marcus Bull, University of Bristol
Howard B. Clarke, Dublin
Simon Coates, London
Edward Coleman, University College Dublin
Antonio Collantes de Téran, University of
    Seville
Barbara Crawford, University of St Andrews
Sally Crumplin, University of St Andrews
Sumi David, University of St Andrews
E. Patricia Dennison, University of Edinburgh
Gary Dickson, Edinburgh
David Ditchburn, University of Aberdeen
Sally Dixon-Smith, The Tower of London
Clare Downham, University of Aberdeen
Marilyn Dunn, University of Glasgow
Susannah C. Humble Ferreira, University of
    Guelph
Robin Frame, Durham
Edda Frankot, University of Groningen
Robert I. Frost, University of Aberdeen
Manuel González Jiménez, University of
    Seville
Anthony Goodman, Edinburgh
Alexander Grant, University of Lancaster
Philip Hersch
John C. Higgitt, University of Edinburgh

Richard A. Hodges, University of East Anglia
Michael C.E. Jones, Nottingham
Ewan Johnson, University of Lancaster
Hugh N. Kennedy, University of St Andrews
Derek Lomax (deceased)
Raymond McCluskey, University of Glasgow
Alastair J. Macdonald, University of Aberdeen
Jennifer McDonald, University of Bergen
Angus MacKay, Edinburgh
Martin L. McLaughlin, University of Oxford
Simon MacLean, University of St Andrews
Norman Macleod, University of Edinburgh
M. Michèle Mulchahey, University of St
    Andrews
Malyn D.D. Newitt, King's College London
Richard Oram, University of Stirling
Esther Pascua, University of St Andrews
Theo Riches, University of Birmingham
Andrew P. Roach, University of Glasgow
Richard K. Rose
Michael L. Ryder, Edinburgh
Ross Samson, Glasgow
Elina Screen, University of Cambridge
Julia M.H. Smith, University of Glasgow
Clive R. Sneddon, University of St Andrews
Angus D. Stewart, University of St Andrews
Roger Tarr, Edinburgh
Alfred Thomas, Harvard University
Elspeth M. Turner, University of Edinburgh
Ian Wei, University of Bristol
Björn Weiler, University of Wales,
    Aberystwyth
Christopher J. Wickham, University of Oxford
Alex Woolf, University of St Andrews

PHYSICAL EUROPE

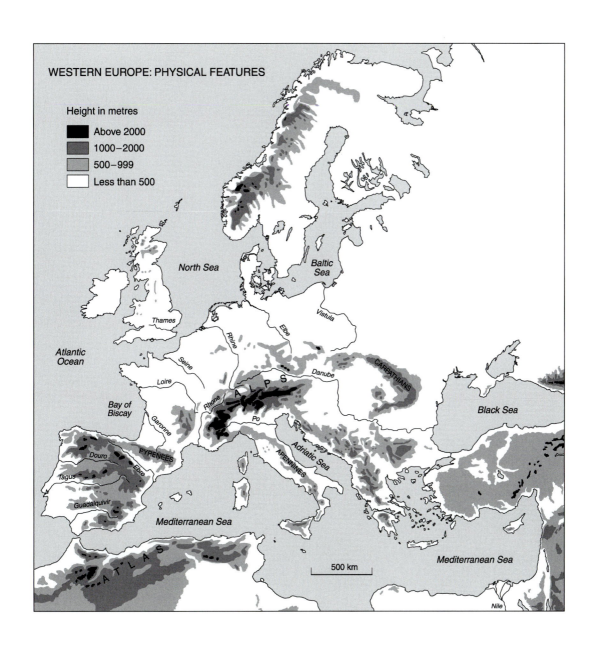

WESTERN EUROPE: PHYSICAL FEATURES

Height in metres

- Above 2000
- 1000–2000
- 500–999
- Less than 500

North Sea

Baltic Sea

Atlantic Ocean

Thames

Vistula

Rhine

Elbe

Seine

Loire

Danube

CARPATHIANS

Bay of Biscay

Garonne

Rhône

A L P S

Po

Black Sea

Douro

Ebro

PYRENEES

Adriatic Sea

Tagus

APENNINES

Guadalquivir

Mediterranean Sea

A T L A S

500 km

Mediterranean Sea

Nile

THE EARLY MIDDLE AGES,
c. 395–*c.* 1050

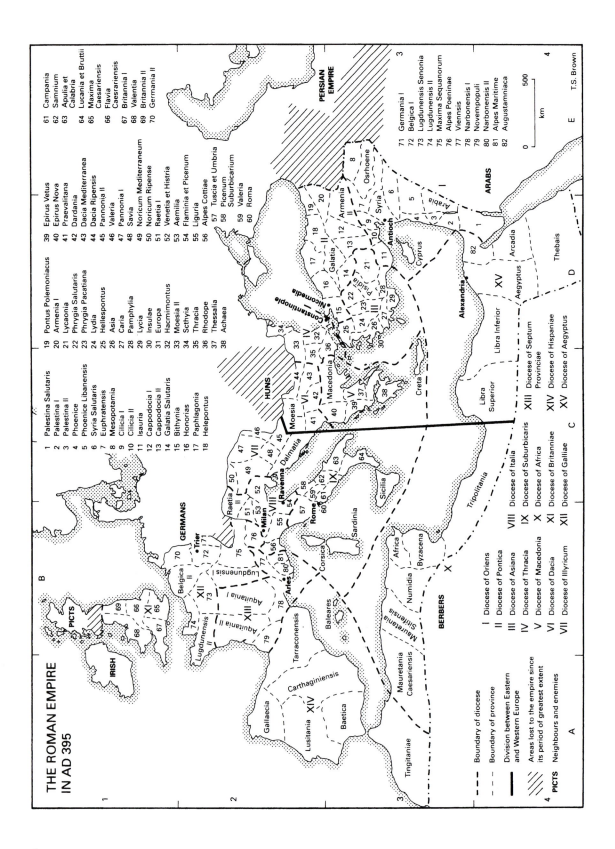

THE ROMAN EMPIRE
IN AD 395

1	Palestina Salutaris	39	Epirus Vetus
2	Palestina I	40	Epirus Nova
3	Palestina II	41	Praevalitana
4	Phoenice	42	Dardania
5	Phoenice Libanensis	43	Dacia Mediterranea
6	Syria Salutaris	44	Dacia Ripensis
7	Euphratensis	45	Pannonia II
8	Mesopotamia	46	Valeria
9	Cilicia I	47	Pannonia I
10	Cilicia II	48	Savia
11	Isauria	49	Noricum Mediterraneum
12	Cappadocia I	50	Noricum Ripense
13	Cappadocia II	51	Raetia I
14	Galatia Salutaris	52	Venetia et Histria
15	Bithynia	53	Aemilia
16	Honorias	54	Flaminia et Picenum
17	Paphlagonia	55	Liguria
18	Helepontus	56	Alpes Cottiae
19	Pontus Polemoniacus	57	Tuscia et Umbria
20	Armenia I	58	Picenum Suburbicarium
21	Lycaonia	59	Valeria
22	Phrygia Salutaris	60	Roma
23	Phrygia Pacatiana	61	Campania
24	Lydia	62	Samnium
25	Hellespontus	63	Apulia et Calabria
26	Asia	64	Lucania et Bruttii
27	Caria	65	Maxima
28	Pamphylia	66	Flavia Caesariensis
29	Lycia	67	Britannia I
30	Insulae	68	Valentia
31	Europa	69	Britannia II
32	Hacmimontus	70	Germania II
33	Moesia II	71	Germania I
34	Scthyia	72	Belgica I
35	Thracia	73	Lugdunensis Senonia
36	Rhodope	74	Lugdunensis II
37	Thessalia	75	Maxima Sequanorum
38	Achaea	76	Alpes Poeninae
		77	Viennsis
		78	Narbonensis I
		79	Novempopuli
		80	Narbonensis II
		81	Alpes Maritime
		82	Augustamniaca

I	Diocese of Oriens
II	Diocese of Pontica
III	Diocese of Asiana
IV	Diocese of Thracia
V	Diocese of Macedonia
VI	Diocese of Dacia
VII	Diocese of Illyricum
VIII	Diocese of Italia
IX	Diocese of Suburbicaris
X	Diocese of Africa
XI	Diocese of Britanniae
XII	Diocese of Galliae
XIII	Diocese of Septum Provinciae
XIV	Diocese of Hispaniae
XV	Diocese of Aegyptus

- – – – Boundary of diocese
- – – – Boundary of province
- —— Division between Eastern and Western Europe
- ——— Areas lost to the empire since its period of greatest extent
- PICTS Neighbours and enemies

0 — 500 km

T.S. Brown

WAR AND POLITICS

The Roman Empire in AD 395

By AD 395 the Roman Empire had changed considerably since the time of its first emperor, Augustus (27 BC–AD 14). Increased external pressures, deteriorating economic conditions and political disorder, aggravated by dynastic insecurity and the ambitions of generals, led to the abandonment of outlying provinces and a period of prolonged upheaval in the third century. A major reorganization introduced by Diocletian (284–305) and continued by Constantine (306–37) saw the elevation of the emperor into a remote autocrat along Eastern lines, the creation of a large bureaucracy and a division of the army into a two-tier force consisting of elite mobile units and poorer quality local troops. In an attempt to improve local efficiency and to minimize the risk of revolt Diocletian doubled the number of provinces and grouped them into dioceses under *vicarii*, while Constantine established a separation of powers between civil governors and military commanders. After defeating his opponents at the Milvian Bridge (312), Constantine became a Christian. He promoted what had been a minority faith by appointing Christians to key positions and endowing the Church with lands and buildings. Theological divisions remained, however, acute and pagan rites were not proscribed until the reign of Theodosius I (378–95). Constantine's transfer of the capital to the strategic site of Byzantium, re-named Constantinople in 330, reflected both his commitment to his new faith and the increasing importance of the East in the Empire.

These changes produced a measure of political and economic stability although Constantine's dynasty was riven by family disputes. It died out after the death of the short-lived pagan Emperor Julian, fighting the Persians in 363. During the reigns of the succeeding emperors barbarian pressure on the frontiers increased, partly as a result of the arrival of the Hun nomads in Europe in the 370s. The Visigoths successfully requested asylum in the Empire in 376 but ill treatment led them to turn against the Romans and to wipe out a Roman army at the battle of Adrianople (378), in which the Emperor Valens was killed. This defeat was a great blow to Roman prestige but the direct effects were limited. The Goths were granted lands in the Balkans as *foederati* (allies) and order was restored by the staunchly Christian Spanish emperor, Theodosius I.

Following Theodosius' death in 395 a critical stage in the transformation of the Roman world occurred with the division of the Empire between his sons Honorius (West) and Arcadius (East). While the myth of imperial unity was maintained, tension grew between the two courts. The Eastern empire remained relatively powerful as a result of its greater wealth and population and its relative immunity from barbarian pressure and the dangerous influence which German mercenaries exercised in the West. Christianity became strongly entrenched and, despite bitter christological controversies, served to reinforce imperial authority by treating the Empire as an instrument of divine policy. In the West fundamental economic and social weaknesses were aggravated by court intrigues, the self-interest of the senatorial elite and frequent revolts by usurpers. While Roman administration, society and culture remained resilient at the highest levels, the decentralization of the *pars occidentalis* was reflected in the growth of non-Roman cultures (as in Britain and North Africa) and the rise of local political allegiances (as in Gaul) even before the full effects of the barbarian migrations were felt in the fifth century.

T.S. Brown

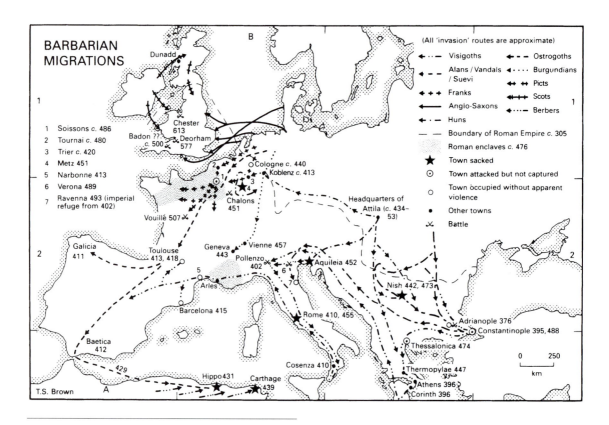

BARBARIAN MIGRATIONS

(All 'invasion' routes are approximate)

- ◄···─ Visigoths
- ◄─── Ostrogoths
- ◄─ ─ Alans / Vandals / Suevi
- ◄···· Burgundians
- ◄ + + Franks
- ◄+─+ Picts
- ◄─── Anglo-Saxons
- ◄+─+ Scots
- ◄─·─ Huns
- ◄···· Berbers
- ── ── Boundary of Roman Empire c. 305
- Roman enclaves c. 476
- ★ Town sacked
- ⊙ Town attacked but not captured
- ○ Town occupied without apparent violence
- • Other towns
- ✕ Battle

1 Soissons c. 486
2 Tournai c. 480
3 Trier c. 420
4 Metz 451
5 Narbonne 413
6 Verona 489
7 Ravenna 493 (imperial refuge from 402)

Dunadd
Chester 613
Badon ?? c. 500
Deorham 577
Cologne c. 440
Koblenz c. 413
Chalons 451
Vouillé 507
Headquarters of Attila (c. 434–53)
Galicia 411
Toulouse 413, 418
Geneva 443
Vienne 457
Pollenzo 402
Arles
Aquileia 452
Nish 442, 473
Barcelona 415
Rome 410, 455
Adrianople 376
Constantinople 395, 488
Baetica 412
Thessalonica 474
429
Cosenza 410
Thermopylae 447
Hippo 431
Carthage 439
Athens 396
Corinth 396

0   250
km

T.S. Brown

Barbarian migrations of the 4th and 5th centuries

The pressure from 'barbarians' (mostly Germans) which the Roman Empire had experienced from the late second century became more intense in the late fourth. This *Völkerwanderung* (wandering of the peoples) involved unstable amalgams of diverse groups, many of whom settled gradually and relatively peacefully. The pressure of steppe nomads such as the Huns from *c.* 370 played a role but probably more important were rivalries among the Germanic peoples, the formation of confederacies under aggressive military leaders from the third century and the opportunities presented to booty-hungry war-leaders and their retinues by Rome's political, military and financial weaknesses and the increasing alienation of Roman provincials from centralized rule.

The first serious case of Germanic penetration occurred after 376, as Visigothic and Ostrogothic tribes living beyond the Danube sought refuge as Roman allies (*foederati*) within the Empire. Tension led to the battle of Adrianople in which a largely Visigothic force defeated a Roman army and killed the Emperor Valens. Although a treaty was soon arranged the Visigoths continued to ravage Greece and Illyricum until, in 402, they entered Italy under the leadership of Alaric. A cat-and-mouse game took place while the imperial government in Ravenna prevaricated in the face of Gothic demands for land and gold. Finally Alaric's exasperation led to the sack of Rome in August 410 – an enormous blow to Roman morale. Alaric died soon afterwards and his brother-in-law, Ataulf, led the Goths to southern Gaul, where they were recognized as *foederati* by a treaty in 416. Under their kings Theodoric I and II and Euric they built a powerful state based on Toulouse which had generally good relations with the Roman aristocracy and established overlordship in Spain.

The Germanic peoples who had remained north of the Danube (Herules, Gepids, Rugi, Skiri and Ostrogoths) became subjects of the Huns, who built a tributary empire under Attila (434–53). While launching regular attacks on the east Roman provinces in the Balkans, Attila remained friendly with Aetius, the dominant force in the west, until he was induced to launch inconclusive raids into Gaul (checked by his defeat at Chalons in 451) and northern Italy. The collapse of the Hun empire following Attila's death in 453 led to renewed pressure by Germanic bands (Ostrogoths, Rugi and others) on the Danube frontier.

Meanwhile, northern Gaul had been thrown into confusion by the rupture of the Rhine frontier in late 406 by a mixed barbarian force dominated by Vandals, Suevi and Alans. While some Alans became Roman allies in Gaul, others joined the Vandal invasion of Spain in 409. The Suevi set up a robber kingdom based on Galicia which lasted until 585. In the face of Visigoth pressure the Vandals sailed to Africa in 429 and were granted the western provinces by a treaty of 435. Their able king, Geiseric, seized Carthage in 439, occupied the rest of Roman Africa and launched a series of lucrative naval raids, occupying Sicily, Sardinia and Corsica and sacking Rome in 455. Following his death in 477 the aggressive and confiscatory policies towards the Roman aristocracy and the Catholic Church gave way to a generally more conciliatory and Romanizing regime.

The collapse of the Rhine frontier in 406/7 had wide repercussions. Britain saw its Roman garrison withdrawn and the assumption of power by rival British chieftains until the Anglo-Saxon invasions in the late 440s. The Burgundians were permitted to set up a kingdom on the upper Rhine in 413. Transferred as federates to the Jura/Lake Geneva area in 443, they built up a Romanized kingdom incorporating the Lyon and Vienne areas from 457. Along the middle and lower Rhine groups of Franks became powerful and attacked cities such as Cologne and Trier. In northern Gaul Roman rule was undermined by obscure rivalries between usurping generals, Bretons, peasant rebels (Bagaudae), Alans and the sub-Roman regimes of Aegidius and his son Syagrius based on Soissons (c. 456–86). The long-term beneficiary of this power vacuum was the Salian Frank dynasty of Childeric (d. 481) and his son Clovis, who gradually expanded from their original centre of Tournai by conquering or allying themselves with rival bands of Franks, including established *laeti* (soldier-farmers).

T.S. Brown

Barbarian kingdoms in the first half of the 6th century

By 500 the Roman Empire in the west had been replaced by powerful Germanic kingdoms. Prominent were the Frankish kingdom, built in northern Gaul by the Frankish rulers Childeric (d. 481) and his son Clovis (481–511), and the Ostrogothic kingdom, established in Italy by Theoderic (489–526). Any semblance of stability in the west was, however, shattered over the next four decades. After his victory over the kingdom of Toulouse at Vouillé in 507 Clovis took over most of south-west Gaul and the Visigoths were compelled to transfer their political base to Spain, with their eventual capital at Toledo. The kingdom of their Ostrogothic cousins fell into decline on Theoderic's death as a result of dynastic uncertainties and tension between pro-Roman and traditionalist elements. Two of the initially powerful kingdoms were conquered in 533–4: the Burgundians' territories in south-east Gaul were

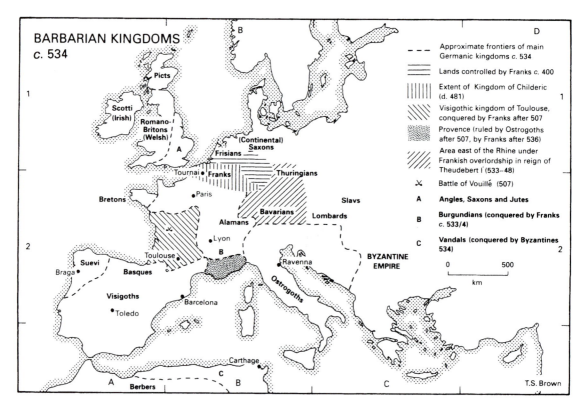

BARBARIAN KINGDOMS
c. 534

- - - Approximate frontiers of main Germanic kingdoms c. 534

Lands controlled by Franks c. 400

Extent of Kingdom of Childeric (d. 481)

Visigothic kingdom of Toulouse, conquered by Franks after 507

Provence (ruled by Ostrogoths after 507, by Franks after 536)

Area east of the Rhine under Frankish overlordship in reign of Theudebert I (533–48)

✕ Battle of Vouillé (507)

A Angles, Saxons and Jutes

B Burgundians (conquered by Franks c. 533/4)

C Vandals (conquered by Byzantines 534)

0   500
        km

Picts
Scotti (Irish)
Romano-Britons (Welsh)
(Continental) Saxons
Frisians
Tournai Franks
Paris
Bretons
Thuringians
Slavs
Bavarians
Lombards
Alamans
Lyon
Toulouse
Suevi
Braga
Basques
Visigoths
Barcelona
Toledo
Ravenna
Ostrogoths
BYZANTINE EMPIRE
Carthage
Berbers
T.S. Brown

incorporated by the Franks and Vandal rule in North Africa was ended by the lightning campaign of the Byzantine general Belisarius. In 534 the Ostrogoths became the next target of the Emperor Justinian's dream of restoring Roman power in the west and Belisarius' forces invaded Italy in 536. Despite fierce resistance by a Gothic army in the north led by Witigis, Belisarius occupied Ravenna in 540. In the 540s the tide turned, thanks to the divisions and corruption of the imperialists. The able Gothic ruler Totila was able to claw back most of the peninsula. By 552, however, new forces dispatched from the east under Narses defeated the Ostrogothic army. Isolated pockets of Gothic resistance held out in the north until the 560s and Italy lay devastated by years of war. Justinian's attempted *reconquista* of the west went a step further in 551, when an enclave around Cartagena was seized from the Visigothic kingdom of Spain and remained Byzantine until the 620s. Nevertheless, economic weaknesses and new pressure from the Avars, Slavs and Persians prevented Byzantium from consolidating its gains. Most of Italy was lost to the Lombards from 568. The dominant power in the west became, not the Empire but its nominal ally, the Catholic kingdom of the Franks.

T.S. Brown

Merovingian Gaul, c. 600

Although Clovis extended the Merovingian kingdom over most of Gaul, for much of the sixth and seventh centuries it was beset by strife, vividly chronicled by Gregory of Tours

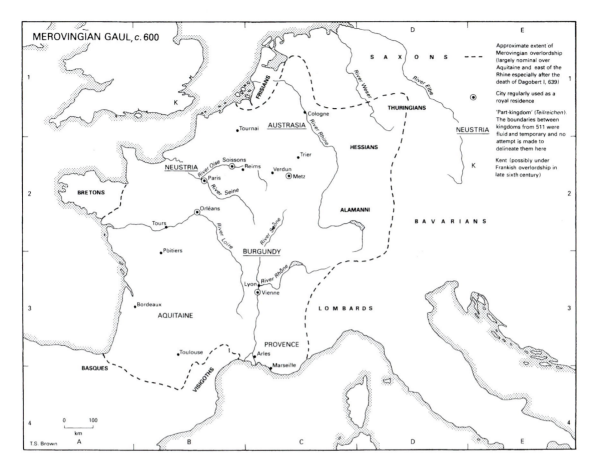

MEROVINGIAN GAUL, c. 600

Approximate extent of Merovingian overlordship (largely nominal over Aquitaine and east of the Rhine especially after the death of Dagobert I, 639)

City regularly used as a royal residence

'Part-kingdom' (Teilreichen). The boundaries between kingdoms from 511 were fluid and temporary and no attempt is made to delineate them here

Kent (possibly under Frankish overlordship in late sixth century)

SAXONS

FRISIANS

AUSTRASIA

Tournai

THURINGIANS

NEUSTRIA

Cologne

River Weser

River Elbe

HESSIANS

Trier

NEUSTRIA

Soissons

River Oise

Reims

Verdun

Paris

Metz

River Rhine

River Seine

BRETONS

Orléans

ALAMANNI

BAVARIANS

Tours

River Loire

Poitiers

BURGUNDY

River Saône

Lyon

River Rhône

Vienne

LOMBARDS

Bordeaux

AQUITAINE

PROVENCE

Toulouse

Arles

Marseille

BASQUES

VISIGOTHS

0   100
km

T.S. Brown

(d. 594). In 511 a complex division took place between Clovis' four sons, hampering efficient royal administration. The Burgundian kingdom was taken over in 534 and Provence in 536. Theudebert I (533–48) expanded his territory east of the Rhine and beyond the Alps but this overlordship collapsed after his death. The kingdom was then reunited under Clothar but partition between his four sons in 561 led to civil war and an increasing sense of identity within each *Teilreich* (part-kingdom).

The murder of King Sigibert of Austrasia in 575 provoked bitter conflict. His powerful widow, the Visigoth Brunhilda, was executed in 613 and the kingdom was reunited under Clothar II of Neustria (584–629). His son, Dagobert I (623–38), proved the last effective Merovingian ruler. Royal power declined with the alienation of rights and estates, the loss of Byzantine subsidies and tribute from client

peoples east of the Rhine and the growing power of counts and other territorial magnates. Subsequent Merovingian 'do-nothing kings' were incapable of ruling personally. Power was assumed by aristocratic factions, one led by the Arnulfings, hereditary mayors of the palace of Austrasia. Under Pepin II this family capitalized on its following in the north-east and its alliance with the Church to become the dominant force throughout the kingdom from 687. A revolt followed Pepin's death in 714 but power over Neustria and the Merovingian puppet-kings was restored by his illegitimate son, Charles Martel (d. 741), who enhanced the power and prestige of his dynasty (the Carolingians) by campaigning against Saxons, Alamans, Thuringians and Bavarians and most famously by his defeat of an Arab force at Poitiers in 733.

The conflicts of the Merovingian period

11

should not obscure its achievements. The kingdom remained the most powerful force in the west as a result of its military strength, its relatively centralized structures, a number of centres of religious and cultural life, and the assimilation which occurred between a small Frankish elite and Gallo-Roman elements prepared to adopt Frankish laws and customs.

T.S. Brown

The Empire of Justinian, 527–65

When Justinian ascended the throne in 527 the Empire had reasonably well-defined frontiers (the Danube, the Euphrates and the Arabian and Egyptian deserts), defended by powerful fortresses (such as Singidunum, Dara and Edessa). Threats, such as the Sassanian Persians in the east, the Bulgars along the lower Danube and the desert tribes, were mostly contained. Internally there were rivalries between circus factions but religious division was more serious. Some valued ecclesiastical unity and the link with the papacy, enshrined at the Council of Chalcedon (451). Others favoured an independent Byzantine Church. The latter had been in the ascendant since *c.* 484, when the Acacian schism separated the Churches of Rome and Constantinople. Even before 527 Justinian worked for communion with Rome. Achieved in 518, this reorientation implied greater interest in the west, now dominated by Germanic tribes which had adopted the Arian heresy. There was some discrimination against native Catholic communities and in North Africa, under the Vandals, outright persecution. Justinian saw himself as the Catholic Church's protector. In 533 he attacked the Vandals. His commander, Belisarius, captured Carthage (the Vandalic capital) and North Africa. Then, in 535, Belisarius seized Sicily and invaded Ostrogothic Italy. Rome was taken in 536. Its successful defence sapped Ostrogothic resistance and he entered the Ostrogoth capital of Ravenna in 540. The Ostrogoths were confined to the Po valley.

These relatively easy victories were tested over the next decade. The Sassanian king of kings, Chosroes I (531–79), sacked Antioch in 540. His armies captured Petra, which commanded access to the Black Sea and control of Lazica. In 544 the city of Edessa beat off a Persian attack and a truce was concluded. Both sides were suffering from the bubonic plague which had struck in 541/2. The death toll at Constantinople was calamitous, with government and economy paralysed. The Ostrogoths then recovered most of Italy and the Slavs, massed along the Danube, raided deep into the Empire's European provinces. Justinian's government slowly recovered its equilibrium. In 550 Slav raiders were removed. In 552 Narses invaded Italy with an army recruited heavily beyond the Danube, from the Herules, the Gepids and Lombards. The Ostrogoths were overwhelmed and Italy reclaimed. Meanwhile, an expedition despatched in 550 recovered southern Spain from the Visigoths and the African coast around Septem (Ceuta). Petra was recovered from the Sassanians in 551 and with it control of Lazica. In the desert war the Ghassanids, an Arab tribe allied to the Byzantines, bested the Lakmids, who were clients of the Sassanians. In 562 a peace was concluded between Persia and Byzantium, designed to last for fifty years. It regulated cross-border trade, trade routes being an element in Byzantine-Sassanian rivalry. The Byzantines were dependent on these for raw silk to feed their industry which was centred on Berytus.

Thanks to heavy investment in fortifications, the Danube frontier held but there was intense pressure from the Slavs and others crowded along it. To counter this, Justinian turned to the Avars, recently arrived from central Asia and settled north of the Crimea. It was a

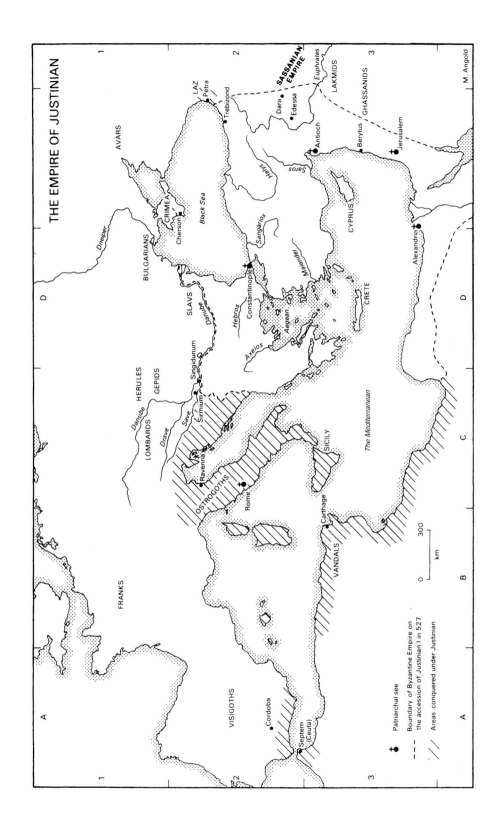

THE EMPIRE OF JUSTINIAN

M. Angold

Patriarchal see
Boundary of Byzantine Empire on
the accession of Justinian I in 527
Areas conquered under Justinian

0   300
km

13

miscalculation. After his death the Avars destroyed the Gepids (567), pushed the Lombards into Italy and intensified Slav raiding of Byzantine territories. The eventual disintegration of Justinian's empire was already apparent in the ecclesiastical field, where independent Churches were emerging in Syria and Egypt. It has been said that 'Justinian's reign witnessed a belated attempt to unify a far-flung Empire that was gradually losing its cohesion'.

M. Angold

The expansion of Islam in the Mediterranean area, 7th–9th centuries

Within ten years of Mohammad's death in 632 the armies of Islam stormed out of Arabia, overwhelmed the Sassanians of Persia and wrested Syria, Palestine and Egypt from the Byzantine Empire. The Arabs were formidable because of their mobility. In 636 they concentrated at Yarmuk beyond the Jordan and completely defeated the Byzantine armies. Victory brought them Damascus, which became their headquarters. In 637/8 Jerusalem fell, followed quickly by Antioch and Edessa. The conquest of Palestine and Syria was completed in 642 when Caesarea was captured. Gaza had already fallen and the conquest of Egypt was completed with the surrender of Alexandria (642).

The Byzantine Empire met the challenge. It contained the Arabs in Anatolia by evolving the *theme* system of defence. Initially this meant dividing Anatolia into three military commands: Opsikion, Anatolikon and Armeniakon. The Opsikion, originally the strategic reserve, was now quartered across the approaches to Constantinople. The Anatolikon was the old army of the East but now withdrawn to defend south-eastern Anatolia. The Armeniakon was the army of Armenia, now established in northern Anatolia and covering the routes from Melitene and the middle Euphrates.

The threat from the Arabs was all the more formidable because they took to the sea. They occupied Cyprus (649–50) and destroyed the Byzantine fleet at Phoinix (655), off the coast of Anatolia. Constantinople was blockaded (674–8) but the attack was beaten off with Greek fire. Another assault failed in 718. From then Constantinople and Anatolia were relatively secure, though there were intermittent raids until the mid-ninth century, some penetrating to within striking distance of Constantinople.

The Byzantines were less successful in holding the Arabs in the Mediterranean. Carthage finally succumbed in 697 and from their new capital of Kairuan the Arabs converted the Berbers. This fuelled the Muslim advance into Spain. Toledo, the Visigothic capital, fell in 711 and by 718 the conquest of Spain was virtually complete. The Muslims advanced northwards but their defeat in 732 by the Franks at the battle of Tours limited further conquests in this area. Their efforts were instead concentrated in the Mediterranean. Crete fell in 824 and a start was made on the conquest of Sicily by the Byzantines. They established a base at Palermo but it was not until 878 that the Byzantine provincial capital of Syracuse fell. In 840 Bari was captured and became the centre of an emirate which terrorized southern Italy and the Adriatic. It was recovered in 876 by the Byzantines and a degree of stability was restored in the central Mediterranean.

The Muslim advance stretched Byzantine resources to their limit, for Byzantium was also involved in the Balkans. In 582 Sirmium fell to the Avars and their Slav tributaries swarmed into the Balkans. They settled on a permanent basis and penetrated as far south as the Peloponnese, where Monemvasia provided a refuge for the native population. In 679 the Bulgarians crossed the Danube and settled the lands to the

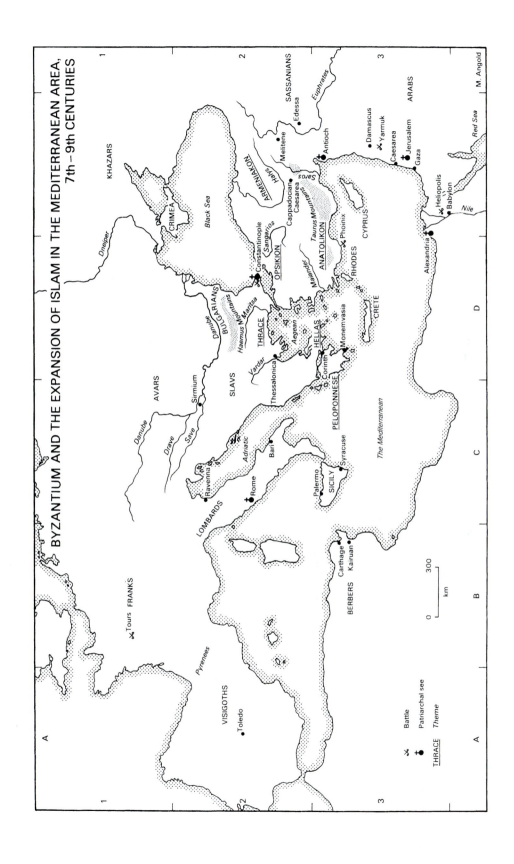

BYZANTIUM AND THE EXPANSION OF ISLAM IN THE MEDITERRANEAN AREA,
7th–9th CENTURIES

M. Angold

15

south. Byzantine territories were now limited to Thrace and a few towns along the fringes of the Aegean, such as Thessalonica, which withstood a series of Slav sieges. To hold these areas the *themes* of Thrace and Hellas were established at the end of the seventh century. From the late eighth century a determined effort was made to strengthen the Byzantine hold in Europe. This culminated in the reoccupation of the Pelopon-nese and the creation (*c.* 805) of the *theme* of the Peloponnese with its headquarters at Corinth.

The Byzantine Empire survived the assaults and losses of territory which occurred from the seventh to the early ninth centuries. In many ways, it emerged stronger, thanks to its capital Constantinople and the evolution of the *theme* system.

M. Angold

Italy in the 8th century

The invasion launched by war-bands of Lombard and other peoples led by Alboin in 568 had a decisive effect on the map of Italy for centuries. Much of the north was conquered, including Milan (569) and Pavia (572). Inadequate Byzantine garrisons were thrown into disarray and Lombard raiding parties penetrated Tuscany and the Rome area. Semi-autonomous duchies were set up at Spoleto and Benevento. Gradually the Empire put up more effective resistance by exploiting Lombard divisions, bribing the Franks to invade the Lombard kingdom, recruiting Lombard rene-gades as mercenaries and concentrating authority in the hands of one military governor, known by 584 as the Exarch. By 603, when a truce was declared, the Empire retained secure control of Rome, Ravenna, a corridor along the Via Amerina through Umbria, and coastal enclaves around Venice, Genoa, Naples and other southern cities.

For much of the seventh century the frontier remained static, broken by King Rothari's capture of Genoa (643) and the defeat of the Emperor Constans' expedition against Benevento (663/4). As the Empire became increasingly endangered in the east, more power within the Byzantine territories was exercised by local military garrisons, their leaders and (in the case of Rome) by the pope. In the Lombard kingdom dynastic instability did not prevent increasing prosperity and adoption of Roman institutions. By *c.* 680 the Lombards had dropped their Arian and pagan beliefs in favour of Catholic Christianity and secured recognition from the Empire. Gradually their pressure on the imperial provinces increased, as the Romans became discontented with the religious and taxation policies of the eastern Empire. King Liutprand (712–44) tried to unite Italy under Lombard rule. Resistance was led by the popes, who remained essentially loyal to Byzantium although they were unable to gain substantial aid from their imperial 'protectors'. Following the Lombard Aistulf's capture of Ravenna (751), and threats to Rome, Pope Stephen II (752–7) obtained the intervention of the Frankish king, Pepin III. He defeated Aistulf and recognized sweeping papal claims in central Italy (Donation of Pepin, 756). Threats were renewed by Aistulf's successor, Desiderius, against Pope Hadrian I (772–95), who called on Pepin's son, Charlemagne, to intervene in 773. In 774 he captured Pavia and became king of the Lombards. The Lombard kingdom retained its distinctive social and governmental institutions and only gradually did an influx of Frankish officials and an increase in the wealth and power of the Church take place.

The political map of Italy remained confused in the late eighth century. Benevento (unlike Spoleto) remained outside effective Frankish control. It became a principality and a centre of traditional Lombard legitimacy under Desiderius' son-in-law, Arichis, often allying itself with Byzantium to preserve its independence.

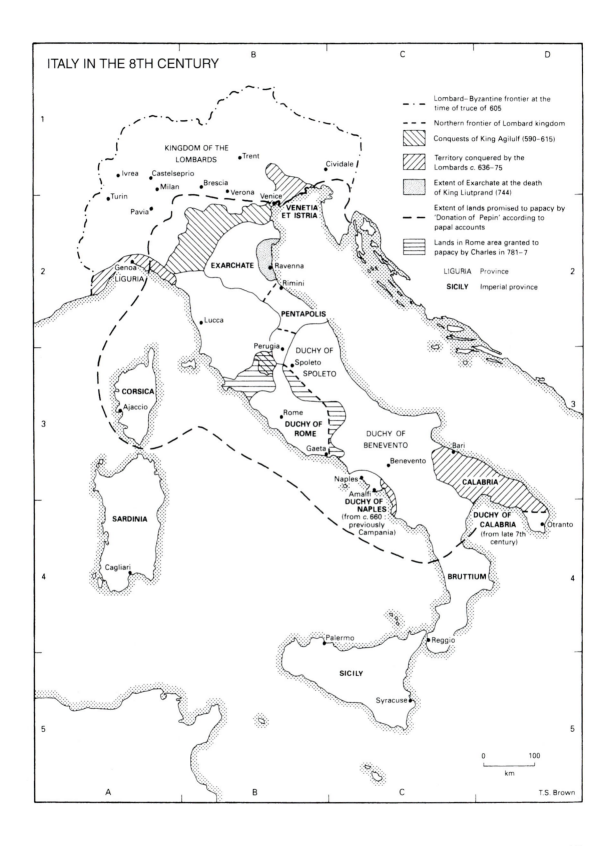

ITALY IN THE 8TH CENTURY

- - · - Lombard–Byzantine frontier at the time of truce of 605
- - - Northern frontier of Lombard kingdom
Conquests of King Agilulf (590–615)
Territory conquered by the Lombards c. 636–75
Extent of Exarchate at the death of King Liutprand (744)
Extent of lands promised to papacy by 'Donation of Pepin' according to papal accounts
Lands in Rome area granted to papacy by Charles in 781–7

LIGURIA   Province
SICILY   Imperial province

KINGDOM OF THE LOMBARDS

Trent
Cividale
Ivrea
Castelseprio
Milan
Brescia
Verona
Turin
Venice
Pavia
VENETIA ET ISTRIA
Genoa
LIGURIA
EXARCHATE
Ravenna
Rimini
Lucca
PENTAPOLIS
Perugia
DUCHY OF SPOLETO
Spoleto
CORSICA
Ajaccio
Rome
DUCHY OF ROME
Gaeta
DUCHY OF BENEVENTO
Bari
Naples
Benevento
Amalfi
DUCHY OF NAPLES
(from c. 660 : previously Campania)
CALABRIA
DUCHY OF CALABRIA
(from late 7th century)
Otranto
SARDINIA
Cagliari
BRUTTIUM
Palermo
Reggio
SICILY
Syracuse

0   100
km

T.S. Brown

17

The Empire retained Sicily and footholds in Calabria and Apulia, together with the nominal allegiance of the maritime cities of Amalfi, Gaeta, Naples and Venice. Istria fell to the Franks in the late eighth century. The papacy's claim to much of central Italy, including southern Tuscany, Spoleto, the duchy of Rome and the old Exarchate, was zealously propagated by Lateran officials on the basis of the Donation of Constantine (a contemporary forgery), as well as the vague promises of the Frankish kings. In no sense was this, however, a papal state. In many areas the papacy was more concerned with estates and rights than overall jurisdiction. In others the Franks were induced by bribes or *Realpolitik* to leave power in the hands of local figures such as the archbishop of Ravenna. Even in the duchy of Rome, the papacy's authority was not secure, as shown by the revolt against Pope Leo III (795–816) which led to the latter's appeal to Charlemagne for aid and the Frankish king's assumption of the imperial title in St Peter's on Christmas Day 800.

T.S. Brown

The Empire of Charlemagne, 768–814

Charles Martel (mayor of the palace 715–41) and Pepin III (mayor 741–51, king 751–68) established the dominance of the Arnulfing/ Carolingian family in Francia by military success against Arabs, Aquitanians, Frisians and various peoples east of the Rhine, by building networks of aristocratic support and by forging a close alliance with the Church. Following his election as king, Pepin launched two expeditions against the Lombards. He then campaigned against the Aquitanians and Saxons. On his death the kingdom was divided

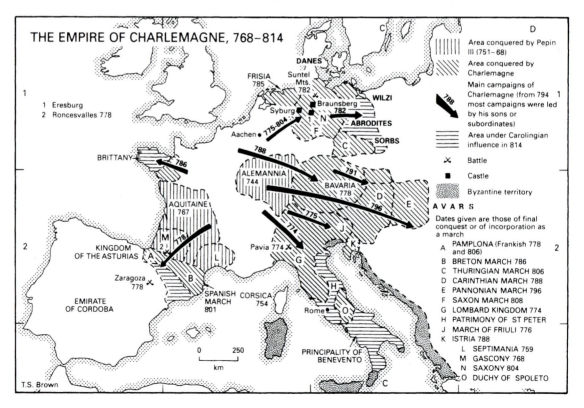

THE EMPIRE OF CHARLEMAGNE, 768–814

1 Eresburg
2 Roncesvalles 778

|||| Area conquered by Pepin III (751–68)
Area conquered by Charlemagne
Main campaigns of Charlemagne (from 794 most campaigns were led by his sons or subordinates)
Area under Carolingian influence in 814
✗ Battle
■ Castle
Byzantine territory

Dates given are those of final conquest or of incorporation as a march

A PAMPLONA (Frankish 778 and 806)
B BRETON MARCH 786
C THURINGIAN MARCH 806
D CARINTHIAN MARCH 788
E PANNONIAN MARCH 796
F SAXON MARCH 808
G LOMBARD KINGDOM 774
H PATRIMONY OF ST PETER
J MARCH OF FRIULI 776
K ISTRIA 788
L SEPTIMANIA 759
M GASCONY 768
N SAXONY 804
O DUCHY OF SPOLETO

T.S. Brown

between his sons but when the younger, Carloman, died (771), the elder, Charlemagne (Charles 'the Great'), became sole king. An energetic and charismatic war-leader, he exploited the superior numbers and technology of the Frankish army in campaigns against the Saxons (772, 775, 776) and Lombards (whose kingdom he took in 774) and against the Spanish Muslims, an unsuccessful expedition culminating in the massacre of his rearguard by Basques in 778. The 780s saw campaigns against the Saxons (780, 782, 784, 785); visits to Italy to see his close ally the pope and to intimidate the Lombard duchy of Benevento (781, 787); and the deposition of Duke Tassilo of Bavaria (788). In the 790s Charlemagne turned his attention to the powerful tributary empire of the Avars, which he destroyed in campaigns in 791, 795 and 796.

Charlemagne also became increasingly involved with non-military matters. His court attracted scholarly advisers, such as the Englishman Alcuin in 782. Charlemagne constructed a new palace complex at Aachen (his main winter residence from 794) and expressed his theological views in the *Libri Carolini* (794). Diplomatic ties were made with the Caliphate of Baghdad and Byzantium (with whom marriage alliances were planned). The Empress Irene's seizure of power in 797 and the blinding of Pope Leo III in 799 proved the catalysts for the most controversial event of his reign – intervention in Rome and coronation as Roman Emperor by the restored pope on Christmas Day 800.

The imperial title was less the culmination of Charlemagne's policies or a key stage in the formation of a distinct Western identity than the product of particular, mainly local factors.

The idea of a Christian Roman Empire had an appeal to Charlemagne's ecclesiastical advisers. An emphasis on imperial *renovatio* is evident in art, coins, charters, writings associated with the 'Carolingian Renaissance' and the issue of new more ambitious capitularies. In practice, however, the imperial title proved a hindrance, tying Charlemagne's office too closely to the papacy and antagonizing Byzantium. Disenchantment is reflected in Charlemagne's *divisio regnorum* between his three sons in 806, which makes no mention of an empire, and his personal coronation of Louis the Pious in 813. No serious attempt was made to create a new universal identity for Charlemagne's subjects. Instead a clear ethnic distinction was stressed between Franks and other groups by the writing down of separate laws for each people ruled by Charlemagne. The machinery for administering the 'empire' remained crude, with minimal central bureaucracy and dependence on powerful local counts. Innovations such as the use of capitularies, inspectors (*missi*) and legal advisers (*scabini*) were largely ineffective. Government depended more on success in war, with its flow of land and booty, and on personal ties such as oaths and grants of benefices to royal vassals and others.

Charlemagne's later years were marked by feelings of decline, succession concerns and threats from Danes, Arabs and Slavs. The empire's fragility became evident during the reign of his son, Louis the Pious (814–40). Fundamental structural weaknesses should not, however, obscure the overriding commitment of Charlemagne and his advisers to learning, justice and Church reform, aspirations which were only realized in part but served as lasting ideals for later medieval rulers.

T.S. Brown

Division of the Carolingian Empire, 843

The mismatch between administrative weaknesses and ideological aspirations in Charle-

magne's empire gave rise to problems in the reign of his son, Louis the Pious (814–40).

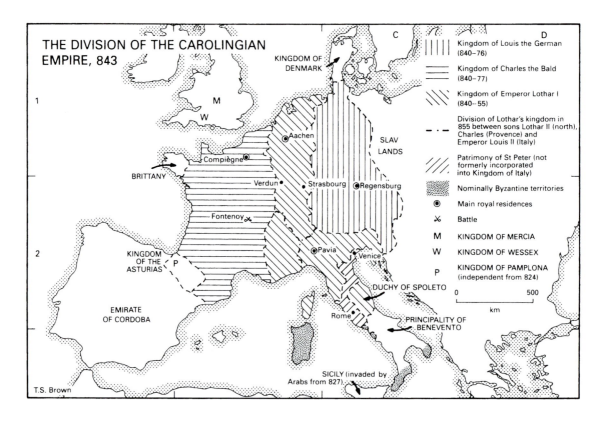

THE DIVISION OF THE CAROLINGIAN EMPIRE, 843

KINGDOM OF DENMARK

SLAV LANDS

Aachen
Compiègne
BRITTANY
Verdun
Strasbourg
Regensburg
Fontenoy
KINGDOM OF THE ASTURIAS
Pavia
Venice
DUCHY OF SPOLETO
EMIRATE OF CORDOBA
Rome
PRINCIPALITY OF BENEVENTO

SICILY (invaded by Arabs from 827)

T.S. Brown

Kingdom of Louis the German (840–76)

Kingdom of Charles the Bald (840–77)

Kingdom of Emperor Lothar I (840–55)

Division of Lothar's kingdom in 855 between sons Lothar II (north), Charles (Provence) and Emperor Louis II (Italy)

Patrimony of St Peter (not formerly incorporated into Kingdom of Italy)

Nominally Byzantine territories

Main royal residences

Battle

M   KINGDOM OF MERCIA

W   KINGDOM OF WESSEX

P   KINGDOM OF PAMPLONA (independent from 824)

0   500
        km

Louis's early rule was conscientious but personal and party conflicts provoked civil war between the king and his sons from 830. After Louis' death his eldest son, Lothar, based in Italy, sought to impose his power as emperor north of the Alps, aiming to deprive his half-brother, Charles the Bald, of his inheritance in west Francia. This encouraged Charles to ally with his other half-brother, Louis the German. Together they defeated Lothar at Fontenoy in 841. The alliance was consolidated by oaths taken by each king's followers at Strasbourg in 842. Lothar was compelled at Verdun in 843 to agree to a division of the Empire into three approximately equal parts. Lothar kept his imperial title and lands stretching from the North Sea to Italy, which incorporated the imperial centres of Aachen, Pavia and Rome, while Charles obtained the west Frankish lands and Louis those east of the Rhine. This arrangement was not envisaged as replacing the Empire by nascent nation-states but in practice centrifugal pressures were increased by rivalries between the rulers and the pressures of aristocratic supporters to regain offices and lands lost in the division.

Lothar's kingdom lacked viability and was divided in 855 among his three sons, none of whom had male heirs. As a result the kingdom of Lothar II (855–69) in the Low Countries was carved up between his uncles, Louis the German and Charles the Bald. In west Francia Charles fought manfully against viking invaders and aristocratic separatism and succeeded in becoming emperor after the death of his nephew, Louis II, in 875. After Charles's death in 877 his descendants were unfortunately short-lived. Louis the German proved the strongest king until his death in 876. His sons too died prematurely, although the youngest, Charles the Fat, managed to reunite the Empire in 884. His deposition in 887 as part of a succession dispute caused the end of the Empire as a territorial unit and terminated the Carolingian family's monopoly on royal status.

T.S. Brown

The Moravian Empire, c. 830–c. 900

'Slav' is a term of convenience used to describe the heterogeneous peoples of medieval central and eastern Europe. The Slavic peoples shared some linguistic and cultural traits but there were also many differences between them. Their differences were increasingly accentuated in the

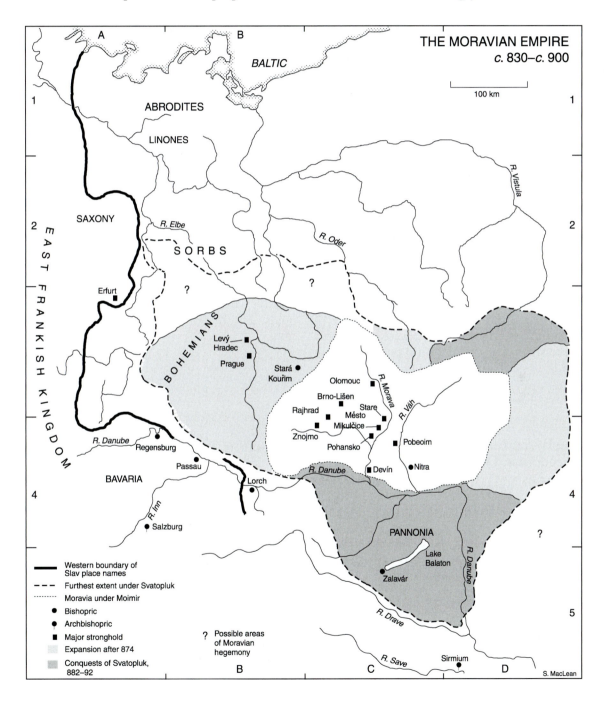

THE MORAVIAN EMPIRE
c. 830–c. 900

100 km

BALTIC

ABRODITES

LINONES

SAXONY

R. Elbe

SORBS

Erfurt

?   ?

R. Vistula

R. Oder

EAST FRANKISH KINGDOM

BOHEMIANS

Levý Hradec

Prague

Stará Kouřim

Olomouc

Brno-Lišen

Rajhrad

Znojmo

Mikulčice

Pohansko

R. Morava

R. Váh

Stare Město

Pobeoim

Devín

Nitra

R. Danube

Regensburg

Passau

BAVARIA

Lorch

R. Inn

Salzburg

R. Danube

PANNONIA

Lake Balaton

Zalavár

R. Danube

?

R. Drave

R. Save

Sirmium

Western boundary of Slav place names
Furthest extent under Svatopluk
Moravia under Moimir
● Bishopric
◕ Archbishopric
■ Major stronghold
Expansion after 874
Conquests of Svatopluk, 882–92
? Possible areas of Moravian hegemony

A   B   B   C   D

S. MacLean

21

eighth and ninth centuries when cultural and social transformations can be observed in the archaeological record. Demographic and economic growth were intensified by increased contact between the west Slavs and the Franks subsequent to Charlemagne's final conquests of the Avars (796) and the Saxons (804). Diplomatic and economic links across the frontiers encouraged the stratification of Slavic societies, as did Frankish attempts to enforce tributary status. These dynamics contributed to the emergence in the mid-ninth century of the so-called Moravian Empire, which dominated central Europe for several decades. This realm, focused on the Morava valley in the territory of the modern Czech Republic, was controlled by a dynasty known as the Moimirids and named after the ruler Moimir I (c. 830–46). Moimir and his successors, Rastislav (846–70) and Svatopluk/Zwentibold (870–94), extended Moravian hegemony by annexing territories held by the Bohemians and the east Franks. The power of the Moravian rulers is manifest in their construction of major earth and timber strongholds, some of which were improved with stone in the ninth century. Around thirty of these fortresses have been excavated, the most impressive being the Moimirid political centre at Mikulčice. The building of such fortifications

became widespread in the west Slav lands about this time and reflects the growing power of Slav rulers and the emergence of increasingly pronounced social hierarchies. The forts featured prominently in Moravian military resistance to Frankish imperialism. Although Frankish sources sometimes depict the Moravians as alien 'others', the Moravians seem to have been culturally quite similar to their Frankish neighbours, particularly in the ethos of their warrior aristocracy. Because of this, they are frequently found supporting one or other side in Frankish internal disputes. The Moravians were Christian and during the later ninth century Rome and Constantinople both fought long and hard to win their ecclesiastical allegiance. By-products of this dispute included the creation of a Slavic vernacular liturgy and the re-establishment of the ancient archbishopric at Sirmium. Nevertheless, the Moravian polity quickly collapsed after the death of Svatopluk. Encouraged by the Frankish ruler Arnulf (887–99), Magyar horsemen from the Carpathian basin launched massive attacks on the Moravian strongholds, effectively destroying the Empire by 906.

S. MacLean

The Byzantine Empire under the Macedonian Dynasty, 9th–11th centuries

From the mid-ninth century Byzantium took the offensive, responding to changes beyond its frontiers. After the battle of the Bishop's Meadow (863) the Arabs were never a real threat to Anatolia. Along the eastern frontier petty emirates emerged, not all of them in Muslim hands. Tephrike, for example, was held by the heretical Paulicians. Its capture in 878 brought the Byzantines within striking distance of the upper Euphrates. Advances were consolidated by creating new border *themes*

such as Mesopotamia and Lykandos (c. 900). Melitene, key to the middle Euphrates, fell in 934, and Theodosioupolis (Erzerum) in 949, allowing the Byzantines to influence Armenian lands, where a policy of piecemeal annexation was pursued. In 968 the Armenian principality of Taron was annexed and turned into a *theme*. These advances were complemented by the conquest of Tarsus and Cilicia (965). Antioch fell in 969 and the city of Aleppo was put under tribute. The eastern frontier thus advanced from

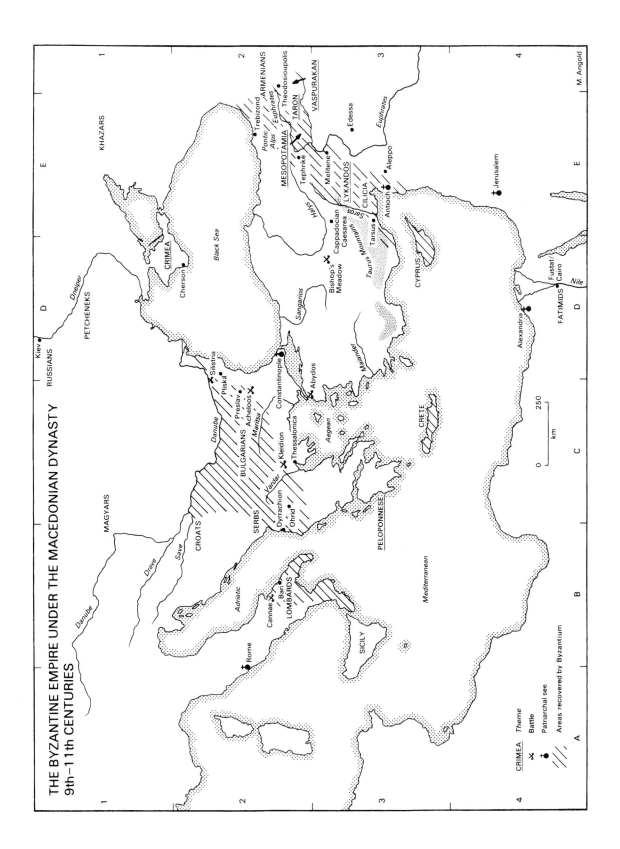

THE BYZANTINE EMPIRE UNDER THE MACEDONIAN DYNASTY
9th–11th CENTURIES

CRIMEA *Theme*
✗ Battle
✝ Patriarchal see
● Areas recovered by Byzantium

0   250
km

M. Angold

23

the Taurus Mountains and the Pontic Alps to northern Syria and the lands of the middle and upper Euphrates.

In the Mediterranean the Byzantines were still on the defensive in the early tenth century but the Arab corsairs of Crete were driven out in 960/61 and Cyprus was taken in 965. Further successes in the eastern Mediterranean were checked by the arrival of the Fatimids in Egypt (969). They quickly extended into Palestine and Syria.

Conditions had also changed rapidly north of the Black Sea. Since the seventh century Byzantium had relied on alliance with the Khazars. By the early ninth century the Russians controlled the rivers leading from the Baltic and the Caspian. Byzantium reacted by creating a *theme* in the Crimea centred on Cherson (833). This did not prevent a Russian attack surprising Constantinople (860). Other Russian attacks followed in 907 and 941 but Byzantium countered by offering the Russians valuable trading concessions.

The Russians also had to contend with the Petcheneks, the dominant power on the steppes. Byzantium cultivated them – they could cut the Russian trade route down the Dnieper from Kiev and they also threatened the Bulgarians across the Danube. After their conversion to Orthodoxy in 865, the Bulgarians might have been brought within the Byzantine orbit but the Bulgarian tsar, Symeon (*c.* 893–927), was a more able opponent than his pagan forebears. He won notable victories over the Byzantines,

including the battle of Acheloos (917), and in 921, 922 and 924 advanced to the walls of Constantinople. He mastered the Balkans and even penetrated the Peloponnese. After 927 Byzantium hastened to make peace with his son Peter (927–69). Over the next forty years the balance of power swung towards the Byzantines. In 967 the Russian prince of Kiev, Svjatoslav, was called in against the Bulgarians but he determined to conquer Bulgaria himself. The Russians were finally defeated by the Byzantines at Silistria on the Danube (971) and Bulgaria was annexed. The returning Russians were caught by the Petcheneks and Svjatoslav was killed. It was a text-book demonstration of Byzantine diplomacy. Svjatoslav's death prepared the way for the conversion of his son Vladimir to Christianity.

Vladimir helped the Emperor Basil II (976–1025) deal with a rebellion by the eastern *themes*, thus contributing to his victory at Abydos (989). These internal problems allowed the Bulgarians to establish a new state centred on Ohrid in Macedonia. Basil's victory over the Bulgarians at Kleidion (1014) was decisive and by 1018 all resistance had collapsed. Basil now extended Byzantine control in Armenia, annexing Vaspurakan (1021). He also strengthened Byzantium's hold in southern Italy, defeating the Lombards at Cannae (1018). It was an imposing achievement which his successors found hard to defend.

M. Angold

Vikings

Between 800 and 1100 the Scandinavian peoples were transformed from an Iron Age into a medieval society. This profound development is reflected in adventurous expeditions abroad and in the use of silver at home. Before 800 silver wealth was stored in jewellery, often huge arm rings or brooches. We assume many of these circulated as gifts, bride wealth, blood

money and plunder. By the twelfth century kings had coins minted bearing their likeness and most silver, in the shape of coins, was used in straightforward financial exchanges or as payment of rent, taxes or tithes. Whether silver was the motor of social change or simply an indispensable element of political and social competition in an increasingly hierarchical

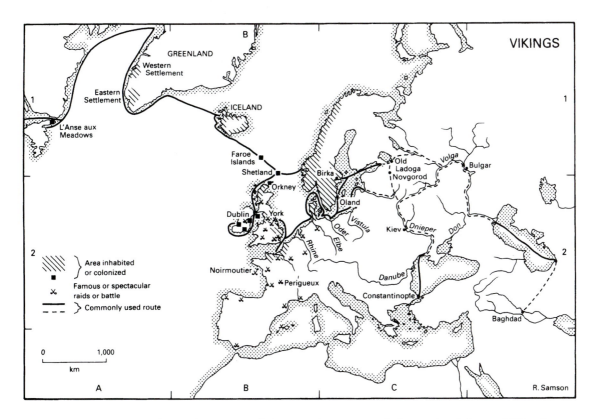

VIKINGS

R. Samson

Scandinavian society, vikings burst out of their homeland dramatically and often terrifyingly in search of it.

In the ninth century they raided and traded for silver but to call these early vikings merchants is anachronistic. In Iceland's famous *Njálssaga*, a main character attempts to obtain hay from a neighbour, asking if he would sell it to him (denying any social relationship between them), next if he would give it to him as a gift (offering future friendship), and finally he had to threaten to take it (confirming their enmity).

In the east Swedes travelled huge distances trading and swapping, buying and selling, gifting and stealing at Old Ladoga, Novgorod, Kiev and Bulgar. The major Russian rivers (the Dnieper, Don and Volga) were their highways. At the end of these rivers lay the Byzantine Empire but more importantly the caliphate of Baghdad and tons of Islamic silver. More than 85,000 Arabic coins have been found in Scandinavia. Although little appreciated today, contact with German and Slavic regions, along

the coast and down the Oder and Vistula, was probably equally intense. More than 70,000 German coins have been discovered in Sweden.

While vikings traded around the British Isles, much of the silver they acquired was probably the fruit of violence. From the raid on the monastery at Lindisfarne in 793 or at Noirmoutier to the battle of Stamford Bridge in 1066, the violence grew from plundering raids of single boats to huge invasion armies. Even the big armies were interested primarily in silver, extracting tribute, the so-called Danegeld. Between 991 and 1014 they received more than 150,000lbs of silver officially, which is equal to 36 million coins!

The change from raids of small bands to huge armies reflects changes in the Scandinavian societies. As political power became more centralized, economic and social organization in Scandinavia came to resemble that of other European nations. The final Scandinavian invasions resembled the wars of their neighbours; they aimed at conquest. Northmen would rule

Normandy and give it their name; Danish law would run for much of eastern England (hence Danelaw); Cnut would later become king of all England (1017–35).

Tensions within Scandinavia during this period of accelerated political centralization perhaps explain why many Norwegians left to settle Shetland, Orkney, the Hebrides, Man, the Faroes, Greenland and even North America. Certainly this is one of the mythical reasons the Icelandic sagas give for departure from Norway. In these new lands the Norse may not have found identical climates and landscapes but they were similar enough to allow old lifestyles to be perpetuated. Moreover, these islands were uninhabited or only sparsely inhabited.

The distances the vikings travelled, their 'primitiveness' and their paganism impressed and frightened the peoples of more settled Europe of the ninth and tenth century. Their incomprehension has left us the vikings of myth and legend.

R. Samson

Magyars

Where the Magyars came from we shall never know. Their language, of a Finno-Ugrian type, is said most closely to resemble that of some aboriginals from Siberia. The Hungarians (Magyar is their own name for themselves) first appear in written sources dated to 833, when they attacked the Khazars around the Sea of Azov. Thirty years later a Magyar raiding expedition reached German borders. In 896 they entered the great Alföld basin, between the

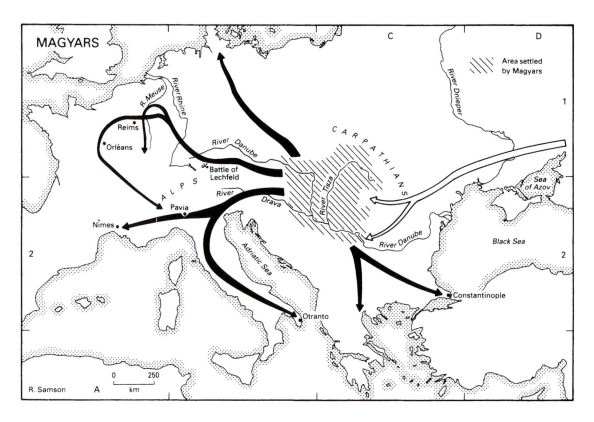

26

Danube and the Tisza, ringed by the Beskidy in the north, Carpathians in the east, Alps in the west, and Dinaric Alps in the south. These plains had been home to nomadic and semi-nomadic peoples since later prehistory. Like the Huns and the Avars before them, the Magyars were accomplished horsemen. They plundered and pillaged far and wide. In 899 they attacked settlements along the Po River; in Italy they raided as far south as Otranto. In 900 they plundered Bavaria; and Germany was to bear the brunt of their unwanted attention. After 917 they regularly pillaged northern Gaul; and in 924 they attacked the area of Nîmes.

Henry I of Germany had fortifications built against the Magyars. His son, Otto I, charged frontier guardians with protecting the Empire from their incursions. Although little else (such as a replication of Charlemagne's massive invasion of the Avar kingdom) was done to lessen the threat, in 955 Otto I defeated a band of Magyar marauders at Lechfeld, as they returned home with booty.

The decline in Magyar incursions owed less to the Ottonian victory at Lechfeld than it did to internal developments on the Alföld plain, where the medieval Hungarian state was developing. The conversion to Christianity had begun with the work of Bishop Pilgrim of Passau (971–91). In 1001 Vaik, with the baptismal name of Stephen, took the title of king. By papal consent Hungary received its own metropolitan, thereby escaping the rival claims of Passau and the Orthodox Church, which had also sent missionaries.

When next Hungarians and Germans did battle, it was in wars between neighbouring kingdoms.

R. Samson

The East European states, *c.* 1000

Although there were few precise frontiers, by 1000 the political map of eastern Europe was becoming better defined. This was outwardly a matter of the conversion of the peoples of the region to Christianity and of the advance of dynastic claims at the expense of tribal loyalties. It also involved the question of political affiliation with the Byzantine and/or German empires. Bulgaria provides a precocious example. Caught between the two empires, its ruler Boris finally accepted Christianity from Byzantium in 865 and with it Byzantine claims to overlordship. He concentrated on the conversion of his people, both the Bulgar elite and the Slav tributaries. It helped both to strengthen his dynastic authority and to unify his people. It was left to his son Symeon to challenge Byzantium. He assumed the imperial title and claimed patriarchal status for the Bulgarian Church. His ambitions led to war with Byzantium. His death in 927 temporarily ended hostilities but Byzantium could not tolerate so potentially dangerous a competitor on its doorstep. The Byzantines finally destroyed all Bulgarian resistance in 1018 and annexed the country.

The Russians too were a threat, on occasion attacking Constantinople. They were originally Scandinavian freebooters who controlled the river routes from the Baltic to the Caspian and the Black Sea. They made Kiev their main centre and put the surrounding Slav tribes under tribute. Their warrior ethos militated against conversion to Christianity, which was delayed until the years 987–9, in the course of which Vladimir, the prince of Kiev, accepted Christianity from Byzantium. This he did on his own terms, because of the temporary weakness of the Byzantine emperor. He obtained the hand of the emperor's sister in marriage, which gave him enormous prestige. These circumstances meant that Byzantine political claims over Russia were always muted. It meant that there was no need for the prince of Kiev to claim

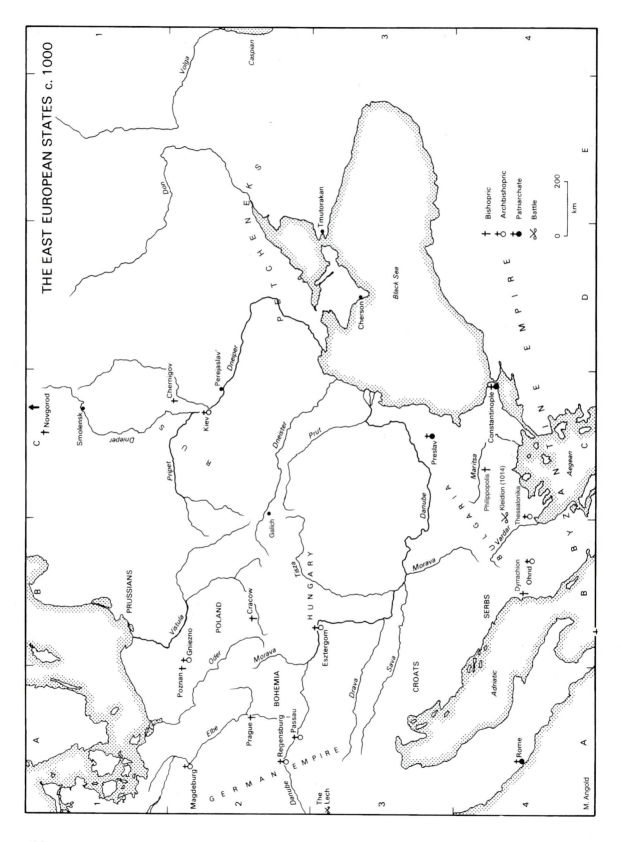

THE EAST EUROPEAN STATES c. 1000

	Bishopric
	Archbishopric
	Patriarchate
	Battle

0   200
km

M. Angold

28

imperial status. Power remained in the hands of the ruling family. The Russian lands continued to be divided into a series of shifting principalities over which the prince of Kiev merely presided as senior member. At the head of the Russian Church was the metropolitan of Kiev. He may have been appointed from Constantinople but there was a close identification of the Church with the ruling family: Vladimir was revered as its founder and his murdered sons, Boris and Gleb, were venerated as martyrs.

The Russians thus managed to solve the dilemma which led to the destruction of the Bulgarian Empire: how to avoid the political entanglements involved in conversion to Christianity. This dilemma was also apparent in the dealings of the western Slavs with the German Empire. Bohemia had to accept a large measure of German domination. In 973 its ruler recognized the suzerainty of the German emperor, Otto I, and the see of Prague was subordinated to Mainz but the native Přemyslid dynasty continued in power thanks to the posthumous reputation of Duke Wenceslas, who was murdered in 929 and was soon revered as the national saint of Bohemia.

In the face of German encroachment the pagan Polish ruler tried to learn from the experience of Bohemia. He married a Bohemian princess and in 966 accepted Christianity voluntarily rather than have it forced upon him. Shortly before his death in 992 he made the 'Donation of Poland' to the papacy in order to block German claims over the Church in Poland. Under his brother Bolesław the independence of Poland was formally recognized by the German emperor, Otto III, in 1000, at a ceremony to inaugurate the Polish archbishopric of Gniezno, though no royal title was accorded.

The ceremony was solemnized by the translation of the relics of St Adalbert of Prague, recently martyred by the pagan Prussians. Adalbert came from a noble Bohemian family and was made bishop of Prague in 982. Most of his energies were devoted to evangelizing the lands to the east. He worked among the Poles and among the Hungarians, who had terrorized far and wide until their defeat in 955 by Otto I at the battle of the Lech. In 995 Adalbert baptized the Hungarian ruler Geza and his son, the future St Stephen, who in 1000 obtained a royal crown from the papacy. A Hungarian archbishopric was established at Esztergom. There are clear parallels between Hungary and Poland. Both turned to the papacy as a means of countering German domination. Bolesław of Poland would follow St Stephen's example and in 1025 obtained the royal crown denied him by the Germans from the papacy.

M. Angold

The Ottonian Empire

With the virtual extinction of the Carolingian line, in 911 the dukes of the eastern (German) kingdom chose one of their own, Conrad of Franconia, as king. On his deathbed Conrad nominated Henry of Saxony as his successor. The dukes of Swabia and Bavaria opposed Henry and it was not until the reign of his son, Otto, that both were pacified. During Otto's reign (936–73) the German kingdom became the most powerful political force in Europe.

Otto was crowned emperor in 962 and is regularly compared to Charlemagne. Otto was in many ways an inheritor of Charlemagne's political legacy. The core of the Ottonian Empire was built directly on the German portion of the subdivided Carolingian Empire. Otto's German empire was, however, far removed from the earlier Carolingian state.

Following the subdivisions of Charlemagne's Empire, the western French-speaking portions tended to fragment. By contrast the German-speaking east revealed stronger unity. The

THE OTTONIAN EMPIRE, 962

MARCH OF THE BILLUNGS

NORTH MARCH

SAXONY

FRIESLAND

SAXONY

MARCH OF LAUSITZ

MARCH OF MEISSEN

FRANCONIA

LORRAINE

BOHEMIA

MORAVIA

MARCH OF AUSTRIA

SWABIA

BAVARIA

MARCH OF STYRIA

CARINTHIA

MARCH OF CARNIOLA

KINGDOM OF BURGUNDY

KINGDOM OF ITALY

PAPAL STATE

Schleswig
Oldenburg
Hamburg
Lüneburg
Bremen
Wildeshausen
Verden
Havelberg
Brandenburg
Utrecht
Osnabrück
Minden
Braunschweig
Magdeburg
Hildesheim
Munster
Herford
Goslar
Halberstadt
Nijmegen
Essen
Paderborn
Corvey
Quedlinburg
Werden
Antwerp
Memleben
Merseburg
Meissen
Liège
Fritzlar
Naumburg
Zeitz
Cologne
Aachen
Hersfeld
Cambrai
Malmedy
Stablo
Koblenz
Fulda
Prague
Prüm
Frankfurt
Mainz
Bamberg
LORRAINE
Trier
Würzburg
Metz
Worms
Lorsch
Gorze
Speyer
Regensburg
Verdun
Weissenburg
Eichstatt
Niederalteich
Toul
Passau
Strasbourg
Ulm
Augsburg
Freising
Vienna
Chiemsee
Salzburg
Basel
Reichenau
Tegernsee
Constance
St Gall
Chur
Brixen
Lyon
Milan

Archbishopric
Bishopric
Abbey
Kingdoms, duchies and Marches

0   100
km

R. Samson

30

differences cannot be ascribed to the problems caused by the vikings. The Magyars proved to be a comparable nuisance to German kings, and political rivals were seen by both the late Carolingians of the French west and the new kings of the German east as greater threats. Indeed this endemic violent political competition ensured that the simple vagaries of inheritance and succession could not be the sole cause of such different fates.

The German kingdom was more primitive than its western neighbour and perhaps much like the Frankish kingdom inherited by Charlemagne. When Otto was crowned emperor the last two hundred years had seen the conversion to Christianity, the development of a diocesan organization (albeit incomplete at the borders), the foundation of abbeys and the collection of tithes. The minting of coins east of the Rhine had not long been established. The exploitation of the countryside by ecclesiastics, lay magnates and the king based on land ownership and farming estates worked by servile peasants represented a departure from the more personal forms of authority and the renders of tribute that had gone before. Unlike Carolingian royal estates, some of which may even have gone back to Roman villas, Saxon royal villas (the densest concentration in the Harz hills, among them Tilleda, Goslar, Werla, Quedlinburg and Otto's

'new Rome' Magdeburg) were relatively new foundations. Only some regions (such as Bavaria and Lorraine) had long histories of developed political and social organization.

Just as Charlemagne's Empire was partly held together by eastward expansion against less developed German neighbours, Otto's in part maintained cohesion by attacking its Slavic neighbours. Frontier principalities ('marches') were created in this process. From centres such as Brandenburg and Meissen these areas were brought under German political control and 'civilized'. The extension of centralized political power was largely achieved through the Church. By 951 Otto successfully declared eighty-five 'royal' monasteries and all the bishoprics exempt from all secular authority: they became 'immune' from ducal administration and their lands could not be sub-enfeoffed without royal authority.

Rule of the Italian kingdom came when the pope invited the king to help drive out his political rival, Berengar II. The campaign was quick and easy and in 962 Otto was made emperor by the pope although Italy did not figure as prominently in Otto's political programme as it would in that of later German emperors.

R. Samson

The Scandinavian kingdoms, *c.* 1000

By the early eleventh century Scandinavia was being transformed from a largely pagan, tribal society to a land of unitary kingdoms. The Danes had teetered on the brink of this transition since the Roman period but its final successful phase began under Harald Blue-tooth (*c.* 958–87) and culminated under his son, Sveinn (*c.* 990–1014), and grandson, Cnut (1019–35). Trading centres at Ribe and Hedeby in Jutland emerged as towns and the episcopacy, tenuously enforced under Ottonian hegemony, took root. In Cnut's time an unsuccessful

attempt seems to have been made to elevate Roskilde, near the pagan cult site of Leire, to metropolitan status. The Danish dynasty did not, however, allow one core region to develop at the expense of others. Hedeby, the commercial centre, lay in south Jutland, Viborg, the site of royal inauguration in the north and Lund, the chief mint, in Scania on the Scandinavian mainland.

Harald Blue-tooth's dynasty managed sporadically to enforce its hegemony over much of Scandinavia. In Norway a local dynasty had

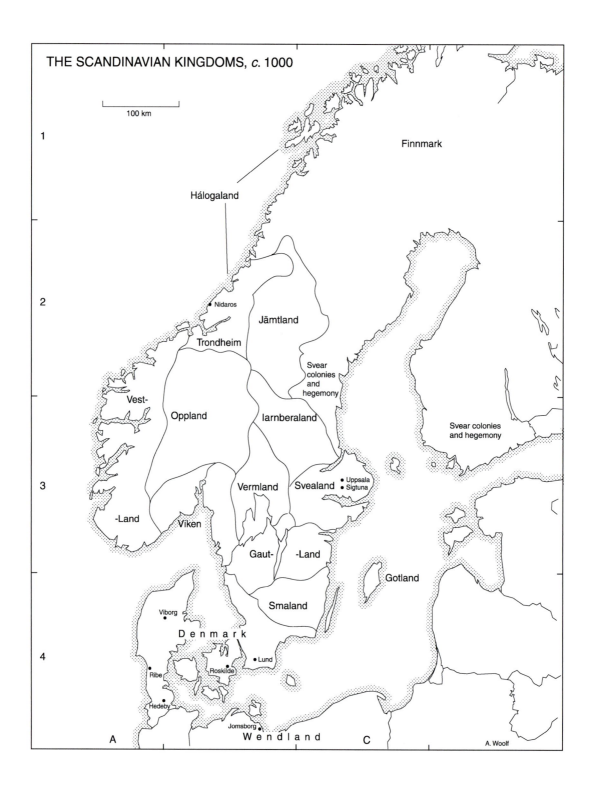

THE SCANDINAVIAN KINGDOMS, c. 1000

100 km

1

Finnmark

Hálogaland

2

● Nidaros

Jämtland

Trondheim

Svear
colonies
and
hegemony

Vest-

Oppland

Iarnberaland

Svear colonies
and hegemony

3

Vermland

Svealand

● Uppsala
● Sigtuna

-Land

Viken

Gaut-

-Land

Gotland

Smaland

Viborg
●

D e n m a r k

4

● Lund

Ribe
●

Roskilde
●

Hedeby
●

Jomsborg
●

A

W e n d l a n d

C

A. Woolf

32

risen to power in the tenth century under Harald Fine-hair and his heirs. Its core territories lay in the Vestland. In Viken, Danish hegemony probably prevented expansion and the north, in Trondheim, seems to have been ruled by semi-regal Hlaðir jarls. Oppland, the interior, was divided between small chieftaincies into the eleventh century. Norway also experienced emigration, with settlers heading west to Iceland and the British Isles, east to the heavily forested Jämtland and north up the coast of Hálogaland. This last province was inhabited by Finnish and Sami tribes from whom the settlers extorted furs and Arctic wares. In the early 970s competition in Viken led to war between Harald Blue-tooth and the Vestland king, Harald Grey-cloak. The Norwegian dynasty was annihilated. Danish hegemony was enforced through the alliance with Hakon Sigurðsson, the Hlaðir jarl.

Resistance to Danish domination was led by Erik the Victorious, king of the Svear (?970–4/5). Svealand (around Lake Mälar and with its cult site at Uppsala) was rich but politically less precocious than Denmark. Its rulers had long controlled trade in Arctic goods from northern Norway, which passed to eastern Europe via Jämtland, Sigtuna and the Baltic. Just as Norwegian settlers colonized Jämtland and Iceland in the early Viking Age, so Svear opened up Värmland and Iarnberaland ('Iron-bearing-land') to the west and the shores of the Baltic. Royal hegemony over these lands remained loose, at best, with small-scale chieftains competing for influence at provincial althings (assemblies).

South of the Svear lay the lands of the Gautar. By the late eleventh century West and East Gautland (separated by Lake Vättern) seemingly went their separate ways. It is a moot point if they had ever been a single polity. Earls of these provinces appear in the sources but were perhaps a product of competing Danish and Svear hegemonies. The local preference was for 'farmer republics' headed by an elected lawman. Legendary history, found in the Icelandic sagas and the Old English poem *Beowulf*, ascribed a pre-viking royal dynasty and the structures of a kingdom to Gautland but it is unclear if this was simply fantasy. Eventually Svear hegemony prevailed but Danish influence in West Gautland was strong.

After Erik's death Sveinn of Denmark married his widow and exerted hegemony over his stepson, Olaf (*c.* 994–1022). Nevertheless, just as Scandinavia seemed on the brink of unification, Norway escaped. Olaf Tryggvason (*c.* 995–9) and Olaf Haraldsson (*c.* 1016–30), sons of minor chieftains from Viken and the Oppland region, returned from England with Danegeld, warriors and separatist aspirations. Although neither was successful, the 'counter-insurgency' efforts of Cnut's regime united the Norwegians. In 1033 some formerly pro-Danish chieftains fetched Olaf Haraldsson's infant son, Magnus, from Russia. With the support of Cnut's alienated nephew, the Svear king Önundr, Norwegian independence was asserted around the figurehead of Magnus.

A. Woolf

The Mercian supremacy

Successful English kingdoms expanded at the expense of neighbours. By the eighth century Northumbria's earlier dominance was declining and Mercia had begun to conquer the kingdoms of the English midlands and south-east. Profiting from the commercial consciousness developing in southern England, the warlike Offa (757–96) was the first king to issue a royal coinage on a really significant scale. He used monastic property to consolidate royal power in newly subordinated kingdoms, holding a tight stranglehold over Kent and temporarily appointing an archbishop at Lichfield. The Mercians were, however, soon to lose their hegemony, following defeat by the rising kingdom of Wessex at Ellendun in 825. Offa's most enduring legacy was the great dyke built on the Welsh border which was less a negotiated frontier and more a basis for future raids.

S. Coates

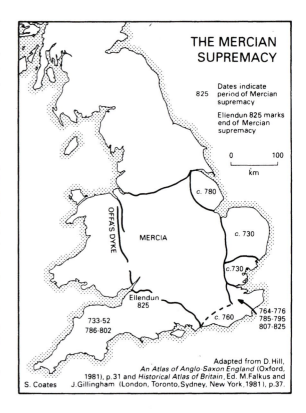

THE MERCIAN SUPREMACY

825 Dates indicate period of Mercian supremacy

Ellendun 825 marks end of Mercian supremacy

0   100
km

OFFA'S DYKE

MERCIA

c. 780

c. 730

c.730

Ellendun 825

733-52 786-802

c. 760

764-776 785-795 807-825

Adapted from D. Hill, *An Atlas of Anglo-Saxon England* (Oxford, 1981), p.31 and *Historical Atlas of Britain*, Ed. M.Falkus and J.Gillingham (London, Toronto, Sydney, New York, 1981), p.37.

S. Coates

England, *c.* 1000

This map shows England during the reign of Athelred II (r. 978–1013, 1014–16). During the tenth century successive kings of Wessex had expanded the boundaries of their realm to include most of the English-speaking areas of Britain. Their main rivals in this endeavour were the Scandinavian kings of York, whose power was finally eclipsed in 954, giving the Wessex rulers full control of England. The continuation of strong regional traditions was recognized in law, as England was divided into three areas (Wessex, Mercia and Danelaw) each with its own code. The Danelaw was an area where Scandinavian customs prevailed, reflecting the pattern of ninth- and tenth-century viking settlement. The names of earlier English kingdoms were also preserved in the regional units allocated to ealdormen. These officials were appointed by the king to enforce

law and oversee local military levies. The sparsity of ealdormen and bishops (who also acted as royal agents) for the area of Danelaw is notable.

England's borders with Celtic and Celto-Scandinavian polities were far from static. Cornwall had been incorporated into England by AD 900 (as indicated by the will of King Alfred) and the extreme north-east of Wales was secured under English rule by the construction of a borough at *Cledemutha* in 921. For the most part Offa's Dyke continued to mark the border between English and Welsh territory. England's northern borders are less than clear and they remained in dispute for centuries. Edinburgh fell into Scottish hands during the reign of Idulb (954–62) and Lothian may have been incorporated into Alba at the same time or, at the latest, during the reign of

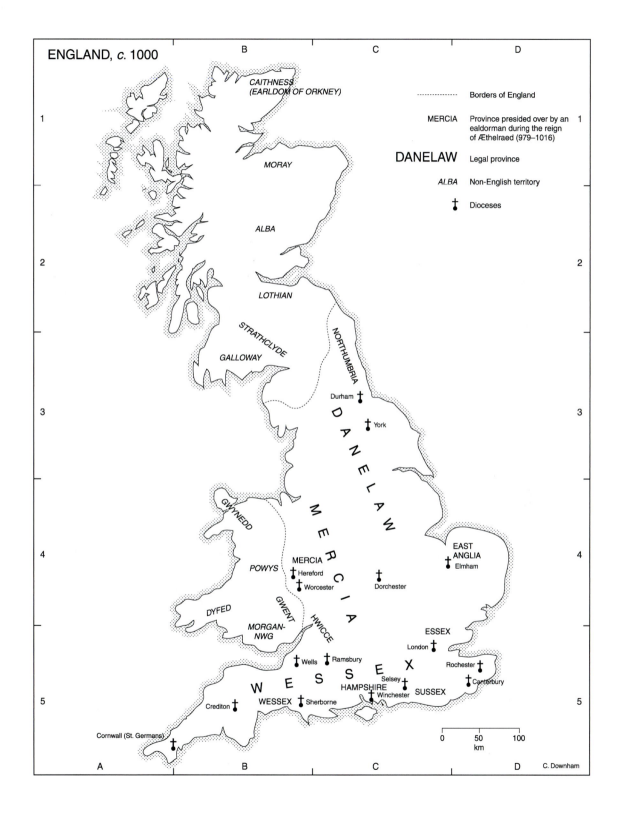

ENGLAND, *c.* 1000

···········	Borders of England
MERCIA	Province presided over by an ealdorman during the reign of Æthelraed (979–1016)
DANELAW	Legal province
ALBA	Non-English territory
†	Dioceses

CAITHNESS
(EARLDOM OF ORKNEY)

MORAY

ALBA

LOTHIAN

STRATHCLYDE

GALLOWAY

NORTHUMBRIA

Durham †

† York

D A N E L A W

M E R C I A

GWYNEDD

POWYS

MERCIA
† Hereford
† Worcester

† Dorchester

EAST
ANGLIA
† Elmham

DYFED

GWENT

MORGAN-NWG

HWICCE

ESSEX
London †

† Wells   † Ramsbury

W E S S E X

Rochester †
† Canterbury

Selsey
†

HAMPSHIRE
† Winchester   SUSSEX

Crediton †   WESSEX   † Sherborne

Cornwall (St. Germans)
†

0   50   100
km

C. Downham

35

Malcolm II (1005–34). In the north-west the boundary between England and Strathclyde is a matter of scholarly debate. This kingdom collapsed in the eleventh century and its lands were divided between England and Alba. Athelred's successor, Cnut, reorganized the provinces of ealdormen and the diocese of Cornwall was merged with Crediton, thus marking further changes to England's political geography.

C. Downham

Ireland, *c.* 1000

Ireland was geographically divided between multiple population groups, each of which could have their own king (or kings). Law codes describe a hierarchy by which the king of a single people (*tuath*) was subject to a local overking, who was in turn subject to a provincial overking. While the most powerful overkings vied for supremacy over Ireland, few rulers held such authority without opposition. The most successful overkings before the eleventh century were members of Uí Néill. This dynasty was divided into two main competing groups: a southern branch (based in Meath) and a northern branch (see map). In the late tenth century Dál Cais of Munster rose to power. Their overking, Brian Ború, subjected both branches of the Uí Néill in 1012. By breaking the hegemony of Uí Néill, Brian paved the way for greater rivalry between provincial overkings in the eleventh century. The most important economic centres in Ireland *c.*1000 were viking ports and ecclesiastical settlements.

C. Downham

France and its principalities, *c.* 1000

The political shape of France in the Central Middle Ages was determined by events in the tenth century. No king after 877 exercised the power wielded by Charles the Bald. Mints and fiscal estates fell out of royal control and Carolingian methods of government, such as *missi* and capitularies, were abandoned. The kingdom remained threatened by viking attack until the 920s and the crown oscillated between two families, the Carolingians (Charles the Simple, 898–929; Louis IV, 936–54; Lothar, 954–86; Louis 986–7) and the Robertian counts of Paris (Odo, 888–98; Robert I, 922–30; and the latter's son-in-law, Ralph of Burgundy, 930–6). Although energetic, Louis IV and Lothar could not stop the Robertian Hugh the Great, 'duke of Franks', from building considerable authority over the counts of Neustria and the coronation of his son, Hugh Capet (987–96), established a lasting 'Capetian' dynasty.

In the tenth century the main beneficiaries of weakening royal power were the 'princes', dynamic personalities who accumulated power by various means: favourable marriages, obtaining titles such as *dux*, amassing bundles of counties, establishing networks of *fideles*, assuming many of the financial and judicial functions of the *bannum* (Carolingian public authority) and exercising effective military leadership. Durable principalities included the duchy of Aquitaine, dominated by the counts of Poitou from *c.* 930; the duchy of Burgundy, built up by Richard the Justiciar (d. 921) but reduced by *c.* 960 to a rump ruled by a cadet branch of the Capetians; Flanders, whose counts capitalized on their military strength to build castles and exploit the vast economic potential

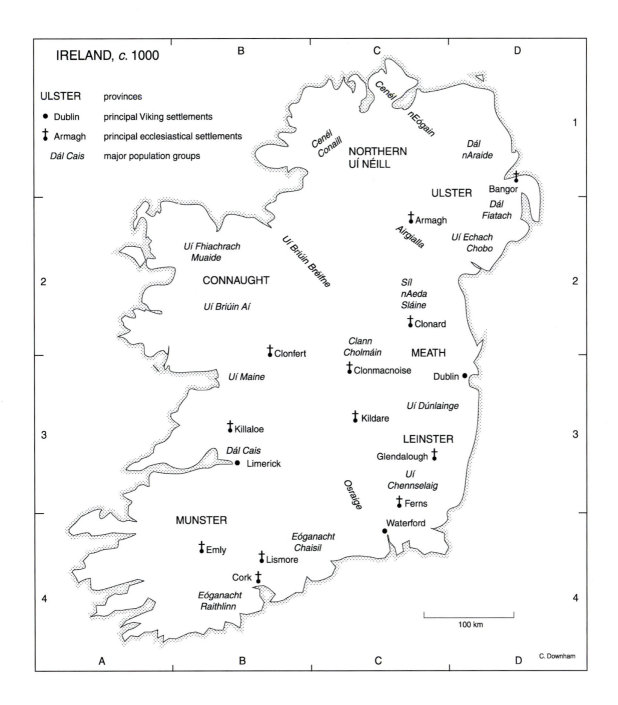

IRELAND, *c.* 1000

ULSTER   provinces
● Dublin   principal Viking settlements
✝ Armagh   principal ecclesiastical settlements
Dál Cais   major population groups

Cenél nEógain

Cenél Conaill

NORTHERN
UÍ NÉILL

Dál nAraide

ULSTER

Bangor ✝

Dál Fiatach

✝ Armagh

Airgialla

Uí Echach Chobo

Uí Fhiachrach Muaide

CONNAUGHT

Uí Bríúin Bréifne

Síl nAeda Sláine

Uí Briúin Aí

✝ Clonard

✝ Clonfert

Clann Cholmáin

MEATH

✝ Clonmacnoise

Uí Maine

Dublin ●

Uí Dúnlainge

✝ Killaloe

✝ Kildare

Dál Cais

LEINSTER

● Limerick

Glendalough ✝

Uí Chennselaig

Osraige

✝ Ferns

Waterford ●

MUNSTER

Eóganacht Chaisil

✝ Emly

✝ Lismore

Cork ✝

Eóganacht Raithlinn

100 km

C. Downham

of their county; and Toulouse, whose counts also ruled Gothia. Some other principalities were weakened by a ruler's untimely death, such as the Vermandois block of counties in north-east France which collapsed after Herbert II's death in 943. The duchy of Brittany remained weak despite its distinctive identity and often fell under the overlordship of neighbouring rulers. Catalonia was a powerful unit under the counts of Barcelona but drifted out of the French orbit from *c.* 987, as did much of the duchy of Gascony. Normandy's origins as a viking buffer

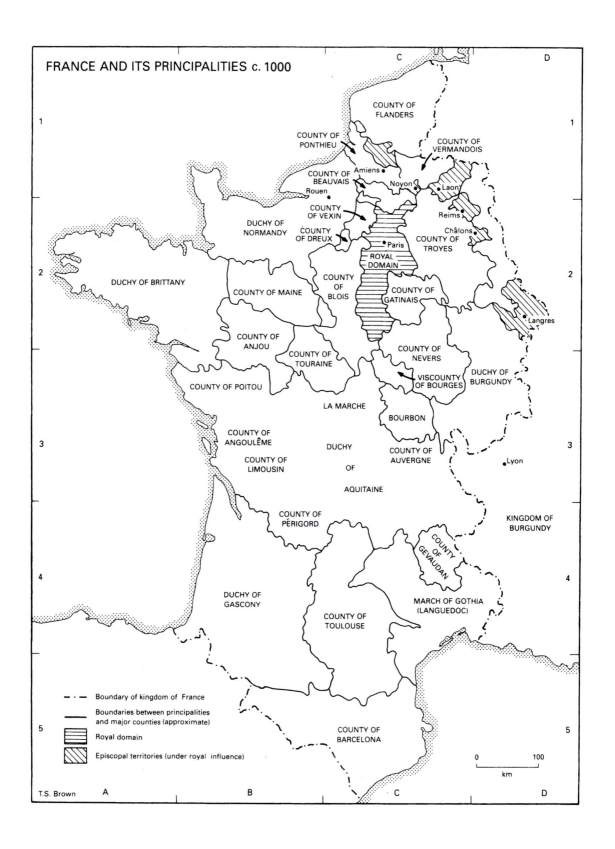

FRANCE AND ITS PRINCIPALITIES c. 1000

COUNTY OF FLANDERS

COUNTY OF PONTHIEU

COUNTY OF VERMANDOIS

COUNTY OF BEAUVAIS

Amiens

Rouen

Noyon

Laon

COUNTY OF VEXIN

Reims

COUNTY OF DREUX

Châlons

DUCHY OF NORMANDY

Paris

ROYAL DOMAIN

COUNTY OF TROYES

DUCHY OF BRITTANY

COUNTY OF MAINE

COUNTY OF BLOIS

COUNTY OF GATINAIS

Langres

COUNTY OF ANJOU

COUNTY OF TOURAINE

COUNTY OF NEVERS

VISCOUNTY OF BOURGES

DUCHY OF BURGUNDY

COUNTY OF POITOU

LA MARCHE

BOURBON

COUNTY OF ANGOULÊME

DUCHY

COUNTY OF AUVERGNE

Lyon

COUNTY OF LIMOUSIN

OF

AQUITAINE

COUNTY OF PÉRIGORD

KINGDOM OF BURGUNDY

COUNTY OF GEVAUDAN

DUCHY OF GASCONY

MARCH OF GOTHIA (LANGUEDOC)

COUNTY OF TOULOUSE

COUNTY OF BARCELONA

- · - Boundary of kingdom of France

Boundaries between principalities and major counties (approximate)

Royal domain

Episcopal territories (under royal influence)

0   100
km

T.S. Brown

state made it distinctive but its dukes pursued familiar policies of reviving Carolingian-style administration, building up followings and co-operating with churchmen.

In parts of Francia other types of polity existed, including largely independent bishoprics (such as Langres, Cahors, Reims and Laon), independent counties (such as the Rouergue) and areas which came under the weak rule of local counts and lords (such as the Auvergne, Berry and Picardy).

In the eleventh century royal judicial and fiscal rights remained limited and the authority of kings such as Robert the Pious (996–1031) and Henry I (1031–60) was largely honorary. Although Carolingian lands around Laon and Reims were incorporated in the demesne, and the Church was a useful support, vassals such as the counts of Anjou and Blois became powerful figures and frequent rivals; Normandy proved an ally for a time but Duke William I's expansionist policies after 1047 provoked royal hostility.

The late tenth and early eleventh centuries also saw socio-economic changes, including a general recovery and a proliferation of castles. Some castles were built on allodial land by lower aristocrats, or 'new men', reflecting a breakdown of the semi-public power of the counts. In many areas, such as Berry, the Auvergne and the Maconnais, castellans took over the public rights of the *bannum* and initiated a regime of oppression. This development partly reflected the growing importance of mounted warriors (*milites* or knights), bound to their lords by ties of vassalage. Contrary to traditional views formal vassalage was not widespread or uniform among the aristocracy early on but the wider use of the term 'fief' in the eleventh century led to increased legal precision in relationships and ultimately enhanced the position of the king as feudal overlord.

T.S. Brown

Southern Italy in the 11th century

In 1000 southern Italy was politically divided: Calabria and Apulia were part of the Byzantine Empire, which also nominally controlled the duchies of Naples, Amalfi and Gaeta; Sicily was controlled by competing Muslim factions; and there were three Lombard principalities: Salerno, Benevento and Capua. A loose political unity was imposed upon the region during the eleventh century by northern French knights, the majority from the duchy of Normandy. The Normans were not a unified force. Individual Normans served under any leader who could reward them. During the initial phase of their activity these leaders came from the established regional powers. At this stage the only territorial gain made by Normans was Aversa, granted to Rainulf in 1030. Sizable territorial acquisitions followed the invasion of Byzantine Apulia in 1040–2 and expansion into other

Byzantine areas over the next two decades. During this period two Norman leaders proved particularly able to attract support: Robert Guiscard and Richard, son of Rainulf of Aversa. Their defeat of a combined papal-German army at Civitate in 1053 left the Normans free to continue their expansion in the peninsula. By 1058 Richard had seized Capua and Guiscard had consolidated his holdings in the south, leading to a formal papal recognition of both conquests at Melfi in 1059. That grant included the island of Sicily, where Norman campaigning began under Guiscard and his brother, Roger, with the capture of Messina in 1061. Guiscard, however, withdrew his troops to enforce control in Apulia, to capture Bari in 1071 and to press his claims to Salerno in 1076. Roger's smaller force, occasionally aided by his brother, captured Palermo in 1072 and then

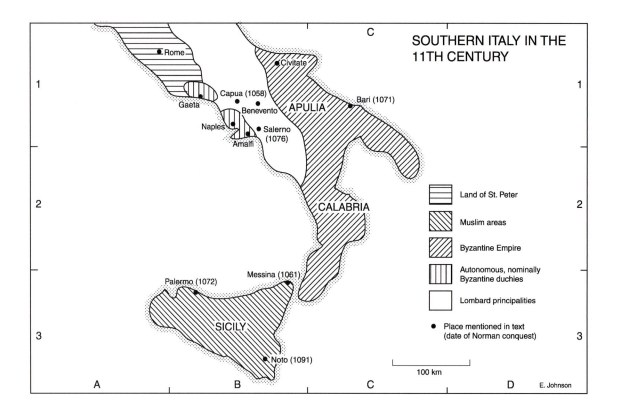

slowly secured the rest of the Sicily, culminating in the capture of Noto in 1091. By 1091 most of southern Italy was under Norman rule, if not yet united by a single governmental system.

E. Johnson

Al-Andalus: Muslim Iberia

Muslim forces invaded southern Spain in 711 and soon defeated the Visigothic king Rodrigo. Their army of largely Berbers was mainly commanded by Arabs. In five years they conquered most of Iberia and until defeat at Poitiers in 732 they conducted frequent raids across the eastern Pyrenees to France. The Muslim areas of Spain and Portugal were known in Arabic as al-Andalus. Although Muslim armies reached the north coast of Spain, settlement was more restricted. By the late eighth century the Muslims occupied Portugal south of the Mondego and Spain south of the Sierra de Guadarrama. There seems to have been an extensive area of

no man's land between Muslim frontier settlements at Talabira and Talamanka and Christian-held areas north of the Duero. Further east, Muslims settled the Ebro basin up to the 1000-metre contour along the Pyrenees. Here Muslim and Christian outposts were only a few kilometres apart. In general Arabs settled in larger cities like Saragossa and Seville and in fertile river valleys while the Berbers predominated in upland areas of the central Meseta. The Muslim capital was established at Cordoba.

In the early eleventh century the caliphate of Cordoba disintegrated and a number of small *taifa* kingdoms emerged. The south was

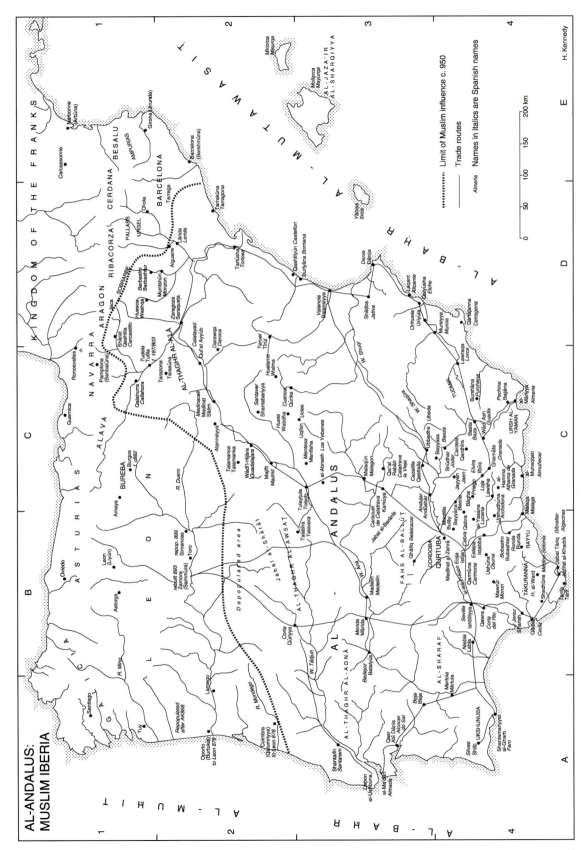

AL-ANDALUS: MUSLIM IBERIA

KINGDOM OF THE FRANKS

AL-BAHR AL-MUHIT

AL-BAHR AL-MUTAWASSIT

AL-BAHR

- **·········** Limit of Muslim influence c. 950
- ——— Trade routes
- *Almería* Names in italics are Spanish names

0 50 100 150 200 km

Narbonne (Arbūna)
Carcassonne
Guernica
Guerica
CERDANA
BESALU
AMPURIAS
UGEL
PALLARS
RIBACORZA
SOBRARBE
ARAGON
NAVARRA
ALAVA
ASTURIAS
BUREBA
Girona (Jirunda)
Barcelona (Barshilūna)
Oliola
Tarrega
Tarrakūna / Tarragona
Lārida / Lérida
Barbastro / Barbashtur
Alguaire
Muntshūn / Monzon
Huesca / Washqa
Shant Qashīla / Carcastillo
Zaragoza / Saraqusta
al 187/803
Tudela / Tutila
Tarasuna / Tarazona
Pamplona (Banbaluna)
Roncevalles
Amaya
Astorga
Oviedo
Leon (Liyūn)
repob. 899
Toro
Simancas
(Sammura)
rebuilt 893
Zamora
Burgos c.882
R. Duero
Qalahurra / Callahora
Madīnat Salīm / Medinaceli
AL-THAGHR AL-A'LÀ
Qal'at Ayyūb / Calatayud
Darawqa / Daroca
Teruel / Tirūl
Santaver / Shantabariyya
Cuenca / Qūnka
Huete / Wabdha
Uqlish / Uclés
Montesa / Mantisha
Atansiyya
Wādī-l-Hijāra / Guadalajara
Talamanca / Talamanka
Majrīt / Madrid
Tulaytula / Toledo
Talabīra / Talavera
al-Abrash / Los Yebenes
AL-ANDALUS
Burtiyāna / Bornana
Qashtīliyūn / Castellon
Valencia / Balansiyya
Shātiba / Jativa
Denia / Dānja
Lūcant / Alicante
Qalyūsha / Eliche
Orihuela / Uryūla
Mursiyya / Murcia
Lawraqa / Lorca
Qartajanna / Cartagena
TUDMĪR
Bushāna / Purchena
Pechina / Bajjāna
al-Māriyya / Almería
Basta / Baza
Wādī Āsh / Guadix
URSH AL-YAMAN
Ubbadha / Ubeda
Bayyāsa / Baeza
Shūdhar / Jódar
Qal'at Rabāh / Calatrava la Vieja
Castalla / Qashtalla
Cazalila / Cazalila
Ghamāta / Granada
Alhama de Granada / al-Hamma
Ilbira / Elvira
Jayyān / Jaén
Priego / Bāgha
Loja / Lawsha
Ardajar / Andujar
Malagon / Malaqūn
W. SHAT
W. SHAT
Medallin / Medellin
FAHS AL-BALLŪT
Jabal al-Barānis
Caracuel
Ghāfiq / Belalcazar
CORDOBA / QURTUBA
Medina al-Zahra
Qabra / Cabra
Istabba / Estepa
Ishbīliyya / Seville
Qawra / Coria del Rio
Ushūna / Osuna
Mawrūr / Moron
Qarmūna / Carmona
Ecija / Istija
Baylish
al-Yasāna / Lucena
Rayya
Bobashtir / Bobastro
al-Munakkab / Almuñecar
Mālaqa / Málaga
Shadhūna / Medina Sidonia
Jabal Tāriq / Gibraltar
Qādis / Cadiz
Tarīf / Tarifa
Jazīrat al-Khadrā / Algeciras
TAKURANNÀ
H. al-Ward
Jerez / Xeres
Shārish
Niebla / Labla
Mertola / Mārtula
AL-SHARAF
Badajoz / Batalyūs
Merida / Mārida
Coria / Qūriyya
Lamego
Oporto (Burtukāl)
Coimbra (Qulumriyya)
to Leon 878
Depopulated area
Jabal a-Sharāt
AL-THAGHR AL-AWSAT
W. Arā
R. Miño
R. Mondego
R. Sal
Qasr Abī Dānis / Alcacer do Sal
Silves / Shilb
Shantamariyyat al-Gharb / Faro
UKSHUNUBA
Beja / Baja
Shantarīn / Santarem
al-Ushbūna / Lisbon
al-Madā'in / Almada
Toy
Santiago
AL-THAGHR AL-ADNÀ

H. Kennedy

dominated by Seville, ruled by the Abbasids (a family of Andalusi origin) and Granada, ruled by the Berber Zirids. They gradually absorbed smaller kingdoms like Carmona and Cordoba. The centre of the peninsula was dominated by Badajoz in the west, Toledo in the centre and Valencia in the east. In the Ebro valley the kingdom of Saragossa, ruled by the Hudid dynasty, emerged as the major power.

Toledo's capture by Alfonso VI of Castile in 1085 was a disaster for al-Andalus. The city was of great strategic importance and its fall led to Christian occupation of much of the central peninsula. Under the Almoravids (1086–c. 1145) Saragossa was lost. Seville, with its easy communications to North Africa, now replaced Cordoba as the effective capital of al-Andalus; and Granada, on a naturally fortified site, grew in importance. The mid-twelfth century witnessed more disintegration and a new generation of *taifas*. The invasion of the Berber Almohads from North Africa put an end to most of these but it was not until 1172 that Valencia was finally taken from its local ruler, Ibn Mardanish, and incorporated into the Almohad empire.

Until 1212 the Almohads, based in Marrakesh and Seville, stabilized the frontiers but after defeat at Las Navas de Tolosa the great Muslim cities of Cordoba (in 1236), Seville (in 1248) and Valencia (in 1236) were lost by Islam. From 1250 to 1492 al-Andalus was confined to the kingdom of Granada, which held on to the mountainous terrain between Almeria and Algeciras. Under the Nasrid dynasty the kingdom survived repeated Christian attacks and Granada itself, now the major Muslim town in the peninsula, became an important commercial centre, much frequented by Genoese merchants. Christians gradually encroached on the frontiers and by 1492 and the final assault on Granada the area under Muslim control had shrunk to the town's immediate environs.

The culture of Muslim Spain was essentially urban. The great mosque in Cordoba is the major monument of the first phase of al-Andalusian history. In the eleventh century several *taifa* courts became important cultural centres and the Aljaferia Palace in Saragossa remains as testimony to their wealth and taste. The greatest monument of the twelfth century is the Almohad minaret known as the Giralda, now the bell tower of the cathedral in Seville. The Almohads were also responsible for building great fortresses at Torre del Oro in Seville and Alacala de Guadaira. The last great monument of al-Andalus is the palace-city of the Alhambra in Granada.

H. Kennedy

The Spanish and Portuguese reconquest to *c.* 1140

Conquered by the Muslims in 711–15, Iberia was ruled after 756 by an independent Ummayad emir of Córdoba, whose control varied enormously in different periods and regions. When central government was weak the emir's Christian enemies made their greatest advances. These enemies first rose in Asturias (*c.* 718), where their leader, Pelayo, defeated a Muslim expedition at Covadonga (*c.* 722) and established an independent kingdom. His descendants annexed Cantabria and

Galicia and ravaged the area between the Cantabrian and Guadarrama mountains, turning it into a no man's land behind which they could shelter from Muslim raids and build up their power. They claimed to descend from the Visigoths who had ruled in Toledo before 711 and to inherit from the whole peninsula; thus they proposed to liberate their country, that is, to 'reconquer' Spain.

Similar centres of resistance arose in Pamplona (740) and Aragon, though little is

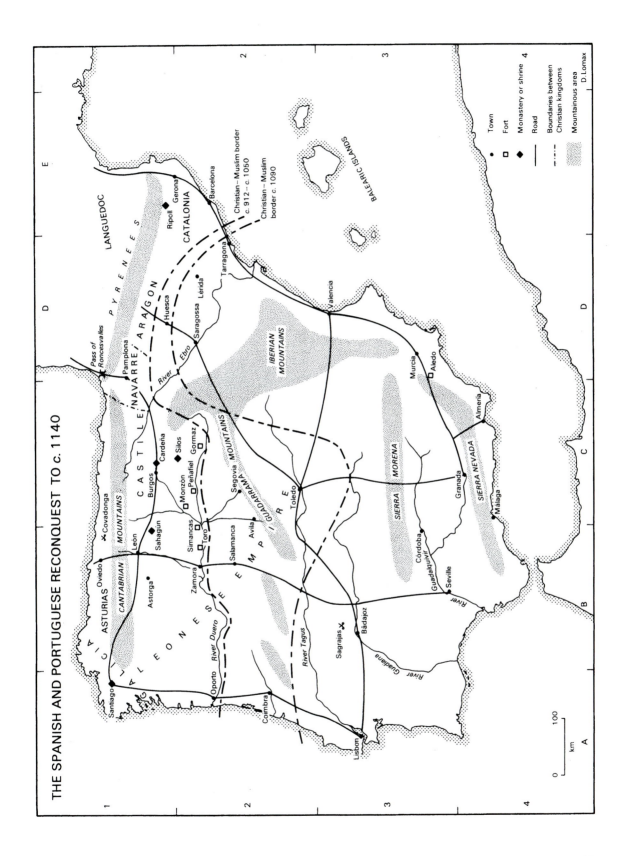

THE SPANISH AND PORTUGUESE RECONQUEST TO c. 1140

LANGUEDOC

PYRENEES

CATALONIA

Ripoll ◆
Gerona ●
Barcelona ●

Christian–Muslim border c. 912–c. 1050

Christian–Muslim border c. 1090

Tarragona ●

Lerida ●

Huesca ●

Saragossa ●

River Ebro

NAVARRE ARAGON

Pass of Roncesvalles ✕
Pamplona ●

CASTILE

IBERIAN MOUNTAINS

Valencia ●

BALEARIC ISLANDS

Cardeña ●
Silos ◆
Gormaz □
Peñafiel □
Monzón □
Burgos ●

Segovia ● MOUNTAINS

GUADARRAMA

Murcia ●
Aledo □

Almeria ●

CANTABRIAN MOUNTAINS
Covadonga ✕

León ●
Sahagún ◆
Simancas □
Toro □
Zamora ●
Salamanca ●
Avila ●

Oviedo ●
Astorga ●

ASTURIAS

GALICIA

LEONESE EMPIRE

Toledo ●

SIERRA MORENA

Granada ●

SIERRA NEVADA
Málaga ●

Córdoba ●
Guadalquivir
Seville ●
River

River Duero
Oporto ●

River Tagus

Sagrajas ✕
Badajoz ●

River Guadiana

Santiago ●

Coimbra ●

Lisbon ●

● Town
□ Fort
◆ Monastery or shrine
Road
Boundaries between Christian kingdoms
Mountainous area

D. Lomax

0   100
km

1   2   3   4

A   B   C   D   E

known of them. To the east, the Franks expelled the Muslims from Languedoc (751), took Gerona (785) and Barcelona (801) and organized Frankish Spain as an imperial March under the count of Barcelona. When the Carolingian empire disintegrated, his descendants became hereditary rulers of the March, now called Catalonia, though they were unable to push the frontier much beyond Barcelona until 1120, when they captured Tarragona.

Meanwhile, inspired by the discovery of the alleged tomb of St James at Santiago de Compostela (c. 810), the Asturians plundered in the emirate and exploited its civil wars to resettle the Duero plains, including the towns of Oporto (868), Zamora (893) and León (856). The Duero became their new frontier, protected by fortresses and by villages settled with peasant-knights and organized often by the great abbeys, such as Sahagún, Cardeña and Silos. It remained the frontier for a century, for Abd al-Rahman III (912–61) emerged as victor of the civil wars and caliph (929) with immense power; the Christian kings became his clients and later the victims of continual raids by the military dictator, al-Mansur (976–1002).

Alfonso VI's conquest of Toledo (1085) ended another period of balance and showed that León now had the strength and the strategic basis to conquer all Muslim Spain. In desperation the Spanish Muslims begged the Almoravid rulers of north-west Africa for help. After routing Alfonso at Sagrajas (1086) the Almoravids launched a holy war to recover the lands taken by the Christians. They met resistance from Rodrigo Díaz de Bivar, 'el Cid', who held Valencia (1094–9) and blocked their way up the east coast; and from thousands of French crusaders who came to defend Aragon, Navarre and Catalonia and who helped to reconquer Huesca (1096), Saragossa (1118) and the rest of the Ebro valley. As a result, a new state was formed in the north-east, Aragon-Catalonia, which would rival León and ensure that the reconquest continued to be a movement of divided, and sometimes conflicting, political forces. The fulcrum continued, however, to be Toledo. There the Almoravids made their principal attacks between 1086 and 1139. It was Toledo's resistance (plus the Almohad rising in Morocco) which finally broke their energies and enthusiasm for the holy war. Meanwhile, the Christians had been building up their strengths between the Duero and the Tagus – demographic, military, political and (with the influence of the papacy and a thoroughgoing Europeanization) spiritual. In 1140 they were poised for further advances as the Almoravid Empire began to disintegrate.

D. Lomax

GOVERNMENT, SOCIETY AND ECONOMY

Royal Carolingian residential villas

Carolingian kings possessed many palaces, villas and estates but they only resided at some of them. Only a partial picture of the farming estates of Carolingian kings can be painted because records survive for only a few of the farms given away to churches. Since long distance, overland transport of food was expensive, we assume that most agricultural estates were not far from places of residence, though vineyards were an exception and sometimes more distant. Once it became more common to pay rent in coin, distance became less problematic.

Royal estates were, however, more than sources of financial gain or places to sleep. They possessed political significance too. The great Carolingian villas of Aachen, Compiègne, Frankfurt, Herstal, Ingelheim, Nijmegen, Paderborn, Quierzy and Thionville were centres of government and monuments to royal authority. Within their walls charters were witnessed, ambassadors met, great assemblies and even church synods were convened and laws were enacted. The concentration of estates along the Rhine and between the Meuse and Moselle reflects the homeland of the Carolingian family. Visits to estates east of the Rhine reflect political activity, such as the planning of campaigns against the Saxons. The rarity of sojourns in southern France reveals both the lack of personal wealth in that region and an

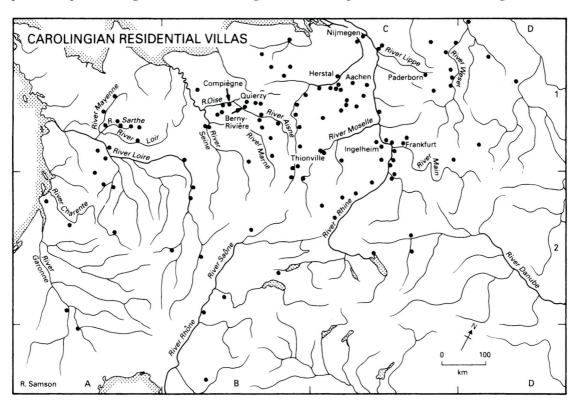

45

absence of important political threats or interests. As estates and palaces grew old, kings favoured newer residences. The favourite royal Merovingian palaces, such as Berny-Rivière, were still owned by Carolingian kings but rarely visited. Charlemagne and his son's most loved palaces (Aachen and Ingelheim) were those they had built anew. It used to be thought that Carolingian power declined due to massive alienation of estates, but the evidence for this theory is very ambiguous.

R. Samson

Carolingian and Ottonian mints

While the silver penny remained the main denomination throughout the ninth and tenth centuries, significant changes in minting occurred at the end of the ninth. Until then

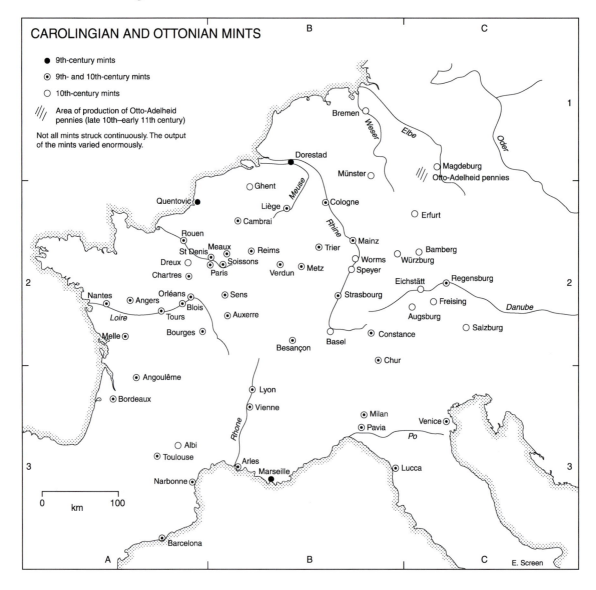

CAROLINGIAN AND OTTONIAN MINTS

● 9th-century mints
◉ 9th- and 10th-century mints
○ 10th-century mints

/// Area of production of Otto-Adelheid pennies (late 10th–early 11th century)

Not all mints struck continuously. The output of the mints varied enormously.

E. Screen

Carolingian rulers regulated the coinage closely. Hoards show that Charlemagne, Louis the Pious and Charles the Bald introduced new coin types and removed older coins from circulation very effectively. Under Charlemagne and Louis the Pious coins circulated rapidly throughout the Empire. After the division of the Empire in 843 the hoards show regional circulation patterns developing, which continued into the tenth century. The Rhine was the effective border for minting and coin use. Major Carolingian mints included Dorestad (to *c.* 850), Mainz, Melle, Orléans, Quentovic, Paris and the Italian mints of Milan and Pavia. The number of mints varied widely, from perhaps forty-five under Louis the Pious to around ninety during Charles the Bald's *Gratia Dei Rex* coinage.

In the tenth century issuing coinage was no longer an exclusively royal privilege. Alongside royal issues, the so-called 'feudal' coinages began to be struck by counts, bishops and abbots across the former Carolingian realms. Many of these coins initially retained the king's name and familiar Carolingian designs such as the 'Carolus' monogram. In the 930s some counts, including William Longsword, count of Rouen (927–43), began to issue coins in their own name. By the end of the tenth century at least fifty royal and 'feudal' mints were striking very different coinages in France. The tenth century also saw the geographical extension of minting, as coins began to be issued in substantial numbers throughout Germany. By Otto III's death in 1002 there were some seventy mints (royal, ecclesiastical and lay) in Germany. The royal Otto-Adelheid coinage struck near the newly discovered silver mines in the Harz mountains was one of the largest. The map shows a selection of mints from the period, illustrating the extension of minting.

E. Screen

Aristocratic landholding in the 9th century

The high nobility dominated the political and social landscape of the Carolingian world. Although the acquisition of offices from the king was crucial to any high-profile aristocratic career, power derived at least as much from the control of land. Land was not merely an economic resource: it also brought power over people (the semi- or unfree families attached to individual estates) and played a crucial role in constructing family status and identity. The top stratum of the nobility is often referred to as the 'imperial aristocracy', a group distinguished by its ability to retain political influence across the generations. These families maintained control of widely scattered properties, even after the division of the Empire in 843. This is illustrated by the lands described in the will of Count Eberhard of Friuli and his wife Gisela (863–4). Eberhard was the scion of a prominent noble family who had risen high enough to marry Gisela, a daughter of the Emperor Louis the Pious (814–40). As well as treasure, books and other movables, they divided their lands up among seven of their eight children (the other was a nun). Despite problems of identification (not all of the lands were specifically named and the location of others is debated), the extent and significance of these estates are unmistakable. The will grants valuable insights into family strategy and structure. The eldest son, Unroch, received a disproportionately large and coherent chunk of property, including everything the family owned in Friuli. It was specified that the other three brothers should receive exactly equal portions of land, a consideration that helps explain the fragmentary nature of their estates. The daughters also inherited land but (despite evidence that Ingeltrude was in fact the eldest of the eight) in smaller amounts and less coherent blocks. The monastery of Cysoing,

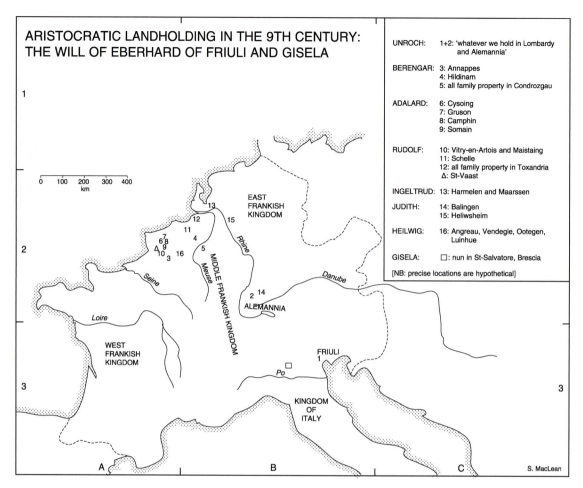

**ARISTOCRATIC LANDHOLDING IN THE 9TH CENTURY:
THE WILL OF EBERHARD OF FRIULI AND GISELA**

UNROCH:	1+2: 'whatever we hold in Lombardy and Alemannia'
BERENGAR:	3: Annappes
	4: Hildinam
	5: all family property in Condrozgau
ADALARD:	6: Cysoing
	7: Gruson
	8: Camphin
	9: Somain
RUDOLF:	10: Vitry-en-Artois and Maistaing
	11: Schelle
	12: all family property in Toxandria
	Δ: St-Vaast
INGELTRUD:	13: Harmelen and Maarssen
JUDITH:	14: Balingen
	15: Heliwsheim
HEILWIG:	16: Angreau, Vendegie, Ootegen, Luinhue
GISELA:	□: nun in St-Salvatore, Brescia

[NB: precise locations are hypothetical]

bequeathed to the third son Adalard, was important to the family's identity (they referred to it as 'our church') and probably also played a part in coordinating the management of family lands in northern Francia. This presence must have been bolstered by Rudolf's control of the non-familial abbeys of St-Vaast and St-Bertin. However impressive this widely dispersed patrimony appears, it must be remembered that routine management of estates was carried out in very local contexts. The second map shows the area of Flanders around Cysoing, and underlines the complexity and competitiveness of land-management in this agriculturally varied zone. The imperial aristocracy was rooted in regional landscapes such as this and it was on such local stages that high political power operated.

S. MacLean

Burhs and mints in late Anglo-Saxon England

Coinage provides major insights into the administrative and organizational abilities of late Anglo-Saxon England. Maintenance of the integrity of the coinage was a factor of

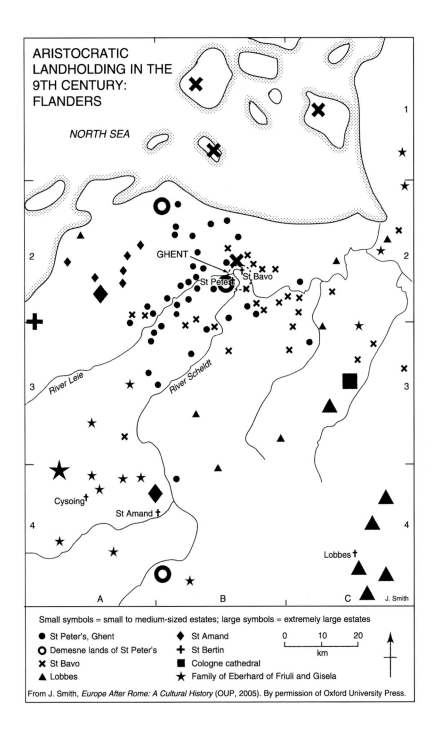

ARISTOCRATIC
LANDHOLDING IN THE
9TH CENTURY:
FLANDERS

NORTH SEA

GHENT

St Peter's   St Bavo

River Leie   *River Scheldt*

Cysoing †

St Amand †

Lobbes †

A   B   C   J. Smith

Small symbols = small to medium-sized estates; large symbols = extremely large estates

● St Peter's, Ghent   ◆ St Amand   0   10   20
○ Demesne lands of St Peter's   ✛ St Bertin   km
✕ St Bavo   ■ Cologne cathedral
▲ Lobbes   ★ Family of Eberhard of Friuli and Gisela

From J. Smith, *Europe After Rome: A Cultural History* (OUP, 2005). By permission of Oxford University Press.

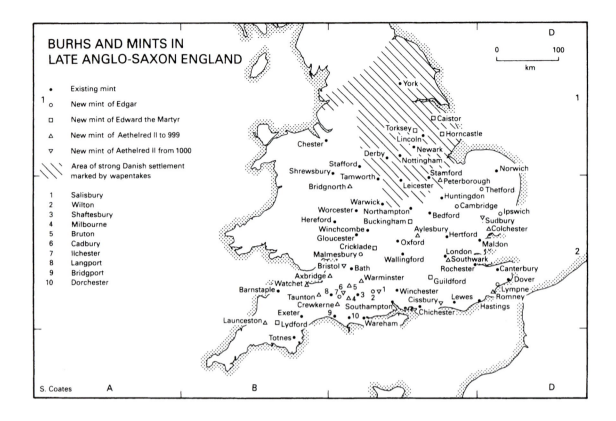

BURHS AND MINTS IN LATE ANGLO-SAXON ENGLAND

- • Existing mint
- ○ New mint of Edgar
- □ New mint of Edward the Martyr
- △ New mint of Aethelred II to 999
- ▽ New mint of Aethelred II from 1000
- ╲╲╲ Area of strong Danish settlement marked by wapentakes

1 Salisbury
2 Wilton
3 Shaftesbury
4 Milbourne
5 Bruton
6 Cadbury
7 Ilchester
8 Langport
9 Bridgport
10 Dorchester

S. Coates

considerable importance to royal prestige. Minting rights were completely regalian and counterfeiters were heavily punished. In the second quarter of the tenth century Athelstan decreed that each burh should have a mint and attempted to limit the number of moneyers. A major reform of coinage took place in 973 under Edgar, who decreed that 'there shall run one coinage throughout the realm'. Under Athelred there was a tremendous increase in the output of mints, partly due to the need to pay off large sums of money demanded by the Danes. Great national mints existed at London, Lincoln, Winchester and York. There were provincial centres at Exeter, Stamford and Chester, while Oxford and Shrewsbury were shire centres.

Burhs were originally fortified, walled towns which had proliferated in Alfred's reign (871–99) and served a military purpose. They were royal in nature and if the king so wished could be made into mints or markets. They became increasingly important as mercantile centres with the development of trade and possessed their own laws and administration. The extension of English authority into territories held for a generation or more by the Danes was heavily reliant on burhs. Hertford, Northampton, Huntingdon and Cambridge had been fortified headquarters of Danish armies.

Local administration was marked by the divisions known as shires which came under the charge of an 'ealdorman', later a shire reeve or sheriff. Shires were not systematically organized and did not settle into more permanent moulds until the reign of Edward the Confessor. They possessed their own courts and were further split into territorial divisions known as hundreds where courts were also held. In areas of strong Danish settlement these were known as wapentakes.

S. Coates

Royal itineraries: 11th-century France and Germany

Most medieval kings were itinerant. They did not reside for long periods in one place or govern from fixed capital cities but journeyed continually from place to place. There were several reasons for this. Economically, it might be cheaper and more convenient to move the king, his retinue and their horses to the supplies of food, drink and fodder rather than *vice versa*. The itinerant court thus consumed the produce of royal manors or received 'hospitality' from bishops, abbots or others on whom the obligation lay, before moving on to its next source of sustenance. Obviously, as the European economy became more monetized and commercialized, such an economic rationale for itinerant kingship grew less pressing: market solutions were now available to meet the problem of supply. There were, however, also political advantages to itineration. In an age of low rates of literacy, when local bureaucracies were rudimentary or non-existent, the physical presence of the king was the surest way of making royal authority a reality. Medieval government, it has been said, was 'a government of the roadside'.

The map shows the places visited during their long reigns by two contemporary rulers, Philip I of France (1060–1108) and Henry IV of Germany (1056–1106), as they are revealed by contemporary documents. Both kings were constantly on the move but the patterns of their itineraries show significant variation. First, much more is known about the movements of Henry IV than Philip I, partly because the number of royal documents from the German king's reign is much greater than that from the French king's (491:171), partly because Henry was a controversial figure and excited the chroniclers' attention. Also clearly visible is the fact that the German kings of the eleventh century acted on a far vaster scale than their French contemporaries. Henry moved regularly throughout Germany, was deeply involved in Italy and campaigned south of Rome, east of Austria and north of the Meuse. The extreme limits of his journeyings produce an axis of around 1,500 km. Not all of this was happy: the concentrations of activity in Saxony and north Italy represent prolonged attempts to subdue opposition. Nevertheless, the geographical range of Henry IV's activities indicate the ambitious scope of the German monarchy.

In contrast, the Capetian king was limited to a relatively small area, especially the zone between the three main royal centres of Orléans, Paris and Laon. Outside this region the king travelled almost as a foreign prince in his own kingdom. His visits to Poitiers and Dol, for example, which took place in 1076, were to seek a military alliance with the duke of Aquitaine and to relieve a castle besieged by William, duke of Normandy – he was treating with equals or enemies rather than subjects. The virtual autonomy of the great French princes in the eleventh century, compared with the relatively greater subordination of the German dukes to royal authority, is reflected in the itineraries of the two kings.

The map demonstrates the basic geographical pattern of royal power in the two kingdoms: in France a royal demesne in the Ile-de-France which was the only real arena for Capetian power; in Germany a monarchy deeply embedded in the Rhine valley and south-east Saxony (the homelands, respectively, of the Salian dynasty and their predecessors, the Ottonians) but which sought also to maintain a hold over the Po valley and Rome. Within two centuries these patterns would be fundamentally altered as the Capetians extended their power beyond the Ile-de-France while the German monarchy saw its lands and powers disintegrate.

R. Bartlett

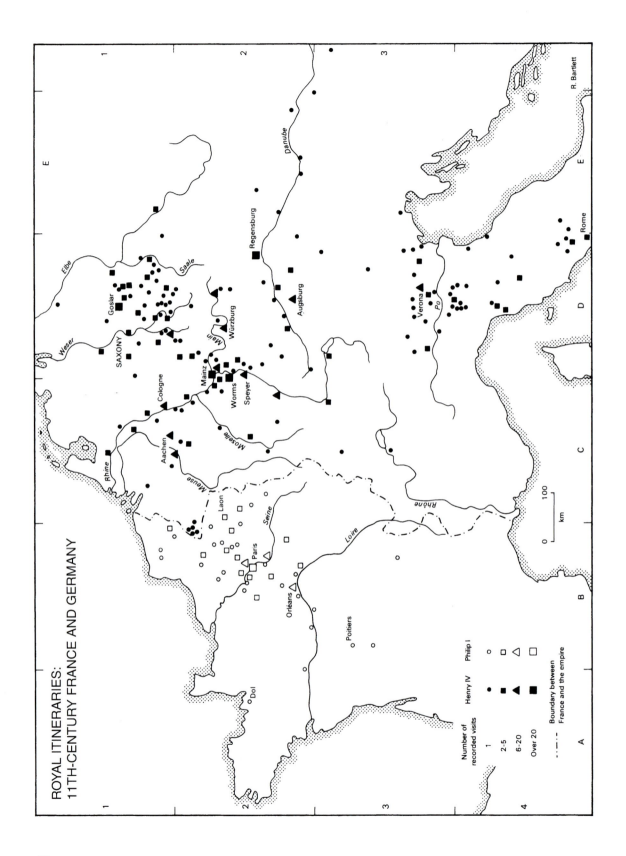

ROYAL ITINERARIES:
11TH-CENTURY FRANCE AND GERMANY

Number of
recorded visits   Henry IV   Philip I

1   ●   ○

2-5   ■   □

6-20   ◤   ◁

Over 20   ■   □

Boundary between
France and the empire ·—·—·

R. Bartlett

England under William I

The Norman Conquest was a momentous event in English history. England received a new royal dynasty, a new aristocracy, a new language, a new architecture and a virtually new church. A tenurial revolution extinguished many noble English families, leaving less than half a dozen Englishmen amongst the 180 tenants-in-chief when the Domesday Book was made in 1086. In theory, all land was held directly from the king although in practice much of the land acquired by the adherents of William I (1066–87) was acquired privately.

Landed wealth and political power were concentrated in the hands of a small number of men such as Odo of Bayeux, Robert of Mortain and Hugh d'Avranches, who were bound to the king through close bonds of blood and personal loyalty. Military considerations led to substantial changes in patterns of land-holding in frontier areas. Unlike their Anglo-Saxon counterparts, the great Norman lords possessed their seats of power and a substantial portion of their land along the edges of the kingdom and not in the heart of England. The king demanded knight-service and financial aid from his tenants-in-chief and knight-service was also imposed on the Church.

Before the Conquest, England possessed very few castles and these were built by Edward the Confessor's Norman or French favourites. The Normans were great castle builders. Castles were built at strategic points on roads and in centres of population. Early post-conquest castles, where possible, attempted to make use of existing fortifications and were swiftly constructed of earth and timber. Often the castle was marked by the distinctive motte or mound and a surrounding bailey or enclosure. The Bayeux Tapestry depicts the speed of castle building showing the construction of a motte at Hastings although the army was only there for fifteen days. It was only after military urgencies had passed that the Normans constructed more elaborate castles.

S. Coates

Scandinavian settlement in the British Isles

The impact of Scandinavian settlement was significant in both eastern England and north and west Scotland, as well as sporadic in eastern and south-west Scotland, Wales and Ireland. The incidence of Norwegian and Danish settlement was, however, very different in all these areas and can only be understood against the background of what is known about the viking raids throughout the British Isles.

The Danish settlement in eastern and northern England resulted from different sections of the 'great army' taking over possession of the land in 876–80, after having been a mobile army of conquest for twelve years. The numbers of Danish place-names (those ending in -*by* or -*thorpe*) are surviving witness to this process throughout East Anglia, Lincolnshire and Yorkshire. In north-west England the settlement was a result of Scandinavian speakers moving in from the north and west, across the Irish Sea – a zone dominated more by Norwegians who had taken over the Northern and Western Isles in an undocumented phase of settlement. Ireland was never densely settled by either Norwegians or Danes, despite having suffered many raids, but the viking impact was nonetheless long-lasting for they founded the trading cities of Dublin, Waterford, Wexford, Cork and Limerick, which were to be important economic, manufacturing and slaving centres adding substantially to the wealth of the controlling dynasty.

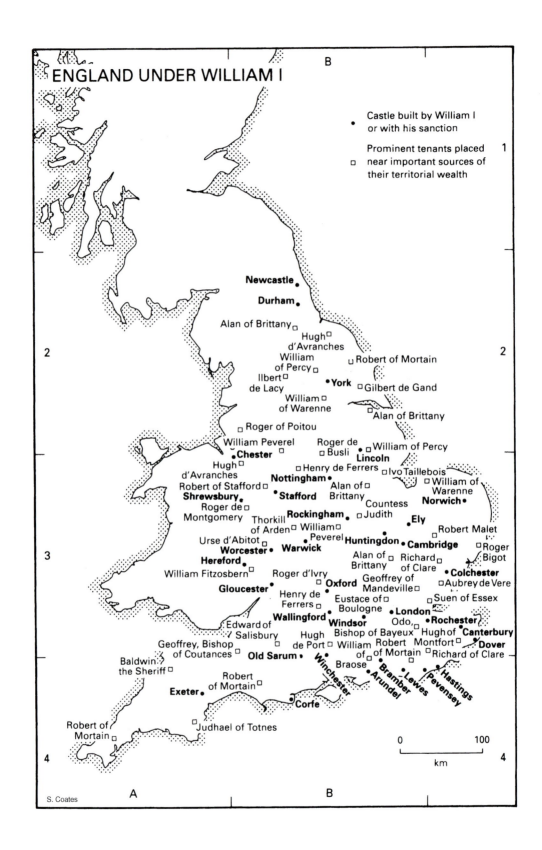

ENGLAND UNDER WILLIAM I

Castle built by William I
or with his sanction

Prominent tenants placed
near important sources of
their territorial wealth

Newcastle

Durham

Alan of Brittany

Hugh
d'Avranches
William
of Percy   Robert of Mortain
Ilbert
de Lacy
York   Gilbert de Gand
William
of Warenne   Alan of Brittany

Roger of Poitou

William Peverel   Roger de   William of Percy
Chester   Busli
Lincoln
Hugh   Henry de Ferrers   Ivo Taillebois
d'Avranches   William of
Robert of Stafford   Nottingham   Warenne
Shrewsbury   Stafford   Alan of
Roger de   Brittany   Norwich
Montgomery   Thorkill   Rockingham   Countess
of Arden   William   Judith   Ely
Urse d'Abitot   Peverel   Huntingdon   Cambridge   Robert Malet
Worcester   Warwick   Roger
Hereford   Alan of   Richard   Bigot
William Fitzosbern   Roger d'Ivry   Brittany   of Clare   Colchester
Geoffrey of   Aubrey de Vere
Gloucester   Oxford   Mandeville
Henry de   Suen of Essex
Ferrers   Eustace of
Boulogne   London
Wallingford   Windsor   Odo,   Rochester
Bishop of Bayeux   Hugh of   Canterbury
Edward of   Hugh   William Robert   Montfort   Dover
Salisbury   de Port   of   of Mortain   Richard of Clare
Geoffrey, Bishop   Old Sarum   Braose
of Coutances   Winchester   Bramber   Hastings
Baldwin   Lewes   Pevensey
the Sheriff   Robert   Arundel
Exeter   of Mortain
Corfe
Robert of
Mortain   Judhael of Totnes

0   100
km

S. Coates

A   B

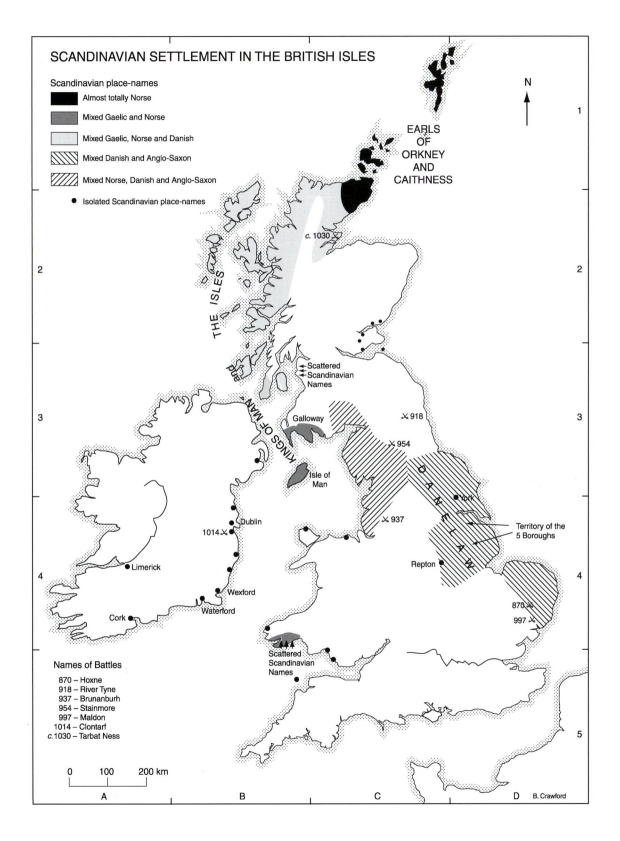

SCANDINAVIAN SETTLEMENT IN THE BRITISH ISLES

Scandinavian place-names

- **Almost totally Norse**
- Mixed Gaelic and Norse
- Mixed Gaelic, Norse and Danish
- Mixed Danish and Anglo-Saxon
- Mixed Norse, Danish and Anglo-Saxon
- • Isolated Scandinavian place-names

N

EARLS
OF
ORKNEY
AND
CAITHNESS

THE ISLES

and MAN

KINGS OF MAN

c. 1030 ✕

✕ 918

✕ 954

D A N E L A W

York

✕ 937

Repton

870 ✕

997 ✕

Territory of the
5 Boroughs

Scattered
Scandinavian
Names

Galloway

Isle of
Man

Dublin

1014 ✕

• Limerick

• Wexford

Waterford

Cork •

Scattered
Scandinavian
Names

Names of Battles

870 – Hoxne
918 – River Tyne
937 – Brunanburh
954 – Stainmore
997 – Maldon
1014 – Clontarf
c. 1030 – Tarbat Ness

0   100   200 km

A   B   C   D   B. Crawford

The vikings' remarkable mobility by sea continued even after they had settled on the land and created urban communities. The famous viking city of York (Jorvik) was even controlled by the same dynasty which ruled Dublin and the 'grandsons of Ivar' formed an economic nexus spanning the Irish Sea and the waterways of north England and south Scotland. Archaeological evidence has filled out the sparse historical picture in both these towns as well as in the 'Five Boroughs' of east Mercia; while in the far north and west farming settlements have revealed much about the life of the colonial Norse communities.

How culturally distinct were these different and various settlements in England, Scotland, Ireland (and Wales, where the site of Llanbedrgoch in Anglesey is newly discovered)? Did they maintain their Norse language, pagan beliefs and way of life? For a period probably yes, but in the areas where they settled among the native population they soon adopted the beliefs of the Christian majority and were eventually absorbed into the unified kingdom of England. Their own laws and customs marked out the settlement zone of eastern and northern England as the 'Danelaw', while in the Northern Isles Norse settlers retained their own language and, along with the Western Isles, remained part of the kingdom of Norway for many centuries to come.

B. Crawford

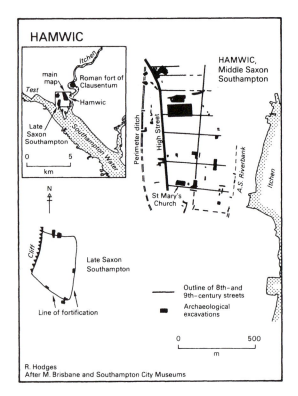

HAMWIC

R. Hodges
After M. Brisbane and Southampton City Museums

Hamwic: Anglo-Saxon Southampton

Anglo-Saxon Hamwic has been discovered by a large number of archaeological excavations in the St Mary's district of Southampton. These show that the town covered an area of about 45 hectares within a deep perimeter ditch, and was laid out with a grid of streets. The principal or high street was nearly 15m wide and may have served as a market place. Most of the many buildings were occupied by various kinds of artisans but traces of Frankish merchants who may have visited the town have been found near the likely beaching places for boats alongside the River Itchen. Hamwic was probably founded *c.* 690 by King Ine of Wessex, and flourished during the eighth and early ninth centuries before it was sacked by vikings in 842. In the late ninth century, if not before, the town was largely deserted in favour of the new fortified town of Southampton to the west, or King Alfred's capital at Winchester.

R. Hodges

Dorestad

The emporium of Dorestad was commonly mentioned by travellers from the seventh to ninth centuries. The site was identified in the nineteenth century by L.D.F. Janssen and substantially excavated by J.H. Holwerda after the First World War, and then by W. a. Van Es between 1967 and 1976. The excavations show that this sprawling town, covering in excess of 50 hectares, lay at the confluence of the Rivers Rhine and Lek, in which were constructed substantial timber docks. Behind the docks lay a row of commercial properties including warehouses but the heart of the settlement was composed of many farms typical of this part of Frisia. The vast amount of Middle Rhenish trade goods indicate that Dorestad acted as an entrepot for trade around the North Sea between the later seventh and mid-ninth centuries. The town was abandoned after viking raids and the silting up of the Rhine in the 860s. A museum in modern Wijk bij Duurstede displays the discoveries made in medieval Dorestad.

R. Hodges

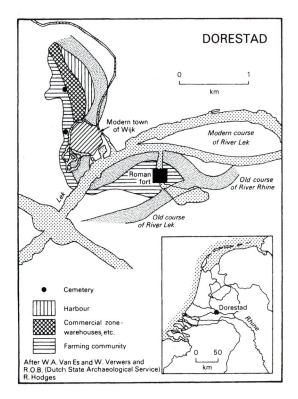

DORESTAD

0   1
km

Modern town of Wijk

Modern course of River Lek

Roman fort

Old course of River Rhine

Old course of River Lek

●   Cemetery

▦   Harbour

▩   Commercial zone - warehouses, etc.

▤   Farming community

After W.A. Van Es and W. Verwers and R.O.B. (Dutch State Archaeological Service)
R. Hodges

Dorestad

Rhine

0   50
km

Dublin

Before Scandinavians first settled at Dublin in 841 two native settlements already existed. Áth Cliath ('hurdleford') was a ridge-top cluster and focal point of long-distance highways above a ford across the Liffey. The 'hurdles' were probably rafts of light timber deposited on mud-flats on either side of the river channel. Dubhlinn (early Irish Duiblinn, 'black pool') was an ecclesiastical complex within a typical ovoid enclosure. The Old Norse form Dyflinn was clearly derived from the latter name and late ninth-century habitation levels have been recovered archaeologically from the defended township (Irish *dún*, 'stronghold'). An assembly site (Thingmót) was established by the shore of Dublin Bay and nearby stood a ceremonial marker, the Long Stone, commemorating the taking of this major Scandinavian settlement. Some early churches were pre-viking while others may reflect Christian observance outside the *dún* prior to the official acceptance of Christianity *c.* 1030 and the construction of a cathedral due west of it.

H.B. Clarke

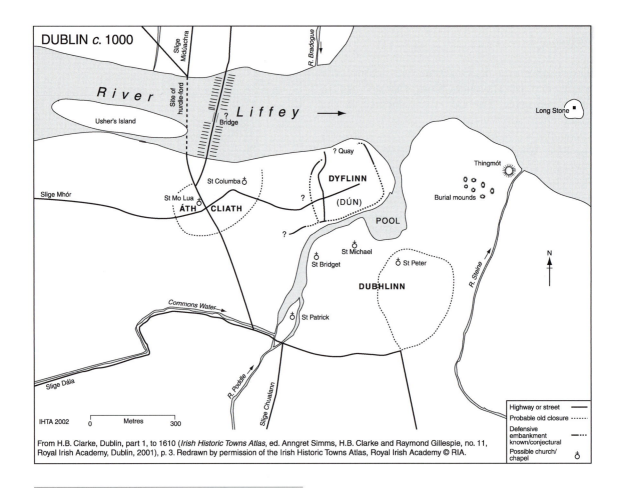

DUBLIN *c.* 1000

Slige Midúachra
R. Bradogue
R i v e r
Site of hurdle-ford
Usher's Island
? Bridge
L i f f e y →
Long Stone
? Quay
St Columba ♂
Slige Mhór
St Mo Lua ♂
ÁTH CLIATH
?
DYFLINN
(DÚN)
Thingmót
Burial mounds
POOL
?
?
St Michael ♂
St Bridget ♂
St Peter ♂
R. Steine
N
DUBHLINN
Commons Water
St Patrick ♂
Slige Dála
R. Poddle
Slige Chualann
IHTA 2002
0 Metres 300

From H.B. Clarke, Dublin, part 1, to 1610 (*Irish Historic Towns Atlas*, ed. Anngret Simms, H.B. Clarke and Raymond Gillespie, no. 11, Royal Irish Academy, Dublin, 2001), p. 3. Redrawn by permission of the Irish Historic Towns Atlas, Royal Irish Academy © RIA.

Highway or street	——
Probable old closure	······
Defensive embankment known/conjectural	—·—·—
Possible church/chapel	♂

Constantinople

Constantinople was chosen in 324 by Constantine as the capital of the Roman Empire in the east. It stands on a peninsula at the meeting point of the Bosphorus, the Golden Horn and the Sea of Marmora, at the hub of the main routes connecting Europe and Asia. Though Constantine wanted his capital to conform schematically to Rome, with its seven hills, twelve regions and forums, its layout was radically different, even before the construction of the Theodosian Walls in 413. It was articulated around the *Mese*, the great avenue which proceeded from the Golden Gate, the ceremonial entrance to the city, through a series of forums to the Augousteion. This was the heart of the city, surrounded by the Imperial Palace, the cathedral of St Sophia and the Hippodrome.

It suffered extensive damage during the Nika riots of 532 but this allowed Justinian to reconstruct many public buildings, including St Sophia, thus setting his stamp on the city. Particular attention was paid to the water supply with its aqueducts and cisterns. This was a necessity with a population approaching half a million. Population declined rapidly from the seventh century, however, and only in the ninth century did the city recover some of its prosperity, a new feature being the foreign 'factories' established along the Golden Horn, which was the commercial centre of the city. Permanent decline set in after its fall to the fourth crusade in 1204.

M. Angold

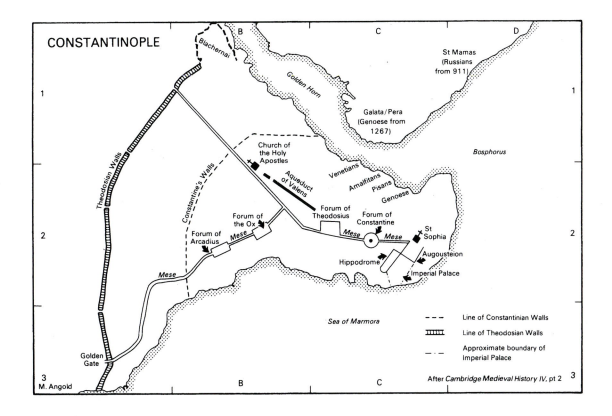

CONSTANTINOPLE

St Mamas
(Russians
from 911)

Galata/Pera
(Genoese from
1267)

Golden Horn

Bosphorus

Blachernai

Theodosian Walls

Constantine's Walls

Church of
the Holy
Apostles

Aqueduct
of Valens

Venetians

Amalfitans

Pisans

Genoese

Forum of
Theodosius

Forum of
Constantine

Forum of
the Ox

Forum of
Arcadius

Mese

Mese

Mese

Mese

St
Sophia

Augousteion

Hippodrome

Imperial Palace

Mese

Sea of Marmora

Golden
Gate

M. Angold

- - - Line of Constantinian Walls

ⅢⅢⅢ Line of Theodosian Walls

- · - Approximate boundary of
Imperial Palace

After *Cambridge Medieval History IV*, pt 2

Rome

Although Rome ceased to be a regular imperial residence by the fourth century, it retained great prestige as the seat of the senate and the papacy. Numerous churches were built, including martyr-shrines, transformed houses of earlier private patrons (*tituli*), and major imperial foundations. Despite sacking by Visigoths and Vandals and Germanic rule after 476, its wealth, population and artistic production remained high until the mid-sixth century, when the Gothic War (535–54), the eclipse of the Senate and the Lombard invasion (568) led to precipitate decline. The city was capital of a Byzantine duchy *c.* 536–727 but the papacy exercised increasing control over the city from the pontificate of Gregory I (590–604). Although habitation was largely confined to the river banks beneath the Palatine, it remained culturally important because of the many Greek monasteries manned by eastern refugees and

churches which continued to be built to serve as charitable complexes (*diaconiae*), or to cater for a growing number of relics and pilgrims.

Following conflicts with Byzantium over iconoclasm, taxation and the Empire's inability to resist Lombard encroachments, the popes strove from *c.* 727 to set up an autonomous papal state. A close alliance was built up with the Franks, culminating in the imperial coronation of Charlemagne in St Peter's (Christmas Day 800). Although relations were often uneasy and Byzantine cultural and social influence remained strong, Rome's enhanced political and jurisdictional role led to increased wealth and building activity. This was reaffirmed (and the endemic problem of local noble violence was partly reduced) by the imperial coronation of the Saxon king, Otto I, in 962.

T.S. Brown

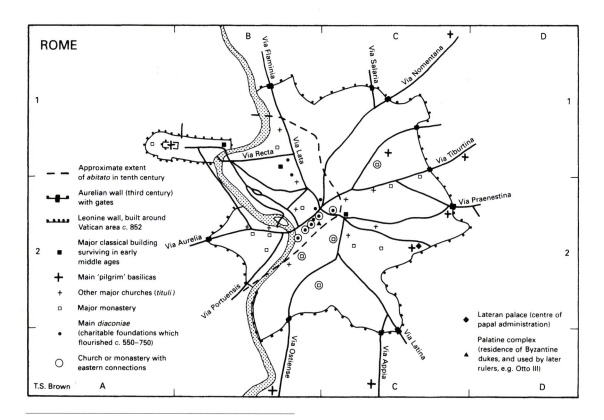

ROME

Legend:

- - - - Approximate extent of *abitato* in tenth century

■█■ Aurelian wall (third century) with gates

⊥⊥⊥⊥⊥ Leonine wall, built around Vatican area *c.* 852

■ Major classical building surviving in early middle ages

✛ Main 'pilgrim' basilicas

+ Other major churches (*tituli*)

□ Major monastery

• Main *diaconiae* (charitable foundations which flourished *c.* 550–750)

○ Church or monastery with eastern connections

◆ Lateran palace (centre of papal administration)

▲ Palatine complex (residence of Byzantine dukes, and used by later rulers, e.g. Otto III)

T.S. Brown

Roads labelled: Via Flaminia, Via Salaria, Via Nomentana, Via Lata, Via Recta, Via Tiburtina, Via Praenestina, Via Aurelia, Via Portuensis, Via Ostiense, Via Appia, Via Latina

Ravenna

Roman Ravenna, with its port of Classe, was an important naval base. The security and good communications afforded by its surrounding marshes and canals encouraged the Emperor Honorius to transfer the imperial capital there in 402 and the size of the city increased dramatically, during its 'first golden age' (lasting until the fall of the western empire in 476 and reflected in richly decorated buildings such as the Mausoleum of Galla Placidia and the Baptistry of the Orthodox).

Ravenna continued to flourish as the capital of the Italian kingdom under King Odoacer (476–93) and his Ostrogothic successors (493–540), whose commissions include the Arian baptistry, the Gothic cathedral, Theoderic's palace and its chapel (later renamed S. Apollinare Nuovo) and the same king's mausoleum. The city's status was matched by the power of its bishops, whose foundations include the octagonal S. Vitale and the basilica of S. Apollinare in Classe (only completed after the Byzantine conquest (540) when such decoration as the court mosaic of the Emperor Justinian and Empress Thedora was added).

The city's affluence and artistic production declined after Justinian's death (565) because of the Lombard invasions, weakening links with the east and the silting up of its harbour. It remained politically important as the residence of the exarch (first mentioned 584). This imperial garrison became a powerful force as it put down local roots and led a number of revolts from the early seventh century. The patronage of external rulers and pious locals helped the archbishops to become *de facto* rulers of the Romagna and Marches after Ravenna's capture by the Lombards in 751 and subsequent incorporation in the papal state. For three or more centuries the city remained an important local capital, despite its commercial and cultural decline.

T.S. Brown

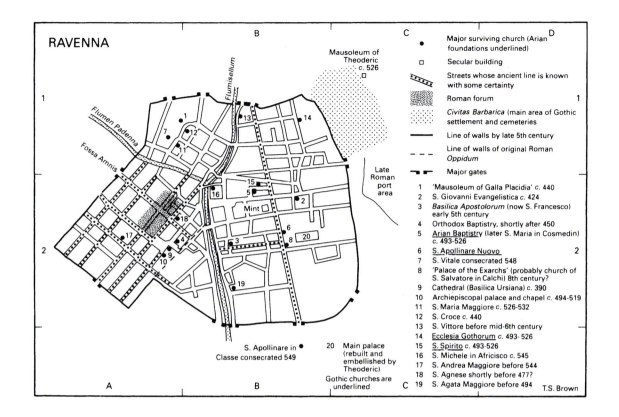

RAVENNA

Mausoleum of Theoderic *c.* 526

Late Roman port area

- ● Major surviving church (Arian foundations underlined)
- □ Secular building
- Streets whose ancient line is known with some certainty
- Roman forum
- *Civitas Barbarica* (main area of Gothic settlement and cemeteries)
- Line of walls by late 5th century
- Line of walls of original Roman *Oppidum*
- Major gates

1 'Mausoleum of Galla Placidia' *c.* 440
2 S. Giovanni Evangelistica *c.* 424
3 *Basilica Apostolorum* (now S. Francesco) early 5th century
4 Orthodox Baptistry, shortly after 450
5 Arian Baptistry (later S. Maria in Cosmedin) *c.* 493-526
6 S. Apollinare Nuovo
7 S. Vitale consecrated 548
8 'Palace of the Exarchs' (probably church of S. Salvatore in Calchi) 8th century?
9 Cathedral (Basilica Ursiana) *c.* 390
10 Archiepiscopal palace and chapel *c.* 494-519
11 S. Maria Maggiore *c.* 526-532
12 S. Croce *c.* 440
13 S. Vittore before mid-6th century
14 Ecclesia Gothorum *c.* 493-526
15 S. Spirito *c.* 493-526
16 S. Michele in Africisco *c.* 545
17 S. Andrea Maggiore before 544
18 S. Agnese shortly before 477?
19 S. Agata Maggiore before 494

S. Apollinare in Classe consecrated 549

20 Main palace (rebuilt and embellished by Theoderic)

Gothic churches are underlined

T.S. Brown

Trade routes of the Carolingian Empire

The trade routes of the Carolingian Empire can only be reconstructed with some difficulty from the written sources of the period. As a result, before archaeological evidence was available, there was much debate about whether the Carolingians engaged in trade on any scale at all. In the past thirty years archaeological investigations of the major trading towns at Dorestad (The Netherlands), Haithabu (Germany), Ribe (Denmark), Quentovic (France), Ipswich, London, Hamwic and York (England) have, however, made it possible to reconstruct the trading activities in which the Carolingians played a direct role. In addition, excavations of comparable settlements around the Baltic Sea reveal the far-flung influence of the Empire, while current research in Italy begins to point to small-scale trade connections between

Beneventum and the Aghlabid dynasty of the Maghreb.

The pattern of trade in this period is most conveniently described in terms of commercial networks embracing (a) the North Sea, (b) the English Channel, (c) the Baltic Sea and (d) the Mediterranean.

Archaeological evidence indicates that traders operated between the Austrasians (in the Rhineland), the Frisians, the Danes and the Anglo-Saxon kingdoms of Kent and East Anglia as early as the sixth century. This trade was probably on a small scale, involving prestige goods. But late in the seventh century a large Frisian trading community was founded at Dorestad, near the mouth of the Rhine, from where Rhenish manufactured goods were shipped to new ports as far as Ribe, London and

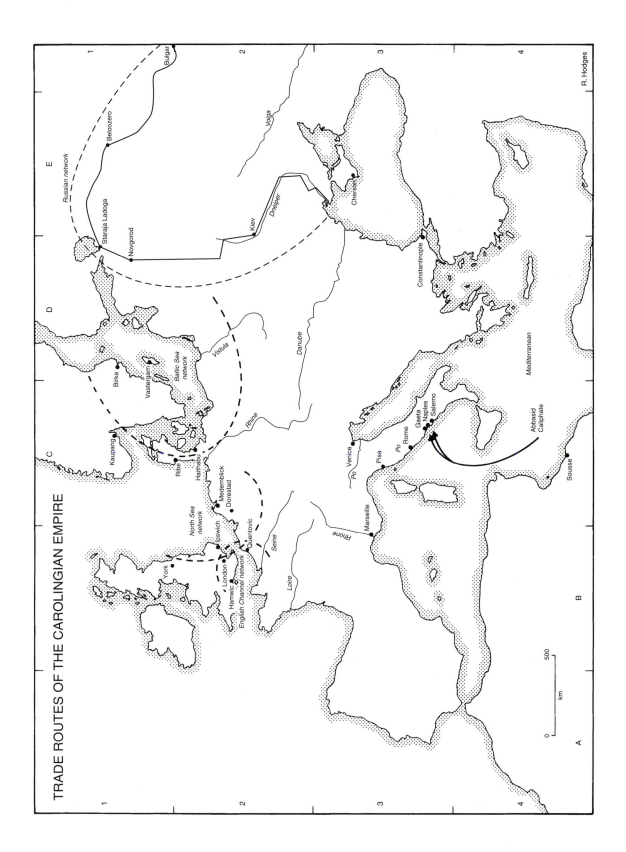

TRADE ROUTES OF THE CAROLINGIAN EMPIRE

R. Hodges

Russian network

Bulgar

Beloozero

Staraja Ladoga

Novgorod

Kiev

Cherson

Constantinople

Volga

Dnieper

Danube

Vistula

Rhine

Birka

Vastergarn

Baltic Sea network

Kaupang

Ribe

Haithabu

Medemblick

Dorestad

North Sea network

Ipswich

Quentovic

York

Hamwic

London

English Channel network

Seine

Loire

Rhône

Marseille

Venice

Po

Pisa

Po

Rome

Gaeta

Naples

Salerno

Mediterranean

Abbasid Caliphate

Sousse

500

km

0

Ipswich, serving the kingdoms of Denmark, Mercia and East Anglia respectively. By Charlemagne's time the commerce had grown and was of considerable political importance. At this time Ribe was replaced by the new port at Haithabu, where the North Sea and Baltic trade networks intersected. After about 830 the North Sea network declined, however, and it was not fully revived until the eleventh century.

Carolingian traders also maintained a largely separate trade network from northern France (the old kingdom of Neustria) to Kent and Wessex. The principal Carolingian port was Quentovic, near Montreuil-sur-Mer, and Hamwic, Anglo-Saxon Southampton – a planned town spread out over 45 hectares – was the main port on the opposite side of the Channel. The history of this system ran parallel to the North Sea network, and it too went into decline after *c.* 830.

Trade across the Baltic Sea existed on a small scale between the later Roman period and *c.* 790, when Scandinavians made contact with the Abbasid caliphate. At this point small trading towns, handling oriental silver and prestige goods, as well as Scandinavian slaves and furs, were founded in several territories around the Baltic, of which Staraja Ladoga (Russia), Birka (Sweden), Vastergarn on Gotland and Kaupang (Norway) are the best-

known. It is likely that several distinct trade networks embraced this large region, linking merchants who plied the rivers of western Russia in the east to those who operated out of Haithabu and dealt with North Sea and west Scandinavian traders. This pattern of trade continued intermittently until the later tenth century.

Little evidence exists for trade across the Mediterranean between the late seventh century and the early eleventh century. Nevertheless, the Abbasid caliph, Harun al' Rashid, gave Charlemagne an elephant which he sent by ship from Egypt to Pisa late in the eighth century, which may indicate the path of small-scale connections at this time. Certainly, a number of Carolingian written sources point to a trade route from Sousse and other North African ports to Gaeta, Naples and Salerno in the kingdom of Beneventum. This may explain the source of the large amounts of gold and silver that the kingdom of Beneventum was obliged to pay as tribute to the Carolingians. The connection, though, was short-lived and faltered once the Empire disintegrated. The demise of this trade route in the 830s may have spurred the Arabs to raid for what previously they had traded, much as their counterparts, the vikings, were doing in the North Sea.

R. Hodges

The economy of San Vincenzo al Volturno

The Benedictine monastery of San Vincenzo al Volturno was founded in the foothills of the Apennines in *c.* 703. Its history can be reconstructed from a twelfth-century chronicle (*Chronicon Vulturnense*) and from archaeological excavations. Like its close neighbour, Monte Cassino, its foundation was perhaps supported by the Lombard dukes of Beneventum. Until *c.* 780 San Vincenzo was small, with some land in the upper Volturno valley and a few minor estates in the high mountain zone (the Abruzzo)

to the north. In 787 it came under Carolingian jurisdiction. It was granted privileges and immunities from taxation. New buildings were erected, accommodating a large body of monks.

Following the election of Abbot Joshua (792) a grand new abbey, guest quarters, churches and other buildings were created. Up to 500 monks and similar numbers of lay brethren lived there but the abbey depended upon non-local labour and resources. The villages in its upper Volturno *terra* were largely unaffected by the

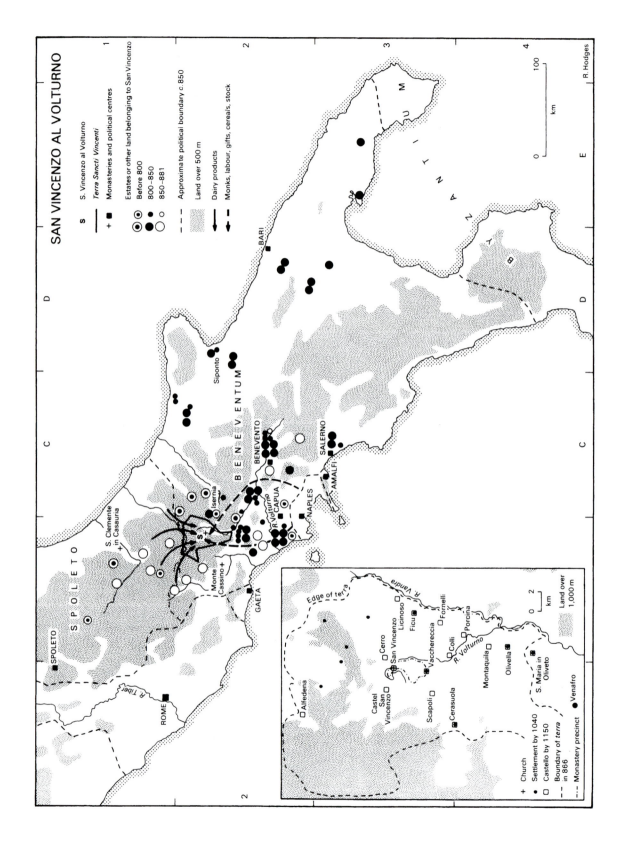

SAN VINCENZO AL VOLTURNO

s   S. Vincenzo al Volturno

Terra Sancti Vincenti

■   Monasteries and political centres

+

Estates or other land belonging to San Vincenzo

	Before 800	800–850	850–881
⊙	⊙	●	○
	⊙	●	○

- - -   Approximate political boundary c. 850

Land over 500 m

↓   Dairy products

⇣   Monks, labour, gifts, cereals, stock

SPOLETO

R. Tiber

ROME

GAETA

S. Clemente
in Casauria

Monte
Cassino +

Isernia

B E N E V E N T U M

Siponto

BARI

BENEVENTO

R. Volturno

CAPUA

NAPLES

SALERNO

AMALFI

M
U

Z

A

R. Hodges

0   100
km

Inset map

Edge of *terra*

R. Vandra

Licinoso

Cerro

Ficu

Fornelli

San Vincenzo

Vaccherecchia

Porcina

Colli

R. Volturno

Castel
San Vincenzo

Alfedena

Scapoli

Cerasuola

Montaquila

Olivella

S. Maria in
Oliveto

Venafro

0   2
km

Land over
1,000 m

+   Church

●   Settlement by 1040

□   Castello by 1150

Boundary of *terra*
in 866

- - -   Monastery precinct

abbey's new affluence. Instead, San Vincenzo obtained more distant estates from the lower-ranking aristocracy of Beneventum. These made it one of Italy's richest landowners.

From these estates, it is proposed, San Vincenzo obtained a workforce to build the new monastery, and also younger sons of the aristocracy to be monks. These lived in timber dwellings in a large *borgo*, as extensive as the monastery, outside the monastic precinct. The *Chronicon* records that columns for the abbey-church were taken from a local Roman site. Craftsmen, too, may have been lent to the abbey. In addition, whereas the villages of the *terra* contributed little to the abbey, archaeological evidence suggests the other estates were developed: stock-breeding and cereal production were intensified.

San Vincenzo may have capitalized on its location to exchange upland dairy products for cereals and animal products of the coastlands. The monastery's own industries may have been used to obtain donations and gifts. Glass vessels, ivories and fine liturgical metalwork were made in its workshops and were perhaps given to donors. By Joshua's death (817), San Vincenzo had become affluent. Its ambitions did not stop. His successor, Talaricus, probably acquired the bones of St Vincent of Saragossa in Spain. With these, he was able to build the resources for a new crypt in the abbey-church, an elevated façade and an atrium to house the cemetery of the monks.

San Vincenzo acquired more estates in the 820s but donations then waned. After civil war in the 840s it was sacked by an Arab war-band on 10 October 881. The monks returned in *c*. 916 but made few repairs before 1000. Instead, the monastery sponsored the development of villages (*incastellamento*) in its *terra*, creating a network modelled on those of the ninth century in the heartlands of the kingdom. The leases granted to these villages indicate that settlers were attracted to clear woodland and developed a mixed farming regime. Their rents and a revival of popular support for monasticism helped San Vincenzo to rebuild its abbey-church and cloisters, and to obtain new estates in the mountains and coastal littoral. In economic terms, it was now a prosperous magnate, competing in the incipient market economy with other ecclesiastical and secular magnates.

San Vincenzo was a model for the transformation of some Italian monasteries into monastic towns. Fragmentary remains from Monte Cassino indicate similar developments, which are also evident at Farfa in the Sabine Hills, Novolesa near Susa and Nonantola near Modena. Indeed, excavations at the Mola di Monte Gelato and Santa Cornelia in north Latium demonstrate the application of a similar strategy on papal estates from the late 780s. Likewise excavations of villages at Miranduolo, Montarrenti and Poggibonsi in western Tuscany indicate that the local aristocracy was also responding to the new economic order, investing in new manor-houses to control previously under-developed communities.

R. Hodges

RELIGION AND CULTURE

Christianity and paganism in the West, c. 350–750

Before and after the conversion of the Emperor Constantine (312–37) Christianity was less established in the West than the East. The problem of the strength of paganism was compounded by the less urban character of the West, lack of local pastoral institutions and of clear hierarchical organization, theological divisions in the Church, and the increasing pressure from barbarian settlers, most of whom were either pagan or Arian (following the conversion of the Goths by Ulfila). The close alliance between Church and state in the East was not replicated in the West and the sack of Rome by the Visigoths in 410 led to a bitter debate between Christian and pagan apologists. Nevertheless, Christianity did much to strengthen its hold on the West from the late fourth century. The western emperor, Theodosius I (379–95), took a firm line against Arianism and paganism. A formidable series of Latin theologians, such as Ambrose (d. 397) and Augustine (d. 430), strengthened the Church's doctrinal position and the conservative senatorial aristocracy finally abandoned paganism in the early fifth century. By the pontificate of Leo the Great (440–61) the see of Rome had built a complex bureaucratic structure. It emerged as the spokesman of the West in disputes with the East and, on the basis of its Petrine origins, claimed special authority in the West, including final ecclesiastical jurisdiction and the right to confirm appointments. The weakening of imperial institutions led to an enhanced political role for the bishops in Rome and other cities. Bishops took over social and charitable services in their cities, negotiated as the representatives of the Roman communities with barbarian leaders and reinforced their hold over their flocks by skilful manipulation of cere-

monies and the cult of saints. The migration from the East of monastic leaders, such as Athanasius and John Cassian, helped spread the phenomenon of monasticism. Although it differed in being more aristocratic and urban, individual monastic figures, such as St Martin of Tours (d. 397) and St Severinus of Noricum (d. c. 470), played an important role in the leadership of their local communities and in evangelizing the countryside.

The collapse of the Empire led to a general extension of the Church's power but its position in particular areas in the sixth century varied according to political circumstances. Southern Britain was one of the few areas where an almost complete disruption of ecclesiastical structures is evident. In Africa, Spain and Italy, the predominantly Arian regimes of the Vandals, Visigoths, Ostrogoths and Lombards restricted the Church's influence although outright persecution was rare. In the Celtic north-west, conversion of southern Scotland and of Ireland had been undertaken in the fifth century by the missionary bishops Ninian and Patrick but in the sixth century the kin-based, non-urban nature of society promoted the emergence of an increasingly monastic form of church. On the continent, new sees were founded, councils regularly convoked and supervisory powers accorded to the heads of provinces (metropolitans or archbishops). With the spread of monastic rules, such as that of St Benedict (d. 547), missionary work became increasingly the preserve of more disciplined and committed monks. Examples include the Irishman Columba, who initiated the conversion of the Picts from Iona c. 565; St Augustine, sent by the powerful Pope Gregory the Great to evangelize the English in 597; and Columbanus

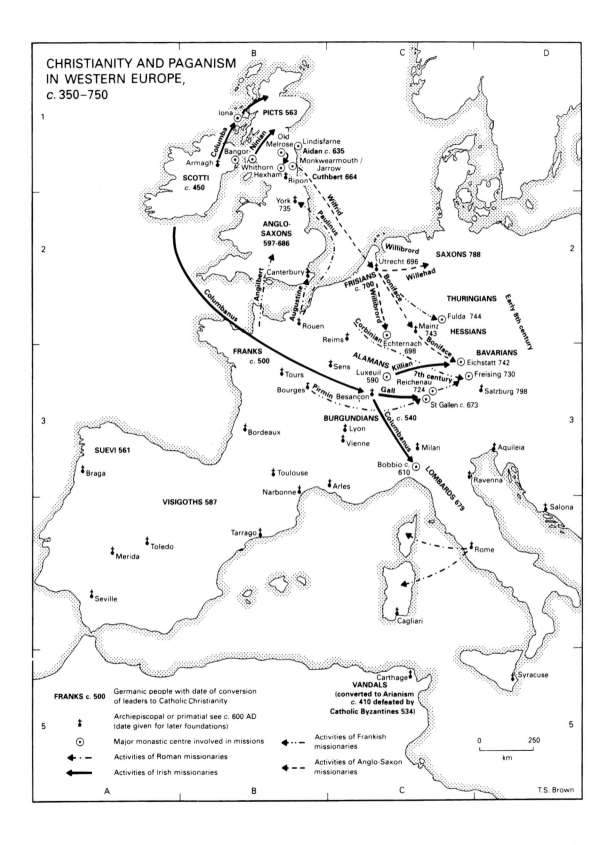

CHRISTIANITY AND PAGANISM
IN WESTERN EUROPE,
c. 350–750

PICTS 563

Iona
Columba
Ninian
Old
Melrose
Lindisfarne
Bangor
Aidan c. 635
Armagh
Whithorn
Hexham
Monkwearmouth /
Jarrow
SCOTTI
c. 450
Ripon
Cuthbert 664
York
735
Wilfrid
Paulinus
ANGLO-
SAXONS
597-686
Willibrord
Canterbury
Saxons 788
Angilbert
Utrecht 696
Augustine
Willehad
FRISIANS
c. 700
Boniface
Columbanus
Rouen
Willibrord
THURINGIANS
Early 8th century
Reims
Corbinian
Fulda 744
Mainz
743
HESSIANS
Echternach
698
Boniface
FRANKS
c. 500
Sens
ALAMANS
Killian
BAVARIANS
Eichstatt 742
Tours
Luxeuil
590
7th century
Reichenau
724
Freising 730
Bourges
Pirmin
Besançon
Gall
St Gallen c. 673
Salzburg 798
BURGUNDIANS
Columbanus
c. 540
Bordeaux
Lyon
SUEVI 561
Vienne
Milan
Braga
Toulouse
Bobbio c.
610
LOMBARDS 679
Aquileia
VISIGOTHS 587
Narbonne
Arles
Ravenna
Tarrago
Salona
Toledo
Merida
Seville
Cagliari
Rome
Carthage
Syracuse

FRANKS c. 500   Germanic people with date of conversion
                  of leaders to Catholic Christianity

              Archiepiscopal or primatial see c. 600 AD
              (date given for later foundations)

              Major monastic centre involved in missions

              Activities of Roman missionaries

              Activities of Irish missionaries

              Activities of Frankish
              missionaries

              Activities of Anglo-Saxon
              missionaries

VANDALS
(converted to Arianism
c. 410 defeated by
Catholic Byzantines 534)

0   250
         km

T.S. Brown

(d. 615) whose austere Irish foundations in Gaul and Italy extended the appeal of Christianity among Germanic aristocrats. The extension and organization of the English Church were largely the work of monks, either Irish-inspired, such as Aidan at Lindisfarne, or Roman in allegiance, such as Wilfrid at York. By the late seventh century Irish and Anglo-Saxon missionaries were winning converts and setting up sees east of the Rhine, the most prominent leaders being Willibrord and Boniface.

By 750 little headway had been made in converting pagans outside the old Roman Empire. Nominal Christians remained attached to traditional Germanic values and superstition remained widespread in the countryside, partly because local parish structures did not yet exist. By vastly improving its hierarchical organization, its writings and the quality of its trained personnel the Church had, however, done much to spread its ideals.

T.S. Brown

Early monasticism to 547

The recorded history of Christian monasticism begins in the Middle East in the late third or fourth century. Although not the first Christian solitary, the Copt Antony (?251–?356) is regarded as the father of Christian eremitism (*eremos* = desert in Greek), spending many years in prayer and contemplation on the edge of the Egyptian desert and latterly retreating to his 'Inner Mountain'. By the mid-fourth century at Nitria, near the mouth of the Nile, at Scetis to the south and in the Thebaid in Upper Egypt colonies of several hundred hermits could be found: such a grouping was known as a *lavra* (from the Greek for a lane or passage). Its inhabitants lived in separate cells but there were common buildings including a church where all gathered on Saturdays and Sundays for communal prayer and mass. The *lavra* spread to Syria and Palestine as did the coenobium (from the Greek *koinos bios* = common life), also Egyptian in origin and founded by another Copt, Pachomius (*c.* 292–346). The first Pachomian community was at Tabennisi on the Upper Nile: such communities were very large and the monks (or nuns) lived together in a number of houses and supported themselves by handicrafts. Coenobitism was spread to the eastern empire and was further refined by the intellectual and theologian Basil of Caesarea (329–79), who entered the monastic life at Annesi and who eventually achieved a more

integrated community than that of Pachomius. He stressed the need for the monk to exercise Christian charity towards his fellows. It is generally held that the monastic movement in the Western Empire began its real evolution under the influence of the East although there already existed an independent tradition of Christian virginity and asceticism and it is possible that the description of the Antonian or *lavra*-style monasticism established at Liguge and Marmoutier by the 'father' of Gallic monasticism, Martin of Tours (d. 397), stemmed from his hagiographer's knowledge of the East as much as Martin's own practice. The visits of the exiled Archbishop Athanasius of Alexandria to Trier and to Rome (335–7 and 339–46) may have inspired western monasticism but possibly even more influential was the translation in the fourth century into Latin of his *Life of Antony* which would become a classic of hagiography and a model for the ascetic life, and was the first of several works about the 'desert fathers' to reach the West. Augustine's conversion to a Christian life followed his introduction at Milan to the *Life*; he founded his own monastery at Tagaste in his native North Africa in 388 and wrote an eastern-influenced *Rule* for his sister's community of nuns. Eastern ascetic ideals were imported into the West by Jerome, who founded his own monastery in Bethlehem in 385 and by Honoratus who founded Lérins

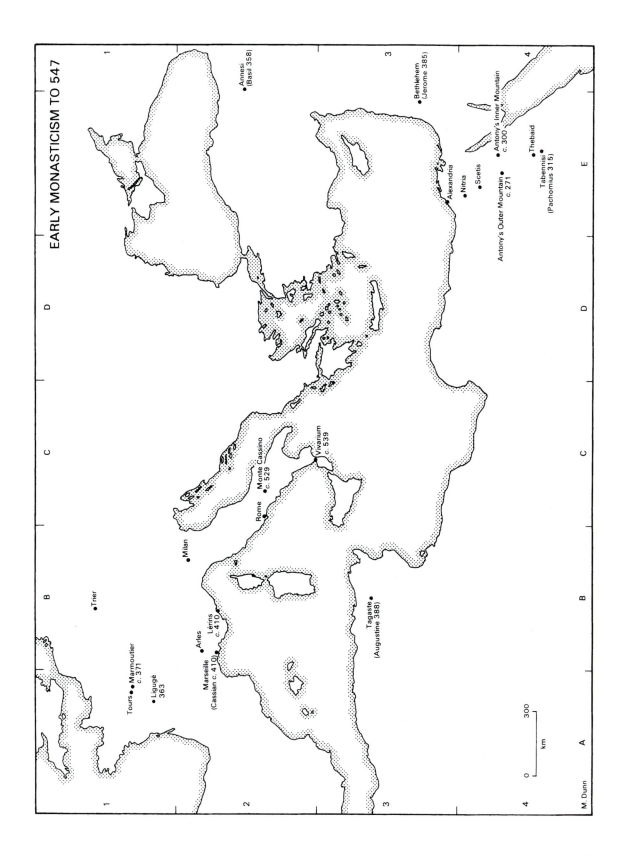

EARLY MONASTICISM TO 547

Annesi
(Basil 358)

Bethlehem
(Jerome 385)

Alexandria
Nitria
Scetis
Antony's Outer Mountain
c. 271
Antony's Inner Mountain
c. 300
Thebaid
Tabennisi
(Pachomius 315)

Trier

Milan

Rome
Monte Cassino
c. 529
Vivarium
c. 539

Tagaste
(Augustine 388)

Tours
Marmoutier
c. 371
Ligugé
363
Marseille
(Cassian c. 410)
Arles
Lérins
c. 410

0   300
km

M. Dunn

c. 410 on his return from travels in the East. About the same time, John Cassian, who had spent a considerable time in eastern monastic communities, and who compiled the *Conferences* of the desert fathers, founded two coenobitic houses at Marseille. His *Institutes* represent the earliest surviving work of monastic instruction composed in western Europe which gave detailed descriptions of the practice of the East. In the sixth century, southern France and Italy produced a number of coenobitic *Rules* including those by bishops Caesarius (*c.* 470–542) and Aurelian (d. 552) of Arles and the (perhaps surviving) compilation of Eugippius of Lucullanum. More controversial is the *Rule of the Master* which is said to have influenced Benedict of Nursia, the founder of Monte Cassino (*c.* 480–*c.* 547). Benedict's *Rule* was not, in any case, an isolated work but reflects both contemporary practice and earlier teaching. It divided the day of the monk between worship (eight offices), reading (*lectio divina*) and work. At Vivarium, founded by Cassiodorus, monastic life was combined with a well-organized programme of studies.

M. Dunn

Northern European monasticism

One of the disciples of Martin of Tours, Ninian (d. 432), began the evangelization of south-west Scotland from his monastery at Whithorn. Martin's monasticism was influential in western France, while the east was dominated by Lérins and Marseille. Radegund, wife of Chlothar I, founded the Convent of the Holy Cross in Poitiers which followed the *Rule* of Caesarius of Arles. Irish monasticism had begun its own development, supposedly influenced, directly or indirectly, by the East, and the mid-sixth century saw the foundation of a cluster of important monasteries, including Clonard (founded by Finian), Clonfert (Brendan), Bangor (Comgall) and Clonmacnoise (Ciaran). Columba (or Colmcille, *c.* 521–97) founded Durrow and Derry and in the 560s migrated to Iona, where he established a monastic centre which also undertook missions among the Scots and Picts. Irish-style monasticism also spread to Melrose and Lindisfarne. About 590 Columbanus travelled from Bangor in Ireland to the continent, where he established Luxeuil under the patronage of the Merovingian court. His *Rule* and accompanying *Penitential* are the earliest surviving documents of this kind from an Irish background and despite the severity of his regime, both Luxeuil and his Italian foundation, Bobbio, attracted recruits. Parts of the *Rules* of Benedict, Columbanus and Caesarius of Arles appear in conjunction in Donatus' seventh-century *Rule* for nuns at Besançon. The use of 'mixed rules' apparently characterized other Frankish foundations, particularly those made in Neustria and Austrasia by some reforming bishops and by the Merovingians and their court – houses such as Rebais, St Wandrille, Jumièges, Pavilly, Fleury and Fécamp. Balthild, wife of Clovis II, founded Corbie with monks from Luxeuil and royal diplomas ensured that older houses such as St Martin, Tours and St Denis (Paris) were free from episcopal financial exactions. Several renowned 'double houses' (i.e. foundations containing both a monastery and a convent) were established in this area and period: the best-known are Faremoutiers, Jouarre and Balthild's own re-foundation of Chelles-sur-Cher. In England continental monasticism arrived from Rome when Augustine and his companions landed in Kent in 597. Traditional assumptions that they followed exclusively the *Rule* of St Benedict have been revised and it is now generally assumed that they too used some sort of 'mixed rule'. In seventh-century England several double houses on the Hiberno-Frankish model were founded, among them Whitby: its first abbess, Hild, presided over the Synod of

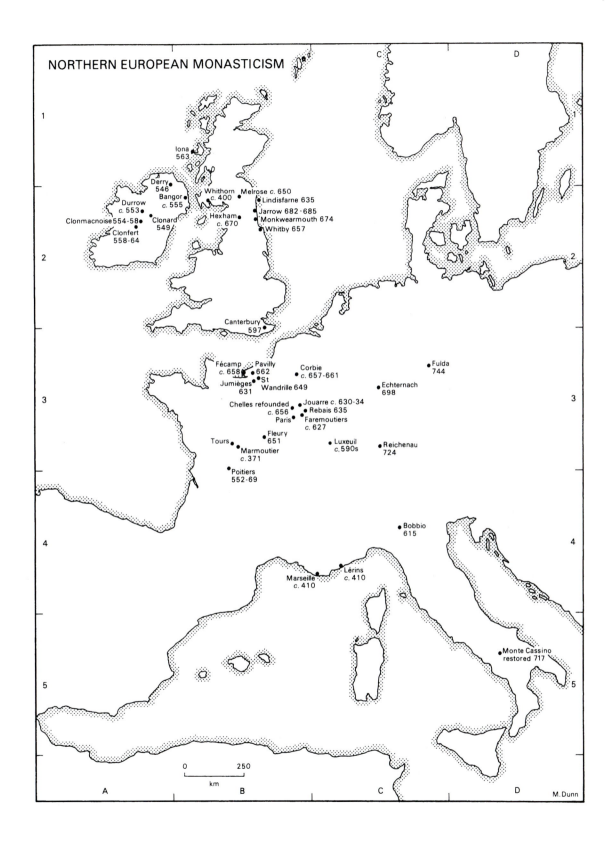

NORTHERN EUROPEAN MONASTICISM

Iona 563

Derry 546
Bangor c. 555
Durrow c. 553
Clonmacnoise 554-58
Clonard 549
Clonfert 558-64

Whithorn c. 400
Melrose c. 650
Lindisfarne 635
Hexham c. 670
Jarrow 682-685
Monkwearmouth 674
Whitby 657

Canterbury 597

Fécamp c. 658
Pavilly 662
St
Jumièges 631
Wandrille 649
Corbie c. 657-661
Fulda 744
Echternach 698

Chelles refounded c. 656
Paris
Jouarre c. 630-34
Rebais 635
Faremoutiers c. 627

Tours
Fleury 651
Luxeuil c. 590s
Reichenau 724
Marmoutier c. 371

Poitiers 552-69

Bobbio 615

Marseille c. 410
Lérins c. 410

Monte Cassino restored 717

0   250
km

A   B   C   D

M. Dunn

71

Whitby (664). Wilfrid, abbot of Ripon and later bishop of York, sought to root out the Celtic practice debated between 'Romans' and 'Celts' at the synod and instituted a more exclusively 'Roman' form of monasticism in his own houses, such as Hexham. At Monkwear-mouth and Jarrow, founded by his friend and contemporary, Benedict Biscop, the customs were based on the Benedictine *Rule* and those of seventeen monasteries (including continental houses) which Benedict Biscop had visited. On the continent, in the late seventh and eighth centuries Frisia, Hessen and Thuringia were evangelized largely by English monks, in particular Willibrord and Boniface: foundations such as Echternach and Fulda showed increased Benedictine influence. So did Reichenau, established by the monk-missionary Pirmin, who may have come from either Ireland or Spain. At the Synod of Aachen (817) Abbot Benedict of Aniane and Emperor Louis the Pious gave formal legislative backing to the Carolingian dynasty's promotion of the Benedictine *Rule*. Despite Benedict of Aniane's encouragement of the use of a 'pure' version of the text of the *Rule*, he also tried to impose a customary with usages in liturgy and practice which often supplemented and surpassed the first Benedict's provisions.

M. Dunn

Irish and Anglo-Saxon centres on the continent

The conversion of the Irish and Anglo-Saxons involved contact with the Christian continent. Communications with Gaul and Italy became frequent after Augustine's mission to Kent (597) and before this the Irish Christian custom of undertaking voluntary, penitential exile had led to the establishment of monasteries abroad. Thus, following Columba's foundation of Iona, Columbanus founded Annegray and Luxeuil in Gaul and Bobbio in Italy. Other important foundations followed at St Gall and Péronne.

From the late seventh century the Anglo-Saxons, whose conversion owed much to the Irish, followed the Irish lead on the continent, although the Anglo-Saxons were primarily concerned with the conversion of their fellow Germans in Frisia and Germany. Amongst the best known of these missionaries are Wilfrid, Willibrord (founder of the monastery of Echternach), Boniface (martyred in 754 and buried at Fulda) and Lull, archbishop of Mainz. The cathedral of Würzburg, an Anglo-Saxon foundation and Irish pilgrimage centre, exemplifies Anglo-Irish contacts. The strongly papal outlook of the Anglo-Saxons could lead to such difficulties as the dispute between Boniface and the Irish Virgil of Salzburg.

Irish and Anglo-Saxon influences on continental Christian culture appear in exegetical, grammatical and other literature and in the transmission of earlier Latin texts. Virgil of Salzburg, Johannes Scottus and Sedulius Scottus were among Irish scholars achieving fame on the continent during the eighth and ninth centuries. Alcuin, a product of the Northumbrian school at York and one of the scholars called by Charlemagne to assist in his ecclesiastical and cultural reforms, worked during his last years at Tours.

The Irish and Anglo-Saxon presence is often indicated by the use in manuscripts of 'insular' scripts and abbreviations. (A ninth-century book-list from St Gall groups such books under the heading *Libri Scottice Scripti*.) More spectacular are the manuscripts decorated in the Hiberno-Saxon style. Some, like the Echternach Gospels or the Irish Gospel books at St Gall, were perhaps imported. Others, like the Cutbercht Gospels (written perhaps at Salzburg), were made on the continent. The initials of such books were widely imitated in Carolingian

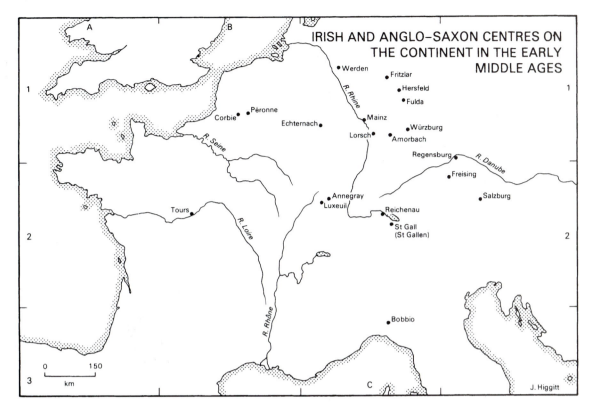

IRISH AND ANGLO-SAXON CENTRES ON THE CONTINENT IN THE EARLY MIDDLE AGES

manuscripts and in the ninth century the style became the basis for the decoration of the 'Franco-Saxon' group of manuscripts.

Such influences cannot easily be mapped. The places selected here are major Irish and Anglo-Saxon foundations and/or centres to which books with insular characteristics have been plausibly attributed.

J. Higgitt

Bede's world

Bede (*c.* 672–735), biblical scholar and 'Father of English History', spent his entire life in the Northumbrian monastery of Wearmouth-Jarrow. His horizons extended, however, far beyond Northumbria. He was something of an armchair traveller. Through texts and travellers he was acquainted with the geography and culture of Europe and as a result Anglo-Saxon England was able to preserve and transmit the Christian culture of the Latin Mediterranean.

Bede described how books, relics, musicians, vestments and glaziers were procured by Benedict Biscop, abbot of Wearmouth, who travelled to Rome six times and was well acquainted with monastic life in Gaul, having received the tonsure at Lérins. Ceolfrith left Wearmouth-Jarrow for Rome with a complete Latin Bible, the *Codex Amiatinus*, but died at Langres. Kings travelled to Rome and sent their daughters to monasteries in Gaul. The turbulent career of Bishop Wilfrid took him to Rome, Gaul and Frisia where the Northumbrian missionary Willibrord later established a bishopric.

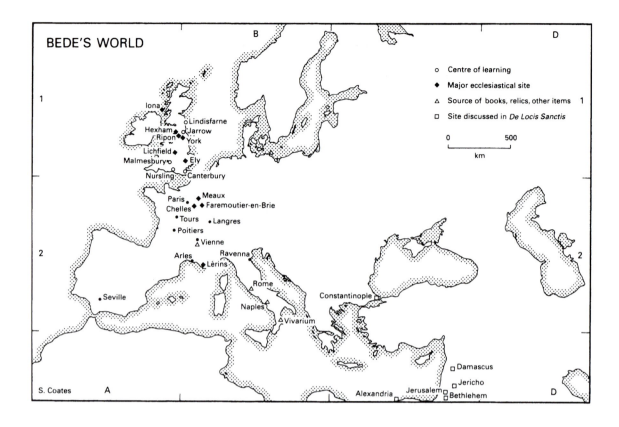

BEDE'S WORLD

- o   Centre of learning
- ◆   Major ecclesiastical site
- △   Source of books, relics, other items
- □   Site discussed in *De Locis Sanctis*

0   500
km

Iona · Lindisfarne · Hexham · Jarrow · Ripon · York · Lichfield · Malmesbury · Ely · Nursling · Canterbury · Paris · Meaux · Chelles · Faremoutier-en-Brie · Tours · Langres · Poitiers · Vienne · Arles · Ravenna · Lérins · Rome · Seville · Constantinople · Naples · Vivarium · Damascus · Jericho · Alexandria · Jerusalem · Bethlehem

S. Coates

Anglo-Saxon England became a notable centre of study through the establishment of schools. Theodore, a Greek monk originally from Tarsus, came to England from an Italian monastery with the African, Hadrian, to become archbishop of Canterbury. He established a school at Canterbury equipped with Greek texts. Foremost among its students was the scholar Aldhelm, who established his own school at Malmesbury. Boniface, the future apostle of Germany, composed his *Ars grammatica* at a school at Nursling and in Northumbria the bishopric and school at Lindisfarne produced an anonymous life of its famous

bishop, St Cuthbert, and a series of lavishly written manuscripts, most notably the Lindisfarne Gospels.

Bede was also aware of the geography of the Holy Land as a result of the travels of the Frankish bishop, Arculf, which were recorded by the ninth abbot of Iona, Adomnan. Adomnan visited Northumbria and enabled Bede to compose his *De Locis Sanctis*. Bede's world was threatened by Arabs. He knew that they had invaded Sicily and that Charles Martel had defeated them at Poitiers in 732.

S. Coates

The cult of St Cuthbert

St Cuthbert was a monk, bishop and hermit of Lindisfarne, the church founded in 630 by the

Northumbrian King Oswald and the Ionan churchman, Aidan. After Cuthbert's death in

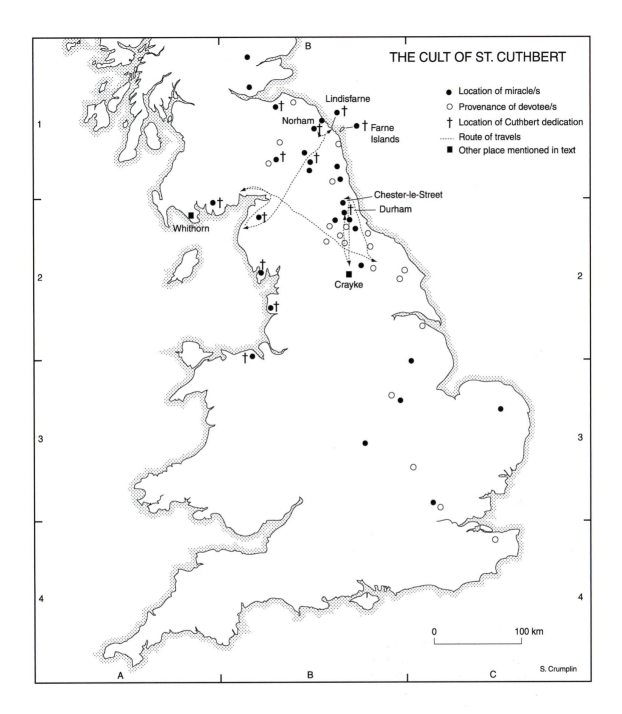

THE CULT OF ST. CUTHBERT

- ● Location of miracle/s
- ○ Provenance of devotee/s
- † Location of Cuthbert dedication
- ⋯⋯ Route of travels
- ■ Other place mentioned in text

Lindisfarne

Norham

Farne Islands

Whithorn

Chester-le-Street

Durham

Crayke

0   100 km

S. Crumplin

687 Lindisfarne gained more strength through his flourishing cult. Indeed, the cult formed the physical focus for the church after its ecclesiastical community had been forced to leave Lindisfarne. From the late eighth century the community moved between the eastern and western seabords and from the Tees to the Forth, asserting its independence in the face of Scandinavian incursions and Anglo-Saxon power struggles. Ultimately it settled at

Chester-le-Street (*c.* 883–995) and then at Durham (995). Cuthbert's cult was central to this church's ability to attract patronage from various kings and nobles, including members of the West Saxon dynasty, Cnut and the Norman King William I. The church was, however, also the focus of massive popular support, as is evident from two twelfth-century miracle collections. The map, based on the rich textual evidence surrounding the cult, illustrates these widespread networks. It shows the travels of Cuthbert's community with his body, from Lindisfarne, possibly to Norham, to Whithorn, south to Crayke, north to Chester-le-Street and then the final move to Durham. These travels are documented in the tenth- and eleventh-century *Historia de sancto Cuthberto* and in Symeon of Durham's early-twelfth-century *Libellus* of the church of Durham. The map also charts the dissemination of Cuthbert's cult in the late twelfth century through the locations of Cuthbertine churches, miracles and pilgrims in Reginald of Durham's miracle collection. St Cuthbert's cult provides an excellent example of the influence that a saint's cult could hold over a wide geographical area, in this particular instance an area that spanned the notional political frontier between England and Scotland.

S. Crumplin

The influx of relics into Saxony

Between 772 and 804, in a long series of bloody campaigns, Charlemagne subjugated the pagan Saxons. A natural corollary to the conquest was a programme of missionary activity and the creation of an ecclesiastical establishment. The heart of Christianity was not, however, formal ecclesiastical structures but rather the cult of the saints and their wonder-working bones. The conversion of the Saxons required the importation of relics (holy bones) from places where they existed in some abundance, such as the churches of northern Francia and, especially, Rome. New monasteries like Corvey and new sees like Hildesheim had to possess such relics as a focus for local devotion and a source of supernatural power. 'The populace can be turned from their superstitions most easily if the body of some famous saint be brought here,' remarked one contemporary Saxon bishop. In 851 the Saxon noble Waltbraht brought the bones of St Alexander from Rome to his monastery at Wildeshausen. The conversion was obviously sending down roots, for Waltbraht was the grandson of Widukind, the hero of the Saxon opposition to Charlemagne.

R. Bartlett

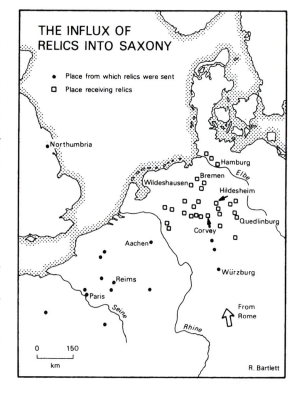

The Carolingian Renaissance

The 'Carolingian Renaissance' is the term conventionally given to a diverse range of reforms and cultural activities sponsored by the Carolingian kings from the mid-eighth century until the end of the ninth. The roots of the phenomenon lay in the notion of a king's duty to 'correct' his people which was internalized by the rulers of the post-Roman West: 'he who does not correct does not rule', as Isidore of Seville put it in his influential seventh-century *Etymologies*. This impulse to correct took on a new intensity under the patronage of the Frankish rulers Pippin (751–68), Charlemagne (768–814) and Louis the Pious (814–40). The aims of these kings were encapsulated in great pieces of written legislation such as the *Admonitio Generalis* of 789, which had as its central theme the obliteration of sin through the correction of religious faith and practice. Reform was not restricted to policing monastic lifestyle and clerical purity: the pursuit of peace, justice and correct faith was supposed to infuse all the institutions of the realm and transform the whole of society. The most spectacular achievement of this drive for standardization was the production of (primarily Latin) texts: over 7,000 manuscripts survive from the ninth-century west, compared to around 1,800 for the previous eight centuries combined. Ninth-century catalogues confirm that many monastic centres quickly acquired extensive libraries: around 400 manuscripts are listed at St Gall and Reichenau and 250 at St Riquier. Naturally, many of these texts were religious. Bibles, canon law, sacramentaries (mass-books) and other authoritative Christian works were produced in large quantities by scriptoria such as Corbie, St-Amand, Orléans, Metz and Tours. Nevertheless, ancient (pagan) literature constituted a significant minority: the earliest copy of almost every major classical author is Carolingian. The library catalogues also show a keen interest in the writing and copying of histories (contemporary and ancient), royal legislation, educational texts and a range of other genres. Formal education played a part, though its benefits were restricted to the elite. It is difficult to pin down the physical location of Carolingian schools, though there were famous teachers at the churches of Fulda, Tours, St-Gall, Auxerre, Liège, Metz, Laon, Salzburg and Rheims. The main areas of intellectual activity correspond with the heartlands of the ruling dynasty: principally northern Gaul between the Loire and Meuse rivers, plus the Rhineland and the Lake Constance region. Members of Charlemagne's court circle were made leaders of important churches in these zones. The main impulses of the Carolingian Renaissance were, however, internalized by subsequent generations of scholars independently of the court and kept alive by a constant stream of correspondence and book-borrowing. Because of this, its chief ideologies continued to influence rulers, church leaders and other patrons of learning for generations, even after the division of the Empire in 843 and its collapse in 887–8. These latter developments also helped diversify the nature of the Carolingian project: the later ninth century witnessed the development of vernacular French and German literatures, and Carolingian political culture also had a profound influence on tenth-century England.

S. MacLean

The correspondence of Lupus of Ferrières

Lupus, monk and later abbot of Ferrières, was one of the most prominent products of the Carolingian Renaissance. Born in central Gaul around 805 to aristocratic parents, he seems to

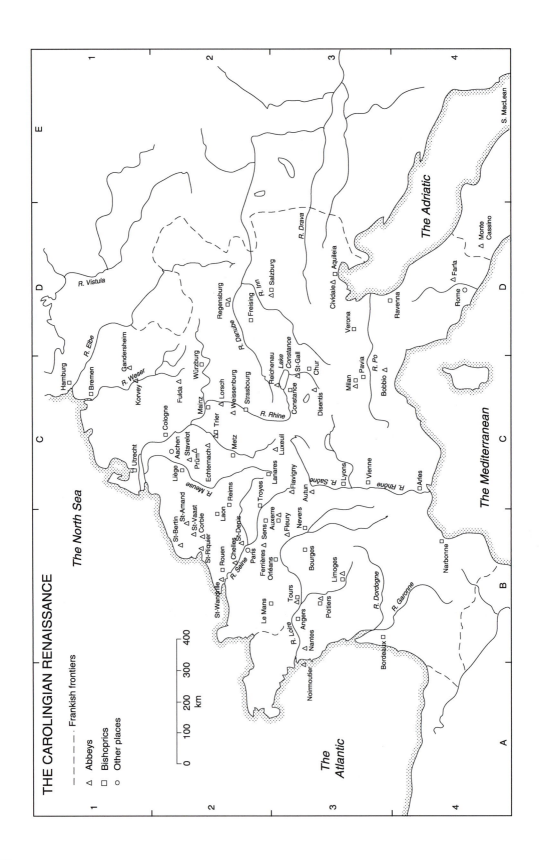

THE CAROLINGIAN RENAISSANCE

- - - - Frankish frontiers

△ Abbeys
□ Bishoprics
○ Other places

0   100 200 300 400
km

The North Sea

The Atlantic

The Mediterranean

The Adriatic

R. Vistula
R. Elbe
R. Weser
R. Danube
R. Rhine
R. Meuse
R. Seine
R. Loire
R. Saône
R. Rhône
R. Garonne
R. Dordogne
R. Drava
R. Inn
R. Po
Lake Constance

Hamburg
Bremen
Gandersheim
Korvey
Fulda
Würzburg
Regensburg
Freising
Salzburg
Cologne
Utrecht
Liège
Aachen
Stavelot
Prüm
Echternach
Trier
Metz
Mainz
Lorsch
Weissenburg
Strasbourg
Reichenau
Constance
St-Gall
Chur
Disentis
St-Bertin
St-Amand
St-Vaast
Corbie
St-Riquier
St-Wandrille
Rouen
Laon
Reims
Luxeuil
Lanares
Flavigny
Autun
Troyes
Sens
Auxerre
Fleury
Nevers
Chelles
St-Denis
Paris
Ferrières
Orléans
Bourges
Limoges
Le Mans
Tours
Angers
Poitiers
Nantes
Noirmoutier
Bordeaux
Narbonne
Lyons
Vienne
Arles
Milan
Pavia
Bobbio
Verona
Cividale
Aquileia
Ravenna
Rome
Farfa
Monte Cassino

S. MacLean

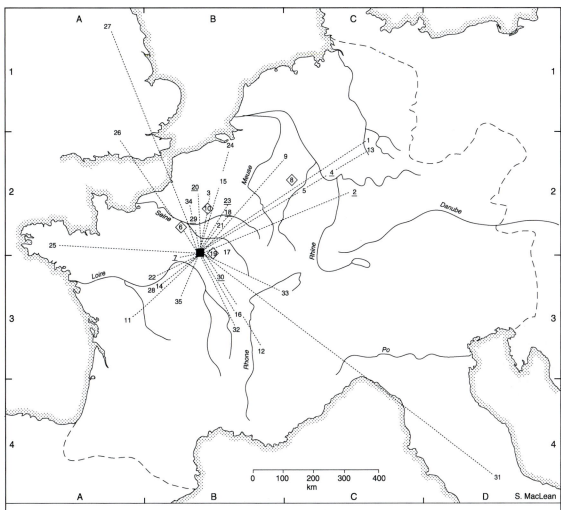

THE CORRESPONDENCE OF LUPUS OF FERRIÈRES

1	Hersfeld (Abbot Bun)	19	Sens (Archbishop Wenilo, Abbot Odo and Count Hugh)	■ FERRIÈRES
2	Seligenstadt (Einhard)	20	Corbie (Abbots Ratbert, Odo and Ratramnus)	2 3 or more letters
3	Noyon (Bishop Immo)	21	Orbais (Gottschalk, a monk)	2 8 or more letters
4	Mainz (Altuin, a monk)	22	Tours (Archbishops Ursmar and Herard)	
5	Trier (Abbot Waldo)	23	Laon (Bishop Pardulus)	
6	St-Denis (Abbot Louis)	24	St-Amand (monks)	
7	Orléans (Bishop Jonas)	25	Brittany (Nominoë, Duke of the Bretons)	
8	Prüm (Abbots Marcward, Eigil and Ansbald)	26	Wessex (King Aethelwulf; Felix, his Archchancellor)	
9	Aachen (Emperor Lothar I)	27	York (Bishop Guigmund and Abbot Altsig)	
10	Compiègne (King Charles the Bald)	28	St-Martin, Tours (Abbot Hilduin)	
11	Poitiers (Bishop Ebroin)	29	Paris (Bishops Ercanrad and Aeneas and the clergy)	
12	Lyon (Archbishop Amulus)	30	Auxerre (Bishop Heribold; monks of St-Germain)	
13	Fulda (Abbot Hrabanus and Hatto, a monk)	31	Rome (Popes Benedict III and Nicholas I)	
14	Cormery (Abbot Odacre)	32	Vienne (Count Gerard)	
15	St-Quentin (Abbot Hugh)	33	Besançon (Bishop Arduic)	
16	Autun (Abbot Usuard)	34	Beauvais (Bishop Odo)	
17	Troyes (Bishops Prudentins and Folcric)	35	Bourges (Bishop Wulfad)	
18	Rheims (Archbishop Hincmar)			

have been destined from the beginning for a career in the church. After entering the monastic life he was sent to study at Fulda, before returning to Ferrières in 836. There he worked as a scholar and teacher before being made abbot in 840 as a reward for supporting Charles the Bald in the Carolingian civil wars. He died in 862. Lupus's modern reputation rests less on his intellectual efforts (which included biblical commentary, legal codification and theological debate) than on the survival of around 130 of his letters. This collection, one of the most significant of the period, illuminates the day-to-day concerns of a Carolingian abbot and scholar. These included the defence of the abbey's properties and privileges: no fewer than thirteen letters from the mid-840s were written to regain the cell of St-Josse that had been lost during the civil wars. The letters also open a window onto the constant exchange of books and ideas that lay at the heart of Carolingian cultural life. Above all, Lupus's careful cultivation of a wide circle of influential friends and

contacts demonstrates the importance of personal networks in politics and intellectual endeavour, especially for figures who built their careers at a couple of removes from direct royal patronage. That some of his most regular correspondents were either relatives (three bishops of Auxerre, possibly Archbishop Wenilo of Sens) or contemporaries from his student days at Fulda (Marcward and Eigil of Prüm, possibly Louis of St-Denis) shows the importance of family and monasteries as nodal points in the construction of such networks. The map shows the extensive nature of Lupus's social circle and thereby illustrates the dynamic nature of communication and learning among the early medieval elite. It can, however, only be impressionistic: the geographical fixing of some recipients (particularly rulers) is somewhat artificial; Lupus wrote a few of these letters on behalf of others; and the map does not include those letters whose recipients cannot be identified with certainty.

S. MacLean

10th- and 11th-century centres of reform

The foundation of the abbey of Cluny in Burgundy in 910 by Abbot Berno and Duke William of Aquitaine was the first step in the creation of the congregation of Cluny. Cluny placed itself directly under the protection of the papacy and eventually became head of a grouping of several hundred monasteries following the Benedictine *Rule* and its own 'customs' (supplementary usages). Another important congregation, also Benedictine in basis but with different emphases from Cluny, was launched in 933 with the reform of Gorze. Brogne brought Benedictine observance to several Flemish monasteries. In England between 940 and the 980s Dunstan, Ethelwold and Oswald, with the backing of the Wessex kings, began a reform at Abingdon and Glastonbury which was partly influenced by the continent (Fleury, Ghent,

Cluny and Gorze) and which led to the composition of the *Regularis Concordia*.

At the beginning of the eleventh century Romuald of Ravenna became the father of an organized eremitical life; after spending time as a hermit in the area of Venice and travelling to the Benedictine house of Cuxa in the Pyrenees, he returned to north-eastern Italy and founded monasteries and hermitages. The most famous of these was Camaldoli, which combined a sort of *lavra* for hermits with a *cenobium* which acted as a buffer between the hermits and the world. A similar organization characterized Fonte Avellana, of which the reformer, Peter Damian, was prior. Around 1039, John Gualbert founded the house – later the congregation – of Vallombrosa, which adhered strictly to the *Rule* of St Benedict and was grouped on federal

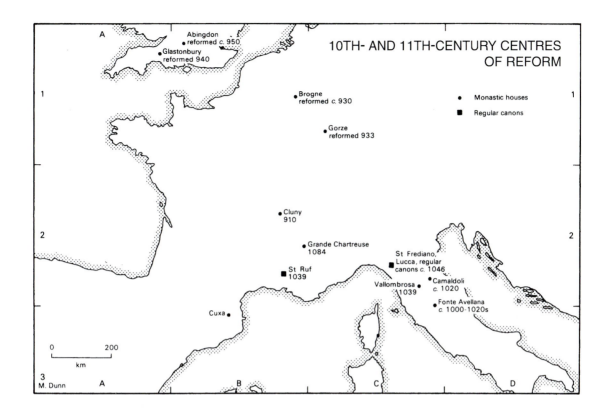

A

Abingdon
• reformed c. 950

• Glastonbury
reformed 940

• Brogne
reformed c. 930

• Monastic houses

■ Regular canons

• Gorze
reformed 933

• Cluny
910

• Grande Chartreuse
1084

St Frediano,
■ Lucca, regular
canons c. 1046

■ St Ruf
1039

• Camaldoli
c. 1020

Vallombrosa •
1039

• Fonte Avellana
c. 1000-1020s

Cuxa •

0   200
km

M. Dunn   A   B   C   D

lines. The foundation of the Grande Chartreuse by Bruno of Rheims in 1084 marked the beginning of an order which, by the early twelfth century, had both eremitic and cenobitic characteristics: the monks lived an austere contemplative life, keeping largely to individual cells which were ranged around a cloister. The idea of a common life for canons, hitherto strongest in the Empire, gained fresh impetus in France and Italy with the foundation of the influential houses of St Ruf and St Frediano.

M. Dunn

The Peace of God

The Peace of God is a name given by modern historians to a series of episcopal councils held in and around west Francia from the late tenth century, which tried to regulate the amount of violence inflicted by the aristocracy on the local population. Warriors were encouraged to swear an oath not to harm certain things and people, typically churches, the defenceless (e.g. women, children, pilgrims and unarmed clerics) and productive capacity (e.g. vineyards, cattle and the peasants of other lords). Lawbreakers, and even those who simply refused to swear the oath, would be threatened with excommunication. By the 1030s the Peace was being joined by what contemporaries called the Truce of God whereby all violence not committed as part of a royal or episcopal host or practised on one's own territories was anathematized during certain lengthy periods of the year.

Until recently the Peace of God was

81

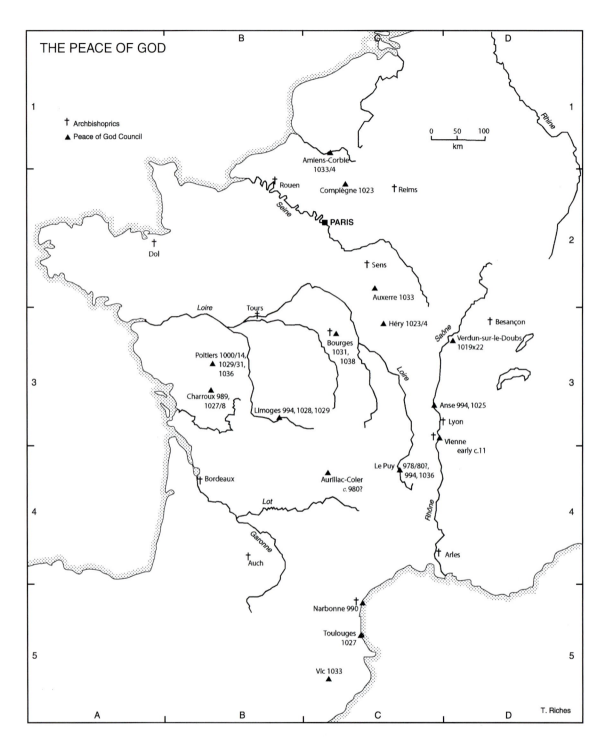

THE PEACE OF GOD

† Archbishoprics
▲ Peace of God Council

Amiens-Corbie
1033/4

† Rouen
Compiègne 1023   † Reims

Seine

■ PARIS

† Dol

† Sens

Auxerre 1033

Loire   Tours
Héry 1023/4   † Besançon

† ▲
Bourges
1031,
1038

Saône   Verdun-sur-le-Doubs
1019x22

Poitiers 1000/14,
▲ 1029/31,
1036

Loire

Charroux 989,
▲ 1027/8

Limoges 994, 1028, 1029

▲ Anse 994, 1025

† Lyon

† ▲ Vienne
early c.11

Le Puy   978/80?,
994, 1036

† Bordeaux

▲ Aurillac-Coler
c. 980?

Lot

Garonne

Rhône

† Auch

† Arles

Narbonne 990   †

Toulouges
1027

Vic 1033
▲

Rhine

0   50   100
km

T. Riches

A   B   C   D

interpreted as an attempt by the reforming Church to control a lesser aristocracy grown anarchic with the collapse of the Carolingian state. The Truce was seen to be more secular-led. Yet recent work has emphasized the co-operation between ecclesiastical and secular magnates, such as the duke of Aquitaine, from the beginning. In this respect the Peace of God can be seen as a continuation, not replacement, of Carolingian tradition.

Some sources describe relics being brought to the meeting place as well as crowds gathering to witness miracles and declaim their support for the Peace. It has been argued that this is evidence of eschatological enthusiasm around the millennia of Christ's birth and crucifixion in 1000 and 1033. Descriptions of relic exhibitions and mass approval are not, however, unique to the peace councils and explicit references to millennial feeling are rare. The sources are in fact very disparate and until they are better contextualized, a satisfactory evaluation of the Peace of God will be stubbornly unforthcoming.

T. Riches

Iconoclasm and the dualist heresies in the Byzantine Empire, 8th–12th centuries

In retrospect, iconoclasm and dualism were the most serious challenges facing the Orthodox Church. Dualism rejected the structure of Orthodoxy while iconoclasm was less about images *per se* as about imperial domination of the Church. Ultimately the triumph of images guaranteed the Church much greater freedom. It was presented as a victory for tradition but was more a radical renewal of Church life, in which monks had a leading role. The iconoclast controversy began in the aftermath of Leo III's successful defence of Constantinople against the Arabs (717/18). To restore imperial authority, Leo restricted the uncontrolled veneration – and sometimes worship – of images. It was a moderate and conservative measure which had general support. Opposition came from the fringes of the Empire. The papacy protested, as did John of Damascus from the monastery of St Sabas, outside Jerusalem. The latter provided image veneration with an effective theological defence, which retrospectively cast doubt on Leo III's actions. To counter this, Leo's son and successor, Constantine V (741–75), convened a church council in the palace of Hiereia (754), which formulated an 'iconoclast' theology. This famously asserted that the veneration of images was doubly heretical because they either confounded the humanity and divinity of Christ in the manner of the Monophysites or separated them in the manner of the Nestorians. Unlike his father, Constantine resorted to the wholesale destruction of icons and persecuted those – mostly monks and nuns – who objected. His actions revealed the depth of popular attachment to images which, despite bitter opposition from the army, his daughter-in-law the Empress Irene (780–802) exploited to restore images at the second Council of Nicaea (787). Supporters of images now took command of the Orthodox Church, supplying patriarchs, bishops and abbots. They were in a strong position when in 813 a military coup brought an increasingly repressive iconoclast regime to power. This lingered on until 843, when the widow of the last iconoclast emperor gave in to pressure within the court and administration to restore images. The military excepted, there was now almost no popular support for iconoclasm.

Paradoxically, dualism did have sporadic popular support. The medieval phase of dualism properly begins in the early eighth century with the Paulicians, who established themselves on Byzantium's eastern frontier, with their headquarters at Tephrike. Tacit support from Leo III suggested that they were originally extreme iconoclasts whose distaste for material images encouraged a dualist outlook, which considers

83

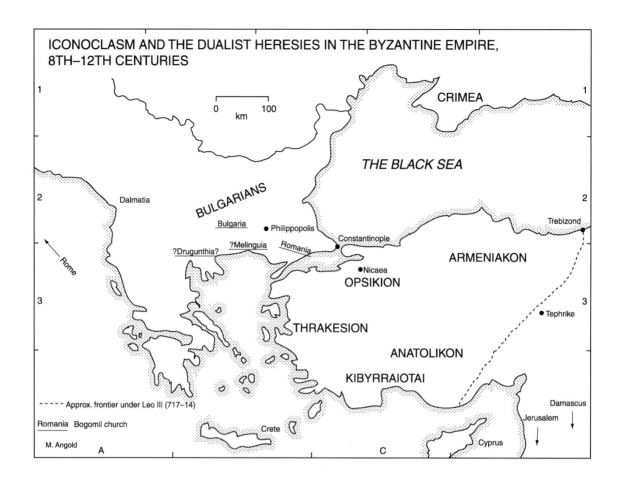

ICONOCLASM AND THE DUALIST HERESIES IN THE BYZANTINE EMPIRE, 8TH–12TH CENTURIES

CRIMEA

THE BLACK SEA

Dalmatia

BULGARIANS

Bulgaria ● Philippopolis

Constantinople

Rome

?Drugunthia? ?Melinguia Romania

ARMENIAKON

●Nicaea

OPSIKION

THRAKESION

Trebizond

● Tephrike

ANATOLIKON

KIBYRRAIOTAI

Damascus

Jerusalem

Crete

Cyprus

- - - - Approx. frontier under Leo III (717–14)

Romania Bogomil church

M. Angold

0   km   100

matter evil, in contrast to the world of the spirit. From the time of the early church dualism represented a counter-culture which bubbled up spontaneously in response to the problem of evil, to which Christianity had no proper answer. Dualism also appealed to a desire for more direct lay participation in religious life, thus challenging the hierarchical ordering of society. It is conceivable that the Paulicians played some kind of coordinating role. Their missionary activities became more important after 878 when the Emperor Basil I destroyed their base at Tephrike and deported large numbers of them to Philippopolis, on the frontier with Bulgaria, where communities of dualists

soon appeared. Known as Bogomils (beloved of God) – a term applied to Byzantine dualist communities – their members called themselves the 'pure (*katharoi*) in spirit'. By the early twelfth century they were organized into five independent churches – Romania, Bulgaria, Dalmatia, Drugunthia and Melenguia. They took as their model the seven churches of Asia, underlining their identification with the early Church. The church of Drugunthia established links with dualist groups in northern Italy and southern France, whose expansion in the twelfth century certainly owed something to the work of missionaries from the Byzantine Empire.

M. Angold

Byzantine missions among the Slavs

The beginnings of this work are closely associated with the brothers Constantine and Methodius, the 'Apostles of the Slavs'. Their first joint mission was in 860 when they were sent to Byzantium's Steppe-allies, the Khazars. Although primarily political, this visit provided them with missionary experience. They put the case for Christianity to the Khazars, who were converting to Judaism. Constantine and Methodius had limited success but were the obvious choice when in 862 the ruler of the Moravians turned to Byzantium for missionaries to counter the Frankish priests working from Passau and Salzburg. Coming from Thessalonica, Constantine and Methodius had the great advantage of knowing the Slavonic language. Their first task was to translate the liturgy and parts of the gospels into Slavonic for use among the Moravians. This angered the Frankish clergy who insisted that there could be

no addition to the number of sacred languages. Constantine and Methodius went to Rome to put their case and secured the support of the papacy. After Constantine's death in 869 Methodius was appointed to Pannonia and the see of Sirmium. The immediate results of his work were unpromising. He was hampered by Frankish hostility and the Hungarian invasion of 895 left almost no trace of his work among the Moravians. After his death in 885 the remnants of his mission were welcomed by the Bulgarian ruler Boris, who was unhappy with the ascendancy of the Greek clergy following his forced conversion in 865 in the aftermath of a Byzantine invasion. Recourse to the papacy was not a success but with the help of Methodius' followers, Clement and Naum, the Bulgarian Church became the main centre of Slavonic Christianity. Much of this achievement passed to the Russians after the baptism at

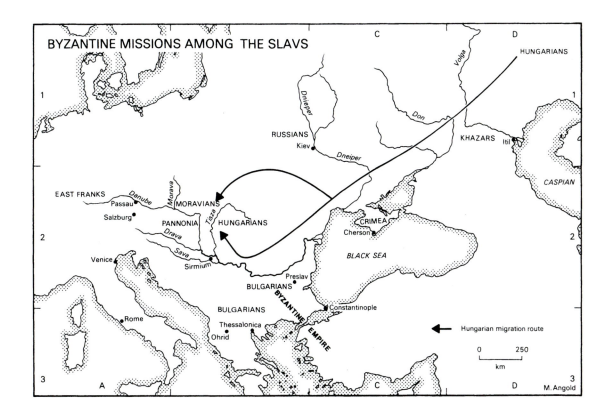

BYZANTINE MISSIONS AMONG THE SLAVS

HUNGARIANS

Volga

Dnieper

Don

RUSSIANS
Kiev
Dneiper

KHAZARS Itil

CASPIAN

EAST FRANKS
Passau
Salzburg
Danube
Morava
MORAVIANS
Tisza
PANNONIA HUNGARIANS
Drava
Sava
Venice
Sirmium

CRIMEA
Cherson

BLACK SEA

Preslav
BULGARIANS

BULGARIANS

Rome

Thessalonica
Ohrid

BYZANTINE EMPIRE

Constantinople

Hungarian migration route

0   250
km

M. Angold

Cherson in 989 of Vladimir, the prince of Kiev. The success of Byzantine missions to the Slavs owed much to the use of Slavonic. It also allowed Slavonic Christianity to develop independently of Byzantium.

M. Angold

Papal authority and the eastern schism

Until the ninth century the Church of Constantinople was willing to accept that the Church of Rome was the ultimate arbiter in matters of Orthodoxy. They were joined in a common allegiance to the creed of Chalcedon (451), with its Roman insistence that Christ has two natures: 'distinct but indivisible'. Time and again from the fifth to the eighth centuries Constantinople broke with Rome, only to return to the fold. In the ninth century Rome's addition of the *filioque* to the creed was not something that Constantinople could overlook because it underlined fundamental disagreements in Trinitarian teaching. Whereas Constantinople remained loyal to the notion that the Holy Spirit proceeded from the Father alone, Rome now posited a double procession from the Father and Son (*filioque*). Among other things this suggested that the pope was presuming on his own authority to alter the creed established by a general council of the church. It alerted Constantinople to the claims being made for papal primacy: that it was not just a matter of precedence but of judicial authority. These differences explain the clash in 1054 between the Byzantine patriarch, Michael Keroularios (1043–58), and the papal legate, Humbert, cardinal of Candida Silva. Over the next hundred

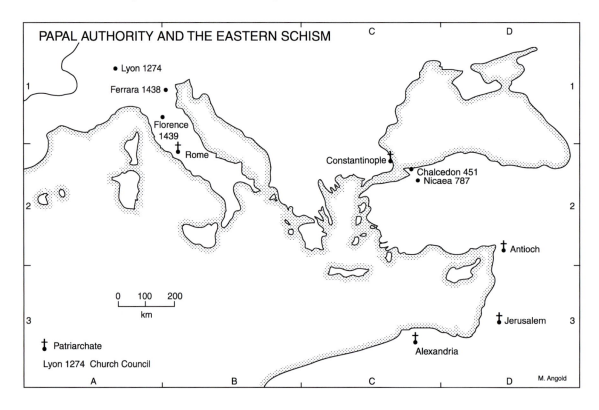

PAPAL AUTHORITY AND THE EASTERN SCHISM

• Lyon 1274

Ferrara 1438 •

• Florence 1439

✝ Rome

Constantinople

• Chalcedon 451
• Nicaea 787

✝ Antioch

✝ Jerusalem

✝ Alexandria

0 100 200
km

✝ Patriarchate

Lyon 1274 Church Council

M. Angold

odd years sincere efforts on both sides to resolve these differences only revealed how far apart the churches were. The crusader conquest of Constantinople in 1204 made the situation still worse. The Byzantines condemned it as religiously motivated, which it was not, but papal support for the establishment of a Latin Church of Constantinople confirmed their worst fears. Despite the recovery of Constantinople (1261) Byzantium remained increasingly dependent on western aid, the price of which was recognition of papal authority. The Byzantines put their faith in a general council of the church but the reunion of churches agreed at the second Council of Lyon (1274) was on terms dictated by the papacy and was soon repudiated by the Byzantines.

By the mid-fourteenth century the position of the Byzantine Empire was so parlous that in 1369 John V Palaiologos (1354–91) travelled to Rome in order to make a personal submission to the pope. He hoped to obtain aid, which was not forthcoming. His son, Manuel II Palaiologos (1391–1425), also sought western help but was saved from the humiliations inflicted on his father by a chance defeat of the Ottomans in 1402. He warned his son, John VIII (1425–48), against the reunion of the churches, advice the latter ignored because he was confident that he could exploit differences between the papacy and the conciliar movement. In 1438 John attended a church council at Ferrara (then adjourned to Florence). This time there was free debate of outstanding differences. The papacy made some concessions but not on the central issues of Trinitarian doctrine and papal authority. When the Byzantine delegation returned home in 1439 its members could not disguise that they had been forced to accept reunion on papal terms. The ensuing demoralization and division made the Ottoman conquest in 1453 more or less inevitable. The union of Florence bore fruit in the southern Russian lands (later known as Ukraine), which were then part of the Polish kingdom. There a uniate church was in existence by 1458. It accepted the teaching and authority of Rome but preserved the Orthodox rite. Its position was officially endorsed at the Council of Brest Litovsk (1596).

M. Angold

Episcopal sees in Europe at the end of the 10th Century

The martyrdom on the Baltic of Adalbert, bishop of Prague, at the hands of the Prussians in 997 marked the drawing to a close of more than two centuries of sustained missionary activity, which gradually brought about the conversion of the pagans of northern and central Europe. The persistent threat that had hitherto been posed to Christian Europe by these pagans, vikings and Slavs, with all the trouble they had brought on the Church, was coming to an end as their rulers chose to adopt Christianity. A period of consolidation and reform led by the papacy followed during which the process of Christianization was advanced throughout the territories inhabited by both the old and the new adherents of the Latin Church.

Politics and religion were closely intertwined on the frontiers of the German kingdom, as its rulers sought to dominate the nascent churches of neighbouring peoples. Missionaries were sent forth from the province of Hamburg-Bremen in the north to convert the Danes, which resulted in the creation of several new sees in the mid-tenth century. Otto I's pet project in this field was the archbishopric of Magdeburg, founded in 968 in the wake of the German settlement of the lands between the Elbe and the Oder, and a new see was erected in the heart of Polish territory, at Poznan, as a suffragan. But with the creation of the metropolitan see of Gniezno in 1000, Poland obtained a Church independent of German control, just as politically it remained

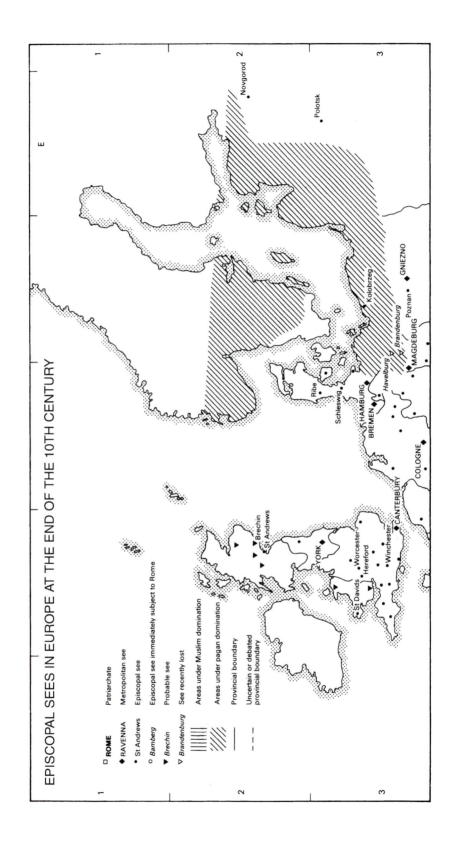

EPISCOPAL SEES IN EUROPE AT THE END OF THE 10TH CENTURY

□ **ROME**   Patriarchate

◆ **RAVENNA**   Metropolitan see

• St Andrews   Episcopal see

○ *Bamberg*   Episcopal see immediately subject to Rome

▼ *Brechin*   Probable see

▽ *Brandenburg*   See recently lost

   Areas under Muslim domination

   Areas under pagan domination

   Provincial boundary

   Uncertain or debated provincial boundary

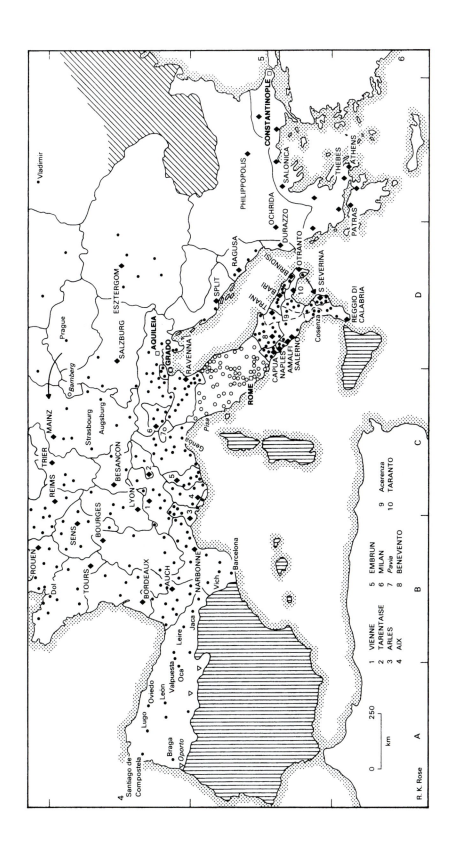

R. K. Rose

outwith the bounds of the Empire, though for a short time jurisdiction over Poznan was retained by the German archbishop. The Hungarian experience was similar. The Bavarian province of Salzburg was most active in the evangelization of the Bohemians, Moravians and Hungarians. The Bohemian diocese of Prague (973) was subjected to Mainz and remained so until the fourteenth century but Hungary, like Poland, achieved an independent Church with the creation of the metropolitan see of Esztergom in 1001.

The eastern and western Churches were in competition with one another for the allegiance of the Slavs and while Rome had gained most of central Europe, the Byzantines had successfully established the Bulgarian and, more recently, the Russian Churches. Tension between Latins and Greeks, due to complex reasons of which theological differences were a part, was most evident in southern Italy. Here the Byzantines held sway over Apulia, Basilicata and Calabria, with a considerable Greek population in the extreme south, which belonged to the partriarchate of Constantinople. On the western side of the peninsula the Lombards of Campania observed the Latin rite. The German Ottonian emperors (962–1002) had ambitions to wrest the region from Byzantine control, which would have effected its union with the Roman or western patriarchate but it was not until some years after the Norman conquest that the entire south was subordinated to Rome. By 1000 there were five southern Italian provinces in the Constantinopolitan obedience: Reggio di Calabria, St Severina, Otranto, Taranto and Brindisi-Oria. Apulia was an area of mixed population and technically pertained to Rome. Nevertheless, the metropolitans of the province of Bari-Canosa were as likely to recognize the authority of Constantinople as that of Rome and from the mid-tenth century they frequently also held the archbishopric of Brindisi-Oria. Moreover, the decision to erect the archbishopric of Trani (by 987) was taken in Constantinople rather than Rome and may have been a reaction against Rome's creation of the province of Benevento in 969. Pope John XIII (965–72),

at the request of Otto I, seems to have expressly established Benevento, with its many suffragans, as a Latin outpost. The same at least might be said of Salerno, if indeed its foundation cannot be described as an outright attempt to eat into the Greek patriarchate. In 989 Pope John XV (985–96) gave the new archbishop jurisdiction over Acerenza and the Calabrian sees of Bisignano, Malvito and Cosenza. Acerenza, although also technically belonging to Rome, had already been assigned with four other sees in 968 to the province of Otranto by Polyeuctes, patriarch of Constantinople, and Bisignano, Malvito and Cosenza had at the beginning of the tenth century been listed among the suffragans of Reggio di Calabria. Continual confirmation of these sees to Salerno by successive popes casts some doubt on the ability of the archbishops to command the obedience of their occupants and such difficulties probably lay behind the Norman Robert Guiscard's agreement with Pope Nicholas II (1058–61) in 1059 to subject the churches of any territories he might conquer to Rome. In any event, Acerenza and Cosenza were erected into metropolitans by the mid-eleventh century and Bisignano and Malvito were made immediately subject to Rome by the mid-twelfth.

From the early eighth century the chief threat to the Christian Church in the Mediterranean was Islam. As well as the greater part of the Iberian Peninsula and its outlying islands, the Arabs held Sicily, Sardinia and Corsica and these were used as bases to harry the coasts of Europe. In the early eleventh century the Pisans and Genoese cleared them out of Sardinia and Corsica and by the 1070s the Normans had taken control of Sicily. In Spain provincial organization had broken down as a result of the Muslim conquest. The surviving sees of Catalonia, which had formerly belonged to the province of Tarragona, were eventually attached to that of Narbonne, across the Pyrenees, but elsewhere in the Christian north the bishops were not formally subjected to any metropolitan authority until the end of the eleventh century. Nevertheless, in the kingdom of Asturias-León the bishop whose see was to be found in the same place as the seat of royal power (first at Lugo, then Oviedo and finally León) performed the functions of, and was in all but name, the metropolitan. Similarly, in the eleventh century the bishop of Jaca was known in official documents as bishop of Aragon and the bishop of Burgos as bishop of Castile. These associations point clearly to the great degree of control the Spanish Christian rulers maintained over ecclesiastical affairs. As the old centres of metropolitan authority were taken from the Muslims during the course of the *Reconquista*, provincial organization in the normal way was re-established: at Toledo in 1088, at Tarragona in 1091 and at Braga in 1104. The growing importance and prestige of Santiago de Compostela as a place of pilgrimage made it, too, a natural site for an archiepiscopal see (1120).

North of the Pyrenees the provincial boundaries that had come into being by the early ninth century remained unaltered until the Late Middle Ages. Under Charlemagne metropolitan authority was reaffirmed in 779. Furthermore, Charlemagne favoured metropolitan bishops' assumption of the honorific title of archbishop, which had earlier been accorded to the missionary Boniface by Pope Gregory III (731–41). By 1000 those sees that had been disrupted by the viking invasions were all restored. In England the two provinces of Canterbury and York, established at the end of the sixth and seventh centuries, remained but the distribution of episcopal sees had been worse affected here with the permanent loss of several sees. Moreover, to some extent the Normans further changed the episcopal geography of England. In Wales and Scotland a territorial episcopate had not yet completely emerged and only at St Davids and St Andrews were there undoubtedly bishops' sees of this kind. The fuller development of a territorial episcopate took place in the eleventh and twelfth centuries under Norman influence. Similarly, the territorial division of Ireland into diocese and provinces was not begun until the mid-twelfth century.

R.K. Rose

Medieval cartography

Isidore, bishop of Seville, compiled an encyclopedia of knowledge in *c.* 630. It included a so-called T-O map, actually a diagram, dividing the earth into Asia, Europe and Africa. Each area was assigned to one of Noah's sons, Sem (the eldest) receiving the largest share. East was located at the top and the land masses were divided by a 'T' of water. Many of the world maps produced in the Central Middle Ages, such as that now in Hereford Cathedral, follow a similar outline, adorned by much greater detail. On the Psalter Map, reproduced on the cover of this volume, east (and paradise) remains at the top, with Jerusalem at the centre. The 'T' is coloured green, with Rome marked 'north' of the Mediterranean. Other striking features include the red-coloured Red Sea and the figures on the circumference. Of limited navigational use, these maps were of

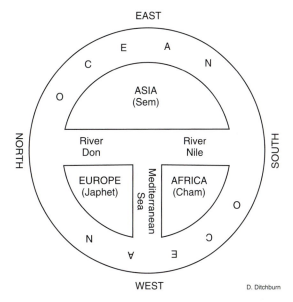

enormous cultural, devotional and iconographic importance.

D. Ditchburn

91

THE CENTRAL MIDDLE AGES
c. 1100–*c.* 1300

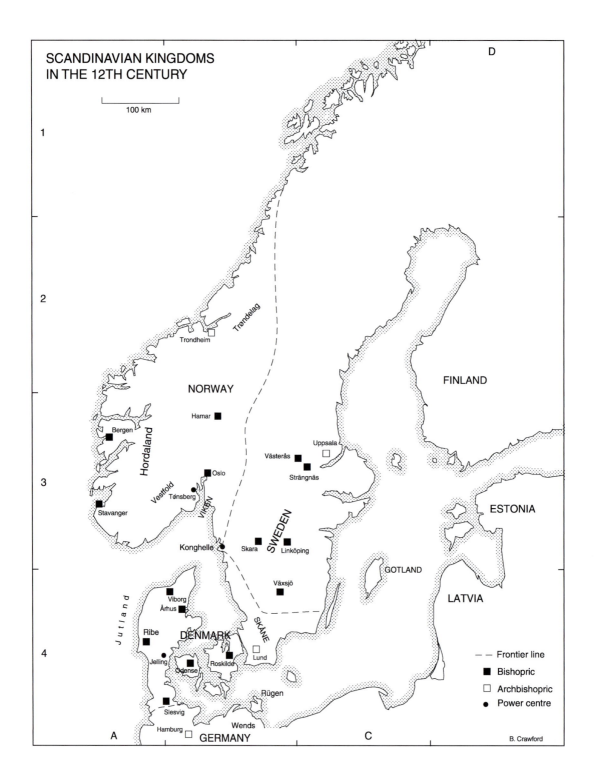

SCANDINAVIAN KINGDOMS
IN THE 12TH CENTURY

100 km

D

1

Trøndelag

Trondheim

NORWAY

FINLAND

Hamar

Bergen

Hordaland

Uppsala

Västerås

2

Oslo

Strängnäs

Vestfold

Tønsberg

Stavanger

VIKEN

ESTONIA

3

Konghelle

Skara

SWEDEN

Linköping

GOTLAND

Växsjö

LATVIA

Viborg

Jutland

Århus

Ribe

DENMARK

SKÅNE

Jelling

Lund

Odense

Roskilde

4

Rügen

Slesvig

Hamburg

Wends

GERMANY

C

— Frontier line

■ Bishopric

□ Archbishopric

● Power centre

B. Crawford

A

94

WAR AND POLITICS

Scandinavian kingdoms in the 12th century

The twelfth century was a time of great cultural achievement for Scandinavia. The fluid societies of the Viking Age were consolidated into three national entitities, each with a royal dynasty which exercised power more or less effectively over territorial kingdoms. The conversion of the pagan north to Christianity was mostly completed and an ecclesiastical framework was established over all parts of Scandinavia, with clearly demarcated dioceses and by mid-century archbishoprics in each kingdom. Full integration into Christendom is shown by the participation of kings and many of their subjects in pilgrimages and the crusading movement.

The process of internal territorial unification and development of centralized political government did not proceed equally smoothly in all areas. The establishment of single monarchies and primogeniture was a hard-fought battle. Danish struggles over the succession dominated the first half of the century while civil wars in Norway continued almost unabated from the 1130s to the 1240s. The kings of Sweden were elected and royal power was often contested by pretenders who had support among the Svear (in the east) or the Götar (in the west). For most of the period c.1130–1250 there were two contending dynasties and royal control of both Svealand and Götland was rarely maintained. The Church strove to stabilize the political situation through its own diocesan framework, especially after the founding of the archbishopric of Uppsala in 1164.

Once internal harmony was established the kings were able to embark on foreign expeditions and expand overseas. As had been the case in the Viking Age the three kingdoms expanded in different directions: Norway looked west towards the British Isles and the kings led expeditions west-over-sea when internal conditions allowed and circumstances beckoned. Sweden looked east to Finland and the eastern Baltic for its colonial ventures, while Denmark expanded its frontier in north Germany and along the south Baltic coast. These aggressive policies towards the pagan Slavs by Sweden and Denmark were recognized by the papacy as crusades.

A notable feature of the religious and political development of all three kingdoms was the elevation to sainthood of murdered members of the royal families, who thus became symbols of national unity. This helped the ideological standing of the kings, whose status was enhanced by coronation and unction, and who became the dispensers of justice and legislators for their whole kingdom, even though the popular assemblies (*thing*) continued to play an important role in all Scandinavian societies.

B. Crawford

The Hohenstaufen Empire, c. 1150–1250

The Hohenstaufen (or Staufen) dynasty, which ruled the Holy Roman Empire (1138–1268), Sicily (1194–1268) and Jerusalem (1225–54), began to play a role in imperial politics during

THE HOHENSTAUFEN EMPIRE, c. 1150–1250

NORTH SEA

Oldenburg
Lübeck
Mecklenburg
Hamburg
Ratzeburg
Lüneburg
Bremen
Verden
Wildeshausen
MARCH OF BRANDENBURG
FREISLAND
DIOCESE OF UTRECHT
DUCHY OF SAXONY
Brunswick
Brandenburg
Osnabrück
Hildesheim
Magdeburg
Utrecht
Münster
Herford
Goslar
Nijmegen
Paderbom
Corvey
BRABANT
Duisburg
Antwerp
Werden
LANDGRAVATE OF THURINGIA
MARCH OF MEISSEN
Bruges
Cologne
Aachen
FLANDERS
Liège
Fulda
HAINAULT
Prague
Cambrai
Mainz
Gelnhausen
KINGDOM OF BOHEMIA
Frankfurt
Bamberg
Trier
Worms
FRANCONIA
Nuremberg
MARCH OF MORAVIA
Reims
Speyer
Regensburg
DUCHY OF AUSTRIA
Wissemboorg
Hagenau
Eichstätt
Niederalteich
Passau
Toul
Strasbourg
Hohenstaufen
Freising
DUCHY OF BAVARIA
Vienna
Ulm
Augsburg
DUCHY OF SWABIA
Munich
Salzburg
Budapest
KINGDOM OF FRANCE
Besancon
Zürich
St Gall
DUCHY OF STYRIA
KINGDOM OF HUNGARY
COUNTY OF BURGUNDY
Berry
DUCHY OF CARINTHIA
Graz
Fribourg
Geneva
PATRIARCATE OF AQUILEIA
MARCH OF CARNIOLA
SAVOY
Vicenza
Treviso
Lyon
Bergamo
Verona
Vienne
Tarentaise
Brescia
Padua
Venice
KINGDOM OF BURGUNDY
Turin
Milan
MARCH OF VERONA
Valence
Asti
Cremona
Mantua
Ferrara
ADRIATIC SEA
Piacenza
Parma
Ravenna
Genoa
EMILIA
Bologna
Rimini
KINGDOM OF ITALY
MARCH OF ANCONA
Avignon
Pisa
Florence
Ancona
Arles
PROVENCE
Siena
Aix
TUSCANY
Perugia
Marseilles
DUCHY OF SPOLETO
Spoleto
Sutri
Farfa
KINGDOM OF SICILY
MEDITERRANEAN SEA
Corsica
PATRIMONY OF ST PETER
Tivoli
Rome
Anagni

0   km   150

From B. Weiler, *King Henry III of England (1216–72) and the Staufen Empire*, Woodbridge, 2006.

B. Weiler

the late eleventh century, when Conrad III become emperor-elect. It was, however, under Conrad's nephew and successor, Frederick I Barbarossa (1152–90), that Staufen power reached its peak. Barbarossa began his reign by seeking to restore an ideal *status quo ante* of imperial lordship and the *honor imperii* (honour of the Empire). While this posed few difficulties in Germany, Frederick's attempts from 1158 to reclaim imperial rights in Italy were viewed by many communes as an unwarranted restriction of their liberties. Those rejecting Frederick's claims, led by Milan, formed the Lombard League, which wrought concessions from Frederick in the Treaty of Constance (1183). The League was revived in 1226, when Barbarossa's grandson, Frederick II (1212–50), tried to impose his authority over the towns.

Barbarossa's clashes with the communes soon involved the papacy. From the late eleventh century successive popes sought to strengthen their independence from, and oversight over, the secular princes of the West. More importantly, since the pope crowned kings of the Romans as emperor, popes increasingly sought to use this right to delineate the emperor's role and authority. When, after 1197, the German princes were unable to decide on a successor to Emperor Henry VI (1190–7), resulting in a double election, Pope Innocent III (1198–1216) took it upon himself to investigate the suitability of the rival candidates. This was no mere formality: Innocent was deciding who would rule Germany. Papal interference reached its peak in 1245, when Pope Innocent IV (1243–54) decided that, as he could crown emperors, he could also depose them.

The seeds of this conflict had been sown in the twelfth century. In 1154 relations between the pope and Barbarossa reached a nadir when a papal legate reportedly described Frederick's imperial office as a papal fief. This was one reason why much of Barbarossa's reign was dominated by the emperor's attempts to prevent recognition of Pope Alexander III (1159–81): Alexander had drafted the 1154 document. All this made the affairs of the Staufen a matter of European importance. Contemporaries could not stand by when Barbarossa sought to replace Alexander III; or when, in 1227, 1239 and 1245, Popes Gregory IX (1227–41) and Innocent IV sought candidates to challenge Frederick II for the imperial crown.

The international dimension to imperial affairs had important repercussions for the imperial heartlands. Distracted by events elsewhere, Frederick II only visited Germany three times during his reign and never made it to Burgundy. While absentee English kings could govern through the administrative apparatus inherited from their Anglo-Saxon forebears, the Staufen looked to the princes. It was no coincidence that an elite group of electoral princes (those who chose an emperor-elect) emerged under the Staufen. This should not be viewed as a wilful surrender of imperial power. Barbarossa was quite capable of making, as well as unmaking, great princes and Frederick II could humiliate princes who challenged his authority or who were unwilling to perform their duties. The dominant role of the princes evident in the Late Middle Ages was not entirely the result of the Staufen system of governance but rather of the political turmoil which characterized Germany between 1245 and 1278. A king ruled unencumbered by a rival claimant for only eighteen months of these years.

B. Weiler

Southern Italy and Sicily in the 12th century

After Robert Guiscard's death in 1085 the centre of Norman power in the south gradually shifted to Sicily. Largely conquered by Guiscard's brother, Roger I (d.1101), the island eventually passed to Roger's son, Roger II (1093–1154). With both Sicily and Calabria under his control he gradually extended his authority over all the Norman territories in

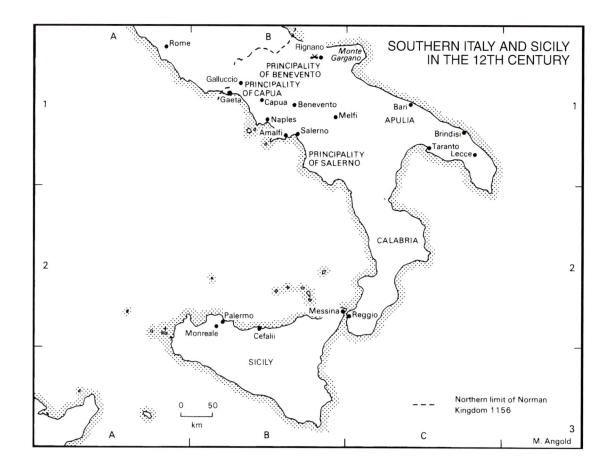

southern Italy, uniting them into a single entity. In 1130 Roger was crowned king at Palermo. The expansion of his power was, however, neither a steady nor uncontested process. Roger faced persistent opposition from other Norman lords, especially in Apulia and Capua, as well as from from popes and emperors in the West and Byzantium in the East. His son, William I (1154–66), periodically encountered similar opposition. Despite capturing Pope Innocent II at Galuccio in 1139, both Roger and William also suffered notable military setbacks: Roger at Rignano (1137) while William saw Bari and Brindisi fall briefly into Byzantine hands (1155). The papacy finally accepted William's rule in 1156, the treaty of Benevento recognizing the inclusion of Salerno, Amalfi and Naples within his kingdom. Greek and

Arab cultural influences remained significant in the kingdom but, although the extent to which either Roger or William remained 'Norman' is questionable, both brought their lands more firmly within the orbit of the West. Following William II's death without direct heirs in 1189 a disputed succession saw the kingdom pass firstly to Roger II's illegitimate grandson, Tancred, count of Lecce (1190–4), and then to the Hohenstaufen (as a result of the marriage between Constance, Roger II's daughter, and the future Emperor Henry VI). All of the Norman kings were great patrons of the arts. Their achievement is still visible in churches and palaces, notably at Palermo, Monreale and Cefalii.

M. Angold

Anglo-Norman penetration of Wales and Ireland

Norman penetration of Wales began soon after the conquest of England (1066). William the Conqueror created strong earldoms along the Anglo-Welsh frontier, centred on Chester, Shrewsbury and Hereford, and gave them to trusted followers. These men and their retainers began encroachment into the lands west of Offa's Dyke, the traditional demarcation between England and Wales. By the 1090s the Normans had built castles along both the north and south coasts of Wales and established footholds as far west as Pembrokeshire and Anglesey, while simultaneously infiltrating the middle march around Brecon and Builth. Not all acquisitions were permanent. Sometimes, as in the case of the advance into the north-west, the Normans were decisively rebuffed by the native rulers. In other parts, especially the south-west, areas went repeatedly back and forth between native and Anglo-Norman rule. Thus, from the eleventh to the thirteenth centuries, Wales was divided between native principalities, of which Gwynedd, Powys and Deheubarth were the most important, and numerous lordships established by Anglo-Norman invaders. These latter gradually assumed a distinctive legal and constitutional identity as 'The March of Wales'.

The lords of the March established their power by building castles, exacting tribute and hostages, and encouraging the settlement of English, French and Flemish immigrants as farmers or as burgesses in the newly created towns. The evidence of place-names and of late medieval surveys and rentals shows that these immigrants settled densely along the southern coastal plain and that areas such as southern Pembrokeshire, the Gower and southern Glamorgan underwent a cultural and ethnic transformation. In other parts, alien colonists existed in heavily fortified enclaves in the boroughs adjoining seigneurial castles.

Despite occasional royal expeditions, the penetration of Wales was largely the result of freelance baronial campaigns. A similar seigneurial expedition took the Anglo-Normans to Ireland. In 1169–70 Richard fitz Gilbert ('Strongbow'), lord of Chepstow and claimant to the earldom of Pembroke, led assorted Anglo-Normans, Welshmen and Flemings in an enterprise that began as a mercenary undertaking in support of the Irish king of Leinster and culminated in Strongbow himself becoming lord of Leinster. The English king, Henry II, could not allow a fractious member of his own aristocracy to set up in quasi-regal state so near to his domains and, in 1171–2, took an army to Ireland and received Strongbow's submission, along with that of the majority of the native Irish kings.

After 1171–2, the situation in Wales and Ireland showed some similarities. In both countries an aristocracy of Anglo-Norman descent had established control over substantial territories, where they built castles, established boroughs and encouraged immigration. But in both countries there survived native rulers, whose power was deep-rooted and might well recover. The English Crown claimed a position of ultimate superiority over both colonial lords and indigenous leaders.

The map shows the approximate distribution of power in 1200. In Wales, the dominant native principality, it was becoming clear, was Gwynedd. Powys and Deheubarth were weakened by divisions and encroachment. The latter, in particular, was hemmed in by the important royal centres of Cardigan and Carmarthen. At this time Glamorgan too was in royal hands. The Marshal earl of Pembroke, Strongbow's successor, and William de Braose, lord of Brecon, were the most important Marcher aristocrats.

In Ireland the situation was more fluid. The Anglo-Normans had only been establishing themselves for a single generation by 1200 and some areas, such as Connaught, were as yet virtually untouched by their expansion. The

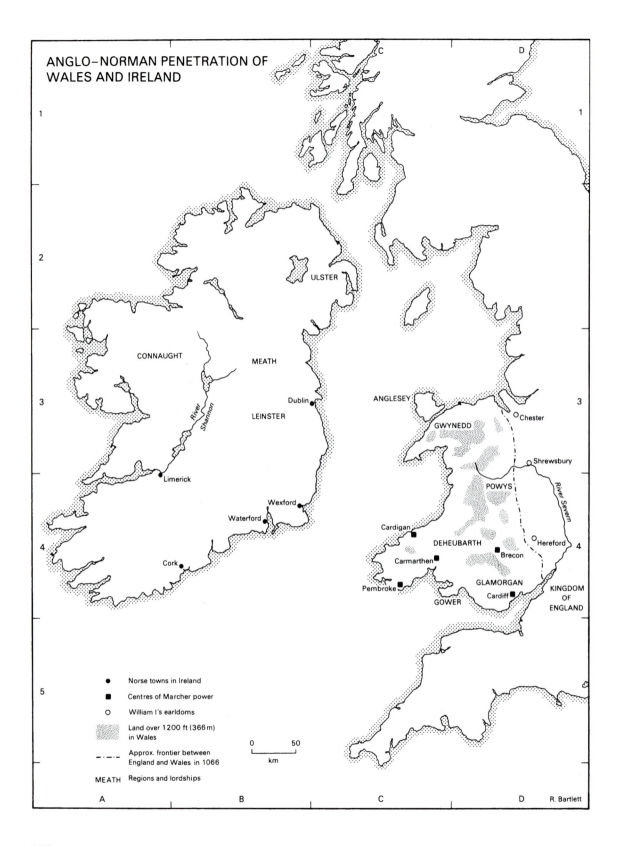

ANGLO-NORMAN PENETRATION OF
WALES AND IRELAND

CONNAUGHT

MEATH

ULSTER

LEINSTER

Dublin

River Shannon

Limerick

Wexford

Waterford

Cork

ANGLESEY

GWYNEDD

POWYS

DEHEUBARTH

Cardigan

Carmarthen

Pembroke

GOWER

GLAMORGAN

Cardiff

Brecon

Chester

Shrewsbury

Hereford

River Severn

KINGDOM
OF
ENGLAND

- Norse towns in Ireland
■ Centres of Marcher power
○ William I's earldoms
Land over 1200 ft (366m) in Wales
-·-·- Approx. frontier between England and Wales in 1066

MEATH Regions and lordships

0   50
km

R. Bartlett

100

great lordships of Leinster and Meath were in the hands of the Marshals and de Lacys, well-rewarded servants of Henry II, while John de Courcy, the paradigm of the maverick *conquistador*, had created his base of power in Ulster. The Norse cities of the south, such as Waterford, Cork and Limerick, were also advanced bases of Anglo-Norman settlement and authority.

R. Bartlett

Scotland in the Central Middle Ages

Medieval Scotland grew out of Gaelic/Pictish Alba, whose core was in the Tay valley, Fife and the north-east coastal plain (map A). Eleventh-century Alba was a collection of local provinces (which became 'provincial' earldoms) under *mormaers* (later, earls); but the term *mormaer*, or 'great steward', implies some superior royal authority, and so does the network of thanages, which were royal estates run by crown agents ('thanes') (map A). From this core, the kingdom of Alba/Scotland expanded to the south, north and west. Southern expansion was at the expense of ancient Northumbria and Strathclyde/Cumbria: Lothian and Strathclyde were gained at around the time of Malcolm II's victory over the Northumbrians at Carham in 1018; while the twelfth century saw the incorporation of Galloway and temporary conquests south of what was becoming the Anglo-Scottish border. In the north, the great province of Moray came directly under the Crown when its ruler, Macbeth, seized the throne in 1042. It was later subjugated after 1130, when the mormaership/earldom was suppressed. Further north, the Norse province of Caithness was also brought within the kingdom during the twelfth century. Pressure westwards came later, chiefly in the thirteenth century; after the Western Isles were surrendered by Norway in 1266 (following the battle of Largs, 1263), the West Highland and Island Gaelic magnates mostly came to accept royal overlordship (map A).

The expansion was partly military, both by external conquest and by defeating frequent internal rebellions, and partly seigneurial, by the installation of effective local agents. The essential basis was already present in the eleventh century but the process was closely associated with the twelfth-century feudalization of Scotland; the best way for rulers to consolidate power was through subordinate feudal knights and castle-based lordships. Scotland's first feudal king was David I (1124–53) – who recruited many Anglo-Norman and English followers – and his example was followed by Malcolm IV (1153–65), William I (1165–1214), Alexander II (1214–49) and Alexander III (1249–86). Great new 'provincial' lordships were created for leading 'Normans' (map B); while individual knights' fees and other feudal tenancies, generally based on mottes and castles, were established throughout southern and eastern Scotland (map C). At the same time the new administrative structure of sheriffdoms was imposed (initially probably for the areas outside the 'provincial' earldoms and lordships but eventually incorporating them); the burghs (trading towns) were created; and many monasteries were founded by both kings and magnates for the new reformed ecclesiastical orders (map D).

Thus Scotland was turned into a fairly typical twelfth-thirteenth-century feudal state. But the transformation of the pre-existing infrastructure was far from absolute. Even the burghs were not all entirely 'new'. In the Church, new foundations were made within an older ecclesiastical framework (many bishoprics dated to before 1100). And no earldoms were granted to incomers; they stayed with native families, only being 'Normanized' through the marriages of heiresses to 'Norman' lords (map B). Similarly, most thanages were held by native thanes during the twelfth and (often) the thirteenth

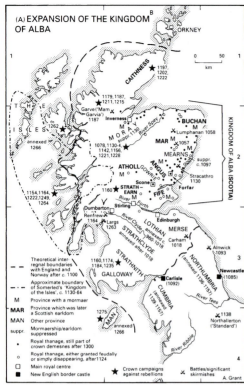

(A) EXPANSION OF THE KINGDOM OF ALBA

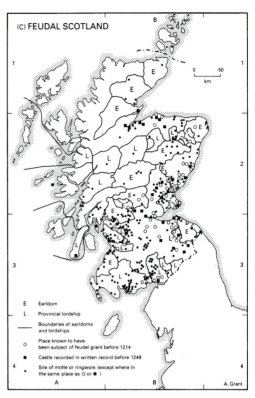

(C) FEUDAL SCOTLAND

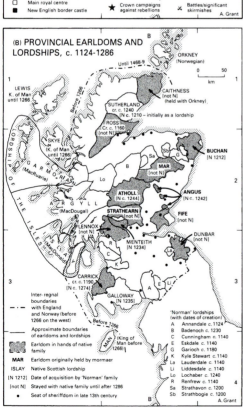

(B) PROVINCIAL EARLDOMS AND LORDSHIPS, c. 1124-1286

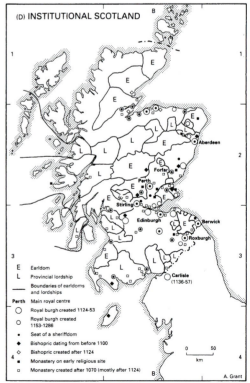

(D) INSTITUTIONAL SCOTLAND

centuries (map A). Thus much native (mostly Gaelic) lordship survived in 'feudal Scotland'. During the Central Middle Ages, in fact, Scotland was a hybrid kingdom, in which Gaelic, Anglo-Saxon, Norman and Flemish elements all coalesced, under the leadership of its 'Normanized' but nevertheless native line of kings. Despite clashes and rebellions (map A), the result was a remarkably successful small kingdom.

A. Grant

Angevins and Capetians in the late 12th century

The relationship between the Angevins and the Capetians illustrates the ambiguities and tensions inherent in the changing feudal structure of the twelfth century. Although the Capetians had held the French throne since 987, by the early twelfth century they had not noticeably expanded their influence beyond their family lands in the Ile-de-France. The great lords who held the neighbouring fiefs, although nominally their vassals, were often just as politically influential and as economically powerful. Indeed, with the invasion of England in 1066, the duke of Normandy became a king in his own right, independent in matters involving his new realm.

The Norman Conquest demonstrates that the Capetians operated within a political kaleidoscope in which dynastic ambition and the wheel of fortune might suddenly produce such unexpected agglomerations of territory that the theoretical superiority of the king of France at the apex of the social hierarchy might bear little relationship to the realities of political power. In the 1150s such a change did indeed occur, for in 1154, following the death of King Stephen, Henry of Anjou was crowned king of England. He had already been accepted as duke of Normandy in 1150 and had inherited from his father, Geoffrey (d. 1151), the lands in western France centred on Anjou, Touraine and Vendôme. Moreover, his wife Eleanor, recently divorced from Louis VII of France, had brought him the duchy of Aquitaine on their marriage in 1152. Nor were these to be the limits of Henry's domains, for the king of Scotland was

his vassal, he claimed authority over the Welsh princes and he had plans for the conquest of Ireland. When his brother, Geoffrey, died in 1158, he invaded Brittany while in 1173 he even received the homage of the count of Toulouse.

Under Henry II (d. 1189) and his son, Richard I (d. 1199) this collection of disparate territories was held together quite successfully although at the cost of continuous vigilance and high expenditure. Despite their theoretical overlordship neither Louis VII (d. 1180) nor Philip II could make any substantial impact. However, the Angevin 'empire' was ultimately dependent on dynastic circumstances, especially when the lands concerned lacked any other real political coherence. Richard's early death left a succession disputed between his brother, John, and his nephew, Arthur of Brittany, with John being accepted in England and Normandy. Arthur gained adherence in Anjou, Touraine and Maine, forcing a wedge across the middle of the Angevin lands. Nevertheless, by 1200 a combination of energetic military action against Arthur and negotiations with King Philip had gained John recognition, which, although it left him in a relatively greater feudal subordination than that of his father or brother, did maintain most of the Angevin lands under his rule.

Yet by 1204 John had lost Normandy and during the next two years, Anjou, Touraine, northern Poitou and Brittany as well. In 1214 at the battle of Bouvines, ten years of strenuous fund-raising and careful alliance-building were brought to nothing when Philip II defeated

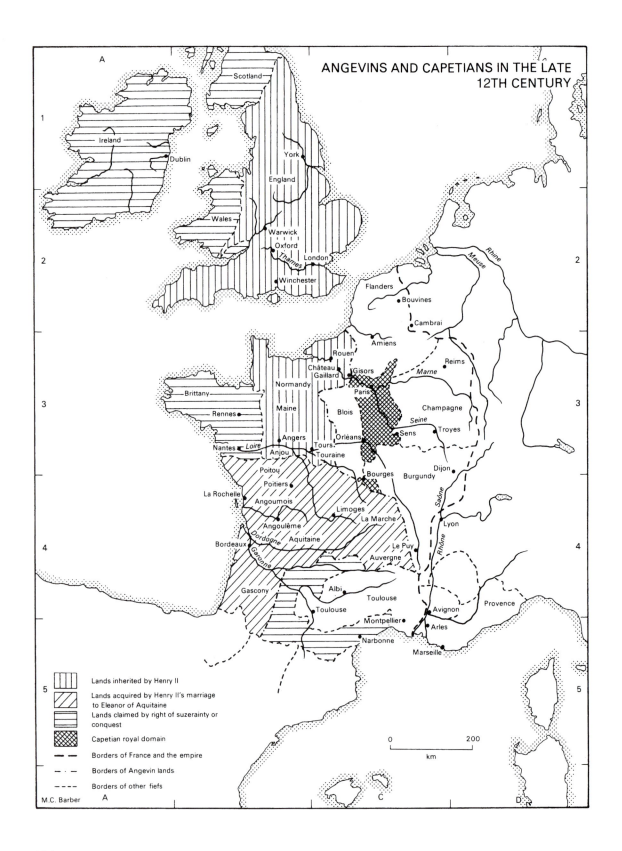

ANGEVINS AND CAPETIANS IN THE LATE 12TH CENTURY

Scotland

Ireland

Dublin

York

England

Wales

Warwick
Oxford
London
Thames
Winchester

Flanders

Bouvines

Cambrai

Amiens

Rouen
Château
Gaillard
Gisors
Paris
Reims
Marne

Normandy

Brittany

Maine

Rennes

Blois

Champagne

Seine
Troyes

Nantes
Loire
Angers
Anjou
Tours
Touraine
Orléans
Sens

Poitou

Bourges
Dijon
Burgundy

Poitiers

La Rochelle

Angoumois

Limoges

Saône

La Marche

Angoulême
Dordogne
Aquitaine

Bordeaux
Garonne

Le Puy

Auvergne

Lyon

Rhône

Gascony

Albi

Toulouse

Avignon
Provence

Toulouse

Montpellier

Arles

Narbonne

Marseille

Rhine
Meuse

Lands inherited by Henry II
Lands acquired by Henry II's marriage
to Eleanor of Aquitaine
Lands claimed by right of suzerainty or
conquest
Capetian royal domain
Borders of France and the empire
Borders of Angevin lands
Borders of other fiefs

0   200
km

M.C. Barber

104

John's allies. John himself was not present, having been driven back to La Rochelle. Philip's shrewd exploitation of John's political and military errors had been enough to prise apart the lands which had been so fortuitously brought together, leaving him master of northern France with access to Norman resources and administrative expertise, a gain which lifted him into a different political league from that of Louis VII.

The limitations of a single map of these changes are evident. Contemporaries did not think in terms of clearly defined borders or of national entities, nor was their authority evenly spread throughout the lands which theoretically owed them allegiance. The constant itinerary of these rulers underlines their awareness of this last point, and the larger the territory, the greater the problems. The map can convey the broad geo-political structure but it is misleading without an awareness of twelfth-century political attitudes.

M.C. Barber

Catalonia, 1080–1180

Between 1080 and 1180 Catalonia evolved from a collection of autonomous counties related by loose dynastic bonds into a principality united under the count of Barcelona. The restoration of the archbishopric of Tarragona in 1117, with authority over the eastern dioceses of the Iberian Peninsula, reinforced Catalonia's coherence as a territory distinct from Castile and Languedoc. The county of Barcelona expanded steadily in three directions: across the Pyrenees to southern France, to the Muslim territories and to Aragon. The counts advanced by means of three key mechanisms: ties of vassalage, warfare and family alliances. The annexation of Pyrenean counties, such as Besalú (1111) and Cerdanya (1117), was the consequence of subtle dynastic policy. The counts developed feudal alliances with several local lords, gaining the submission of the count of Peralada (1128) and, beyond the Pyrenees, of Bernard Atón, count of Carcassonne and Razes (1112). The political primacy enjoyed by the counts until the battle of Muret (1213) culminated in the marriage of Ramón Berenguer III to Dulce of Provence in 1112. Her dowry consisted of Lower Provence, Rouergue, Millau, Gavalda and Carlat.

Expansion to the south gained momentum under Ramón Berenguer III (1086/95–1131) who took Tarragona in 1095. Despite the arrival of the Almoravids, he laid siege to the fortresses of Amposta (1097), Oropesa and Murviedro (1098) and, with the help of the military orders and Pisa, he conquered Mallorca (1114–16). These advances were, however, threatened by Aragon's expanding power. Aragonese kings conquered Saragossa (1118), built the castle of Gardeny in order to attack Lleida (1123), re-settled Monzón (1130), occupied the area of Matarraña in the Ebro basin and planned the conquest of Tortosa and Valencia in 1133. Nevertheless, defeat by the Almoravids at Fraga (1134) and the subsequent death of King Alfonso I threw the Aragonese kingdom into disarray. Diplomatic contacts were soon established and in 1137 marriage between Petronila, daughter of Ramiro II, and Ramón Berenguer IV (1131–62) united the county and the kingdom for good. After several coastal campaigns (Lorca, 1144; Valencia, 1146; and Almeria, 1147), in 1148 Ramón Berenguer IV conquered Tortosa, with the consent of the pope (who granted him a bull of crusade) and the help of the Genoese, Pisans and the military orders. The next year he took Lleida, Fraga and Mequinenza. In 1153 the fall of Siruana and Miravet, the last Muslim fortresses on the lower Ebro, created what a century later would be known as New Catalonia. It is in this context of Catalonian expansion, invigorated by the Aragonese union, that the treaties agreed with Castile at Tudellén (1151) and Cazorla (1177) are best understood: the remaining Muslim

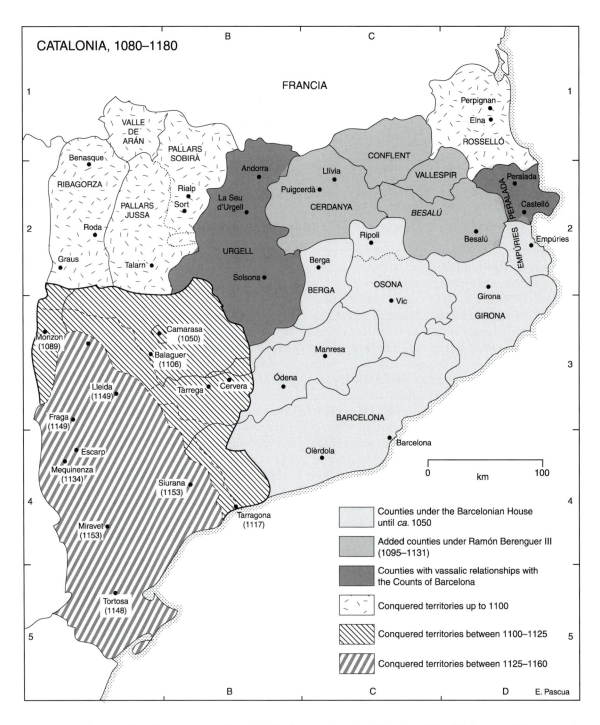

CATALONIA, 1080–1180

FRANCIA

VALLE DE ARÁN

PALLARS SOBIRÀ

Benasque

RIBAGORZA

PALLARS JUSSA

Rialp
Sort

Roda

Graus

Talarn

Andorra

La Seu d'Urgell

URGELL

Solsona

Llívia

Puigcerdà

CERDANYA

Berga

BERGA

CONFLENT

VALLESPIR

BESALÚ

Ripoli

OSONA

Vic

ROSSELLÓ

Perpignan

Élna

Peralada

Castelló

Besalú

Empúries

PERALADA

EMPÚRIES

Girona

GIRONA

Monzon (1089)

Camarasa (1050)

Balaguer (1106)

Lleida (1149)

Fraga (1149)

Escarp

Mequinenza (1134)

Miravet (1153)

Tàrrega

Cervera

Siurana (1153)

Manresa

Ódena

BARCELONA

Olèrdola

Barcelona

Tarragona (1117)

Tortosa (1148)

0   km   100

Counties under the Barcelonian House until *ca.* 1050

Added counties under Ramón Berenguer III (1095–1131)

Counties with vassalic relationships with the Counts of Barcelona

Conquered territories up to 1100

Conquered territories between 1100–1125

Conquered territories between 1125–1160

E. Pascua

areas on the peninsula were to be divided between them.

The settlement of the newly conquered regions differed from that of the core Catalonian territories. North of the Llobregat River, semi-independent peasant communities and Benedictine monasteries used the institution of the *aprisio* to appropriate the land they cultivated.

The middle territories of Manresa, Camarasa and Olerdola were placed under comital power. Ravaged by Muslims and Christians, they were settled in several waves. This gave increasing power to the nobility who created a landscape of castles (*castells termenats*). Meanwhile, in New Catalonia charters of repopulation were granted to peasant communities under the jurisdiction of the count, Cistercian monasteries such as Poblet, Santes Creus and Valldaura or the military orders. The dynamism of urbanized society explains Catalonia's remarkable economic and military presence in the islands of the western Mediterranean, Africa and southern Italy during the next century.

E. Pascua

The Empire of the Comneni, 1081–1185

Alexius I Comnenus (1081–1118) rescued the Byzantine Empire from a period of political difficulties which had meant the loss of southern Italy to the Normans, much of the Balkans to the Petcheneks and Asia Minor to the Seljuq Turks, following the battle of Mantzikert (1071). Alexius dealt with these threats one by one. After an initial setback at Dyrrachion he defeated the Normans at Larissa (1083) and recovered Dyrrachion (1085). Though defeated by the Petcheneks at Dristra (1087), he won a decisive victory over them at Mount Levounion (1091) and restored the frontiers of the Empire to the Danube. His plan to recover Asia Minor from the Seljuqs was complicated by the arrival of the first crusade at Constantinople in 1096. With crusader help he took Nicaea, the Seljuq capital, and then under the cover of the crusader victory at Dorylaion his forces were able to recover the coastlands of western Asia Minor. But involvement with the crusader states was to mean that neither he nor his successors were able to make significant advances into the interior.

His grandson, Manuel I Comnenus (1143–80), established close dynastic ties with the crusader states but this involved him in a costly expedition against Damietta and the Fatimids (1169) and another against the Seljuq capital of Ikonion, which came to grief at the battle of Myriokephalon (1176). Manuel's attempt to recover southern Italy (1156–7) from the Normans was also a failure but it did counter the serious Norman attacks (1147–9) which were directed against the Greek provinces. The Byzantines were more successful along the Danube. The victory over the Hungarians at Sirmium (1167) not only brought Hungary within the Byzantine orbit but also pacified the Serbs. Only in Asia Minor did the territories controlled by the Comneni differ significantly from those held in the mid-eleventh century.

If the Comneni relied more heavily on the indirect exercise of authority than their predecessors, their empire enjoyed a period of great prosperity thanks to the stability they ensured for nearly a century. Agricultural wealth was more fully mobilized and there was a growth of towns. The Venetians had an important role to play. They had been exempted from the payment of customs duties (1082) in return for naval assistance against the Normans and had been given a factory at Constantinople. They contributed to the growth of internal trade, mostly in agricultural goods, within the Empire. They were particularly active at Corinth and Halmyros, which were the main outlets for the agricultural wealth of Greece.

Their presence also produced friction which was largely political in origin. There was a conflict of interests in the Adriatic and the Venetians resented the favours shown to their commercial rivals, the Pisans and the Genoese. This led in 1171 to the arrest of all the Venetians in the Byzantine Empire and the confiscation of their goods. Despite all efforts relations never returned to normal. This contributed to the diversion of the fourth crusade and the fall of Constantinople (1204). There were many

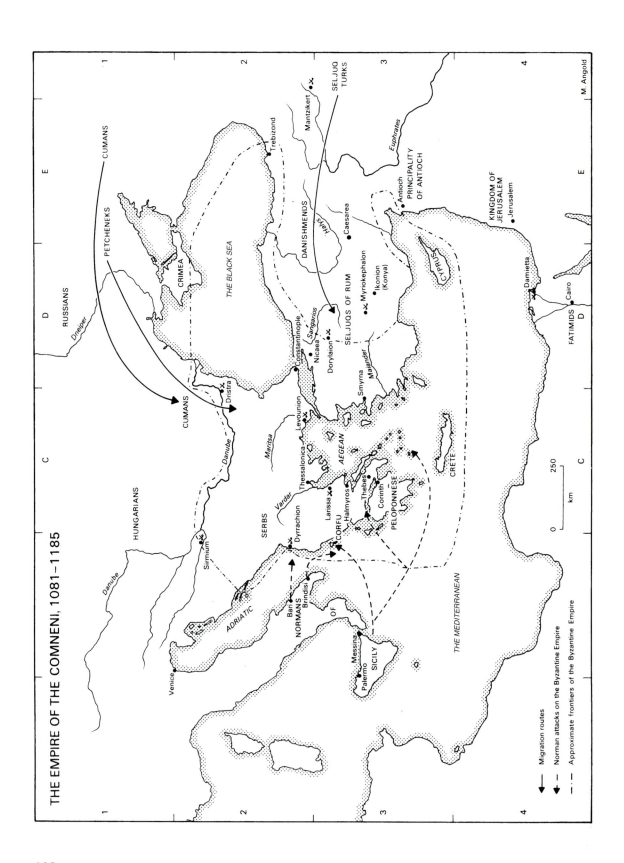

THE EMPIRE OF THE COMNENI, 1081–1185

RUSSIANS
Dneiper

CUMANS

PETCHENEKS

CUMANS

CRIMEA

THE BLACK SEA

Trebizond

Mantzikert ✕

SELJUQ TURKS

DANISHMENDS

Halys

Euphrates

Caesarea

Antioch
PRINCIPALITY OF ANTIOCH

KINGDOM OF JERUSALEM

Jerusalem

SELJUQS OF RUM

Myriokephalon

Ikonion
(Konya)

CYPRUS

Damietta
✕
Cairo

FATIMIDS

Constantinople
Sangarios
Nicaea ✕
Dorylaion

Smyrna
Maiander

HUNGARIANS

Danube

Danube

Sirmium ✕

SERBS

Vardar

Dristra ✕

Maritsa

Levounion ✕
Thessalonica

AEGEAN

Larissa ✕
Dyrrachion ✕
Halmyros
CORFU

Thebes
Corinth
PELOPONNESE

CRETE

Venice

ADRIATIC

Bari
Brindisi
NORMANS

OF

Messina
Palermo
SICILY

THE MEDITERRANEAN

0   250
|————|
km

Migration routes
Norman attacks on the Byzantine Empire
Approximate frontiers of the Byzantine Empire

M. Angold

other factors involved in the collapse of the Empire of the Comneni in the late twelfth century. Perhaps the most important was loss of control at the centre following the death of Manuel I Comnenus in 1180. The ascendancy of the Comneni, which was vital to the stability of the Empire, was undermined in a series of coups and rebellions.

M. Angold

Where did the crusaders come from? Major areas of recruitment to the crusade in the Near East from the Latin West, 1095–1271

The problem of crusade motivation must be put into its geographical context. As one might have expected, there was a strong correlation between the leadership of individual crusades and the regions of crusade recruitment. The first crusade, preached by Pope Urban II at the Council of Clermont in 1095, attracted recruits from virtually all over Christendom. Englishmen, Scots, Scandinavians, Italian merchant-seamen, even Tuscan monks (who were forbidden to go) and Spanish knights (who were told to stay and fight the Moors at home) sought to take the cross. But from the major areas of recruitment came the great feudal nobles, bringing their vassals and assuming leadership positions. The most prominent amongst them were Robert of Normandy, Robert of Flanders, Hugh of Vermandois, Godfrey of Bouillon,

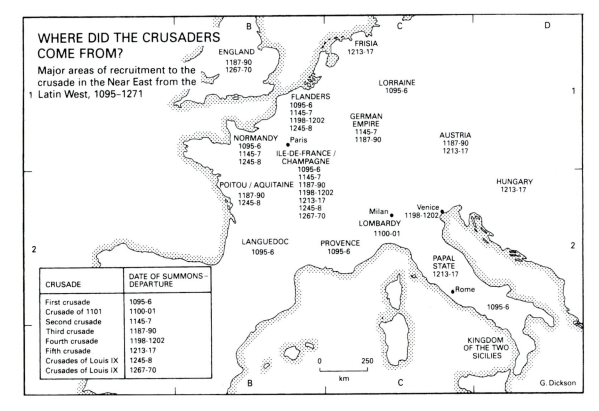

WHERE DID THE CRUSADERS COME FROM?

Major areas of recruitment to the crusade in the Near East from the Latin West, 1095–1271

ENGLAND 1187-90 1267-70

FRISIA 1213-17

LORRAINE 1095-6

FLANDERS 1095-6 1145-7 1198-1202 1245-8

GERMAN EMPIRE 1145-7 1187-90

AUSTRIA 1187-90 1213-17

NORMANDY 1095-6 1145-7 1245-8

Paris

ILE-DE-FRANCE / CHAMPAGNE 1095-6 1145-7 1187-90 1198-1202 1213-17 1245-8 1267-70

HUNGARY 1213-17

POITOU / AQUITAINE 1187-90 1245-8

Milan

Venice 1198-1202

LOMBARDY 1100-01

LANGUEDOC 1095-6

PROVENCE 1095-6

PAPAL STATE 1213-17

Rome

1095-6

KINGDOM OF THE TWO SICILIES

CRUSADE	DATE OF SUMMONS – DEPARTURE
First crusade	1095-6
Crusade of 1101	1100-01
Second crusade	1145-7
Third crusade	1187-90
Fourth crusade	1198-1202
Fifth crusade	1213-17
Crusades of Louis IX	1245-8
Crusades of Louis IX	1267-70

0   250
km

G. Dickson

Baldwin of Boulogne, Bohemund of Taranto, Adhemar of Le Puy (the papal legate) and Raymond of Toulouse. The crusade of 1101 drew a large army of Lombards under Archbishop Anselm of Milan, as well as first-crusaders who had failed to honour their original vow, along with some others. In the second crusade, led by Louis VII of France and Conrad III of Germany, kings and kingdoms became involved for the first time. The champions of the third crusade were Emperor Frederick I, King Richard I Lionheart of England (who also brought his troops from Poitou) and King Philip II Augustus of France. The fourth crusade saw the Venetians join great barons from northern and central France and Flanders, while the fifth crusade – after the first, perhaps the most truly 'international' crusade – aroused Frisians, Rhinelanders, Frenchmen, Italians from the papal state, Austrians, Hungarians and other contingents, too. The crusading armies of King Louis IX of France (St Louis) were overwhelmingly composed of Frenchmen, although his latter expedition attracted far less support than his first. Prince Edward of England's crusading army, which arrived in Tunis after Louis had already died there, must still be counted as part of Louis' crusade. The geography of crusade recruitment may be an essential clue to the psychology of crusade motivation.

G. Dickson

The routes of the First Crusade

Following Pope Urban II's appeal at Clermont in November 1095 the crusaders set out over the next summer for Constantinople. They followed two main routes. The first was through

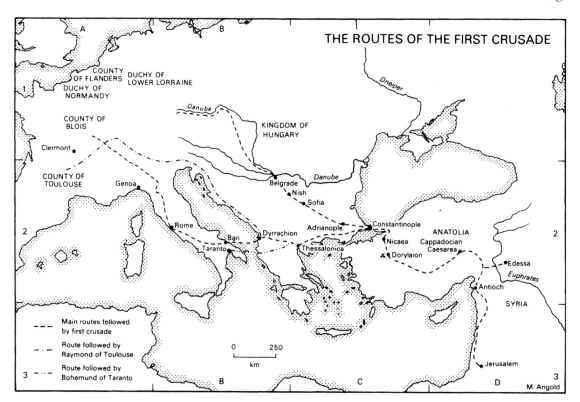

THE ROUTES OF THE FIRST CRUSADE

M. Angold

Hungary to the Byzantine frontier post at Belgrade and then along the military road across the Balkans. This was taken by Peter the Hermit and by Godfrey of Bouillon, duke of Lower Lorraine. Other leaders, such as Robert of Normandy, Robert of Flanders and Stephen of Blois, travelled through Italy and crossed over to Dyrrachion, whence the *Via Egnatia* led to Constantinople. Variants of this route were followed by Bohemund of Taranto and by Raymond of Toulouse, who were the last to arrive at Constantinople (April 1097). The next stage was across Asia Minor which was controlled by the Seljuq Turks. The crusaders captured Nicaea, the Seljuq capital, and then on 1 July 1097 defeated the Turks at Dorylaion. This

victory opened up the routes across the Anatolian plateau to Edessa, which was occupied in March 1098, and to Antioch, which finally capitulated on 28 June 1098. The crusaders set out in January 1099 on their last stage to Jerusalem, which fell after a month's siege on 15 July. Their successes were made possible by help from the Genoese, who dispatched a fleet in July 1097. News of these triumphs prompted the departure of two more crusading expeditions. Both were cut to pieces by the Turks in the summer of 1101. These defeats were decisive. They meant that Anatolia would remain Turkish and that the crusaders' hold in Syria would always be tenuous.

M. Angold

The Second and Third Crusades

The second crusade was a response to the fall of Edessa in 1144. Its inspiration was St Bernard, who in 1146 persuaded Louis VII of France and the Emperor Conrad III to participate. The

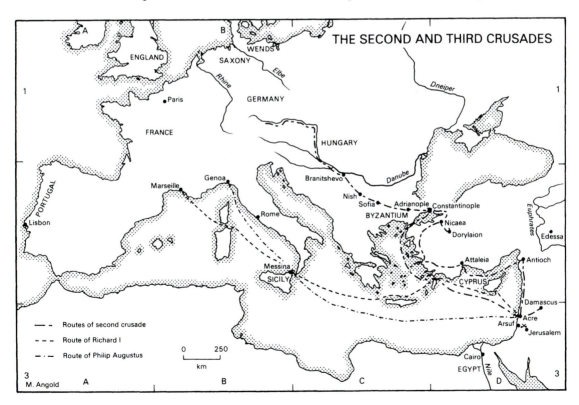

THE SECOND AND THIRD CRUSADES

Routes of second crusade
Route of Richard I
Route of Philip Augustus

M. Angold

111

route chosen was through Hungary and across the Balkans. The Germans reached Constantinople in September 1147 and the French in October. The Germans were turned back by the Turks near Dorylaion and joined the French who were marching down the west coast of Asia Minor. Conrad fell ill and returned to Constantinople, where he took ship to Palestine. Louis fought his way to Attaleia, whence he was ferried by the Byzantines to Antioch. Damascus was chosen as the goal of the crusade. A brief siege (24–28 July 1148) broke up in confusion. As a participant observed, 'if it brought no worldly success, it was good for the salvation of many souls'. Associated with this crusade were an English expedition which captured Lisbon from the Muslims (October 1147) and a Saxon campaign across the Elbe against the Slavic Wends.

The third crusade aimed to recover Jerusalem which had fallen to Saladin on 2 October 1187. The Germans under Frederick Barbarossa set out in May 1189 and followed the traditional route across the Balkans and Anatolia but Frederick died *en route*. The English and French went by sea, wintering at Messina. The French under Philip Augustus arrived before Acre in April 1191; the English under Richard I not until June, having secured Cyprus on the way. Acre fell on 12 July. Philip Augustus then returned home. Richard stayed for another year. Despite his victory over Saladin at Arsuf, Jerusalem eluded him. He only secured a foothold along the coast.

M. Angold

The Fourth Crusade

In 1198 Pope Innocent III was determined to launch a new crusade. With the major rulers of western Europe unavailable, unsuitable or unwilling to participate, Innocent appealed to the noble class which had been so successful in 1099. Three northern French counts – Baldwin of Flanders, Theobald of Champagne and Louis of Blois – negotiated a treaty with Venice to provide transport and provisions for the army. The target, as with later expeditions, was Egypt. Nevertheless, the army that assembled in Venice in 1202 comprised only a third of the 33,500 men envisaged, despite the recruitment of a leading Lombard noble, Boniface of Montferrat, as the new commander-in-chief. Saddled with debt, the crusade leaders agreed to help the Venetians regain Zara. Many left, however, to find their own way to the Holy Land. Those remaining agreed to help the Byzantine prince Alexius oust his uncle, the Emperor Alexius III, from Constantinople, in return for assistance

with the expedition and Byzantine submission to the pope. Alexius III duly fled (July 1203) but Isaac II and his son, the crusader candidate, Alexius IV, were unable to fulfil their promises. Relations deteriorated and a Byzantine aristocrat usurped the throne in February 1204. The crusaders and Venetians attacked the city again, on 12 April. For three days Constaninople was brutally sacked. Baldwin was crowned the new 'Latin' Emperor (16 May) but in 1205 he was defeated by the Bulgarians and Cumans at Adrianople and killed. Byzantine rulers were established in Epiros, Trebizond and Nicaea, the latter ending Latin rule in Constantinople in 1261. The Byzantine Empire was re-established but pockets of western power remained until the fourteenth century and Venetian rule over the islands continued, in some cases until the seventeenth century.

A. Stewart

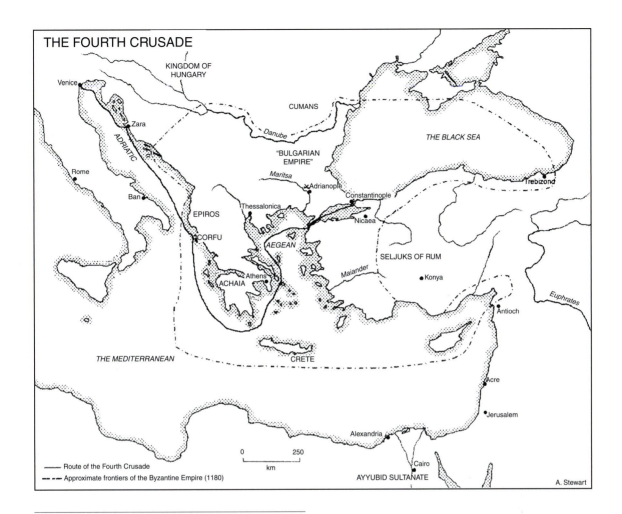

THE FOURTH CRUSADE

The crusades of the Emperor Frederick II and St Louis

As king of Sicily, the Emperor Frederick II was well informed about the Muslim world. He realized that rivalry between the Muslim rulers of Egypt and Syria could be exploited to recover Jerusalem. Even before he set off on crusade in 1228, he was negotiating with the sultan of Egypt, who in February 1229 agreed to the return of Jerusalem. Frederick entered the city and crowned himself king on 18 March. This propaganda coup turned sour, as he found himself condemned. The manner of his recovery of Jerusalem was an affront to the crusading ideal, while the terms left it isolated. It fell in 1244 to the first serious Muslim attack.

This produced a wave of crusading fervour centring on Louis IX of France. In 1249 from his base on Cyprus he launched an attack on Egypt – seen as the key to Jerusalem. Damietta fell in June but Louis delayed his advance against Cairo until the autumn. He won a victory at Mansourah but then found himself cut off. On 6 April 1250 he surrendered. He was released after paying a ransom of 800,000 bezants. To atone for his failure he stayed in the Holy Land until 1254, strengthening its defences. In 1270 he launched another crusade; this time against Tunis. Its ruler was thought to be ready to convert to Christianity.

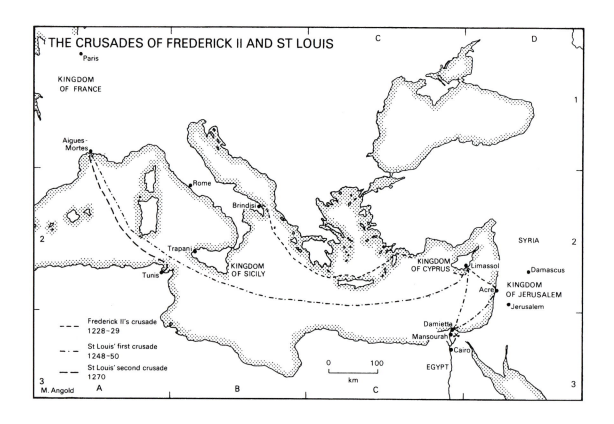

THE CRUSADES OF FREDERICK II AND ST LOUIS

KINGDOM OF FRANCE

Paris

Aigues-Mortes

Rome

Brindisi

Trapani

KINGDOM OF SICILY

Tunis

SYRIA

KINGDOM OF CYPRUS

Limassol

Damascus

Acre

KINGDOM OF JERUSALEM

Jerusalem

Damietta

Mansourah

Cairo

EGYPT

— — — Frederick II's crusade 1228–29

— · — St Louis' first crusade 1248–50

— — St Louis' second crusade 1270

0   100

km

M. Angold

Louis fell ill outside the city and died on 25 August.

St Louis was an idealist who brought meticulous planning to his crusades – down to the construction of the port of Aigues-Mortes. His utter failure did more harm to the cause of the crusade than Frederick's blatant opportunism.

M. Angold

The crusader states

Of the four states the first to be established (1098) and the first to fall to the Muslims (1144) was the county of Edessa. Its position athwart the middle Euphrates left it exposed but provided cover for Antioch, while its crusader princes tried and failed to take Aleppo which blocked expansion inland. After the defeat at the Field of Blood (1119) they were more or less restricted to the coastal plain. To the south the county of Tripoli was similarly confined to the coast, where the plain known as La Bloquée opened up a route inland but it was blocked by Homs. Krak des Chevaliers was built in 1142 to defend the frontier.

This pattern of going onto the defensive after failing to break out into the interior was repeated by the kingdom of Jerusalem but with differences. While a frontier was quickly established along the Jordan from Galilee to the Dead Sea and then in 1115–16 extended as far south as the Gulf of Aila (Aqaba), the coast took much longer to secure. Tyre only fell in 1125; Ascalon not until 1153. The kingdom of Jerusalem thus drove a wedge between the Muslim

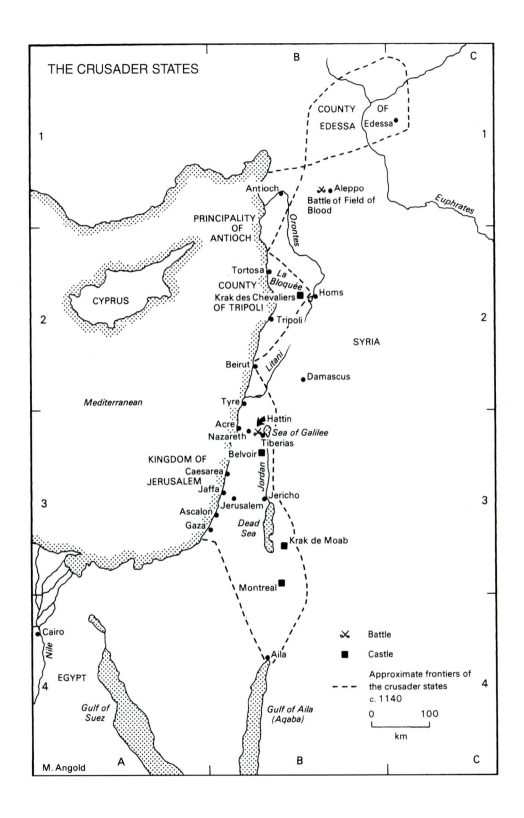

THE CRUSADER STATES

COUNTY
EDESSA OF Edessa

Antioch
⚔ • Aleppo
Battle of Field of
Blood

PRINCIPALITY
OF
ANTIOCH

Orontes

Tortosa
*La
Bloquée*
COUNTY
Krak des Chevaliers ■ Homs
OF TRIPOLI
• Tripoli

CYPRUS

SYRIA

Litani

Beirut

Mediterranean

• Damascus

Tyre

Hattin
Acre
Nazareth ⚔ *Sea of Galilee*
Tiberias
Belvoir ■
KINGDOM OF
Caesarea
JERUSALEM
Jaffa
Jordan

Jericho

Ascalon
Jerusalem
Gaza
*Dead
Sea*
Krak de Moab ■

Montreal ■

Cairo

Nile

EGYPT

Aila

*Gulf of
Suez*

*Gulf of Aila
(Aqaba)*

⚔ Battle

■ Castle

Approximate frontiers of
the crusader states
c. 1140

0   100

km

M. Angold

powers of Egypt and Syria. It threatened both Cairo and Damascus but once these were united by Saladin in 1174 the crusaders were forced on the defensive. Though the kingdom of Jerusalem prospered – Acre was becoming the entrepot of the trade of the eastern Mediterranean – the costs of defence, particularly the construction and maintenance of fortresses, were crippling. The strain contributed to the collapse of the kingdom after Saladin's victory at Hattin in 1187. Though reconstituted by

the third crusade, it was virtually limited to the coast; Jerusalem was only briefly recovered (1229–44). The kingdom survived thanks to the commercial interest of the Italians and divisions among Saladin's successors. Once Egypt passed to the Mamluks (1250), who were dedicated to the revival of the holy war, it was only a matter of time for the crusader states, with Acre finally falling in 1291.

M. Angold

The Templar network

The Templars were founded in 1119 with the limited aim of protecting the pilgrim routes between Jaffa and Jerusalem and the adjacent holy sites. At first they attracted little attention but papal confirmation granted at the Council of Troyes in 1129, followed by a vigorous recruiting drive in the West, set in motion an expansion which, during the twelfth century, transformed them from a small charitable association into an international corporation, possessing estates in all the Christian lands. According to the Rule of the Order their possessions were divided into ten provinces, each governed by a hierarchy of commanders ultimately responsible to the Grand Master. By this means new members were recruited and a set proportion of income sent to the East in the form of responsions. The need to make large sums of money available in the various different parts of Christendom soon led to the development of a complementary banking structure. This vast organization was geared to the protection of the crusader lands in the East where at various times the Order was responsible for at least fifty-three fortified places, ranging from massive castles like Athlit and Safed to small watch-towers in which pilgrims could take refuge. By the 1180s it could muster over 600 knights and 2,000 sergeants in Outremer.

This network was therefore a complex back-up organization for the front-line. Since these

possessions originally derived from the generosity of pious benefactors, there was inevitably a certain random element in the pattern but the map shows the effects of shrewd management unrestricted by the desire for isolation that affected the distribution of Cistercian houses. The Order had houses in the major Atlantic and Mediterranean ports, while its inland possessions clustered around the main trade and pilgrim routes to and from northern Europe: in the east through Champagne, along the Rhône and into Provence and Italy, and in the west through Normandy, Anjou and the Charente into Languedoc and Iberia. Indeed, the expansion of the reconquest in Spain created a second front for the Order, where it became well established in Aragon and, later, Portugal, although the Castilian rulers relied much more upon local military orders. The Templars were least important along Christendom's eastern frontier, dominated first by the Hospital and, from the early thirteenth century, by the Teutonic Knights. Nevertheless, one of the provinces listed by the Rule was that of Hungary which in this period incorporated Dalmatia, a region in which it seems likely that the Templars held many more houses than can at the moment be shown with any certainty on a map. The Order's shipping maintained regular links with Outremer, where the Templars had their own quays and warehouses in all the main ports of the Palestinian and Syrian mainland

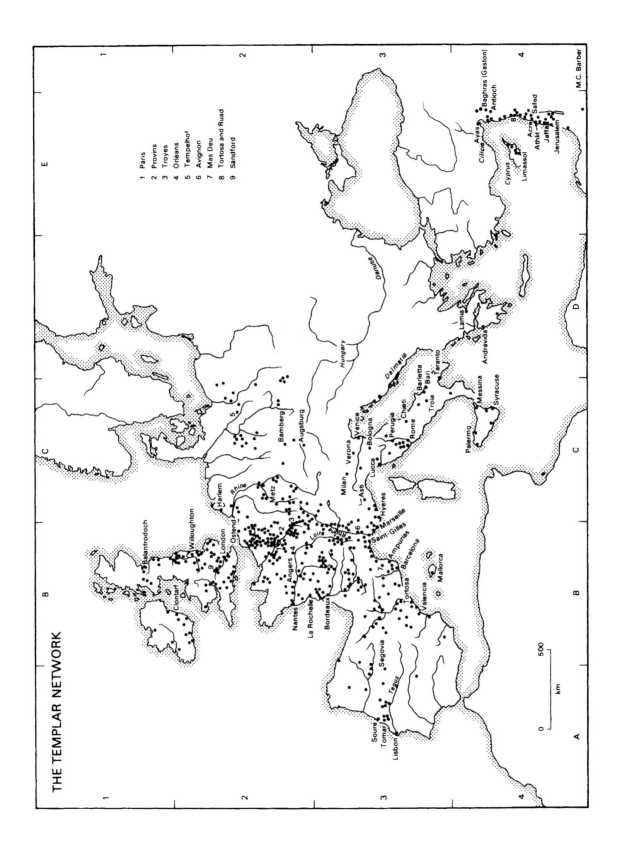

THE TEMPLAR NETWORK

1 Paris
2 Provins
3 Troyes
4 Orléans
5 Tempelhof
6 Avignon
7 Mas Deu
8 Tortosa and Ruad
9 Sandford

M.C. Barber

117

and, in the thirteenth century, in Cyprus and Cilicia as well. In 1307 the Templars were arrested in France, accused of heretical and immoral activity by the government of Philip IV, and during the next two years they were similarly seized in other countries as well. Although there was little substance in the charges, the Order was suppressed by the papacy in 1312 and its lands transferred to the Hospitallers.

At its height the membership is unlikely to have been fewer than 5,000, excluding dependants of various kinds, nor to have had fewer than 800 houses, ranging from great complexes like the Paris Temple to remote rural preceptories administered by perhaps two brothers. A map of this kind should therefore be used with caution, for it cannot mark every single establishment, nor show their relative importance. Moreover, the situation was never static; a more dynamic picture would require several maps.

M.C. Barber

Crusader Jerusalem

In 1099 the crusaders took the Muslim city more or less intact. The outer walls were repaired and the citadel in the Tower of David strengthened. The need was for colonists. At first the crusaders only occupied a single quarter around the Holy Sepulchre, Muslims and Jews having been massacred or expelled. A partial solution was the settlement in 1116 of Christian Syrians from Transjordan, probably in the old Jewish quarter. Repopulation accelerated with the organization of the pilgrim trade. This was largely the work of the Hospital and the Temple, which acquired the Dome of the Rock and the al-Aqsa mosque. There was much rebuilding, notably the enlargement of the church of the Holy Sepulchre, rededicated in 1149, and the construction of the church of St Anne (1140). The covered market was partially reconstructed in 1152. Muslims were much impressed by the city which fell to them in 1187. It briefly returned to the crusaders in 1229–44.

M. Angold

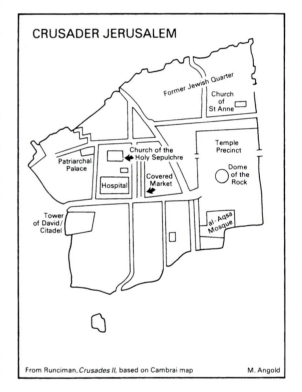

CRUSADER JERUSALEM

From Runciman, *Crusades II*, based on Cambrai map   M. Angold

Crusader Acre

The crusaders captured Acre with Genoese help in 1104. It developed into the main port of the crusader kingdom. Though Italians enjoyed concessions it remained within the royal demesne. Falling to Saladin in 1187, it was recovered in 1191. The single line of walls was now strengthened with a moat and outer wall, incorporating the rapidly developing suburb of Mont Musard. Nominally the capital of the restored kingdom of Jerusalem, Acre was increasingly influenced by the Temple, the Hospital and the Italians after a commune was created in 1232 to defy the vestiges of royal authority. Trade flourished, organized through the *cour de la chaîne*, dealing with seaborne trade, and the *cour de la fonde*, responsible for the market. The latter comprised two Franks and four Syrians, who were increasingly important. The town's topography on the eve of its fall in 1291 is revealed in a map left by Marino Sanudo.

M. Angold

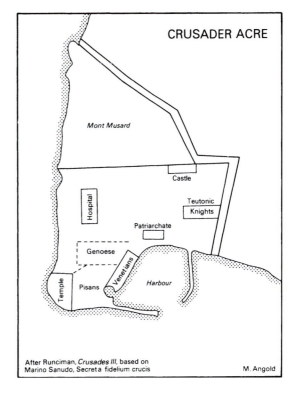

CRUSADER ACRE

Mont Musard

Castle

Hospital

Teutonic Knights

Patriarchate

Genoese

Venetians

Temple

Pisans

Harbour

After Runciman, *Crusades III*, based on Marino Sanudo, Secreta fidelium crucis

M. Angold

The Byzantine Empire in the 13th century

The conquest of Constantinople in April 1204 by the Venetians and the soldiers of the fourth crusade temporarily destroyed the Byzantine Empire. Under Latin rule the empire became a shell, its lands broken up along predictable lines. The Bulgarians brought much of the Balkans under their control. A branch of the imperial house of Angelos established itself in Epiros with its seat at Arta, until strong enough to reconquer Thessalonika (1224). The Ville-hardouins turned the Peloponnese into an independent principality, as did the de la Roches in Athens and Thebes, while the Venetian Sanudos created the duchy of the Archipelago with Naxos at its centre. Venetian energies were largely expended in the face of Genoese competition on securing the islands of Crete and Euboea (Negroponte). In Asia Minor the grandsons of the last Comnenian emperor created a 'pocket' empire in Pontos around Trebizond, while from Nicaea Theodore I Laskaris extended his authority over the western coastlands of Asia Minor.

By the mid-thirteenth century the latter's successors had isolated Latin Constantinople, which they recovered in July 1261. It remained uncertain whether the new emperor, Michael VIII Palaiologos (1259/61–82), could restore the Empire to its late twelfth-century frontiers or whether the divisions that emerged after 1204 would persist. At first it looked as though the lost territories would be recovered without much difficulty. William of Villehardouin, the emperor's prisoner, purchased his freedom

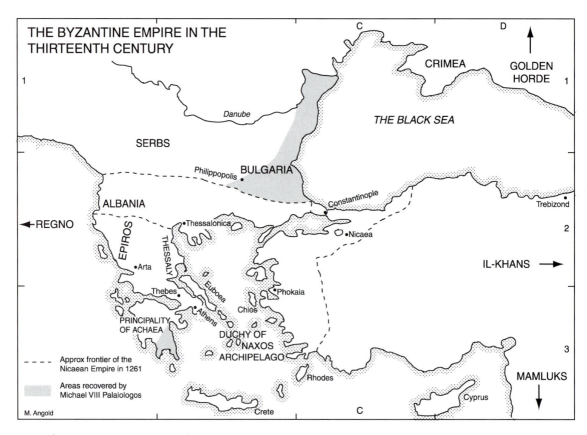

THE BYZANTINE EMPIRE IN THE THIRTEENTH CENTURY

M. Angold

- - - - Approx frontier of the Nicaean Empire in 1261

Areas recovered by Michael VIII Palaiologos

in 1262 with the surrender of the eastern Peloponnese. In the same year Byzantine armies annexed Philippopolis (Plovdiv), the Maritsa valley and the coastlands of Bulgaria as far as the Danube delta. In 1264 the Greek rulers of Epiros and Thessaly acknowledged Byzantine overlordship. Expeditions were mounted against the Venetian bases of Candia in Crete and Negroponte in Euboea. Byzantine privateers recovered the Aegean islands. But the momentum of Byzantine recovery slowed with the appearance of Charles of Anjou, who conquered the *regno* of southern Italy and Sicily in 1266 and set about stiffening Latin resistance. With Angevin backing William of Villehardouin stemmed Byzantine advances in the Peloponnese. Charles rallied the Greek lords of northern Greece and in 1271 was elected king of Albania. Despite arduous campaigning and notable victories the Byzantines were unable to oust the Angevins from Albania. The Venetians equally held on to Crete and Euboea.

Michael Palaiologos's preoccupation with his European provinces meant that he neglected his Anatolian territories, which came under increasing pressure from Turkish raiding. Another pointer to the future was the favour shown to the Genoese adventurer, Benedetto Zaccaria, who received the alum mines of Phokaia (1275) and then seized the island of Chios on his own account. It becomes clear that Michael VIII Palaiologos never quite mastered the situation. This was masked by his wide-ranging diplomacy. He realized that Mongol conquests in Russia and the near East made Constantinople the fulcrum of a new power system. He made marriage alliances with the khans of the Golden Horde, who dominated the steppes, and with the Il-khans of Iran. In 1281 he agreed a peace treaty with the Mamluks of Egypt, which was directed against the crusading ambitions of Charles of Anjou. Earlier he had sought papal support to neutralize Charles's plans for a crusade against Byzantium and was willing to offer a union of churches on papal terms at the second Council of Lyon (1274). Taken as a betrayal of Orthodoxy, this aroused bitter internal opposition. On balance, Michael Palaiologos left Byzantium even more divided than when he came to power.

M. Angold

Italy in the second half of the 13th century

The Italian peninsula can be divided into three politically distinct regions. In the south the Hohenstaufen *regno* ('kingdom') collapsed after the battles of Benevento and Tagliacozzo and the death of the last Hohenstaufen heirs of Frederick II, his grandson Conradin and his illegitimate son Manfred. By 1268 the *regno* had passed to Charles of Anjou, the younger brother of Louis IX of France. Charles had been invited to intervene in the *regno* by the papacy and the 'Guelph' alliance between Charles and the papacy resulted in the cession of Benevento to the papacy after 1263. Once established in the south Charles sought to dominate the north too, by uniting Guelph factions in Lombardy and by assuming the lordship of several Tuscan towns. He also secured influence in Rome. His domination of Italy collapsed, however, following the massacre of French Angevins in Palermo and across the island of Sicily at Easter 1282, an event known as the Sicilian Vespers. The Angevin dynasty continued to hold sway in Naples until the fifteenth century but Sicily now passed to King Pere III of Aragon, whose wife Constance was the daughter of Manfred. The ensuing War of the Vespers between the Angevins and Aragonese was to last for ninety years. Pere's son Jaume later also acquired Sardinia and Corsica from the papacy.

In central Italy the papacy had emerged as the leading political force and Ferrara, Bologna and the towns of the Romagna were formally ceded to the papal states by the emperor-elect, Rudolph of Habsburg, in 1278. A series of short pontificates, however, weakened papal authority in this region. In an attempt to retrieve the situation Boniface VIII (1294–1303) appointed Charles of Valois, brother of Philip IV of France, as vicar of the papal state but his success in reasserting papal authority was limited. Boniface also attempted, with greater success, to establish members of his Caetani family in the Roman hinterland as a basis for support. But this policy alienated others, notably the Colonna family, and in 1303 it joined the now hostile French in kidnapping the pope at Agnani. Unable to pacify the papal state, the papal court was transferred to Avignon in 1307.

In the north, meanwhile, commerce flourished but political factionalism was rife in the vacuum caused by the demise of imperial power. Ostensibly, at least, much of this conflict (both between and within towns) assumed the guise of a contest between 'Guelph' and 'Ghibelline' powers: the pro-papal Guelphs deriving their name from the old Welf opponents of the Hohenstaufen in Germany while the pro-imperial Ghibellines derived theirs from the Hohenstaufen castle of Waiblingen. In the 1250s the papacy led a crusade against Ezzelino da Romano and Oberto Pelavicini (Pallavicini), who, disguised as imperial vicars, between them controlled Cremona, Pavia, Piacenza, Vercelli, Verona, Vicenza and Padua. Ezzelino was killed but, by opportunely changing sides, Oberto built up an even stronger lordship, which briefly included Milan. Thereafter control of that city alternated between the Ghibelline della Torre (1263–81) and Guelph Visconti factions (1281–95). In Tuscany conflict polarized between traditionally Guelph Florence, defeated at Montaperti in 1260, and traditionally Ghibelline Siena. In reality, attachment to these parties depended more on local rivalries than wider loyalties but the parties did at least

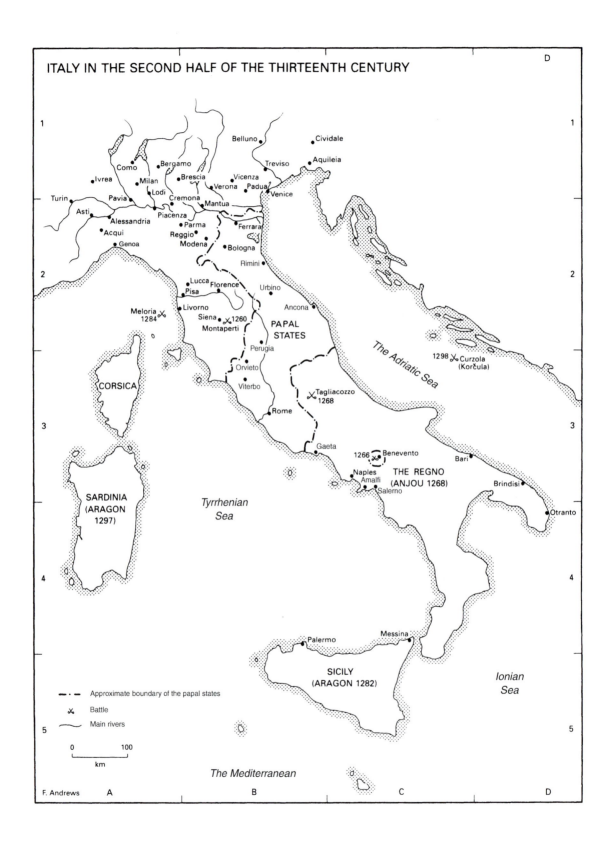

ITALY IN THE SECOND HALF OF THE THIRTEENTH CENTURY

Belluno
Cividale
Como
Bergamo
Treviso
Aquileia
Ivrea
Milan
Brescia
Vicenza
Verona
Padua
Lodi
Venice
Turin
Pavia
Cremona
Mantua
Asti
Piacenza
Alessandria
Parma
Ferrara
Acqui
Reggio
Genoa
Modena
Bologna
Rimini
Lucca
Florence
Pisa
Urbino
Livorno
Ancona
Meloria
1284
Siena
1260
Montaperti
PAPAL
STATES
CORSICA
Perugia
Orvieto
Viterbo
SARDINIA
(ARAGON
1297)
Rome
The Adriatic Sea
1298
Curzola
(Korčula)
Tagliacozzo
1268
Gaeta
1266
Benevento
Bari
Naples
THE REGNO
Amalfi
(ANJOU 1268)
Salerno
Brindisi
Tyrrhenian
Sea
Otranto
Palermo
Messina
SICILY
(ARAGON 1282)
Ionian
Sea

– · – Approximate boundary of the papal states
✗ Battle
⌇ Main rivers

0   100
km

The Mediterranean

F. Andrews   A   B   C   D

provide a measure of cohesion to a politically fragmented region. Elsewhere Pisa, Genoa and Venice fought to defend their trading interests: the Genoese defeated the Pisans at Meloria in 1284 and the Venetians at Curzola in 1298. In the north-west Gugliemo VII of Monferrato extended his power over Piedmont by acquiring authority in Alessandria, Asti, Turin and elsewhere, while in the north-east an alliance of 1262 between Verona, Padua, Treviso and Vicenza was designed to prevent the dominance of one person in any of these cities. Nonetheless, Verona and later Vicenza fell to the della Scala family, Treviso to the da Camino and Padua to the Carrara.

F. Andrews

The *Ostsiedlung*

Between 1100 and 1350 eastern Europe was transformed by a wave of German immigration (the *Ostsiedlung*), which moved the eastern boundaries of the German-speaking world hundreds of miles beyond its former limit on the rivers Elbe and Saale. In some areas, such as Brandenburg, this new settlement came in the wake of conquest by German lords and knights but in many other regions, such as Pomerania and Silesia, it was local Slav princes who encouraged German settlement. National antagonism was not important. The new settlers wanted land and the local rulers were happy to grant it and to profit, directly or indirectly, from the taxes, rents and tithes flowing from the new villages.

The frontier of settlement began to move in the first half of the twelfth century when immigration was actively promoted by such vigorous border lords as Adolf of Holstein, Henry the Lion, duke of Saxony, and Albert the Bear, margrave of Brandenburg. They advertised the attractions of the eastern frontier among the overcrowded inhabitants of western Germany and the Low Countries and soon streams of colonists were arriving in east Holstein, Schwerin, Ratzeburg and Brandenburg. The pace quickened in the thirteenth century as planned and large-scale development was undertaken in Pomerania and the Polish lands.

Rural settlement often involved the layout of entirely new villages, composed of standard, rectilinear farms (*Hufen* or *mansi*). The recruitment and organization of the colonists were the task of a planning entrepreneur (*locator*), who received land and privileges in the new settlement as his reward. Slav peasants were not usually dispossessed (though there are some instances of this), since in general there was plenty of land, especially for those willing to drain marshes or fell forests.

Rural settlement was complemented by new urban foundations. German burgesses formed the core of most of the new chartered towns founded in eastern Europe in these centuries. They brought their language, culture and law with them. Places as significant for German civilization as Lübeck, Berlin and Leipzig were twelfth- or thirteenth-century foundations in previously Slav landscapes. German urban settlement spread far beyond the limits of German peasant settlement and up to the borders of Russia there were German burgesses, living according to German town law, in the midst of native rural populations.

In some regions German conquest and settlement coincided with conversion to Christianity. The Slavs who inhabited Mecklenburg and Brandenburg, for example, were pagan until the twelfth century. In most areas, however, Germans came to lands that were already Christian. But one German settlement was unique in being created and permanently maintained by holy war. This was the domain of the Teutonic Knights, Prussia and Livonia, where German crusaders brought forcible baptism to pagan Baltic peoples. By the fourteenth century,

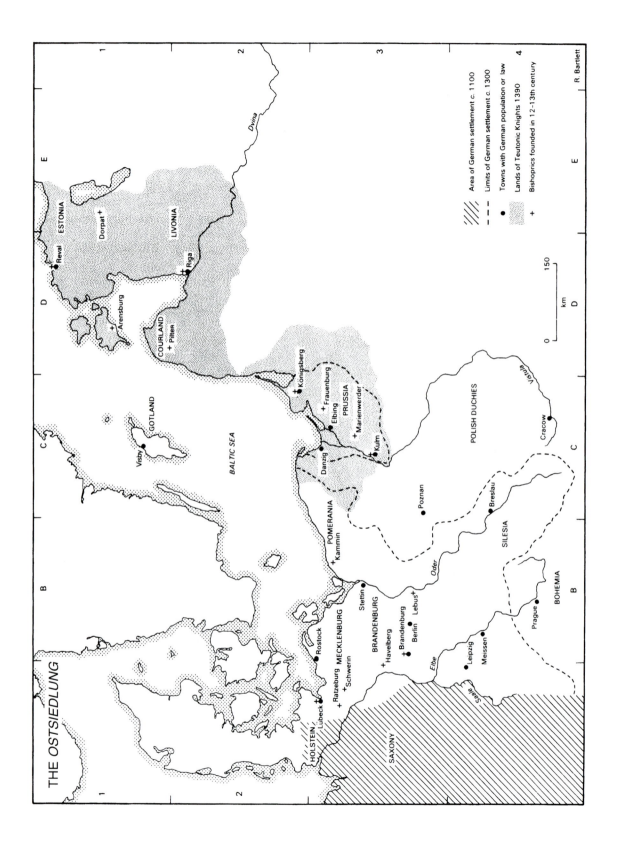

THE OSTSIEDLUNG

Legend:
- Area of German settlement c. 1100
- Limits of German settlement c. 1300
- Towns with German population or law
- Lands of Teutonic Knights 1390
- Bishoprics founded in 12–13th century

R. Bartlett

0 — 150 km

ESTONIA
Dorpat +
Reval
Arensburg +
LIVONIA
Riga +
COURLAND
Pilten +
Königsberg
Frauenburg +
Elbing +
Marienwerder +
PRUSSIA
Kulm +
Danzig
GOTLAND
Visby
BALTIC SEA
POMERANIA
Kammin +
POLISH DUCHIES
Cracow
Poznan
Breslau
SILESIA
Stettin
MECKLENBURG
Rostock
Ratzeburg +
Schwerin +
BRANDENBURG
Havelberg +
Brandenburg
Berlin
Lebus +
Oder
Lübeck
HOLSTEIN
SAXONY
Leipzig
Meissen
Elbe
Saale
BOHEMIA
Prague
Dvina

although the pagan Lithuanians were far from being defeated, a German population of landlords, churchmen, burgesses and (in Prussia) peasants had settled, from Danzig to the Gulf of Finland, under the rule of the crusading knights.

The end result of the *Ostsiedlung* was the Germanization of vast areas east of the Elbe and an increase in their economic productivity. Some of the political units created in the process, like Brandenburg and Prussia, were to have an important role in subsequent European history.

R. Bartlett

Poland in the Central Middle Ages

Pola means 'field', generally taken as a reference to the broad north European plain running eastwards and eventually broadening into steppe. The Carpathians provide a definitive southern boundary and although Polish influence has stretched as far west as the Elbe, the kingdom's heartland was around the Oder and Vistula rivers. The medieval state was largely landlocked apart from the area around Danzig/ Gdansk.

In the mid-tenth century Slavic tribes along the Elbe, Oder and Vistula rivers came together under Mieszko I (962–92). The state depended largely on the nobility's desire to resist Bohemian and German influence and its rallying around Mieszko's Piast dynasty: Bolesław Chrobry, the Brave (992–1025); Bolesław Szczodry, the Munificent (1058–79); and Bolesław Krzywousty, the Wrymouth (1102–38). Rulers augmented their fragile authority through association with powerful churchmen and neighbours. In 1000 Emperor Otto III placed his own crown on the head of Bolesław I, who was recrowned by the archbishop of Gniezno in 1025, and Bolesław II sought a crown from Pope Gregory VII in 1076. Repeated crownings highlight the uncertain status of the early Piasts.

Tenth- and eleventh-century Polish rulers collected taxes and maintained a standing army but their authority was in steady decline until Bolesław III's death heralded the kingdom's division between his sons. Five duchies emerged: Małopolska, Wielkopolska, Mazovia, Silesia and Pomerania. The kingdom was evidently regarded as a dynastic estate. Tales of internecine strife from Poland and Kievan Rus, whose nobilities were heavily intermarried, suggest an acute sense of political community based on the family.

Local churchmen, on the other hand, maintained a collective and distinctly Polish identity. Ever since Mieszko I's conversion (966) rulers and churchmen feared the German archbishopric of Magdeburg whose ambitions were as much territorial as spiritual. Bolesław I used the cult of the martyred missionary Adalbert to win papal approval for a metropolitan see at Gniezno with dependent bishoprics in Kraków, Poznan and Wrocław. These bishoprics quickly became powerful: when in 1079 Bolesław II ordered the death of Stanislaw, bishop of Kraków, he was ultimately forced to abdicate himself. The establishment of Benedictine, Cistercian and Dominican monastic orders also maintained Polish contacts with mainstream western spiritual life. Extensive German immigration meant that Poland became a Catholic country as much by colonization as conversion.

In the thirteenth century the political vacuum encouraged predators. The Mongols raided from the steppes in 1241, sacking Kraków and destroying a Polish army at Legnica. Further raids in 1259 and 1287 emphasized the region's lack of stability and security. This helped the rise of the Teutonic Knights. Driven from the crusader kingdom of Jerusalem, this military monastic order looked to regain God's favour by campaigning against the heathen Prussians on Poland's north-east

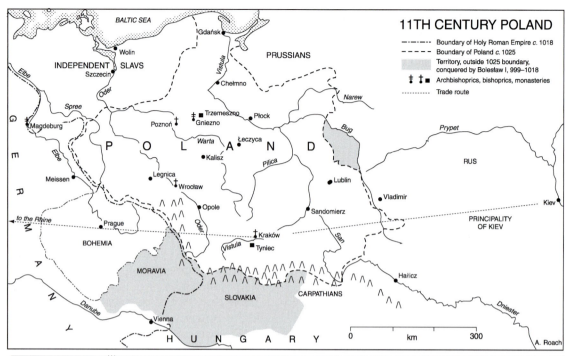

11TH CENTURY POLAND

- — · · — Boundary of Holy Roman Empire *c.* 1018
- — — — Boundary of Poland *c.* 1025
- Territory, outside 1025 boundary, conquered by Bolesław I, 999–1018
- ‡ † ■ Archbishoprics, bishoprics, monasteries
- · · · · · · Trade route

BALTIC SEA

Gdańsk

PRUSSIANS

Wolin

INDEPENDENT SLAVS

Szczecin

Chełmno

Narew

Vistula

Oder

Spree

Magdeburg

‡■ Trzemeszno

Poznań

Płock

‡ Gniezno

Bug

Prypet

P O L A N D

Warta

Łęczyca

RUS

Elbe

Kalisz

Pilica

Meissen

Legnica

† Wrocław

Lublin

RUS

Opole

Oder

Sandomierz

Vladimir

Kiev

to the Rhine

Prague

San

PRINCIPALITY OF KIEV

G E R M A N Y

BOHEMIA

Vistula

† Kraków

■ Tyniec

MORAVIA

Hałicz

SLOVAKIA

CARPATHIANS

Danube

Vienna

Dniester

H U N G A R Y

0   km   300

A. Roach

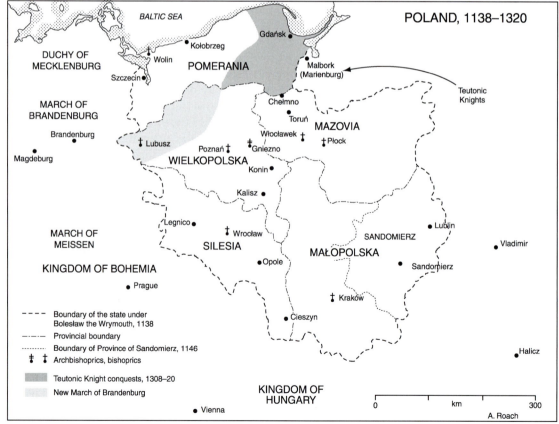

POLAND, 1138–1320

BALTIC SEA

DUCHY OF MECKLENBURG

Kołobrzeg

† Wolin

Gdańsk

POMERANIA

Szczecin

Malbork (Marienburg)

MARCH OF BRANDENBURG

Teutonic Knights

Chełmno

Toruń

MAZOVIA

Brandenburg

Włocławek

Magdeburg

‡ Lubusz

Poznań

‡ Gniezno

† Płock

WIELKOPOLSKA

Konin

Kalisz

MARCH OF MEISSEN

Legnico

† Wrocław

SANDOMIERZ

Lublin

KINGDOM OF BOHEMIA

SILESIA

MAŁOPOLSKA

Vladimir

Opole

Sandomierz

Prague

† Kraków

Cieszyn

- — — — Boundary of the state under Bolesław the Wrymouth, 1138
- — · — · — Provincial boundary
- · · · · · · Boundary of Province of Sandomierz, 1146
- ‡ † Archbishoprics, bishoprics
- Teutonic Knight conquests, 1308–20
- New March of Brandenburg

Halicz

KINGDOM OF HUNGARY

Vienna

0   km   300

A. Roach

frontier. By 1283 they had carved out their own state focused on the colossal fortress at Marienburg. The margraves of Brandenburg also had ambitions in the region and in 1300 Vaclav II of Bohemia had himself crowned king of Poland after a short-lived conquest of Wielkopolska.

External threats encouraged the Polish nobility to resurrect an effective monarchy by adopting the principle of election. Władisław Łokietek (the Short) was crowned king in 1320 at Kraków. His kingdom was a central European state which looked mainly south and east and, like its neighbours Hungary and Bohemia, it was to enjoy an unprecedented flowering in the fourteenth century.

A.P. Roach

The Premyslide-Habsburg conflict in Central Europe

The history of Premyslide Bohemia from its mythical origins under Premysl the Ploughman to the extinction of the native dynasty in 1306 is one long struggle against the German hegemony to the west. The rulers of Germany availed themselves of frequent opportunities to interfere in the affairs of Bohemia while the Premyslide dukes sought to advance their own interests at the expense of the Empire. Successfully resisting the right of the emperor to nominate the holder of the crown, the Czech dukes gradually asserted a position of influence among the seven electors of the Empire. By 1114 the ruler of Bohemia, as hereditary cup-bearer, was in a strong enough position to influence the election of the emperor himself.

The struggle between the Czech and German ruling houses was not racial in character; on the contrary, Czech princes married princesses from Saxony, Swabia and Meissen. Germans held high office within the Bohemian clergy and the Czech rulers, by now kings, invited large numbers of German colonists to Bohemia, granting them special privileges and laws quite separate from those of the indigenous population. This colonization, which reached its height in the second half of the thirteenth century, was in two stages: the first wave of immigrants were farmers contracted to cultivate the heavily wooded border region of the realm; the second wave consisted of skilled artisans, principally miners, who established their own towns, such as Stríbro and Kutná Hora, east of Prague. This colonization was part of a larger economic and political policy to exploit the mineral resources of the kingdom while creating a middle-class wedge between the king and his traditional rivals for power, the nobility.

The first Premyslide ruler to capitalize on dissensions within the Empire was Premysl Otakar I (1198–1230) who obtained from the emperor a 'Golden Bull' (1212) which confirmed the royal title and renounced the imperial right to ratify each successor to the crown. The most powerful member of the dynasty was Premysl Otakar II (1253–78). Already duke of Austria by the time of his accession, Otakar skilfully played off the rivals for the vacant imperial throne while furthering his own dynastic ambitions in central Europe. By a series of brilliant military campaigns, Otakar added Styria, Carinthia, Carniola and Istria to his domains, so that at the height of his power he ruled from Silesia to the Adriatic, revealing as historical reality Shakespeare's claim that Bohemia was once in possession of a coastline.

Otakar's successes attracted the antagonism and resentment of the German princes who in 1273 elected Count Rudolph of Habsburg to the imperial office. In 1274 Otakar's rights to Austria, Styria and Carinthia were annulled at the diet of Regensburg. In 1276 Rudolph, supported by the Hungarians and Otakar's recalcitrant lords resentful of the king's pro-German policies, marched against Otakar. Deserted on

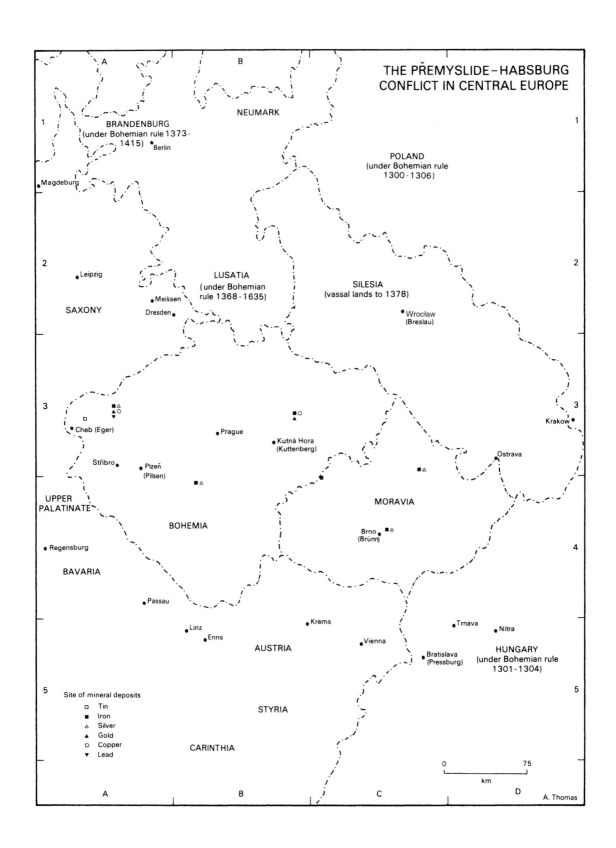

THE PŘEMYSLIDE–HABSBURG
CONFLICT IN CENTRAL EUROPE

NEUMARK

BRANDENBURG
(under Bohemian rule 1373-
1415)
• Berlin

POLAND
(under Bohemian rule
1300-1306)

• Magdeburg

• Leipzig

LUSATIA
(under Bohemian
rule 1368-1635)

SILESIA
(vassal lands to 1378)

SAXONY

• Meissen
Dresden •

• Wrocław
(Breslau)

• Krakow

■ △
▲ O
□
▼
• Cheb (Eger)

• Prague

■ O
▲
• Kutná Hora
(Kuttenberg)

• Ostrava

Stříbro • • Plzeň
(Pilsen)

■ △

■ △

UPPER
PALATINATE

BOHEMIA

MORAVIA

Brno • ■ △
(Brünn)

• Regensburg

BAVARIA

• Passau

• Krems

• Trnava
• Nitra

• Linz
• Enns

• Vienna

AUSTRIA

• Bratislava
(Pressburg)

HUNGARY
(under Bohemian rule
1301-1304)

Site of mineral deposits
□ Tin
■ Iron
△ Silver
▲ Gold
O Copper
▼ Lead

STYRIA

CARINTHIA

0   75

km

A. Thomas

all sides, Otakar appealed in the form of a letter to the dukes of Silesia and Poland, invoking an all-Slav resistance to the German threat. But Otakar's army was routed at the battle of Dürnkrut on the Marchfeld and the king himself was slain. Habsburg rule over Austria was established, enduring until its demise in the twentieth century. Although Bohemia was to prosper under the next king, Wenceslas II (1278–1305), and enjoyed a golden age under Charles IV (1347–78), king of Bohemia and emperor, the real focus of power had shifted southwards to the Habsburgs. While the fortunes of Bohemia waxed and waned over the next three centuries, Habsburg Austria was destined to become one of the major powers on the map of modern Europe.

A. Thomas

The Mongol-Tatar invasions and their impact on the West

Rumours of the conquests made by the Mongols under Ghingis Khan reached the crusader camp at Damietta in 1221, exciting only momentary interest. The Russians paid scarcely more attention, despite being defeated in 1223 by a Mongol reconnaissance force. They were unprepared for the Mongol assault launched in 1237 by Batu. The northern Russian principalities were the first to suffer. Rjazan' was sacked, then Vladimir. Its prince, Jury, died fighting the Mongols on the River Sit' (4 March 1238). The Mongols then turned south, their campaign culminating in December 1240 with the destruction of Kiev. A carefully organized sweep into the heart of Europe followed. While one army was destroying Polish resistance at Liegnitz (9 April 1241), another was crushing the Hungarians at Mohi (12 April 1241). The Mongols met up in Hungary but the danger that they might settle permanently was averted when news came of the death of the Great Khan Ögedei. Batu evacuated his armies to their base north of the Caspian, the better to influence events at the Mongol capital of Karakorum. His withdrawal gave the new pope, Innocent IV, a chance to evaulate the Mongol threat. It came high on the agenda of the General Council he called at Lyon in 1245. He also dispatched the Dominican John of Pian Carpini to the new Great Khan Güyük to discover more about Mongol intentions and to sound out the possibilities of their conversion to Christianity. The reply, brought back in 1247, was scarcely encouraging. The Great Khan claimed world dominion by mandate of the Sky God and demanded the pope's submission. The succession struggle following Güyük's death in 1248 forced the Mongol lieutenant in Persia to adopt a more conciliatory stance when confronted by St Louis IX's first crusade (1248–50). Louis rejected his offer of an alliance, insisting that conversion to Christianity must come first. His caution was justified when his emissary returned with yet another demand from the Great Khan for submission.

Such demands explain why the West remained suspicious of Mongol overtures even when the Mongol Empire began to disintegrate. In Persia the Ilkhans made repeated requests for a western alliance. This Mongol successor state was founded by Hülegü, who favoured the Nestorian Christians and was hostile to Islam. In 1258 he sacked Baghdad and put the caliph to death. He had the support of the Armenian king of Cilicia and the crusader prince of Antioch, who rode in triumph into Damascus in 1260 with the Mongol army. This was almost immediately followed by the defeat of the Mongols at Ain Jalud by the Mamluks of Egypt. Thereafter the Ilkhans found their western flank along the Euphrates under threat from the Mamluks who in 1268 took Antioch. They turned to the West for an alliance, even sending emissaries in 1274 to the second

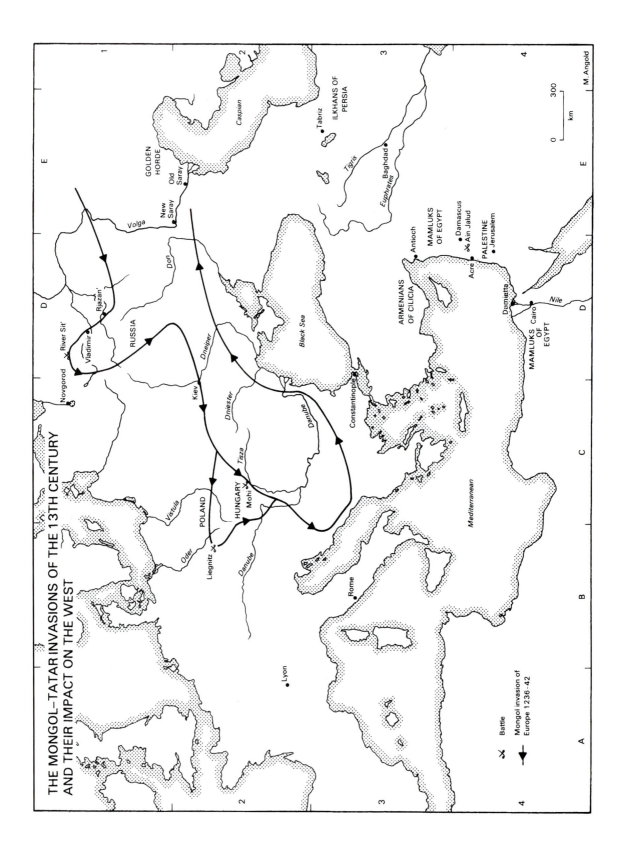

THE MONGOL–TATAR INVASIONS OF THE 13TH CENTURY
AND THEIR IMPACT ON THE WEST

M. Angold

Battle

Mongol invasion of
Europe 1236-42

GOLDEN
HORDE

Old
Saray

New
Saray

Volga

Don

Dnieper

Kiev

Dniester

Vistula

Oder

POLAND

Liegnitz

Danube

HUNGARY

Mohi

Tisza

Danube

RUSSIA

Vladimir

Rjazan'

River Sit'

Novgorod

Black Sea

Constantinople

Rome

Lyon

Mediterranean

Caspian

Tabriz

ILKHANS OF
PERSIA

Tigris

Baghdad

Euphrates

ARMENIANS
OF CILICIA

Antioch

MAMLUKS
OF EGYPT

Damascus

Ain Jalud

PALESTINE

Jerusalem

Acre

Damietta

Nile

MAMLUKS
OF
EGYPT

Cairo

0   300
km

Council of Lyon, where a crusade was being mooted. Religion proved a stumbling block. The Ilkhans therefore sent the Nestorian Rabban Sauma in 1287 to impress the West with their devotion to Christianity. There was talk of the restoration of Jerusalem. The West remained aloof but the Mamluks took the possibility of a western alliance with the Mongols seriously and countered it by occupying the remaining crusader places in Palestine, Acre falling in 1291. The Mongol impact on the West was muted. The *pax mongolica* briefly opened up the Orient to western merchants, the Ilkhan capital Tabriz being a favourite des-tination. It also offered some scope for western missionaries but this quickly reduced with the conversion of the Ilkhans to Islam from the turn of the thirteenth century. For the Russians it was a different matter. Until the fifteenth century they were tributaries of the Golden Horde – the Mongol successor state established by Batu and his descendants, with its capital at Saray. The Mongol yoke allowed Russia to develop in isolation from the West, while Mongol favour to the Orthodox Church enhanced its hold on Russian society.

M. Angold

France in the reign of Philip the Fair

The reign of Philip IV (1285–1314) saw the Capetian monarchy at the height of its powers. There were no spectacular conquests to rival those of Philip Augustus. But in conformity with recent royal policy, Philip consistently built up the royal *domaine* by more peaceful means such as marriage alliances, purchase, *paréage* agreements (obtaining shared jurisdiction with another lord, usually an ecclesiastic, prior to gaining outright control) and the clever manipulation of uncertainties in successoral law, backed up by the judicious but limited use of force. As a result the frontiers of the kingdom were extended, particularly towards the east, whilst the internal authority of the Crown was consolidated. Some acquisitions were permanent additions to the *domaine*. Others were used to endow cadets like Charles of Valois and Louis of Evreux, the king's brothers, or his sons, returning to the Crown for the most part in the next few generations.

By his marriage (1284) to Jeanne, heiress to the counties of Champagne and Brie as well as to the small kingdom of Navarre, Philip obtained extensive properties in eastern France bordering on imperial territory. The acquisition of Valenciennes (1292), recognition of his suzerainty by the count of Bar (1301) and by the archbishop of Lyon for the Lyonnais (1307), together with a *paréage* with the bishop of Viviers in the same year, helped to bring the frontiers of the realm close to those formerly established by the treaty of Verdun (843), with the Meuse and Rhône marking the extent of royal control. By arranging the marriage of the future Philip V with the heiress of the county of Burgundy he was even able to carry this influence across the Saône. Other *paréages* were made with the bishop of Mende for the Gevaudan, the bishop of Le Puy for Velay and the bishop of Cahors for Cahors (all in 1307).

There remained four great feudatories enjoying extensive independent authority: the count of Flanders and the dukes of Guyenne, Brittany and Burgundy. The seizure of Guyenne (1294) and Flanders (1301) proved short-lived triumphs. Philip soon had to release them to their former rulers, gaining only the small Pyrenean *vicomté* of Soule (1306) and the castellanies of Lille, Douai and Béthune (eventually exchanged for Orchies in 1322) as more permanent additions to royal properties. But in all four principalities local power was coming to be circumscribed by the crown and its agents. For in developing a royal doctrine of sovereignty in conformity with Roman law precepts, the

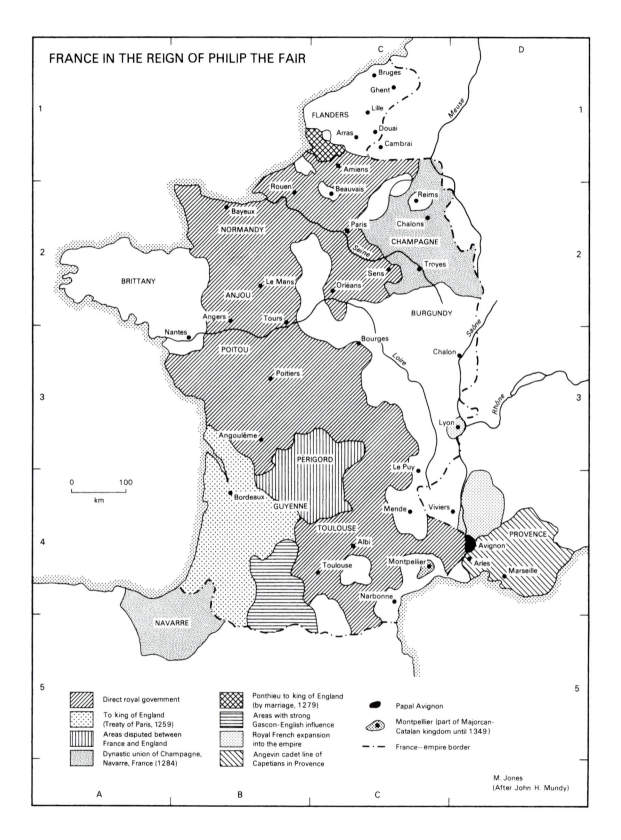

FRANCE IN THE REIGN OF PHILIP THE FAIR

Bruges
Ghent
Lille
FLANDERS
Arras
Douai
Cambrai
Meuse

Amiens
Rouen
Beauvais
Reims
Bayeux
Chalons
Paris
NORMANDY
CHAMPAGNE
BRITTANY
Seine
Troyes
Le Mans
Sens
ANJOU
Orléans
Angers
Tours
BURGUNDY
Nantes
Saône
POITOU
Bourges
Chalon
Poitiers
Loire
Angoulême
Lyon
Rhône
PERIGORD
Le Puy
Bordeaux
Mende
Viviers
GUYENNE
TOULOUSE
PROVENCE
Albi
Avignon
Toulouse
Montpellier
Arles
Marseille
Narbonne

NAVARRE

0   100
km

Direct royal government

To king of England
(Treaty of Paris, 1259)

Areas disputed between
France and England

Dynastic union of Champagne,
Navarre, France (1284)

Ponthieu to king of England
(by marriage, 1279)

Areas with strong
Gascon-English influence

Royal French expansion
into the empire

Angevin cadet line of
Capetians in Provence

Papal Avignon

Montpellier (part of Majorcan-
Catalan kingdom until 1349)

France–empire border

M. Jones
(After John H. Mundy)

132

Parlement of Paris now exercised the right to hear appeals from provincial courts, the king issued *ordonnances* for general application and royal officials kept a close eye on local princely governments, frequently intervening. Ties between the crown and leading vassals were also often given more definite form. In 1297, for instance, the duke of Brittany was made a peer of France, emphasizing his prestige but also his liege status and carefully defining the services he owed.

An authoritarian streak marked many royal actions, especially in attacks on vulnerable minorities like the Jews and Lombard financiers. It was most spectacularly displayed in the persecution of the Order of the Temple whose members were, with few exceptions, seized in a remarkable country-wide operation on 13 October 1307. It is perhaps not surprising that Philip's death was followed by a widespread provincial reaction against the centralizing tendencies that had so strongly marked his policies, calling into question the Capetian achievement.

M. Jones

The Spanish and Portuguese reconquest in the 12th and 13th centuries

In the 1140s the Almoravids were overthrown by the heretical sect of the Almohads as rulers of the Maghreb and Muslim Spain. During the interregnum various towns were taken by the Christians: Lisbon (1147) by the newly independent kingdom of Portugal; Tortosa (1148) and Lérida (1149) by the newly united realm of Aragon-Catalonia; and Almería (1147), temporarily, by León. The Spanish Muslims tried to create their own independent kingdom, based on Murcia and Valencia, but this was absorbed by the Almohad Empire in 1172. Thenceforward, Portugal, León, Castile (independent from 1157), Navarre and Aragon-Catalonia were frequently targeted by the Almohad caliph's holy wars. They were relieved only by his equally frequent need to suppress Muslim dissidents in Tunis and Mallorca. To resist his attacks, the Templars and Hospitallers garrisoned fortresses on the highways leading north. When they failed, Iberian military orders were created for the same purpose. The Order of Calatrava (founded in 1158) defended the approaches to Toledo at Calatrava and Zorita; that of Santiago (founded in 1170) defended Toledo at Uclés and Mora, Lisbon at Palmela, and the Seville-León road at Cáceres. Other highways were defended by the friars of Evora (later Avis) and Alcántara. No help was received from foreign crusaders, except those sailing to the Holy Land who helped capture Lisbon, Silves (1189) and Alcácer (1217).

At Alarcos (1195) Alfonso VIII of Castile (1158–1214) suffered a great defeat but at Las Navas de Tolosa (1212) he avenged it, routing the caliph and breaking Almohad morale. After 1224, as the Almohad Empire disintegrated in a war of succession complicated by religious, racial and tribal hatreds, the Spanish Muslims again fought to set up a state independent of both Christians and Africans. They achieved this, although under nominal Castilian suzerainty, in the kingdom of Granada (1232–1492). The Christians, with papal help, profited from Muslim dissensions to conquer almost all southern Iberia. Alfonso IX of León (1188–1230) took Cáceres (1229) and Badajoz (1230). His son, St Ferdinand III of Castile (1217–52), inherited León (1230) and deployed Leonese-Castilian forces to conquer the Guadalquivir valley, including Córdoba (1236), Jaén (1246) and Seville (1248), and to make the Muslim successor states of Murcia (1243), Granada (1246) and Niebla his vassals. Ferdinand's son,

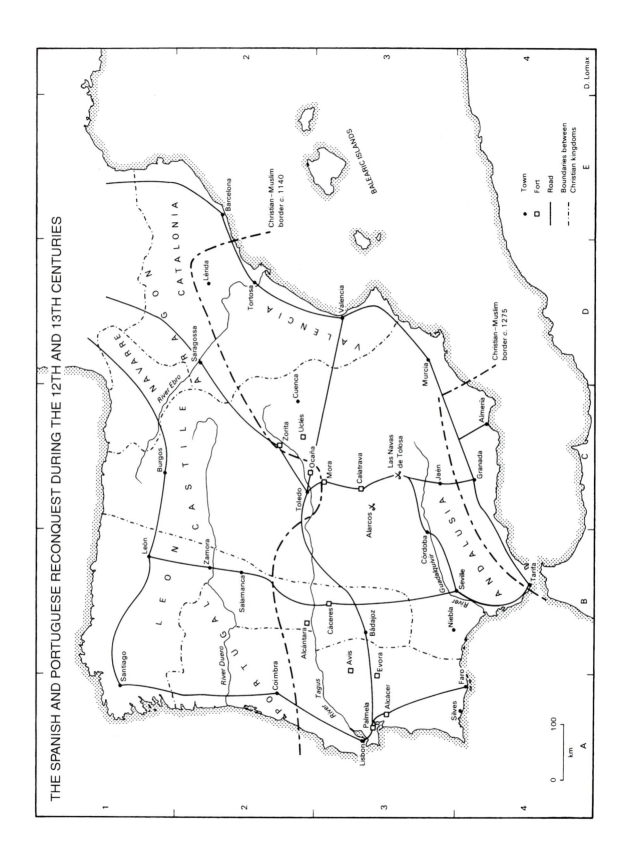

THE SPANISH AND PORTUGUESE RECONQUEST DURING THE 12TH AND 13TH CENTURIES

Town •
Fort ☐
Road ——
Boundaries between Christian kingdoms —·—·—

Christian–Muslim border c. 1140
Christian–Muslim border c. 1275

BALEARIC ISLANDS

NAVARRE
ARAGON
CATALONIA
LEON
CASTILE
PORTUGAL
VALENCIA
ANDALUSIA

Barcelona
Lérida
Tortosa
Valencia
Saragossa
Cuenca
Murcia
Almería
Granada
Zorita
Uclés
Ocaña
Mora
Calatrava
Las Navas de Tolosa
Jaén
Toledo
Alarcos
Córdoba
Seville
Guadalquivir River
Niebla
Tarifa
Burgos
León
Zamora
Salamanca
Cáceres
Badajoz
Alcántara
Ávis
Évora
Alcácer
Palmela
Lisbon
Coimbra
Santiago
Faro
Silves
River Ebro
River Duero
River Tagus

km
0   100

D. Lomax

Alfonso X (1252–84), annexed Murcia and Niebla, expelled most Muslims from Castilian Andalusia and replaced them with Christians. When the Moroccan Banu Marin dynasty invaded Iberia (1275–1340) it was unable to reconquer territory because it was opposed by a solid mass of peasant warriors, who would defend Castile against Muslim irredentism until the Catholic Monarchs, Ferdinand V and Isabella I, led them to conquer the last Muslim stronghold in the Peninsula, Granada (1492).

Meanwhile, in Portugal the Palmela peninsula and Alcácer (1217) were captured by the military orders and Rhenish crusaders. King Sancho II (1223–48) reconquered most of the area to the Algarve coast, leaving only Faro (1250) to be taken by his successor, Afonso III (1248–79). With the exception of certain towns on the south coast, the rest of the territory was given to the military orders and developed mainly for cattle-ranching.

To the east, James I of Aragon, 'the Conqueror' (1213–76), captured the Balearic Islands (1229–35) and the city (1238) and kingdom of Valencia. In the kingdom he expelled the Muslims from the towns, replacing them with Christian settlers. Muslim peasants remained in the countryside, almost untouched by Christian immigration, but reduced to near-serfdom under a new landowning aristocracy from Aragon and Catalonia. Thus James strengthened the nobility throughout his realms. He inhibited Catalan migration, except to Murcia and the overseas islands which his descendants were to conquer, and ensured that, whereas the peasantry enjoyed ever more favourable conditions in Castile, the reverse was true in Catalonia.

D. Lomax

GOVERNMENT, SOCIETY AND ECONOMY

Provisioning war in the 12th century

In the twelfth and thirteenth centuries some western European monarchies began to produce documents which recorded their activities in a more sustained and detailed way than before. From this period it is thus possible to reconstruct the practical workings of government. One of the best-documented of medieval governments was that of England and the map shows the kind of detailed information that can be drawn from twelfth-century English records. In this case the information is drawn from the Pipe Rolls. These were accounts of the sums rendered by the sheriffs and other royal officials to the exchequer, the central financial institution. When the king took goods from the localities directly, these were credited to the sheriff's account. Plotted on the map is the amount of foodstuffs and materials provided for Henry II's expedition to Ireland in 1171–2.

This expedition, which brought an English king to Ireland for the first time, had been made necessary by developments in Ireland over the previous two years. In 1169 Norman-Welsh adventurers had landed in Leinster, initially serving as auxiliaries in the never-ending warfare of the Irish kings. In 1171, however, their leader, Richard fitz Gilbert ('Strongbow') had taken over Leinster itself. Henry II had no desire to see a new, independent principality so close to his own territories, especially one ruled by a politically suspect member of his own aristocracy. His expedition of 1171–2 secured both Strongbow's submission and the recognition of his overlordship by the Irish kings. It was the beginning of a political connection which survives, in part, to this day.

The king maintained an army of about 10,000 men in Ireland for six months. This included a prolonged stay during the winter months in Dublin, where a timber palace was constructed. An army of this size, especially if sedentary for any length of time, could not live off the land and hence a great quantity of provisions had to be collected in England and transported to Ireland. The map shows how a successful twelfth-century monarchy could mobilize large-scale resources for warfare. Thousands of quarters of grain and hundreds of hogs were sent from virtually every part of the kingdom. Beans and cheese (not plotted) were collected. Ships' gear, such as canvas, was procured and seamen were levied from a dozen counties. Axes, shovels and nails were also dispatched – 60,000 nails and a thousand shovels came from the Forest of Dean, England's most important iron-working centre.

Bristol and Chester were the most important shipping points but oats and other products of the northern counties were sent directly from Cumbrian ports. Naturally more food and material was raised in the counties nearer to Ireland but the existence of water routes meant that even the eastern counties could contribute: grain was sent by river from Cambridge to Lynn, for example. The initial contact between Normans and Irish had been a matter of ambitious frontiersmen on a freelance expedition. From 1171 the English state was involved and hence the resources of a much larger area could be applied to support military or political involvement in Ireland. The food chain was extended; the acorns of Norfolk were being excreted in Dublin.

Other monarchs of this period also launched large-scale military expeditions. The kings of Germany, for example, repeatedly took armies of thousands southwards across the Alps. They left, however, no complex bureaucratic record of

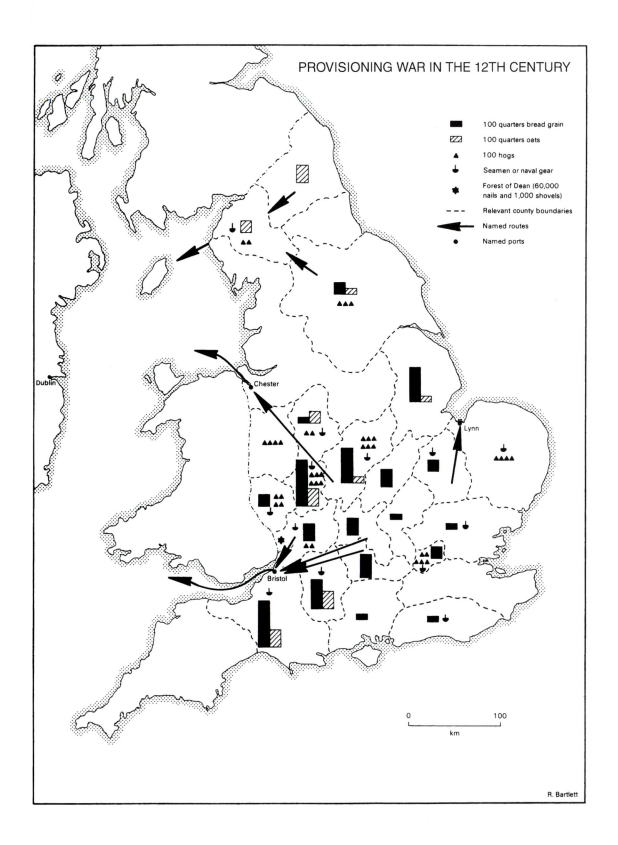

PROVISIONING WAR IN THE 12TH CENTURY

■	100 quarters bread grain
▨	100 quarters oats
▲	100 hogs
⚓	Seamen or naval gear
✶	Forest of Dean (60,000 nails and 1,000 shovels)
- - -	Relevant county boundaries
←	Named routes
•	Named ports

Dublin

Chester

Lynn

Bristol

0   100
km

R. Bartlett

137

the provisioning of these troops. England is unique in the scope of its records rather than the scale of its undertakings. The existence of these records, however, enables us to anatomize some of these undertakings and produce a map illustrating a sophisticated twelfth-century state at work in one of its most characteristic activities.

R. Bartlett

Castles

Castles provide an impressive physical reminder of medieval Europe and are often presented as one of the defining features of the medieval landscape. They were built within the heartlands of Europe and accompanied the expansion of 'Latin' or 'Frankish' rule into areas from Iberia to the Baltic. In the 1180s the missionary bishop of Livonia, Meinhard, offered the pagan Livs castles for protection from Lithuanian raiders in return for their conversion to Christianity. Castles could thus be emblematic of acculturation to western models.

Castles are distinguished from Roman legionary or post-medieval garrison forts as much by function as form. Castles were the fortified residences of lords or constables of lords. They were a development of the militarization of aristocratic society, a symptom of political instability and a reflection of the localization of power. The appearance of great military strength should not, however, obscure their residential function. The great 'donjon' or 'keep' was where lords located their halls, necessary for the entertainment and maintenance of followers or peers. Often too there were private apartments above, perhaps with a chapel. Castles were thus symbols of lordship and social and administrative foci. Many were located in valleys, in the centre of a lord's land, rather than on isolated outcrops. Nevertheless, much warfare focused on castles. Castles were an instrument of occupation, as in the Norman conquests of England; castles could be used to encircle a town until its surrender; small siege castles could be built to attack larger castles. As siege technology improved, so did the defensive design of castles – from simple earth and timber 'mottes' to the great concentric strongholds of the thirteenth century. As their costs escalated, so their possession was restricted to princes and the greater lords: symbols of independent robber-barons became bastions of royal authority.

A. Stewart

The expansion of French royal control, 1180–1226

Although politics in the reigns of Philip II Augustus (1180–1223) and Louis VIII (1223–6) were largely conducted by the traditional means of warfare, ritual, marriage alliances and diplomacy, this period was also characterized by greater attention to the mechanics of effective government: witness the enormous expansion of Paris as a capital, improved record-keeping and revenue-collection, and more interventionist supervision of royal officials. This increased efficiency made possible the administrative integration of the northern French lands of the 'Angevin Empire', which Philip wrested from King John of England in 1202–4. Greatly improved royal finances, as well as vigilant supervision of the aristocracy, underpinned the

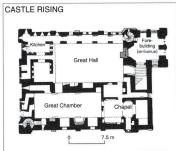

CASTLE RISING

Plan of a mid-twelfth-century hall-style keep at Castle Rising (England), containing in one building the lord's hall, private and other domestic apartments; the keep was surrounded by a bank of earth and stone.

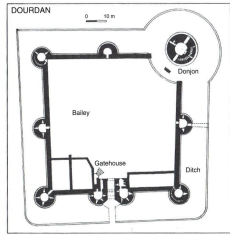

DOURDAN

A typical castle of the early thirteenth century (Dourdan, France; c. 1222) – the keep/donjon has become: higher, with the apartments arranged vertically rather than horizontally; round, for reasons of defence; and has moved to join the bailey wall defences.

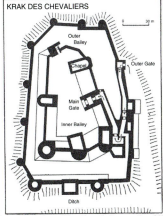

KRAK DES CHEVALIERS

The thirteenth-century plan of the Hospitaller castle of Krak des Chevaliers (Syria), much simplified; with the complex entrance and the successively higher lines of defence, this is a well-known example of the 'concentric' castle.

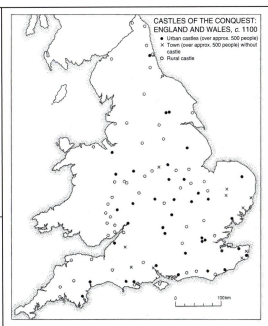

CASTLES OF THE CONQUEST: ENGLAND AND WALES, c. 1100

- Urban castles (over approx. 500 people)
× Town (over approx. 500 people) without castle
○ Rural castle

Map of castles documented in England and Wales, c. 1100; while some castles were intended to defend the new conquest from Danes, Welsh or Scots (and border castles were centres of expansion rather than 'national defences'), most castles were intended to act as fortified centres of new Norman-held estates, or to dominate existing towns; building castles was an integral part of the process of conquest.

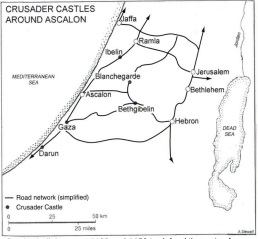

CRUSADER CASTLES AROUND ASCALON

— Road network (simplified)
● Crusader Castle

Castles built between 1130 and 1150 to defend the routes from Ascalon into the heart of the kingdom of Jerusalem, and from which to attack the city's Egyptian garrison; Ascalon fell to the crusaders in 1153.

A. Stewart

139

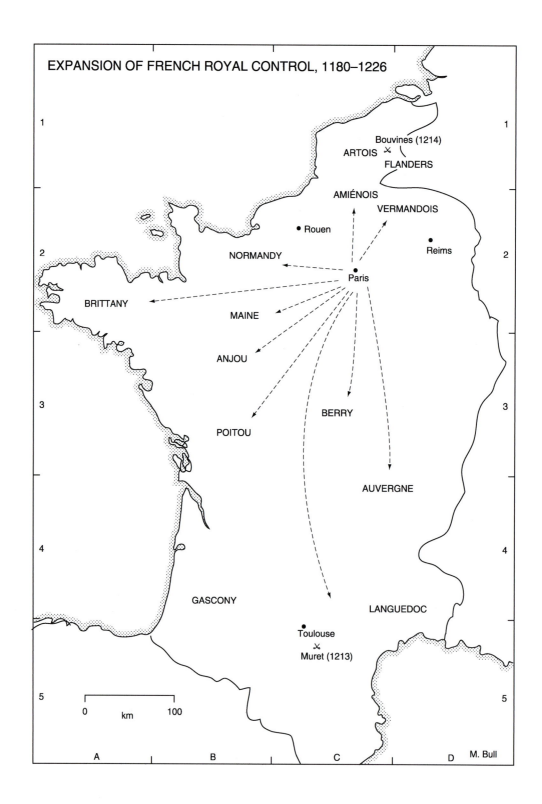

EXPANSION OF FRENCH ROYAL CONTROL, 1180–1226

Bouvines (1214)

ARTOIS

FLANDERS

AMIÉNOIS

VERMANDOIS

● Rouen

● Reims

NORMANDY

● Paris

BRITTANY

MAINE

ANJOU

POITOU

BERRY

AUVERGNE

GASCONY

LANGUEDOC

● Toulouse

Muret (1213)

0   km   100

A   B   C   D   M. Bull

ability of the French crown to inflict a decisive defeat on a coalition of its greatest enemies at the battle of Bouvines in 1214, as well as to begin the process of expansion into southern France, filling a power vacuum left by the Albigensian Crusade (1208–29).

M. Bull

Settlement patterns in medieval Italy: (1) nucleation; (2) dispersal

From the tenth century, Italy, as elsewhere in Europe, saw the development of a network of castles, fixing in place the slowly emerging structures of private political power that succeeded the public world of the Carolingians. In northern Europe castles were usually aristocratic fortifications, dominating pre-existing, often tightly structured, systems of village settlement and field division. In Italy villages were less stable and agriculture often less collectively controlled, without common fields or strip farming. Aristocratic fortifications could have much more impact on settlement, notably in the relatively underpopulated central peninsula. The development of castles (*incastellamento*) could produce a network of fortified villages, which absorbed other rural settlement between *c.* 950 and *c.* 1200. Around and inland from Rome unfortified villages and dispersed farmsteads, which had been common earlier, disappeared; aristocrats moved whole villages and groups of villages inside their fortifications and independent peasants set up and lived in their own castles if they wanted to stay independent.

The first map shows this process at Monte Amiata in southern Tuscany, where political breakdown was relatively slow and castles rare before 1000. Subsequently the major powers on the Amiata developed castles and settlement nucleation is evident. West of the mountain there is a fairly clear pattern of castles replacing open settlements in a one-to-one relationship: Mustia, for example, was a village directly replaced by Montenero. Whether settlements changed in type is unclear: Mustia may have been a nucleated village before Montenero was built. But by *c.* 1200, after *incastellamento*, nucleated settlements predominated: documents show almost no isolated houses on the thirteenth-century Amiata. East of the mountain settlement patterns changed: a scatter of small sites overlooking river valleys were, in the eleventh century, drawn into a smaller number of castles. Then, around 1150 this group focused on a smaller number still. The twenty-odd (some tiny) settlements of *c.* 900 were reduced to two by *c.* 1200, Abbadia S. Salvatore (the castle of the monastery of S. Salvatore) and Radicofani. S. Salvatore could do this because it owned much of the land. This was under-settled and in need of economic reorganization, which the monastery undertook. Settlement change of this sort is usually an indicator of economic organization and of political control – though the monastery found its two big castles extremely difficult subjects and eventually ceded them extensive rights.

Still in Tuscany, the Casentino shows similar localization of private power across the same period but in a very different environment. It is much closer to a major town, Arezzo (the towns near the Amiata were weak): landowning by lay aristocrats and churches was much more fragmented here and peasant owners numerous. Local lords built many *castelli*, more indeed than on the Amiata; but far fewer of them were population centres. Many were probably little more than fortified residences of petty aristocrats. A tight network of small open settlements survived almost without break. Some of these were highly fragmented, with houses stretching from end to end of their territories. One of the few castles to establish itself as a real population centre was Bibbiena, a major base of

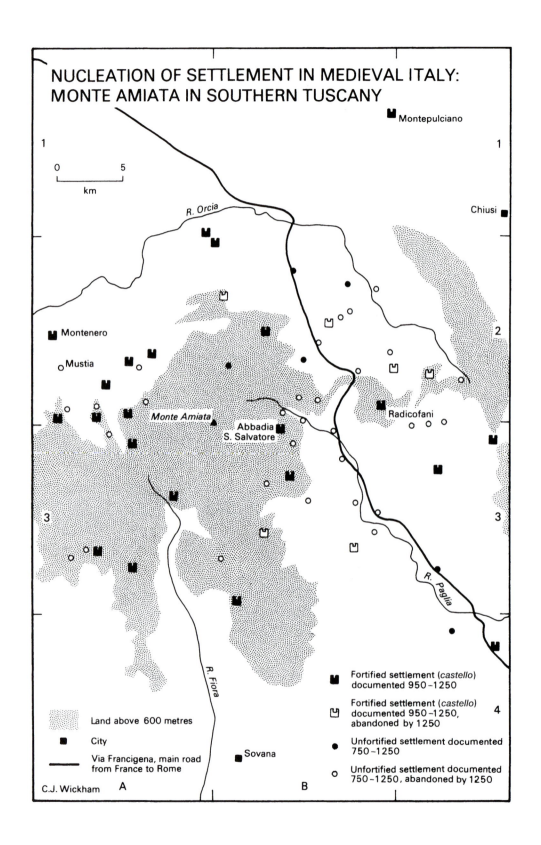

NUCLEATION OF SETTLEMENT IN MEDIEVAL ITALY:
MONTE AMIATA IN SOUTHERN TUSCANY

0 — 5
km

Montepulciano

Chiusi

R. Orcia

Montenero

Mustia

Monte Amiata

Abbadia
S. Salvatore

Radicofani

R. Fiora

R. Paglia

Land above 600 metres

City

Via Francigena, main road
from France to Rome

C.J. Wickham

Sovana

Fortified settlement (*castello*)
documented 950–1250

Fortified settlement (*castello*)
documented 950–1250,
abandoned by 1250

Unfortified settlement documented
750–1250

Unfortified settlement documented
750–1250, abandoned by 1250

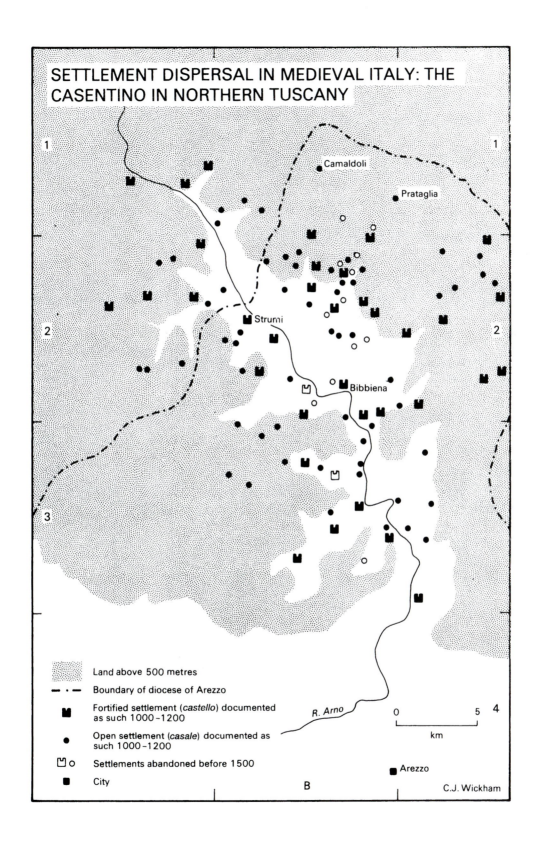

SETTLEMENT DISPERSAL IN MEDIEVAL ITALY: THE CASENTINO IN NORTHERN TUSCANY

Camaldoli

Prataglia

Strumi

Bibbiena

R. Arno

Land above 500 metres

Boundary of diocese of Arezzo

Fortified settlement (*castello*) documented as such 1000–1200

Open settlement (*casale*) documented as such 1000–1200

Settlements abandoned before 1500

City

Arezzo

0   5

km

B

C.J. Wickham

143

Arezzo's powerful bishops. Camaldoli, Prataglia and Strumi, the local monasteries whose archives survive, built no castles at all (though they received several from lay families): a military rhetoric for their power was evidently less necessary than on the Amiata. The importance of Bibbiena underlines the failure of most other local castles to expand: it looks as if aristocrats here never had the hegemony over the population that their peers had in the south. This pattern, of numerous small castles and surviving dispersed settlement, is common in the urbanized areas of the Po plain and northern Tuscany. It seems to indicate relatively fragmented political power and, sometimes, weak seigneurial rights.

C. Wickham

The huerta of Valencia

Although the Cid had taken Valencia in 1094, it was reconquered by the Muslims in 1102 and did not fall definitively to the Christians until James I of Aragon acquired it in 1238. Although these dramatic events created the illusion of a triumphant Christian victory, in reality, the conquerors were prepared to come to terms with the defeated Muslims who remained, and above all to make use of their agrarian institutions and manpower. The kingdom of Valencia after its reconquest contained several predominantly Christian cities, particularly Valencia itself, many towns in which Muslims and Christians lived together

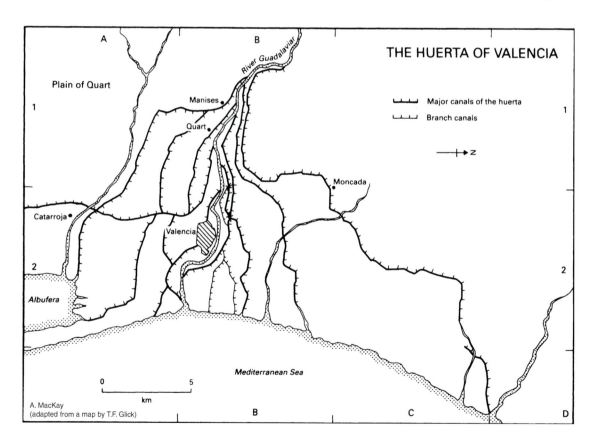

THE HUERTA OF VALENCIA

Plain of Quart

Manises

Quart

Moncada

Catarroja

Valencia

Albufera

Major canals of the huerta

Branch canals

Mediterranean Sea

0   5
    km

A. MacKay
(adapted from a map by T.F. Glick)

and a countryside which, although under the political control of Christian lords, was mainly tenanted by Mudejars (Muslims living under Christian rule).

Along the Levantine coast of Spain some regions, notably those in and around the city of Valencia, were characterized by a rural economy with sophisticated irrigation systems in which thousands of small channels and ditches diverted water from the larger canals, distributing the precious liquid over large areas. Rivers played an important role, particularly the Guadalaviar and the Júcar, but so too did small dams, divisors of currents, branches of canals, *norias* (devices for lifting water, probably of Persian origin) and horizontal wells dispersing water by gravity flow (*qanats*).

The practical effects of irrigation demanded co-operation among those who depended on water distribution and favoured small farms rather than large estates. Before conquering Játiva James I of Aragon himself described the patchwork landscape, the huertas of the area, the villages or *alquerías*, and the water-courses or *acequías* on which the inhabitants depended.

A. MacKay

The 13th-century repopulation of Andalusia

The reconquest of Andalusia was largely due to the Castilian kings Ferdinand III (1217–52) and Alfonso X (1252–84). The former skilfully exploited internal weaknesses in the Almohad Empire, which had been plunged into crisis almost on the morrow of the great defeat it sustained at the battle of Las Navas de Tolosa (1212). Combining military aggression with surrender agreements, the Christians took the leading cities of Andújar (1224), Baeza (1227), Ubeda (1232), Córdoba (1236), Jaén (1246) and Seville (1248). Alfonso X followed these successes by taking Cádiz (*c.*1260), Niebla (1262) and Jerez with its territory (1264). The last significant conquest of the thirteenth century was Tarifa (1292). By then the long-term military objective was already to deprive the Moors of control over the straits of Gibraltar.

Reconquest was followed by repopulation – that is, the introduction of new colonists from the north who recieved massive amounts of land – and by the civil and ecclesiastical reorganization of the conquered territories. As in Valencia and Murcia, the repopulation of Andalusia was carried out according to the model of *repartimiento*. Briefly, this consisted of a royally-ordered distribution of houses, lands and rural properties between those who had participated in the campaigns of conquest and the new Christian colonists. The former – nobles, members of the royal family, leading churchmen, the military orders, soldiers and royal officials – received the best lands. But most of the lands were given to colonists or *repobladores*, awarded properties according to their socio-military status as knights (noble or urban) or plain footsoldiers. The view, widely propagated by even eminent historians, that the Andalusian *latifundios* were created as a result of the conquest and the *repartimientos* is completely erroneous because every colonist was by definition a proprietor. For example, footsoldiers in Carmona or Vejer de la Frontera were assigned some 74 acres.

The Muslim population was systematically expelled from towns and areas of strategic value. Nevertheless, many Muslims remained in the villages and smaller urban nuclei by virtue of surrender agreements which guaranteed them freedom of religion, their own laws and their properties. This continued until the uprising of the subjected Muslims (*mudéjares*) in 1264. With their defeat came the conquest of more territory (Jerez) and the expulsion of most of the *mudéjares* who still remained in Andalusia. Thereafter Muslims were reduced to

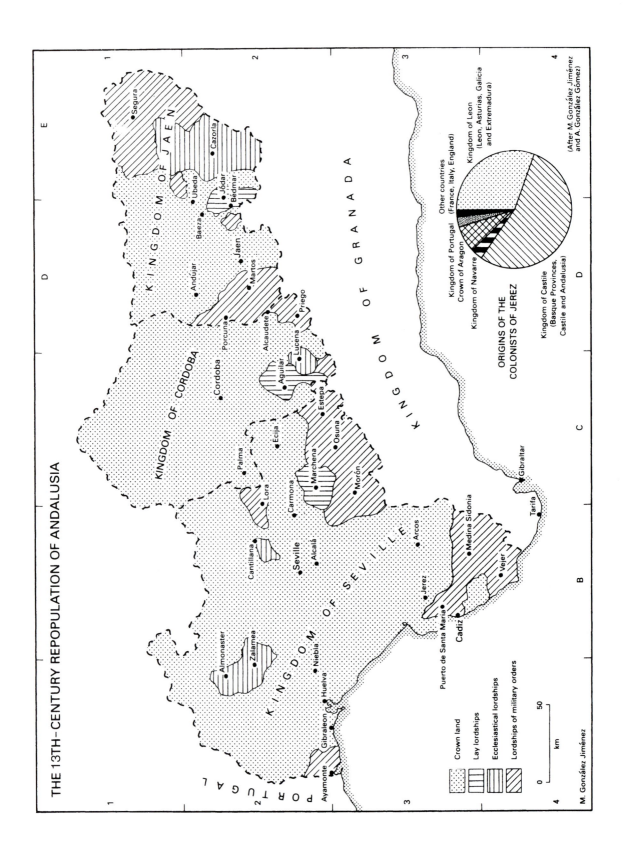

THE 13TH-CENTURY REPOPULATION OF ANDALUSIA

M. González Jiménez

KINGDOM OF JAEN

Segura
Cazorla
Ubeda
Jódar
Bédmar
Baeza
Jaen
Andujar
Martos

KINGDOM OF CORDOBA

Porcuna
Alcaudete
Priego
Cordoba
Aguilar
Lucena
Palma
Ecija

KINGDOM OF SEVILLE

Cantillana
Lora
Carmona
Seville
Alcalá
Marchena
Estepa
Osuna
Morón
Arcos
Medina Sidonia
Vejer
Jerez
Cadiz
Puerto de Santa Maria
Almonaster
Zalamea
Niebla
Huelva
Gibraleon
Ayamonte
Tarifa
Gibraltar

KINGDOM OF GRANADA

PORTUGAL

ORIGINS OF THE COLONISTS OF JEREZ

Other countries (France, Italy, England)
Kingdom of Portugal
Crown of Aragon
Kingdom of Navarre
Kingdom of Leon (Leon, Asturias, Galicia and Extremadura)
Kingdom of Castile (Basque Provinces, Castile and Andalusia)

(After M. González Jiménez and A. González Gómez)

Legend:
- Crown land
- Lay lordships
- Ecclesiastical lordships
- Lordships of military orders

km
0   50

a small minority with little demographic significance.

Andalusia was mainly repopulated by people of Castilian and Leonese origin, although some colonists came from the other Iberian kingdoms. In places well connected with maritime trade – Seville, Jerez, Cádiz, Puerto de Santa María – foreigners appeared: English, French, Bretons and above all Italians, especially Genoese. (The map shows the origins of the first colonists of Jerez de la Frontera.) Nevertheless, Andalusia remained underpopulated in the thirteenth and fourteenth centuries. This was especially evident in the countryside and explains the foundation or repopulation of numerous rural nuclei throughout the later medieval period.

Administratively Andalusia was organized around the three 'kingdoms' of Jaén, Córdoba and Seville. In them royal jurisdiction was initially predominant and exercised through large municipalities or town councils endowed with extensive lands and municipal law codes or *fueros*. Nevertheless, some lordships also appeared, mostly along the frontier with Granada and belonging to the military orders of Calatrava, Santiago and Alcántara.

An ecclesiastical organization was also set up or restored. Initially the region was divided into three diocesan areas: the bishoprics of Jaén and Córdoba, dependent on the archbishopric of Toledo, and the archbishopric of Seville. In 1263 the bishopric of Cádiz, dependent on Seville, was created.

M. González Jiménez

Maritime laws

Maritime law regulated relations between those involved in the transportation of goods on sea vessels. In general a distinction can be drawn between customary sea laws (which applied to an extensive but undefined geographical area) and maritime regulations contained in particular town laws (which applied to the citizens of the town concerned). Significant developments in both types of law occurred from the early thirteenth century, when maritime regulations were initially included in the town laws of Hamburg and Lübeck. In 1299 a separate Lübeck Sea Law appeared which was partly based on the shipping laws incorporated within the Hamburg Town Law. This town law was copied for Riga (1294–97) and then included in the revised Riga Town Law of the early fourteenth century. Maritime regulations also appeared in the Norwegian Town Law of Bergen (1276), introduced by King Magnus Lagaboetir, while in Sweden, the town laws of Stockholm, called *Bjärköarätten* (1285–96), and of Visby (1341–44) formed the basis for the general Swedish Town Law of *c*. 1350. In the

Netherlands, maritime regulations were included in the Kampen town laws from the second half of the fourteenth century.

By contrast, the oldest customary sea laws, known as the *Rôles d'Oléron* (*c*. 1286), have a western rather than northern origin. This compilation was translated from French into Flemish in the late thirteenth or early fourteenth century and into Scots in the second quarter of the fourteenth century. The Flemish translation (known as *Vonnesse van Damme*) was mostly copied together with another customary sea law, the *Ordinancie*, which appeared in the Zuiderzee region in the second half of the fourteenth century. In the late fifteenth century articles of the Lübeck Town Law were added to this compilation, which was subsequently printed in Copenhagen in 1505 and has mistakenly been known as the Gotland Sea Law ever since. Many editions, sometimes with slight variations, followed in the sixteenth and seventeenth centuries.

E. Frankot

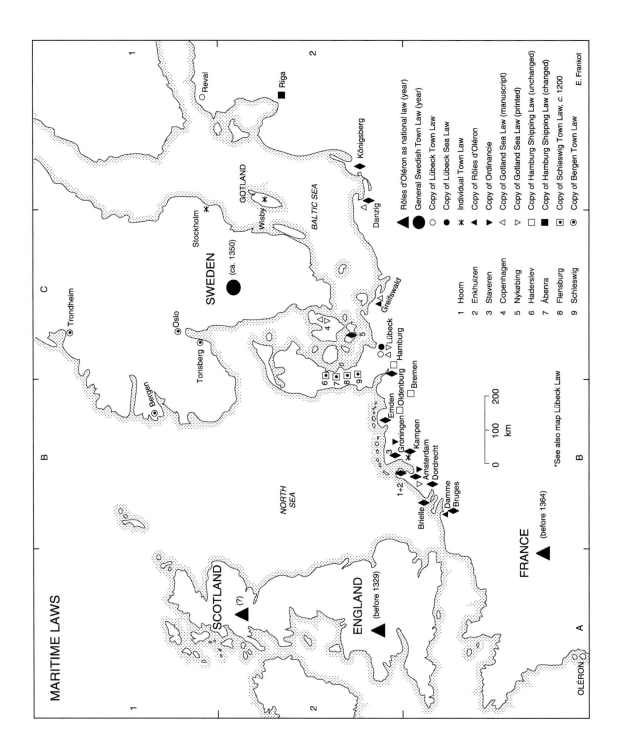

MARITIME LAWS

Rôles d'Oléron as national law (year)
General Swedish Town Law (year)
Copy of Lübeck Town Law
Copy of Lübeck Sea Law
Individual Town Law
Copy of Rôles d'Oléron
Copy of Ordinancie
Copy of Gotland Sea Law (manuscript)
Copy of Gotland Sea Law (printed)
Copy of Hamburg Shipping Law (unchanged)
Copy of Hamburg Shipping Law (changed)
Copy of Schleswig Town Law, c. 1200
Copy of Bergen Town Law

E. Frankot

1 Hoorn
2 Enkhuizen
3 Staveren
4 Copenhagen
5 Nykøbing
6 Haderslev
7 Åbenra
8 Flensburg
9 Schleswig

*See also map Lübeck Law

0   100 200
        km

NORTH
SEA

BALTIC SEA

GOTLAND

SWEDEN
(ca. 1350)

FRANCE
(before 1364)

SCOTLAND
(?)

ENGLAND
(before 1329)

OLÉRON

Reval
Riga
Königsberg
Danzig
Wisby
Stockholm
Greifswald
Oslo
Tonsberg
Bergen
Trondheim
Lübeck
Hamburg
Bremen
Oldenburg
Emden
Groningen
Kampen
Amsterdam
Dordrecht
Brielle
Damme
Bruges

148

Town laws

During the twelfth and thirteenth centuries many new towns were founded and old settlements raised to urban status. One common way of doing this was through the grant of the rights and privileges of an existing town. The result was the creation of 'families' of town law, groups of urban settlements whose legal arrangements were, at least initially, modelled on a 'mother town'. The mother town might be a major economic and political centre, like Lübeck, but some relatively unimportant places, like Breteuil in Normandy, also became the model for many towns spread over wide areas.

The degree of dependence between mother and daughter towns varied. Sometimes the new town was simply granted the customs of an existing town and there was no further connection. In other cases the affiliated town might turn to the mother town for a ruling when some point in the customs needed clarification. An even closer bond existed in town families such as that of Lübeck, whose mother town heard judicial appeals from the courts of daughter towns.

The three families of town law shown here have been chosen to illustrate the variety of the phenomenon. The first, the family of towns with the law of Breteuil, was modelled on the small Norman town of Breteuil, which was enfranchised by its lord, William fitz Osbern, around 1060. After the Norman conquest of England fitz Osbern became earl of Hereford and introduced the law of Breteuil into his Marcher lordship, whence it spread into surrounding areas of England and Wales. The Anglo-Normans who invaded Ireland in the decades after 1169 included many men, like the de Lacys, from this part of the country, and when they founded boroughs, like the de Lacy

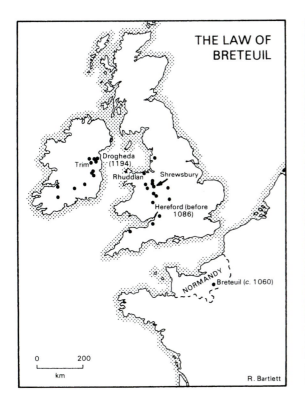

THE LAW OF BRETEUIL

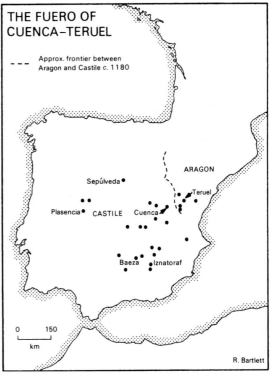

THE FUERO OF CUENCA-TERUEL

- - - Approx. frontier between Aragon and Castile c. 1180

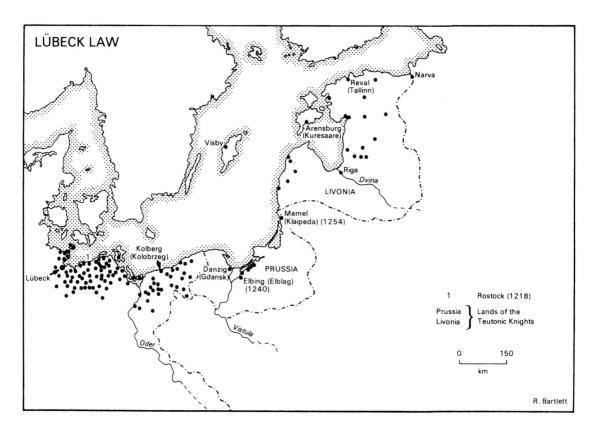

LÜBECK LAW

Narva
Reval (Tallinn)
Arensburg (Kuresaare)
Visby
Riga
Dvina
LIVONIA
Memel (Klaipeda) (1254)
Kolberg (Kolobrzeg)
Lübeck
Danzig (Gdansk)
PRUSSIA
Elbing (Elblag) (1240)
Oder
Vistula

1   Rostock (1218)
Prussia }
Livonia } Lands of the Teutonic Knights

0   150
km

R. Bartlett

foundation of Drogheda, they too granted the laws of Breteuil. In this way, by a series of feudal conquests, the laws of a small Norman town came to be adopted by dozens of settlements in England, Wales and Ireland.

The law of Breteuil did not consist of a large or well-defined body of customs. Indeed, its essence seems to have been the limitation of judicial fines to the low sum of 12*d*. The law or *fuero* of Cuenca was a very much more elaborate affair. It contained almost a thousand clauses, regulating matters as varied as inheritance rights, criminal law, military obligations, Christian–Jewish relations, irrigation and pasturage, the public baths and the penalties for taking roses and lilies from another's vineyard. This comprehensive code was granted by Alfonso VIII of Castile soon after he had conquered the town from the Muslims in 1177. At about the same time a very similar code was granted to Teruel, across the border in Aragon, by Alfonso II of Aragon. Thus the

family of Cuenca-Teruel law spread across political boundaries. As the reconquest pushed south, more towns were granted the *fuero*, some, such as Baeza and Iznatoraf in Andalusia, becoming the mother towns for yet further settlement.

Lübeck law, originating in the twelfth century and codified in the thirteenth, was the basis of the most important of the three families of law shown here. It was a complex set of provisions governing commercial activity as well as criminal law and town government, and it provided the model for over a hundred towns founded along the Baltic shore in the thirteenth century. It served as the basic urban constitution for virtually all the towns of Mecklenburg and Pomerania. Because of its stress on urban independence some rulers found it suspect. The Teutonic Knights, for example, discouraged Lübeck law in their domains, preferring their own, less autonomous code, that of Kulm. Danzig and Memel, which originally had

Lübeck law, were forced to abandon it under pressure from the Knights. Despite this resistance, Lübeck law was in various forms the dominant code of the Baltic, from the mother city itself to the frontiers of Russia.

R. Bartlett

The contado of Lucca in the 12th century

The commune of Lucca is first recorded with consuls in 1119, though it may have been autonomous since the 1080s. Like other Italian cities, it aspired to control the whole of its diocese; like them, it had to fight rural lords and rival cities in order to do so.

The core of the diocese was the rich plain around the city, the Sei Miglia or 6-mile territory, fully ceded to city jurisdiction by Henry IV in 1081; in this area, rival powers were weak, except along the frontier with Pisa, and all were destroyed relatively early (though Ripafratta, taken in 1105, ended up under Pisan control). The major problem the city faced was access to the sea, normally through the territory of its enemy. The Lucchesi and Pisans fought many wars over the issue, particularly when the Lucchesi tried to establish a port in their own diocese on the River Motrone, rather than go through Pisa. These wars reached their height in the 1170s but they are a feature of the whole period. Elsewhere, Lucchese control was helped by the network of episcopal castles, for the bishop was generally a reliable associate of the commune, and by an early tendency for rural lords to live in the city. The military expansion of Lucca was largely along the major road routes east and south-east and up the Serchio valley into the mountains. East and north, the Lucchesi found domination relatively easy and they were only held back by the occasional hostile intervention of German emperors.

The Arno and Era valleys – in a geographical sense Pisa's hinterland – were, however, absorbed into the latter's *contado* in the end, despite the episcopal castles in the area; the Lucchesi made no effective impact here. Hegemony over the rural lordships of the diocese was otherwise pretty complete well before the end of the century; only a rival city prevented it from being fully realized in the south, not any rural aristocrat.

C. Wickham

Communal movements

Risings of townsmen against their ecclesiastical or lay lords not only demonstrated the growing importance of such groups in society but also frequently took on the form of communal movements, as in northern France, northern Spain, northern Italy, Flanders and some of the Rhine towns. A classic account of such a communal struggle in the northern French town of Laon in 1112 is given by the Benedictine Abbot Guibert of Nogent although it tends to be lost among his many stories and observations about miracles and even anecdotes of a folkloric nature. Not that the religious dimension was irrelevant to communal movements. On the contrary, they were frequently influenced by the Christian value of love, also to be found in the Peace of God movements which coincided with the emergence of the early communes and like them aimed to eliminate conflict and vendettas. Indeed, the word 'commune' could

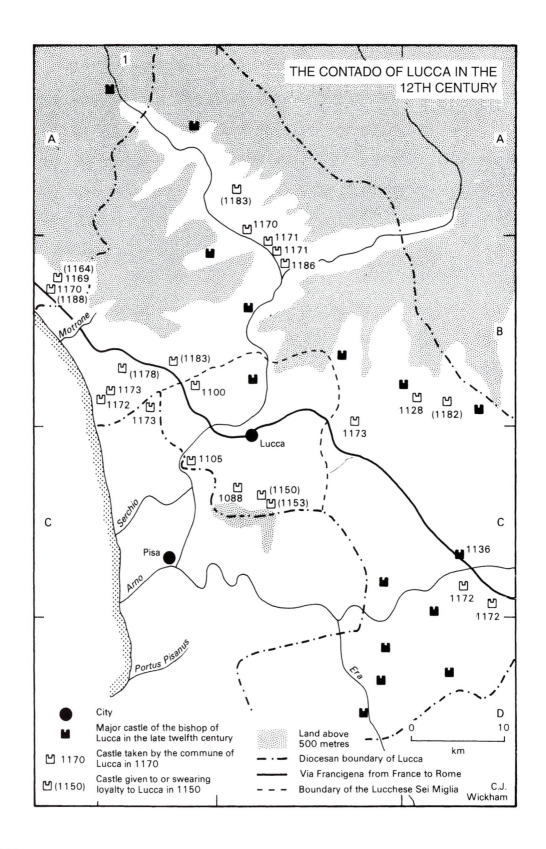

THE CONTADO OF LUCCA IN THE 12TH CENTURY

1

A   A

(1183)

1170
1171
1171
1186

(1164)
1169
1170
(1188)

B

Motrone

(1183)
(1178)
1100
1173
1172
1173   1128 (1182)

1173

Lucca

1105

1088   (1150)
(1153)

C   C

Serchio

Pisa   1136

Arno   1172

1172

Portus Pisanus

Era   D

●   City

■   Major castle of the bishop of
     Lucca in the late twelfth century   Land above
                                              500 metres

⬚ 1170   Castle taken by the commune of
         Lucca in 1170   — · —   Diocesan boundary of Lucca

⬚ (1150) Castle given to or swearing   ———   Via Francigena from France to Rome
         loyalty to Lucca in 1150
                                              - - -   Boundary of the Lucchese Sei Miglia

0   10

km

C.J.
Wickham

152

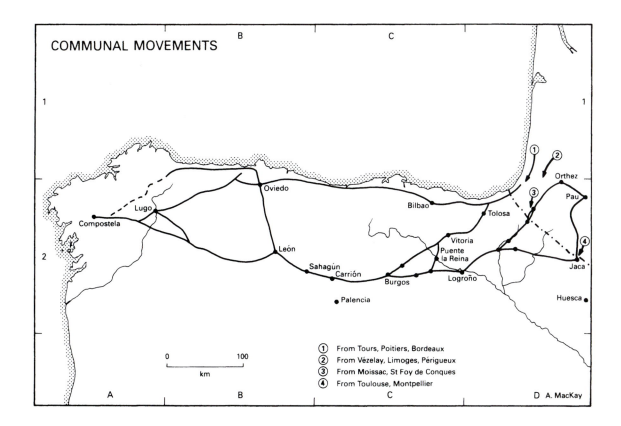

COMMUNAL MOVEMENTS

① From Tours, Poitiers, Bordeaux
② From Vézelay, Limoges, Périgueux
③ From Moissac, St Foy de Conques
④ From Toulouse, Montpellier

D. A. MacKay

be associated with the communion (*communio*) of Christians in the Eucharist and it was not uncommon for the urban authorities of some towns of the later medieval and early modern period to attempt to disperse dangerous urban uprisings by confronting the rioters with consecrated hosts carried in procession by members of the clergy.

The religious dimension was evident in other ways. The emergence of towns is frequently associated with economic causes, such as the growth of trade and the appearance of markets, but these too were influenced by religious factors. The towns which grew up along the famous pilgrim route to Santiago de Compostela are a case in point. The townsmen who settled in Sahagún, for example, included pilgrims and others from the various regions of France and Italy, and even Germans and English. But although many of those who settled in Compostela, Sahagún, Carrión, Burgos and Palencia grew relatively prosperous as merchants and

artisans, they found that their wealth and status were not accompanied by any participation in the local power structure and chroniclers' accounts of some of the ensuing troubles are remarkably similar to that of Guibert of Nogent.

According to the anonymous chronicler of Sahagún, the town had been founded by Alfonso VI of León and Castile (1065–1109). The king had, however, taken care to protect the rights and jurisdiction of the monastery that already existed there. Thus if any townsmen held lands within the lordship of the monastery, they could only do so on the terms and conditions laid down by the abbot; all those with houses in the town were to pay a yearly sum of money to the monastery as a rent and recognition of the monastic lordship; and all bread had to be baked in the monastery's oven. Friction over this latter requirement was resolved by commuting the obligation into yet another cash payment, the townsmen now having to pay one

153

sum at Christmas for the oven and another at All Saints as rent and recognition of lordship.

The townsmen not only resisted the lordship of the monastery but sought to replace its authority by their own. In a typical incident, they forced their way into the monastic chapter, produced a document of new laws and customs which they themselves had drawn up and forced the monks to sign in agreement.

Although the objective of such rebellions was to establish communal power, this was envisaged in practical terms and not as an abstract ideal. Frequently, too, the disturbances were linked to more widespread tensions, such as conflicts between the monarchy and nobility, or the townsmen recruited help from other discontented sectors of society, as they did in Compostela where they exercised *de facto* communal power for a whole year, during which the political and jurisdictional powers of the ecclesiastical lordship virtually ceased to exist.

A. MacKay

Frederick Barbarossa and the Lombard League

Benefiting from a weakening of imperial authority in northern Italy from the late eleventh century, the Lombard towns had established considerable independence as urban republics by the time of Frederick's election as emperor in 1152. Civic powers had never been confirmed by formal grant but by the early twelfth century towns had appropriated for their own uses various imperial dues and services. Such control, it was felt, gave a customary entitlement to possession. Frederick's reassertion of imperial rights at the diet of Roncaglia in 1158 raised the prospect of greater domination than the towns were prepared to accept. His subsequent destruction of Milan in 1162 provoked collective resistance, formalized in 1167 in the Lombard League. Support from the papacy, itself anxious about the reestablishment of imperial power south of the Alps, held the League together in the face of three further imperial campaigns. Finally, at Legnano in 1176, its forces crushed Frederick's army. Forced to recognize that plans for direct rule in Lombardy were unattainable, Frederick, in return for annual tribute, agreed the treaty of Constance (1183), which established the limits of imperial overlordship and effectively confirmed urban independence. Towns received the right to fortify themselves and renew their league. A fiction of imperial approval was established for recognition of consuls whom the towns elected for themselves. It was a face-saving arrangement for Frederick but it could not disguise that any chance of restoring an imperial north Italian power-base had been lost, even though many towns remained proimperial in 1183. More significantly, it granted the power of custom, legislation and the weight of royal authority to the urban republics, ensuring the future spread of civic independence throughout north and central Italy.

R. Oram & E. Coleman

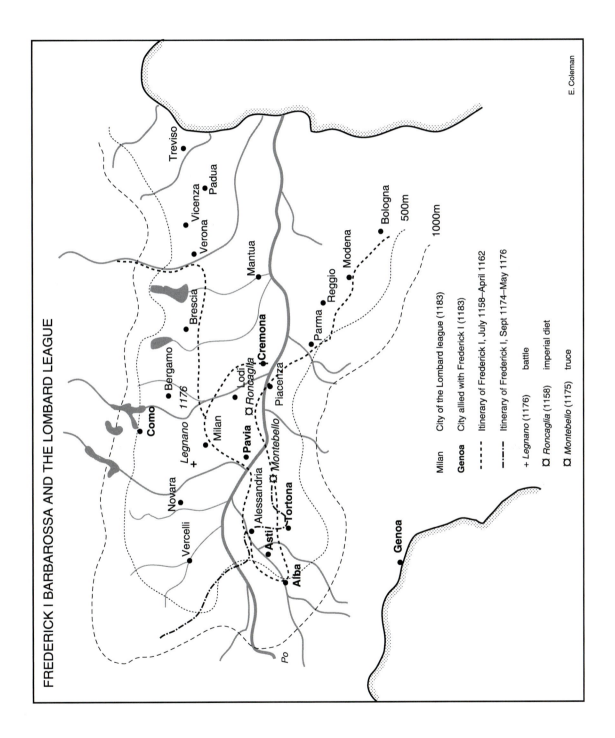

FREDERICK I BARBAROSSA AND THE LOMBARD LEAGUE

E. Coleman

Treviso

Padua

Vicenza

Verona

Mantua

Brescia

Bergamo

Legnano 1176

Como

Milan

Pavia

Lodi

Roncaglia

Cremona

Piacenza

Montebello

Novara

Alessandria

Tortona

Vercelli

Asti

Alba

Genoa

Parma

Reggio

Modena

Bologna

500m

1000m

Po

| Milan | City of the Lombard league (1183) |
| **Genoa** | City allied with Frederick I (1183) |

- - - - - Itinerary of Frederick I, July 1158–April 1162

– · – · – Itinerary of Frederick I, Sept 1174–May 1176

+ *Legnano* (1176)   battle

⌘ *Roncaglia* (1158)   imperial diet

⌘ *Montebello* (1175)   truce

155

Late 13th-century Brunswick

Brunswick, the largest city in Lower Saxony, was one of the earliest examples of a 'multi-town'. Most German 'multi-towns' comprised two or three constituent settlements. Brunswick was unusual in that it had five. The earliest, dating from the tenth century, were at Sack (around the fortified castle and cathedral) and Alte Wiek, a market-based settlement. In the eleventh century a mercantile quarter grew at Altstadt, while Henry the Lion, duke of Saxony, founded Hagenstadt and Neustadt in the twelfth century. The three new towns had their own councils by the thirteenth century (before the two old ones). In 1269 a general council was established to overlook matters of common concern. Although the existence of councils in the component towns, increasingly styled municipalities, was confirmed in 1299, the general council began to dominate internal and external matters.

D. Ditchburn

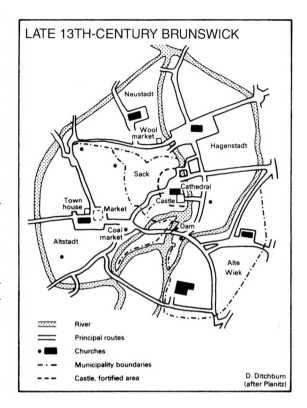

LATE 13TH-CENTURY BRUNSWICK

River	
Principal routes	
Churches	
Municipality boundaries	
Castle, fortified area	

D. Ditchburn
(after Planitz)

The larger towns of Europe

Towns and townspeople provide a contrast to the predominantly rural landscape and agrarian society of the Middle Ages. In many countries walls physically separated towns from the surrounding countryside and, to some extent, townspeople were subject to different laws from others. Economically town and country were, however, more closely integrated: the produce of the countryside was bought and sold in towns and rural areas provided raw materials for urban craft industries. Significant numbers of townspeople, especially in smaller towns, were even engaged in agrarian pursuits. Most medieval towns were, by modern standards, small. Even although the number and size of towns grew to accommodate part of the rising population of the Central Middle Ages, their population was usually numbered in hundreds rather than thousands. Of the largest urban communities,

a disproportionate number were located in northern Italy. In this region about forty towns probably had a population of over 10,000, including four of Europe's largest urban centres, the ports of Genoa and Venice and the manufacturing centres of Milan and Florence. Urban density was probably at least as great in both Flanders and Sicily where towns were generally smaller but more numerous. Calculating the exact population of medieval towns remains, however, difficult. Contemporary chroniclers routinely overestimated their size while little statistical data of the sort used by modern demographers survives for the Middle Ages. Instead, historians have based their population estimates on a variety of other sources, including the physical size of towns, lists of townspeople compiled for taxation or military purposes and even figures of aggregate wine

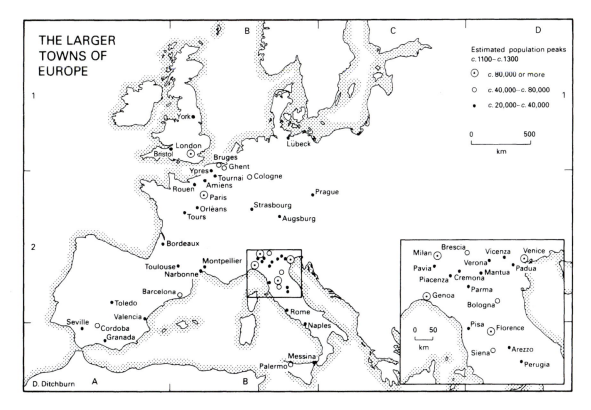

THE LARGER TOWNS OF EUROPE

Estimated population peaks
c. 1100– c. 1300

⊙ c. 80,000 or more
○ c. 40,000–c. 80,000
• c. 20,000–c. 40,000

0   500
km

York•
•London ⊙
Bristol ⊙
Bruges ○○ Ghent
Ypres• •Tournai ○ Cologne
Rouen• Amiens
⊙ Paris
•Orléans
Tours•
Strasbourg
•Augsburg
Prague•
Lübeck•

•Bordeaux

Toulouse• Montpellier
Narbonne•

Barcelona ○
•Toledo
Valencia•
Seville ○ Cordoba
•Granada

Rome•
•Naples
Messina•
Palermo ○

Milan ⊙ Brescia ○ Vicenza Venice ⊙•
Pavia• Verona• Padua•
Piacenza• Cremona• Mantua•
Genoa ⊙ Parma•
Bologna ○
Pisa• ○ Florence ⊙
Siena ○ •Arezzo
•Perugia

0 50
km

D. Ditchburn

purchase. Such figures then require to be multiplied (selecting the appropriate multiplier is itself a controversial matter) to produce a population quotient. Different approaches can lead to gross discrepancies: Lucca's population has been estimated as 15,000 or 23,000; Paris's as 80,000 or 200,000; and London's traditionally as about 40,000 or more recently as at least 80,000. The accompanying map should, therefore, be regarded with caution.

D. Ditchburn

European fairs and trade routes

The Central Middle Ages was, in general, an era of economic vitality. Population grew, more land was brought under cultivation and both the number and size of towns increased. Commercial activity also expanded as individuals sought to sell surplus produce and to purchase commodities which were not available locally. This trade was focused on the markets and fairs. Many of these had developed during the Early Middle Ages, in an *ad hoc* style now difficult to trace, at locations such as castles and monasteries. At specific times of the year large numbers of people congregated in these places for judicial, religious and other purposes and merchants realized that such groups were potential consumers. Here, too, in an age without the resources or requirement for permanent trading centres, merchants could meet and deal with other merchants. In the Central Middle Ages landlords came to recognize that, through the imposition of tolls and other levies, profit could be made from the commercial activity at such gatherings. Licence from a landlord to hold a market or fair could also help to stimulate the

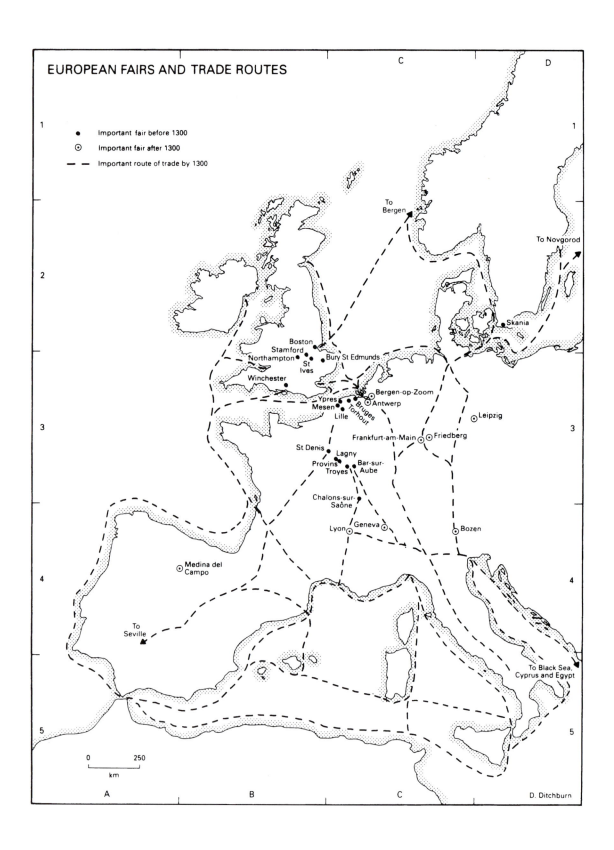

EUROPEAN FAIRS AND TRADE ROUTES

- ● Important fair before 1300
- ⊙ Important fair after 1300
- – – – Important route of trade by 1300

To Bergen

To Novgorod

Skania

Boston
Stamford
Northampton
St Ives
Bury St Edmunds

Winchester

Bergen-op-Zoom
Ypres
Antwerp
Bruges
Mesen
Torhout
Lille

Leipzig

Frankfurt-am-Main
Friedberg

St Denis
Lagny
Provins
Troyes
Bar-sur-Aube

Chalons-sur-Saône

Lyon
Geneva
Bozen

Medina del Campo

To Seville

To Black Sea,
Cyprus and Egypt

0   250
km

A   B   C

D. Ditchburn

economic fortunes of a new town. Consequently markets and fairs became the subject of seigneurial protection and regulation and they came to acquire a legal status. Markets were normally weekly events and mainly of local importance. Fairs, by contrast, were less frequent occasions and in many places were held only on an annual basis. Most were of between several days and several weeks duration and attracted merchants from further afield than the local market. Although some, such as Bozen's wine fair, Medina del Campo's wool fair and Scania's herring fair, specialized in particular commodities, most provided a venue for the exchange of a diverse range of local and more distant wares. While the overwhelming majority of fairs were of a mainly regional significance, a few, facilitated by good communications and developments in transport, rose to international prominence. In some areas cycles of sequential, neighbouring fairs emerged, providing merchants with virtually year-long trading opportunities. One of the earliest cycles had developed in Flanders by the twelfth century, based on the fairs of Ypres, Lille, Mesen, Torhout and Bruges, which were held between February and November. The most famous cycle was, however, located in Champagne. From the Lagny fair in January/February merchants could progress to Bar-sur-Aube, Provins and Troyes, returning to Provins and then the second Troyes fair in November/December. The six Champagne fairs attracted merchants and merchandise from all over western Europe and were especially important as a point where Flemish cloth was exchanged for the commodities brought along the Rhône-Saône route by Italian merchants. In the wake of this commercial activity the Champagne fairs acquired equal significance as a financial centre where money was changed, credit arranged and accounts settled. In the Late Middle Ages other fairs, such as the Antwerp/Bergen-op-Zoom cycle and many in the developing regions of central and eastern Europe, rose to international stature. By contrast, the fairs of Flanders, Champagne and several others of international significance in the Central Middle Ages were in decline by the early fourteenth century. In some instances local political instability contributed to this demise but economic factors were probably more important. The fairs were undermined by the development of the central Alpine passes and direct sea communications between Italy and northern Europe in the later thirteenth century. These new routes by-passed Champagne. The growing sophistication of business and financial techniques made direct personal contact between northern and southern European merchants in Champagne less necessary. More generally, commerce had become a year-long activity in the larger towns of western Europe. While markets remained central to commercial activity throughout the Middle Ages and after, it was no longer necessary to stimulate trading activity by means of a periodic fair.

D. Ditchburn

The Alpine passes

The Alps were a major obstacle to the medieval traveller. Although guides, hospices and road improvements gradually facilitated communication, even in the Late Middle Ages winter journeys remained difficult or impossible and goods could only be transported by pack animals. The lack of maps, avalanches, wild animals and sudden weather changes exacerbated matters. From Carolingian times the Great St Bernard and Mont Cenis passes were used frequently. They provided direct routes between Italy and the Champagne fairs but were also used by imperial armies campaigning in Italy and by pilgrims: over eight thousand horses from northern France and England were recorded on the Great St Bernard in the

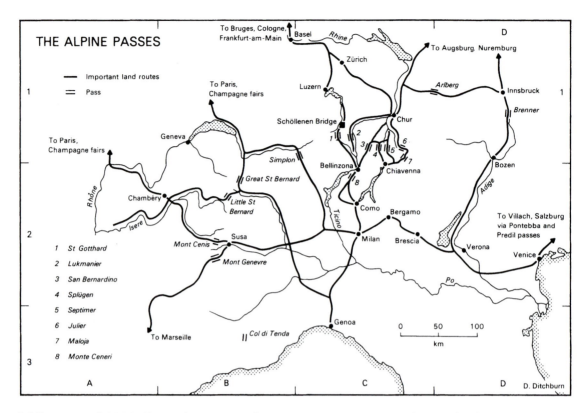

THE ALPINE PASSES

— Important land routes
= Pass

To Bruges, Cologne, Frankfurt-am-Main
Basel
Rhine
Zürich
To Augsburg, Nuremburg
Luzern
Arlberg
Innsbruck
To Paris, Champagne fairs
Schöllenen Bridge
Chur
Brenner
To Paris, Champagne fairs
Geneva
Simplon
Great St Bernard
Bellinzona
Chiavenna
Bozen
Rhône
Chambéry
Little St Bernard
Ticino
Como
Bergamo
Adige
To Villach, Salzburg via Pontebba and Predil passes
Isère
Mont Cenis
Susa
Milan
Brescia
Verona
Venice
Mont Genèvre
Po

1 St Gotthard
2 Lukmanier
3 San Bernardino
4 Splügen
5 Septimer
6 Julier
7 Maloja
8 Monte Ceneri

To Marseille
Col di Tenda
Genoa

0   50   100
km

D. Ditchburn

jubilee year of 1300. From the 1230s, when a bridge was constructed at Schöllenen, the western passes lost traffic to the Gotthard. It was easily reached from the north-west and the increasingly important south German fairs, such as Frankfurt-am-Main. Latterly English wool was also transported across the Gotthard, avoiding passage through hostile France. To the south, Monte Ceneri had a bad reputation for brigandage in the fifteenth century. Other central passes focused on Chur. The Septimer was the most popular but suffered from heavy snowfalls and a steep southern ascent. The central passes were less attractive for military purposes as they converged on Como, Milan and territory traditionally hostile to emperors. Instead, armies increasingly used the Brenner. Its northerly approaches were direct and if necessary Verona could be easily by-passed. Low in height, it was also less susceptible to heavy snowfalls. With its proximity to Venice and the development of the central European economy in the Late Middle Ages, the Brenner was also of growing commercial importance. It was one of the few passes across which wine could be transported and an important wine fair developed at Bozen. Further east, the Pontebba and, from the fourteenth century, the Predil, were used by merchants trading between the Veneto and Carinthia.

D. Ditchburn

Environmental change, *c.* 1000–1300

Europe's landscape is the result of cultural developments starting in the Neolithic Age and peaking intermittently during the Bronze Age, Central Middle Ages, Industrial Revolution and more recently. The transformation of the medieval landscape began with changes to the agro-, silvo- and pastoral systems in the Early Middle Ages. Major land clearance took place around monasteries, royal residences and peasant settlements in the Byzantine Empire, Muslim Spain and Lombard Italy. Palynology reveals an expansion of livestock-raising from the sixth century and the emergence of the typical Mediterranean pollen mix of evergreen oak, cork-oak, small-leaf oak and Pyrenean oak alongside *maquis*. In mountainous regions sweet chestnut had, however, started to oust oak.

Northern Europe also witnessed changes, notably in the clearance of woodlands from parts of Scandinavia, Germany and the British Isles during the early viking period. Meanwhile, the extensive territories between the Rivers Loire and Rhine, and particularly those around the Rivers Meuse and Moselle, became densely populated in the Merovingian and Carolingian era. Here too trees were cleared, tree pollen decreasing from about three-quarters of total pollen to half by 1000.

From 1000 to 1300 environmetal change reached unprecedented levels. Analysis of ice layers and bog growth shows that temperatures rose. Annual averages were one or two degrees higher than today. This 'medieval warm epoch', or 'little optimum', extended the growing range of crops northwards. Rhineland vines grew four degrees further north and 100 metres higher up hillsides. The expansion of Norse settlements in Greenland and Iceland suggests that crop cultivation was possible there too. Warmer weather and growing population encouraged peasants to clear and plant lands and to divert rivers. There was a remarkable agricultural colonization of Europe with Benedictine and Cistercian landlords notable agents of this environmental change.

In coastal and lowland Mediterranean regions there was a steady degradation of evergreen oak. Upland areas felt the impact of human activity for the first time. The ecology of chestnut built a whole civilization in the Apennines, transformed by the *incastellamento*. The growth of sheep transhumance in Spain, Provence, Italy and the Dinaric Alps created the landscape of the *dehesa* (grass enclosure), while in the northern Mediterranean mountains many forests of beech and oak gave way to pasture.

Change was even more remarkable in temperate Europe. East of the River Elbe and in Transylvania land was reclaimed and settled by colonists from the west after 1100. In the Alps, Balkans and Carpathians settlement crept to ever-higher elevations. In coastal regions agricultural reclamation was facilitated by the construction of canals, dikes, dams and sluices. Proto-industrial activities consumed timber from the Basque, Thuringian and Carpathian mountains using ring-barking and burning systems; and in countries bordering the North and Baltic Seas charcoal particles embedded in soils and lake sediments provide evidence of slash-and-burn husbandry from the thirteenth century. Frequent burning of forest, heathland and moorland produced grazing areas and forests dominated by oak, at the expense of beech and birch.

In post-conquest England two generally distinctive landscapes emerged which rarely intermingled: the 'champion' or 'open field' countryside of nucleated villages and communal cereal farming; and the 'ancient' or 'woodland' landscape dedicated mainly to livestock and featuring greater bio-diversity. Large quantities of oak were used for building. Hazel, willow and ash were collected as firewood while oak, ash, alder, willow and yew were used for domestic purposes. Coppicing was practised extensively, often in competition with pastoral exploitation. Elsewhere too dense forests disappeared from the landscape they had once dominated. Only in Poland, Russia, Ireland and the Scottish Highlands did woodlands remain largely untouched by the expansion of European society.

E. Pascua

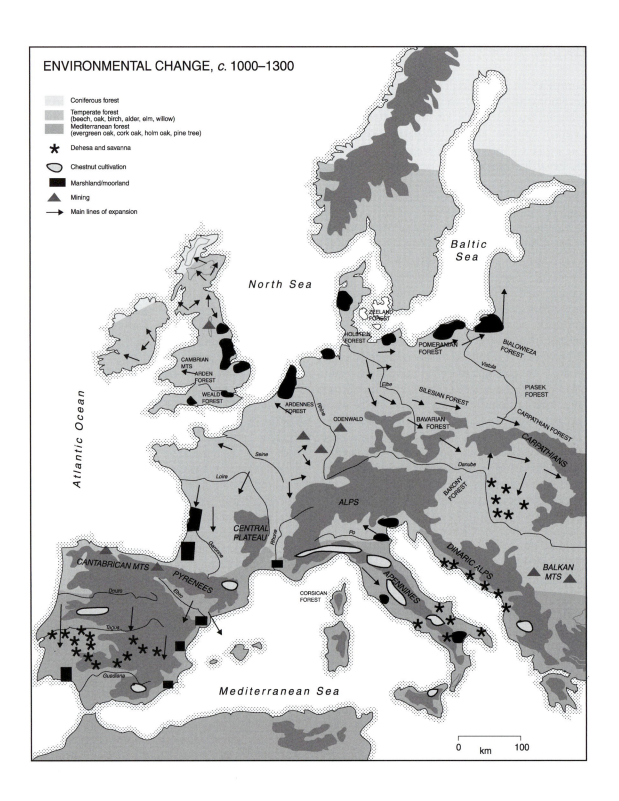

ENVIRONMENTAL CHANGE, *c.* 1000–1300

Coniferous forest

Temperate forest
(beech, oak, birch, alder, elm, willow)

Mediterranean forest
(evergreen oak, cork oak, holm oak, pine tree)

✳ Dehesa and savanna

Chestnut cultivation

Marshland/moorland

▲ Mining

→ Main lines of expansion

Baltic Sea

North Sea

Atlantic Ocean

ZEELAND FOREST

HOLSTEIN FOREST

POMERANIAN FOREST

BIALOWIEZA FOREST

Vistula

PIASEK FOREST

CAMBRIAN MTS

ARDEN FOREST

WEALD FOREST

ARDENNES FOREST

Rhine

ODENWALD

Elbe

SILESIAN FOREST

CARPATHIAN FOREST

BAVARIAN FOREST

CARPATHIANS

Seine

Loire

Danube

BAKONY FOREST

ALPS

CENTRAL PLATEAU

Rhône

Garonne

Po

DINARIC ALPS

BALKAN MTS

CANTABRICAN MTS

PYRENEES

Douro

Ebro

Tagus

CORSICAN FOREST

APENNINES

Guadiana

Mediterranean Sea

0   km   100

162

RELIGION AND CULTURE

Latin episcopal sees at the end of the 13th century

By the end of the thirteenth century Latin Christianity had for the most part reached its furthest limits territorially until the beginning of European expansion overseas two centuries later. The extensive ecclesiastical provinces of central Europe bounded to the east and south upon territories that followed the Orthodox rite and to the north-east upon pagan Lithuania, which did not finally convert to Christianity until the late fourteenth century. The provinces of Gniezno, which corresponded to the Polish kingdom, and of Esztergom and Kalocsa, which were contained within the kingdom of Hungary, had been established in the early years of the eleventh century, between 1000 and 1009, but the creation of new dioceses within them was not far advanced in the years since then. Kalocsa had recently acquired jurisdiction over Bosnia, following its absorption by Hungary in the course of a crusade against the heretics of the region. The diocese of Prague, which together with Olmütz corresponded to the kingdom of Bohemia, was still dependent upon Mainz and was not to be erected into a separate province until 1344. In the north-east a number of episcopal sees had been set up in the early thirteenth century to promote and accommodate missionary activity among the Baltic peoples. With the exception of Reval (now Tallinn), which was attached to the Scandinavian province of Lund, these were consolidated into the province of Riga in 1253. Within Scandinavia itself the process of conversion begun in the tenth century with the Danes had been carried forward and culminated in the erection of the three provinces of Lund (1104), Trondheim (1152) and Uppsala (1164). These were coterminous with the boundaries of, respectively, the kingdoms of Denmark, Norway and Sweden.

Across the North Sea, in the British Isles, several significant changes had been made since the eleventh century. In England the Norman conquerors respected the provincial boundaries but moved several sees from their Anglo-Saxon locations to centres of greater political and economic importance. Edward I's conquest of Wales in the late thirteenth century ended any lingering hopes that the Welsh bishops may have entertained of jurisdictional independence and effectively bound their sees to the province of Canterbury. In Scotland the diocesan confusion of the Early Middle Ages was followed in the twelfth century by the foundation or re-foundation of firmly established sees, which thereafter enjoyed an uninterrupted succession of bishops until the abolition of the episcopate in the Reformation period. The efforts of successive twelfth-century archbishops of York to bring the Scottish Church under their metropolitan jurisdiction failed everywhere but Whithorn. With the exception of Sodor and Man (the Isles) and Orkney, which formed a part of the province of Trondheim, the remainder of the Scottish sees were made immediately subject to the jurisdiction of Rome and given the status of *filia specialis* to the apostolic see in either 1189 or 1192, thus confirming what was in fact a political reality. Eventually the sees of St Andrews and Glasgow were promoted to metropolitan dignity with their own suffragans in 1472 and 1492, respectively, and the sees of Whithorn, the Isles and Orkney were incorporated into the Scottish

Church. Irish diocesan organization along the lines that obtained in the remainder of Latin Christendom was begun in the early twelfth century. The four provinces of Armagh, Cashel, Tuam and Dublin were established at the Synod of Kells in 1152. This took place a number of years before the English subjugation of Ireland but King Henry II was nevertheless able to play upon Roman suspicions of ecclesiastical irregularities in Ireland in order to obtain Pope Alexander III's approval for the conquest of the island.

Whereas provinces or dioceses in central Europe, Scandinavia and the British Isles either came, or had been specifically designed, to correspond with political units, the ecclesiastical structure that had early evolved in the Frankish kingdoms and the Carolingian empire did not so readily reflect political boundaries. The eastern dioceses of the provinces of Reims and Lyon, both of which lay substantially within the kingdom of France, took in tracts of land across the border in the Empire. Moreover, with a few exceptions such as the duchy of Normandy, which was coterminous with the province of Rouen, the boundaries of the various provinces and dioceses did not follow those of the greater fiefs. This could prove troublesome for both lay and ecclesiastical authorities. In particular, the long-standing aspirations of the Breton clergy to form a separate province under the metropolitan jurisdiction of Dol were not finally crushed until 1199, when Innocent III made decisive judgement in favour of the traditional claims of Tours. As in France, the pattern of provinces and dioceses in the kingdom of Germany was well established by the eleventh century. It was only in the eastern and south-eastern marches of the Empire, in the provinces of Bremen-Hamburg, Magdeburg and Salzburg, that new sees were erected in the eleventh, twelfth and thirteenth centuries. Thus, to the province of Salzburg, which at its establishment in 798 had only the three suffragans of Freising, Passau and Regensburg, and soon afterwards Brixen, were added the sees of Gurk (1072), Chiemsee (1215), Seckau (1218) and Lavant (1228). Few major changes

took place in France, the Empire or the central European kingdoms in the following centuries. A few new sees were raised in the eastern provinces. As a measure to combat heresy the diocese of Pamiers was erected in 1295 and in 1317 it and six other new sees were removed from the southern French province of Narbonne and assigned to the new metropolinate of Toulouse, while a few other sees were at the same time established in the provinces of Bourges, Bordeaux and Narbonne itself. In 1475 another new, small province, Avignon, was carved out of Arles.

It was in the Mediterranean that the most significant institutional developments since the early eleventh century took place. The gradual expulsion of the Saracens there opened up extensive territories in which to establish provinces and dioceses. In the Iberian Peninsula, the aim was largely one of the re-foundation of episcopal sees at their ancient sites and the reconquest that enabled this was nearly complete by the end of the thirteenth century, with only the Moorish kingdom of Granada remaining in the extreme south. The latter was eventually conquered and created into a province in 1492, at which time Valencia was also promoted to metropolitan status. In 1318 the province of Saragossa was established with jurisdiction over sees that formerly belonged to Tarragona. The Great Schism brought about the contraction of the province of Braga and the establishment of that of Lisbon, both within the confines of the kingdom of Portugal, which supported the Urbanist line of popes in opposition to neighbouring Castile. Likewise, the Saracen-dominated Sardinia and Corsica were conquered by the Genoese and Pisans and Sicily by the Normans in the eleventh century, which afforded the opportunity in each island for a new ecclesiastical ordering. Rival Pisa and Genoa themselves had each been promoted to metropolitans in 1092 and 1133, respectively. Further subdivision in northern Italy took place with the erection of the provinces of Florence in 1420 and Siena in 1459. The provincial fragmentation of southern Italy continued with the creation in the eleventh century of Rossano,

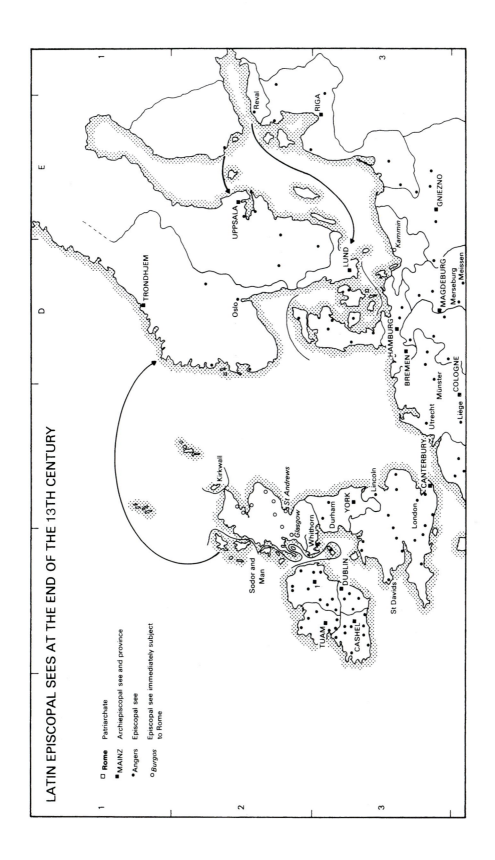

LATIN EPISCOPAL SEES AT THE END OF THE 13TH CENTURY

□ **Rome**   Patriarchate

■ **MAINZ**   Archiepiscopal see and province

• Angers   Episcopal see

○ *Burgos*   Episcopal see immediately subject to Rome

Reval
RIGA
GNIEZNO
UPPSALA
Kammin
TRONDHJEM
LUND
MAGDEBURG
Oslo
Merseburg
Meissen
HAMBURG
BREMEN
Utrecht
Münster   COLOGNE
Liège
Kirkwall
St Andrews
CANTERBURY
Glasgow
Whithorn
Durham   YORK
Lincoln
Sodor and Man
London
DUBLIN
St Davids
TUAM
CASHEL

165

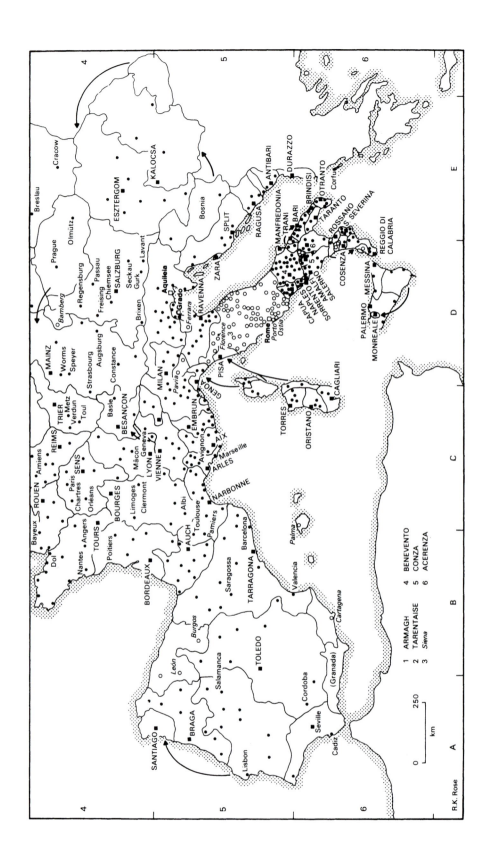

1 ARMAGH
2 TARENTAISE
3 *Siena*

4 BENEVENTO
5 CONZA
6 ACERENZA

R.K. Rose

166

Siponto, later translated to Manfredonia, Acerenza, Cosenza, Trani and Conza. Few changes took place in Italy in the Late Middle Ages beyond the suppression or union of a number of smaller, poorer sees.

R.K. Rose

Cistercians, Premonstratensians and others

The monastery of Cîteaux was founded in Burgundy in 1098 by Robert of Molesme and twenty-one companions. Robert had been abbot of more than one house and was the founder of Molesme, itself the head of a prosperous congregation; but he and his companions now wished to attempt to keep the *Rule* of St Benedict even better than they had previously done. Subsequent Cistercian writings attempted to show that Cîteaux was founded in reaction to the decadence of conventional Benedictinism, typified by Cluny; but although it is popularly supposed that the Cistercians attempted to follow the Benedictine *Rule* without the additional customs which had been developed in the tenth and eleventh centuries, it is now clear that they soon developed customs of their own which were partly based upon those of Cluny. By 1119 the Cistercian way of life had attracted new recruits. Several new houses had been founded and Pope Calixtus II approved legislation for an order as a whole. The Cistercians' originality lay in their rejection of tithes as a fitting source of monastic income; in their insistence on supporting themselves by agriculture and the labour of their own hands, and on only accepting donations of remote and unwanted lands to do this; and in their development of the use of lay brothers – already used to some extent in other new congregations – to help them.

The order was governed on federal lines, by visitation and annual assemblies of abbots in a General Chapter, set out in several versions of a document known as the *Charter of Charity*. The Cistercian habit was undyed (in contrast to the black robes of the earlier Benedictines) and their churches plain and unadorned with, eventually, their own architectural style – in the time of St Bernard of Clairvaux (d. 1153), the famous Cistercian leader, mystic and theologian, they generally had a square and plain east end in contrast to the semicircular ambulatory with radiating chapels found in many other churches. The design of Cistercian monastic buildings became standardized and is remarkable both for the use of diverted streams for sanitation and mills and also for the strict separation of the quarters of the monks and the lay brothers. The Cistercian use of lay brothers to till marginal land put them in the forefront of the process of land clearing and reclamation, particularly on the eastwards-expanding German frontier and in northern England. By the end of 1151 there were over 330 Cistercian houses; the next century saw a steady but less remarkable expansion. The map shows some of the most important houses, or the earliest in their region, or those which had many 'daughter' houses founded from them.

The Premonstratensians, founded in 1120 by the famous preacher Norbert of Xanten (d. 1134), were an order of regular canons who followed not only the *Rule* of St Augustine, which became the most popular rule for canons in the twelfth century, but also customs based partly on those of Cluny and an organization which derived from the Cistercian *Charter of Charity*. They too adopted undyed habits, used lay brothers to help cultivate marginal lands and expanded into the border lands of Germany, although the conversion of the chapter of Magdeburg also meant a succession of Premonstratensian bishops there and elsewhere in Germany. Their numbers and expansion were never as dramatic as those of the Cistercians but they were known throughout Europe. Other

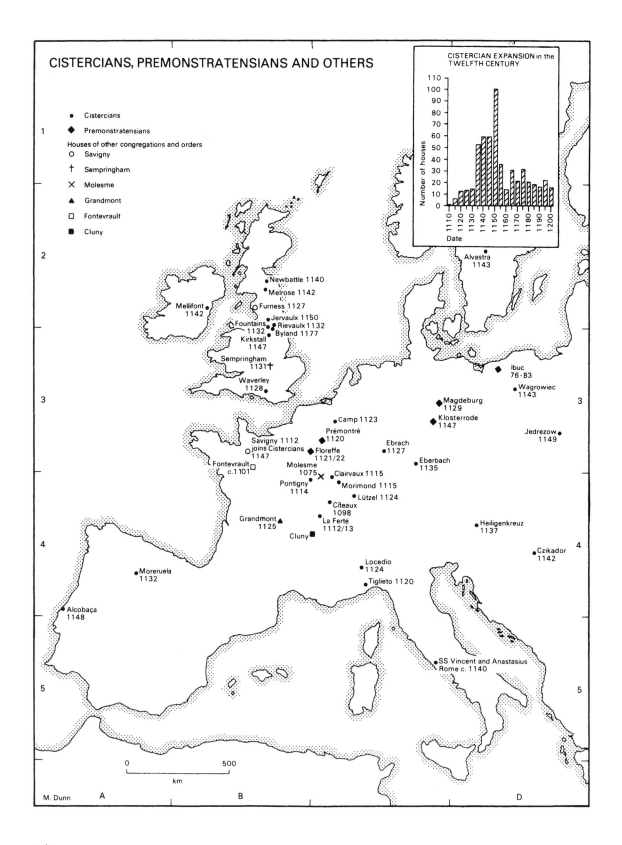

CISTERCIANS, PREMONSTRATENSIANS AND OTHERS

Legend:
- ● Cistercians
- ◆ Premonstratensians

Houses of other congregations and orders
- ○ Savigny
- † Sempringham
- ✕ Molesme
- ▲ Grandmont
- □ Fontevrault
- ■ Cluny

CISTERCIAN EXPANSION in the TWELFTH CENTURY

Newbattle 1140
Melrose 1142
Mellifont 1142
Furness 1127
Jervaulx 1150
Fountains 1132
Rievaulx 1132
Byland 1177
Kirkstall 1147
Sempringham 1131
Waverley 1128
Alvastra 1143
Ibuc 76-83
Wagrowiec 1143
Magdeburg 1129
Camp 1123
Klosterrode 1147
Prémontré 1120
Ebrach 1127
Jedrezow 1149
Savigny 1112 joins Cistercians 1147
Floreffe 1121/22
Eberbach 1135
Fontevrault c.1101
Molesme 1075
Clairvaux 1115
Pontigny 1114
Morimond 1115
Lützel 1124
Cîteaux 1098
Grandmont 1125
La Ferté 1112/13
Cluny
Heiligenkreuz 1137
Czikador 1142
Moreruela 1132
Locedio 1124
Tiglieto 1120
Alcobaça 1148
SS Vincent and Anastasius Rome c. 1140

0   500
km

M. Dunn

A   B   D

important twelfth-century groupings included that of Savigny which joined Cîteaux in 1147; the Order of Sempringham, a small English order founded in the 1130s by Gilbert for women and canons; and the famous house of Fontevrault, founded early in the century by Robert of Arbissel, also for women. The Order of Grandmont, which grew up after the death in 1125 of its 'founder', Stephen of Muret, expanded considerably but almost exclusively in France, in the twelfth century. It evolved its own *Rule* which stressed the need for communal poverty.

M. Dunn

The mendicants

The name 'mendicant' (from *mendicare*, to beg) is applied to religious men and women who have taken vows of common renunciation of goods, chastity and obedience. The earliest orders were the Franciscans (founded by Francis of Assisi *c.* 1172–1226 and approved in 1209) and the Dominicans (founded by Dominic of Caleruega, 1170–1221 and approved in 1216). By the mid-century they also included the Carmelites who had originated from groups of hermits (Order of Our Lady of Mount Carmel) living in Palestine on the slopes of Mount Carmel, who migrated to Sicily, Italy, France and England in the 1240s. In 1247 they approached Innocent IV for a modification in the *Rule* which allowed them to settle anywhere (including the towns), to lead a cenobitical style of life and adopt an active pastoral role. Similarly, groups of hermits in Lombardy, Tuscany and Romagna were united in 1256 with the Bonites, a congregation of penitents, who lived a life of preaching and mendicancy in north Italy. They also ministered to the towns-people of Europe (primarily in Italy but with priories in Spain, Germany, France, England and Scotland) and were renamed the Order of Friars Hermits of St Augustine.

The mendicant orders aimed to introduce the apostolic life of the gospels (or imitation of Jesus and the first apostles) into the growing towns of thirteenth-century Europe. Poverty, voluntarily embraced, was one intention, as was the idea of preaching to the unconverted or those who had strayed. The movement first emerged in Italy and southern France but quickly spread throughout Christendom. The mendicants were generally welcomed with enthusiasm but at times faced opposition from secular clergy who feared their competition, particularly after 1267, when Clement IV renewed the Franciscans' privilege of preaching, hearing confession and accepting burials without having to obtain diocesan consent. Nevertheless, the papacy, usually supportive of the mendicants, sought to resolve conflict, in bulls such as *Super cathedram* (1300), which introduced a licensing sytem for such activities.

At first the friars usually settled on the urban periphery, moving into town centres from the 1230s, to often derelict pre-existing churches which had been lent by a sympathetic local bishop, an individual or an urban corporation. The first purposely built mendicant churches were tiny and simple and were quickly outgrown, thus necessitating rebuilding which was executed in a new architectural style which recalled Cistercian models. This plan was ideally suited to preaching, with a spacious nave (single or aisled), optional transept and terminating in an apse or apsidal chapels at the east end. Apart from their contribution to preaching and education, the mendicant contribution to art was also immense – each mendicant order attracted extensive patronage from families and confraternities which commissioned works of art in return for masses and/or burial.

The Dominicans and Franciscans, in particular, had a considerable impact upon all subsequent forms of religious life, including the

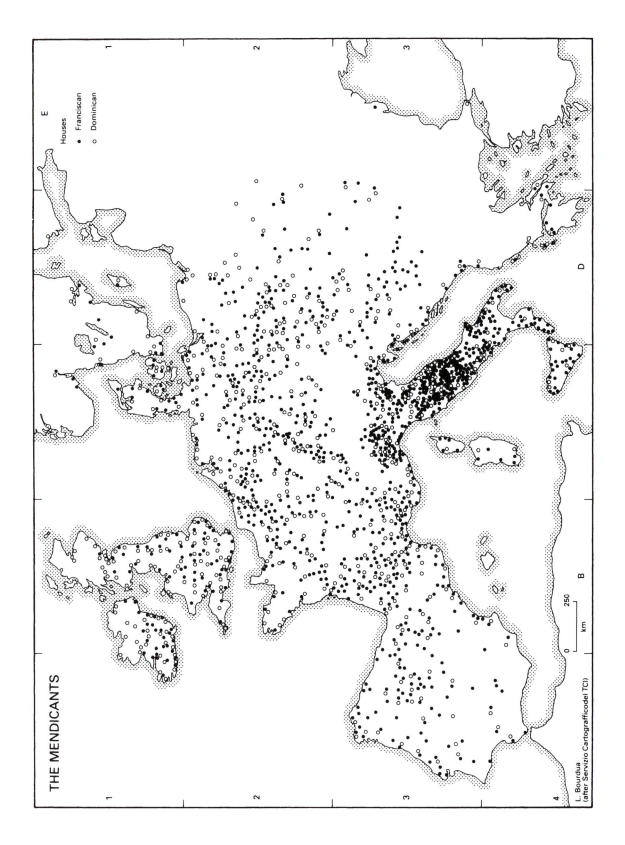

THE MENDICANTS

Houses
● Franciscan
○ Dominican

L. Bourdua
(after Servizio Cartografico del TCI)

Tertiaries. These, the Third Order, were groups of lay people who led a life of piety and charity and continued to live in their homes, married or not, and attached themselves to the mendicants for liturgical services.

L. Bourdua

Béguines and Beghards

Pious women known as Béguines first appeared in the Low Countries and the Rhineland in the early thirteenth century as part of a Europe-wide movement of popular religious revival. They grew rapidly in numbers and spread to northern France, Switzerland and central Europe. Their male counterparts, the Beghards, were much fewer in number and followed rather than led the women. The origin of the names is unknown but was possibly associated with the Albigensian heresy. They were certainly intended to discredit women and men who lived a life of pious devotion but followed no approved rule and took no irrevocable vows.

Recruits included both members of the newly affluent bourgeoisie and poorer women who sometimes lived in Béguine hospitals. They are often elusive in the written records and the style of their communities was subject to regional variation, including some living alone or in small groups in a house or convent, while others inhabited a large Béguinage within an enclosure, or occasionally in Béguine parishes. Béguines and Beghards adopted voluntary poverty, renounced worldly goods, undertook to observe celibacy while in their communities and lived by the labour of their hands, often working in hospitals or cloth manufacture and

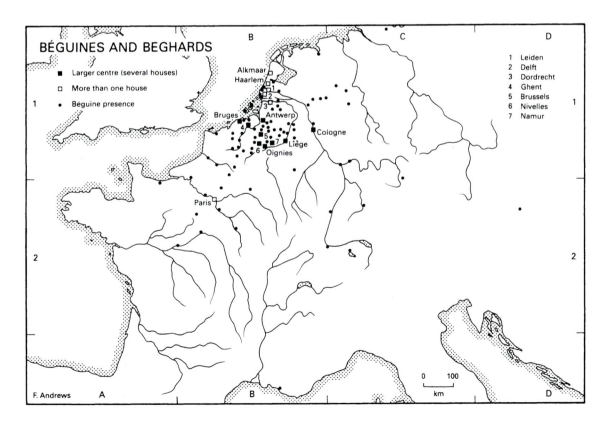

171

occasionally resorting to begging. Their spirituality was frequently mystical, individualistic and marked by visionary experiences, and several were accomplished writers in the vernacular. Initially they were admired and supported by prominent clerics, such as Jacques de Vitry (d. 1240) and Robert Grosseteste (d. 1253), and attracted lay patronage, for example from Louis IX of France, who established a Béguinage in Paris in 1264. As lay women living without a religious order, the Béguines also attracted hostility from some clerics who suspected them of heresy. Thus in 1310 Marguerite Porète was condemned and burnt with her mystical work, *The Mirror of Simple Souls*. The Council of Vienne in 1311–12 issued a broad condemnation of Béguines who 'lose themselves in foolish speculations . . . promise obedience to nobody . . . nor profess any approved rule'. 'Faithful' women who wished to live 'as the lord shall inspire them' were not condemned but the decree forced numerous Béguines into more formal communities: many attached themselves to the houses of friars.

F. Andrews

The Humiliati

The Humiliati or 'humble[d] ones' were one of many products of the so-called 'Evangelical Awakening' of the late twelfth century, a renewed search for a more intense religious experience focused on the life of Christ and the apostles, as described in the Gospels: the *vita apostolica* and the model of the early Church, the *ecclesie primitive forma*. They first emerged in the towns and countryside of northern Italy in the 1170s and the earliest references describe both groups of clerics living in community and lay women and men devoted to the religious life in small *ad hoc* associations promoting the Catholic faith. In November 1184, together with the Cathars, Poor of Lyon and other less well-documented groups, they were anathematized as heretics by Pope Lucius III and Frederick I Barbarossa at the Council of Verona. The most alarming practice of the Humiliati was to insist on preaching without authority, as specified in the text of *Ad abolendam*, the papal decree. They also rejected oathtaking, as is clear from later papal letters, which went to great lengths to explain that swearing oaths was necessary in some circumstances. This heretical labelling of the early Humiliati should not, however, be over-emphasized. They did not err in matters of dogma and unlike the Waldensians, there is no evidence for other unorthodox beliefs and practices developing after rejection by the Church. Indeed, there is very little evidence for action against them as a result of *Ad abolendam* and by the turn of the century they were sufficiently established to approach the pope, Innocent III (1198–1216), in search of approval. By this date three distinct elements were recognizable: married or single lay men and women living a religious life while remaining in their own homes (the first 'tertiaries'); male and female regulars living in common; and clerics following the *ordo canonicus*. In 1201 these groups achieved recognition as three separate orders under one framework of authority, supervised by houses in Viboldone, Vialone, Lodi and Como. The rule adopted by the regular communities, *Omnis boni principium,* was a combination of earlier monastic observances. A particular emphasis on manual labour was expressed by woolworking and cloth production but they also eventually became substantial landowners, following traditional monastic practices and particularly perhaps those of the Cistercians.

The Humiliati preached actively against heretics in northern Italy and by the mid-thirteenth century, the *ordo Humiliatorum* had achieved spectacular growth. In 1278 Bonvesin della Riva, himself a Humiliati Tertiary,

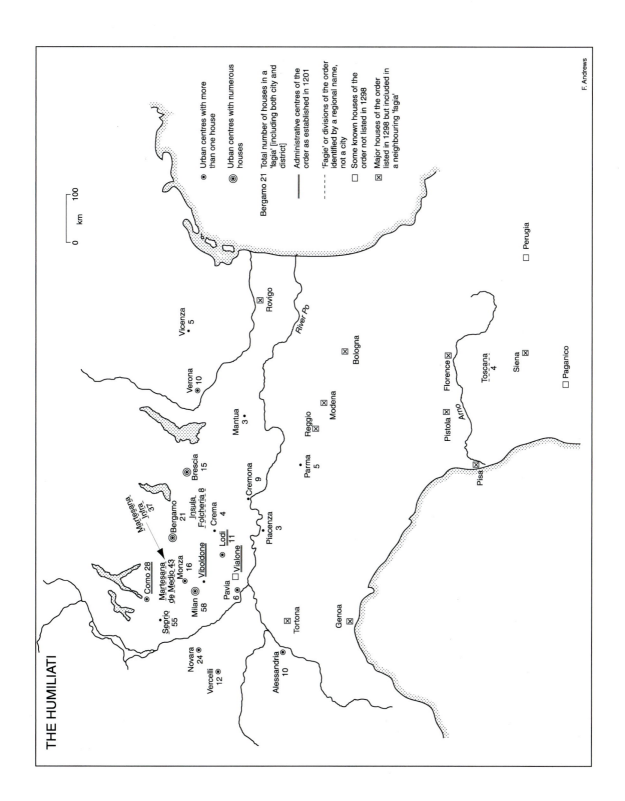

THE HUMILIATI

F. Andrews

- ⊙ Urban centres with more than one house
- ◉ Urban centres with numerous houses

Bergamo 21 Total number of houses in a 'fagia' [including both city and district]

────── Administrative centres of the order as established in 1201

- - - - - - 'Fagie' or divisions of the order identified by a regional name, not a city

- ☐ Some known houses of the order not listed in 1298

- ⊠ Major houses of the order listed in 1298 but included in a neighbouring 'fagia'

0 km 100

Como 28
Septio 55
Novara 24
Vercelli 12
Milan 58
Pavia 6
Alessandria 10
Martesana de Medio 43
Monza 16
Viboldone
Vialone
Martesana intra 37
Bergamo 21
Insula Folcheria 8
Crema 4
Lodi 11
Brescia 15
Piacenza 3
Cremona 9
Tortona
Genoa
Parma 5
Reggio
Modena
Mantua 3
Verona 10
Vicenza 5
Rovigo
River Po
Bologna
Pistola
Florence
Siena
Toscana 4
Paganico
Perugia
Arno
Pisa

173

recorded that there were over 200 houses of the regular 'Second' order and seven *canoniche* of the 'First' in the city and region of Milan alone. A catalogue of 1298, on which this map is based, names 387 houses. The Humiliati had become a major presence in the religious, economic and administrative life of northern Italy. They were invited as expert woolworkers to settle in Perugia and were active administrators in cities such as Bologna, Parma and Novara. In the late thirteenth and early fourteenth centuries in Siena, Florence and elsewhere they regularly served as communal treasurers. Plans to expand into the kingdom of France came, however, to nothing.

In the following centuries the order shrank in both size and prestige. By the early fourteenth century it had already adopted the *Rule of Benedict* and the tertiaries seem to have disappeared in many towns at some point later in that century. In the 1500s the Humiliati were swept aside by the winds of change in the Catholic Reform[ation]. In 1571 the male Orders were suppressed by Pius V. The women, perhaps always numerically more significant than the men, were left to fade out in less dramatic manner in the following centuries.

F. Andrews

The papacy and the conciliar fathers of 1215

In his letter convoking the Fourth Lateran Council of 1215, *Vineam Domini Sabaoth* (19 April 1213), Pope Innocent III sought the widest possible attendance of Church dignitaries, including, for the first time, representatives from the cathedral chapters. Abbots of the monastic orders and lay envoys of the secular powers were also urged to attend. Thus the primacy of Rome as the centre of papal Christendom was to be symbolized by an ecclesiastical parliament on an unprecedented scale.

Besides the crucial issues of Church reform, the struggle against heresy and the forthcoming crusade, the conciliar agenda also included such matters of ecclesiastical politics as the outcome of the German imperial election, the disputed primacy of the Spanish Church and the suspension of the archbishop of Canterbury. A further vexed question involved the rights of the count of Toulouse in the territories won by the Albigensian Crusade. All of these items of Church business influenced the geographical composition of the Fourth Lateran Council.

The gathering at Rome in November 1215 dwarfed previous western ecumenical councils.

Over 1,200 churchmen are known to have been present. Scots and Irishmen mingled with Hungarians, Poles and Sicilians. But the supposed ecumenicism and cosmopolitanism of the Fourth Lateran require some qualification. Oriental Christians absented themselves and the prelates from the Christian East were overwhelmingly transplanted Latins. The large delegations from Spain, Provence and England were in part motivated by specific regional concerns. Above all, the geographical distribution of the conciliar fathers reveals a Mediterranean and especially Italian numerical predominance at the Council although Italian loyalties were fragmented and localized. The Scandinavian countries largely ignored the Council and the politically divided German episcopate was under-represented. Not all of the bishoprics immediately subject to Rome were actually located in Italy but the concentration of Italian churchmen at the Fourth Lateran Council perhaps helps to explain the significance of the papacy's Italian policy, both in the papal states and in southern Italy, in the course of the thirteenth century.

G. Dickson

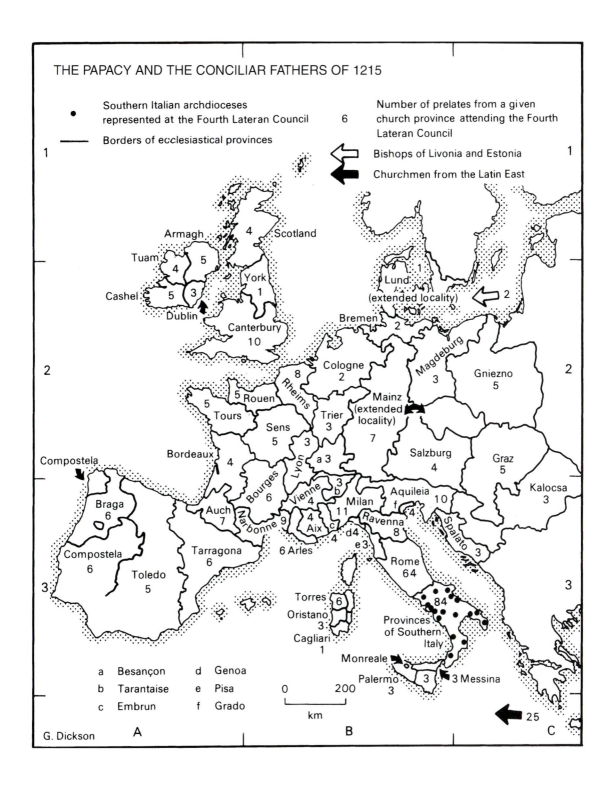

THE PAPACY AND THE CONCILIAR FATHERS OF 1215

• Southern Italian archdioceses represented at the Fourth Lateran Council

—— Borders of ecclesiastical provinces

6 Number of prelates from a given church province attending the Fourth Lateran Council

⇦ Bishops of Livonia and Estonia

⬅ Churchmen from the Latin East

Armagh
Scotland 4
Tuam 5
4
Cashel 5 3
Dublin
York 1
Canterbury 10

Lund 1
(extended locality) 2
Bremen
2

Cologne 2
Magdeburg 3
Gniezno 5

Rheims 8
Rouen 5
Tours 5
Sens 5
Trier 3
Mainz (extended locality) 7
Salzburg 4
Graz 5

Bordeaux 4
Lyon
a 3
Vienne 3
b
Milan 11
Aquileia 10
Kalocsa 3

Compostela
Braga 6
Auch 7
Bourges 6
Narbonne 9
Aix 4
c
Ravenna 8
Spalato 3

Compostela 6
Toledo 5
Tarragona 6
6 Arles
d 4
e 3
Rome 64

Torres 6
Oristano 3
Cagliari 1
Provinces of Southern Italy
84

Monreale
Palermo 3
3 Messina

a Besançon   d Genoa
b Tarantaise   e Pisa
c Embrun   f Grado

0   200
km

25

G. Dickson   A   B   C

175

Shrines and revivals: popular Christianity, *c.* 1200–*c.* 1300

Pilgrimage to the holy shrines of Latin Christendom was a striking feature of popular religious experience from the Early Middle Ages to the eve of the Reformation. Pilgrimages were undertaken to seek a miraculous cure at the tomb of a saint; to perform the penitential rite of the ascetic journey; and to receive the spiritual reward of an indulgence, such as the crusader's plenary indulgence for the Jerusalem pilgrimage. During the first of the medieval Jubilees – the remarkable Holy Year of 1300, the year in which Dante's celebrated *Divine Comedy* is set – Pope Boniface VIII (1294–1303) granted a plenary indulgence to pilgrims who visited designated Roman stational churches. In addition to religious motives for pilgrimage, more secular cravings for travel, adventure or escape also played an important part in directing the footsteps of medieval proto-tourists.

Punitive pilgrimages were imposed by some secular powers, in the Flemish towns, for instance. They were especially utilized by the inquisitorial courts of Carcassonne, Albi and Toulouse as penances for the former heretics of Languedoc. These Inquisitors drew upon an old distinction between 'major' and 'minor' pilgrimage sites. Here the shrines where the 'major' saints were venerated – St James of Compostela, saints Peter and Paul of Rome, the Three-Kings of Cologne and St Thomas Becket of Canterbury – provide us with four outstanding 'high places' of thirteenth-century Christendom. On the other hand, the choice of 'minor' pilgrimage sites is not representative of the great number of regional and local shrines dotted throughout Europe but instead reflects the southern French perspective of the Inquisitors and the locality of the penitent ex-heretics. A few important shrines not mentioned by the Inquisitors have been marked on the map. A complete map of Christian holy places, listing all the miraculous images, translated eastern saints' relics, pieces of the True Cross, venerated hosts and so on – could it be drawn – would be so detailed as to be virtually unreadable. Indeed, by the Late Middle Ages, most localities could lay claim to some saint or sacred object worthy of a pilgrim's devotion.

Like pilgrimage, many thirteenth-century revivals had an itinerant (or at least an ambulatory, processional) character. Like pilgrimage, too, revivals were instances of public, collective and popular religious behaviour. They began with a religious crowd, developed into a movement and sometimes, as with the flagellants of 1260, created durable religious institutions. The flagellant movement of 1260 began in Perugia and completed its transalpine trek in 1261 in northern Poland. It was fundamentally penitential, prophetic and Christocentric in nature although strongly influenced by its crusading context. In contrast, the children's crusade of 1212 and the shepherds' crusade of 1251 were both popular (i.e. unofficial) crusades: the papacy did not authorize them. The children's crusade began with processions, which probably were held at Chartres, to obtain divine support for the threatened Spanish Church. Ultimately, the majority of its adherents settled in Mediterranean cities. The enthusiasts of the shepherds' crusade proclaimed their intent to assist King Louis IX of France against the Saracens of Egypt. This movement turned violent, anti-semitic and anti-clerical and was put down by force. All three of these popular enthusiasms gained recruits along the line of march. These recruits were usually peasants but also included townspeople. The Lombard 'Great Hallelujah' of 1233 was itinerant only in respect of the huge crowds who gathered to hear the sermons of miracle-working friars. It was a revival promoted by Franciscan and Dominican friars, who emphasized preaching. It was a notable medieval peace movement. As with both pilgrimages and crusades, these medieval

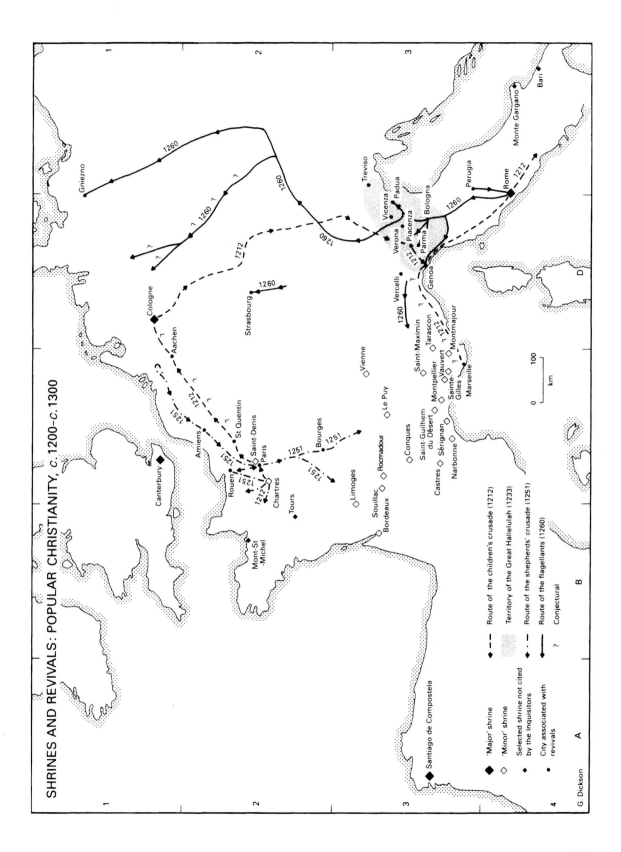

SHRINES AND REVIVALS: POPULAR CHRISTIANITY, c.1200–c.1300

Route of the children's crusade (1212)

Territory of the Great Hallelulah (1233)

Route of the shepherds' crusade (1251)

Route of the flagellants (1260)

Conjectural

'Major' shrine

'Minor' shrine

Selected shrine not cited by the Inquisitors

City associated with revivals

G. Dickson

177

revivals show how religious enthusiasm could mobilize large groups of ordinary believers and influence their behaviour in many ways.

G. Dickson

Heresy, the Albigensian crusade and the Inquisition, *c.* 1200–*c.* 1240

Individuals of questionable orthodoxy as well as heretical sects were scattered throughout much of early thirteenth-century Europe. Paris in 1210 saw the burning of the pantheistic Amalricians, while Strasbourg a year or two later witnessed a greater conflagration, perhaps of the obscure Ortliebians. When the Stedinger peasants of northern Germany refused to pay their tithes to the archbishop of Bremen, they were declared heretical; Pope Gregory IX (1227–41), who believed they were Luciferians, authorized the crusade which crushed them in 1234. Such pockets of heresy did not, however, constitute a major threat to the Church.

What worried a pope like Innocent III (1198–1216) was the danger of large concentrations of religious deviants existing in the midst of Catholic communities, while remaining relatively free to evangelize. The Cathars or Albigensians were dualists who had their own Church. Their holy men and women – known as the perfect – were actively proselytizing from the Pyrenees to the Papal State, almost to the outskirts of Rome. Also, the Poor Men of Lyon (or Waldensians), laymen whose main heresy was to insist upon preaching the Gospel despite ecclesiastical prohibition, were gaining adherents in southern France and in the Lombard cities. The Waldensians and Cathars were opposed to one another but intermingled in southern Europe and, to an extent, in northern Europe as well. There were other heresies; but these were the most formidable. The last Cathar perfect was burnt as late as 1321. The Waldensians of Piedmont survived until the Reformation.

The stronghold of the Cathars (or Albigensians) was in the lands of the count of Toulouse in south-west France. Here, because the heretics were so deeply entrenched in Languedocian society, the Church could not persuade or compel the secular nobility to suppress them on its behalf. Nor was the king of France, Philip II Augustus, willing to act. After the murder of his legate Peter of Castelnau in 1208, Innocent III launched a crusade against the heretics and their supporters – a holy war for peace (against the mercenary *routiers*) and for the faith (against the heretical Albigensians). It was led by papal legates like the Cistercian abbot Arnold Aimery and the northern French baron Simon de Montfort. Towns were sacked, Cathar *perfecti* were massacred and lands were confiscated by the northerners. The crusade continued intermittently through the first half of the thirteenth century although Catharism was by no means eradicated. In 1271 Languedoc passed to the French Crown. The Capetians were the crusade's ultimate beneficiaries.

While the Albigensian crusade was still in progress, in 1212 Innocent III threatened the Milanese with a crusading army if they failed to repress the heretics in their city. Yet the crusade was a blunt instrument. The Inquisition was potentially more selective. Traditionally it was the bishop's job to detect heretics within his diocese. Now specialists were needed. The Franciscan and especially the Dominican friars brought theological expertise and religious zeal to their task. The career of the Dominican Inquisitor, Robert le Bougre, active between *c.* 1232 and 1239, culminated in that year with the mass *auto da fé* of Cathars at Mont-Aimé in Champagne. The secular priest Conrad of Marburg was similarly relentless in his pursuit of Waldensians, Cathars and (alleged) Luciferians in the mid-Rhineland from *c.* 1227 until

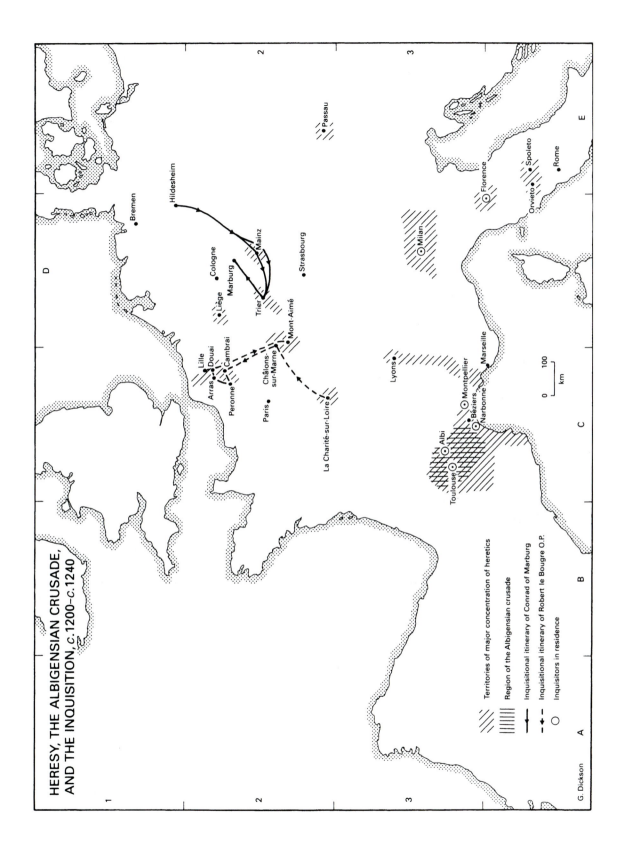

HERESY, THE ALBIGENSIAN CRUSADE,
AND THE INQUISITION, c.1200–c.1240

Bremen

Hildesheim

Cologne
Liège
Marburg
Trier
Mainz
Strasbourg

Lille
Arras
Douai
Cambrai
Péronne
Mont-Aimé
Châlons-sur-Marne

Paris

La Charité-sur-Loire

Passau

Milan

Florence

Orvieto
Spoleto
Rome

Lyons

Montpellier
Marseille

Albi
Béziers
Narbonne
Toulouse

0   100
         km

Territories of major concentration of heretics
Region of the Albigensian crusade
Inquisitional itinerary of Conrad of Marburg
Inquisitional itinerary of Robert le Bougre O.P.
Inquisitors in residence

G. Dickson

his assassination in 1233. Pope Gregory IX, who had commissioned them both, established the Inquisition in Languedoc in 1233. Inquisitors were then based at Toulouse, Montpellier and Albi; at Narbonne there was already a Dominican Inquisitor, an appointee of the archbishop. Fixed inquisitorial tribunals in Italy also date from Gregory IX's pontificate; they become more plentiful thereafter. Particularly effective was the Inquisition of the dead. For a deceased testator to be found guilty of heresy meant that his heirs forfeited their estate. Property proved a powerful stimulus for orthodoxy.

G. Dickson

Anti-semitism, 1096–1306

The Middle Ages began with a fair degree of harmony existing between Jews and Christians. This *modus vivendi* was, however, shattered by the first crusade (1096). According to a Jewish chronicler, many who took the cross reasoned as follows: 'We are going . . . to exact vengeance on the Ishmaelites, yet here are the Jews . . . whose forefathers slew him [Jesus]. First let us take vengeance on them.' By the summer of 1096 much of Rhineland Jewry had either been killed or forcibly converted. Such anti-Jewish violence was frowned on by the Church. According to Innocent III's *Constitutio pro Judaeis* of 1199, Jews were to be tolerated 'in accordance with the clemency that Christian piety imposes'. The Church was concerned, however, to distinguish Jews from Christians physically (by, for example, the 'Jewish badge'), socially (by discouraging all manner of social intercourse) and politically (by prohibiting Jews from exercising authority over Christians). These regulations also found their way into secular law though they did not affect the legal status of Jewry; Jews had to be humbled but they were not legally defined as being of servile status. To be sure, the term *servi regi* was applied to the Jews of Aragon (first to Teruel in 1176) and the term *servi camarae* was applied to the Jews of the Holy Roman Empire (first in Sicily by Frederick II in 1236). These terms were not, however, descriptive of a servile Jewish status; rather they were used to press certain jurisdictional rights over Jews in the face of a competing jurisdiction.

While official ecclesiastical and lay policies for the most part sought to protect Jews, the religious consciousness of people tended to emphasize the demonic nature of the Jew. This was most apparent in the blood libel and in the charge of host desecration, both of which often led to anti-Jewish violence. According to the blood libel, from the time Jesus had been crucified the Jews thirsted, particularly at Easter time, for the pure and innocent blood of Christian children. The libel of host desecration appeared only after the Lateran Council of 1215 had formulated the doctrine of transubstantiation. Jews were thought to bribe Christians into supplying them with a host (the body of Jesus) which they then tortured. Such a charge in Röttingen in 1298 led to a wave of massacres throughout Bavaria and adjoining regions.

The demonic nature of Jewry was further emphasized by the artistic depiction of Jews as *incubi* and the like. In contrast to the sweet-smelling 'odour of sanctity', the foul *foetor judaicus* was ascribed to Jews. That innocent Christians were exploited by Jewish usurers was another charge that found adherents in Church, state and populace. Jews, indeed, were often engaged in money-lending and tax collection; this fact, which was the cause of much antagonism, was itself the result of attempting to leave the practice of money-lending to the Jews, who were not 'brothers' in the mystical body of Christ. Jews could, of course, join this body by converting, and the mendicant orders, particularly the Dominicans, mounted a campaign of

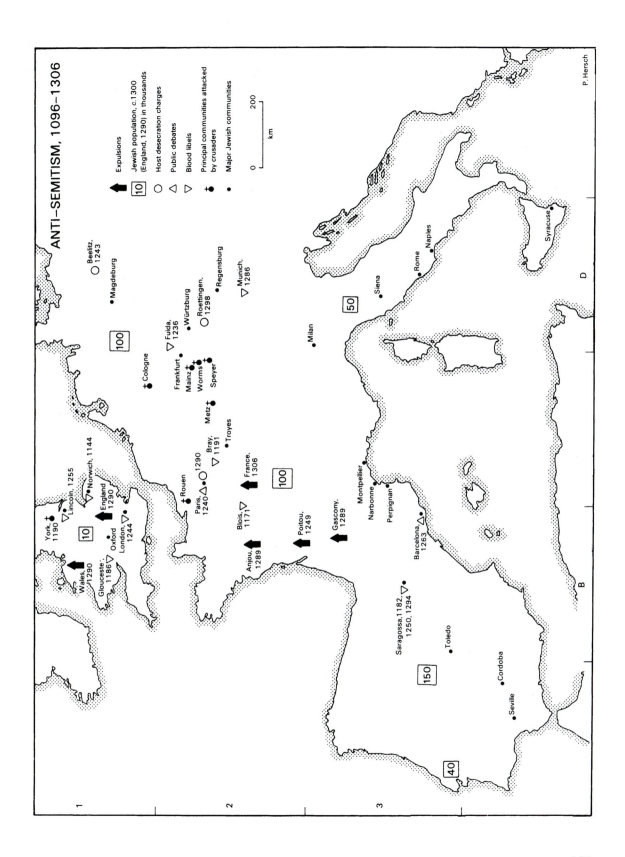

ANTI-SEMITISM, 1096–1306

Expulsions

Jewish population, c.1300 (England, 1290) in thousands

10

Host desecration charges ○

Public debates △

Blood libels ▽

Principal communities attacked by crusaders ✝ ●

Major Jewish communities ●

0 — 200 km

P. Hersch

○ Beelitz, 1243

● Magdeburg

100

✝ Cologne ●

Frankfurt ●
Mainz ✝
Worms ✝
Speyer ●

▽ Fulda, 1236

Würtzburg ●
○ Roettingen, 1298

● Regensburg

▽ Munich, 1286

Metz ✝

● Troyes

● Milan

50

York, 1190 ✝
▽ Lincoln, 1255
○ ● Norwich, 1144
England 1290
10
Oxford ● ▽
Gloucester, London, 1244
1186
✝
Wales, 1290

✝ Rouen

Paris, △ ● ○
1240 1290

▽ Bray, 1191

France, 1306

100

Blois, 1171 ▽

Anjou, 1289

Poitou, 1249

Gascony, 1289

Montpellier ●

Narbonne ●
Perpignan ●

Barcelona, △
1263 ●

Saragossa, 1182, ▽
1250, 1294 ●

150

Toledo ●

Cordoba ●

Seville ●

40

Siena ●

Rome ●
Naples ●

Syracuse ●

D

B

1

2

3

181

conversion in the thirteenth century which manifested itself in conversionist sermons, directed at Jews, and in the staging of public debates, such as that held before the court of James I at Barcelona in 1263. The failure of this 'dream of conversion' led to the more strident view that Jews were unassimilable to the Christian social body and ought, therefore, to be either forcibly segregated or expelled. The latter course was adopted in England in the first general expulsion of the Jews in 1290 and later in France in 1306.

P. Hersch

The 12th-century Renaissance

The 'Twelfth-Century Renaissance' is a convenient historiographical label and, despite re-evaluations, the vision of this cultural achievement published by C.H. Haskins in 1927 remains the starting-point for its study. Haskins outlined a reinvigorated interest in Latin and its ancient classics, the revival of Roman law, greater sophistication in historical writing and the rise of universities. Because of the repercussions for philosophical and scientific thought, he emphasized the translation of texts unavailable to the West for generations.

The pre-eminent centres of translation were in southern Italy and Spain. In Sicily various writings were translated directly from Greek, including Ptolemy's Almagest and works by Euclid and Proclus. With a medical school at Salerno, demand grew for medical texts, especially by Galen. This was met by men like Burgundio of Pisa, a jurist who often visited

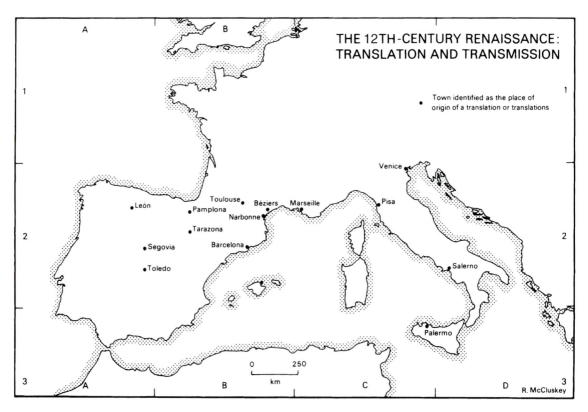

THE 12TH-CENTURY RENAISSANCE: TRANSLATION AND TRANSMISSION

• Town identified as the place of origin of a translation or translations

R. McCluskey

Constantinople. He and others also translated theological works by the Greek Fathers. The main impetus was, however, directed at translating ancient philosophy, often with Arabic commentary, and mathematics and astronomy. Translations from Arabic in Spain were principally devoted to these subjects and, most significantly, to recovering Aristotle's works. Toledo's role as the leading Spanish centre needs qualification – the idea of a 'school' under Archbishop Raymond (1125–52) is premature – but in the second half of the century Toledo undoubtedly attracted scholars of quality, including the enormously productive Gerard of Cremona. Other centres are identifiable: Hugh of Santalla in Tarazona, Plato of Tivoli in Barcelona, Robert of Chester in Segovia. Herman of Carinthia was in León in 1142 and in Toulouse and Béziers in 1143, translating as he went.

It is not fully understood how manuscripts of Aristotle and others were transmitted to the West's intellectual centres. The wandering scholars themselves probably played a major part in dissemination. It fell to men like St Thomas Aquinas (1225–74) to systematize the 'new' knowledge and harmonize it to the fundamentals of Christian theology.

R. McCluskey

The emergence of universities

The first universities emerged after a period of development which began in the late eleventh century. This process can only be understood in the context of economic growth and urban expansion since large numbers of economically unproductive scholars could only gather on a permanent basis when towns could offer adequate accommodation and regular markets at which basic necessities could be bought. From the early twelfth century there were more and more urban schools, centred on cathedrals or individual masters. They were very different from the monastic schools which had long dominated the world of learning. The atmosphere was highly competitive because masters needed to attract and retain the students who paid the fees which enabled the urban schools to survive. It was common for masters to set up school with the intention of poaching a rival's pupils. Institutionally, the situation was highly fluid with masters moving in and out of fashion very quickly. During the twelfth century the schools gradually became more permanent, each school embracing a number of masters. By 1200 the earliest universities had become established at Bologna and Paris. These *studia generalia*, as they were known, were essentially corporations or guilds. In Bologna the guilds were formed by students and the students regulated the lives of the masters. Paris, however, was run by the masters; they formed the corporations and students obtained their rights through association with their masters. Subsequent universities followed one or other of these models more or less closely. Crucial to the emergence of a university was the grant of privileges from pope, emperor, king or commune. These privileges usually included an element of juridical autonomy, the right to elect officers, powers to make statutes and other keys to independence. While grants of privileges to the earliest universities simply recognized and reinforced developments which had already taken place, many later universities were deliberately 'founded'.

Universities very quickly developed a system of faculties. A *studium generale* would have a faculty of arts and at least one other faculty teaching theology, canon law, Roman law or medicine. Key textbooks emerged in what could now be called academic disciplines. Certain basic teaching techniques became established and were used in all disciplines. Lectures consisted of commentary on set texts while disputations involved debate in which the participants were required to take different sides.

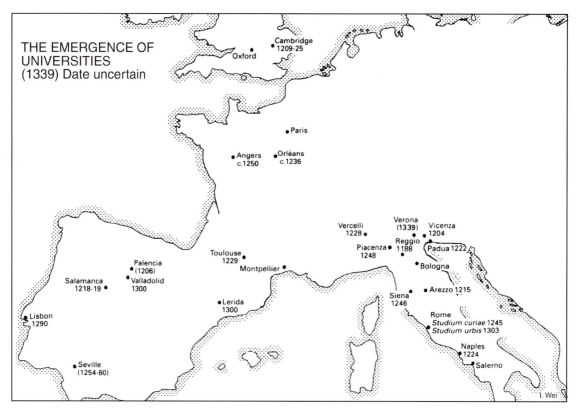

THE EMERGENCE OF
UNIVERSITIES
(1339) Date uncertain

Cambridge
1209-25

Oxford

Paris

Angers
c.1250

Orléans
c.1236

Vercelli
1228

Verona
(1339)

Vicenza
1204

Reggio

Piacenza 1188
1248

Padua 1222

Toulouse
1229

Montpellier

Bologna

Palencia
(1206)

Valladolid
1300

Salamanca
1218-19

Lerida
1300

Siena
1246

Arezzo 1215

Lisbon
1290

Rome
Studium curiae 1245
Studium urbis 1303

Naples
1224

Salerno

Seville
(1254-60)

I. Wei

Scholars who worked in this context developed new ways of thinking in many fields of study.

The process by which universities were set up across Europe was far from smooth. Indeed universities were highly controversial: they had both passionate supporters and vitriolic critics. This is scarcely surprising in view of the roles which many scholars claimed to play in society. Masters of theology at the University of Paris, for example, considered it their responsibility to remove doubt and error, to elucidate the truth, to defend the faith against heretics and to train others how to preach, teach and see to the cure of souls throughout Christendom. Certainly universities had a major impact on many aspects of medieval society. Scholars played an important role in shaping attitudes and opinions in many areas of life. University men also left the academic world to pursue careers in secular and ecclesiastical administration at every level. The culture of the medieval intellectual was thus an essential part of medieval society.

I. Wei

The spread of the Old French epic (the Roland legend)

The skirmish at Roncevaux (15 August 778) at the end of Charlemagne's abortive intervention in the Iberian Peninsula produced a legend of great vitality. Roland's name is first mentioned in connection with the battle in Einhard's early ninth-century biography of Charlemagne. By the eleventh century sufficient myth had accrued round names and events that a note

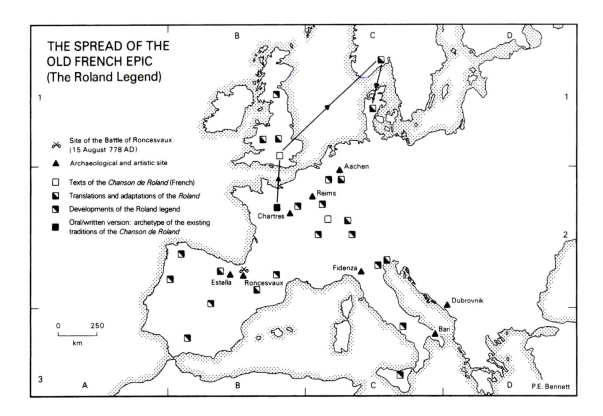

THE SPREAD OF THE
OLD FRENCH EPIC
(The Roland Legend)

✂ Site of the Battle of Roncesvaux
(15 August 778 AD)

▲ Archaeological and artistic site

☐ Texts of the *Chanson de Roland* (French)

◧ Translations and adaptations of the *Roland*

◪ Developments of the Roland legend

■ Oral/written version: archetype of the existing
traditions of the *Chanson de Roland*

Aachen

Reims

Chartres

Fidenza

Estella Roncesvaux

Dubrovnik

Bari

0   250
├──┼──┤
km

P.E. Bennett

appended to a manuscript at the abbey of San
Millán de la Cogolla, near Nájera (Castile),
attributes the defeat not to Basques but to
'Saracens' and has Charlemagne surrounded by
twelve nephews, including Roland, who were
epic heroes drawn from all three main cycles of
Old French epic. The archetype of the existing
versions of the poem was produced *c.* 1100,
probably in Normandy, by a learned poet
exploiting oral traditions and the techniques of
oral poetry. This version gave rise to that in the
oldest manuscript of the *Chanson de Roland*,
copied in England *c.* 1150. In the course of the
twelfth century new material, increasing the
role of Roland's fiancée, Aude, and of the traitor,
Ganelon, generated modernized, romance-
influenced versions of the legend. This version,
the most common, was translated or adapted
into English, Welsh, Middle High German (the
version by Pfaffe Konrad), Provençal (inventing a
troubadour-style love plot between Roland and
the Saracen Queen, Bramimonde), Aragonese
and the Franco-Italian koïné of the Veneto. It

was probably from Plantagenet England,
possibly via Scotland and the Norse earldom of
Orkney, that the legend was transmitted to
Norway and Denmark, where it was incorporated along with legends of the local hero,
Ogier the Dane, into the Old Norse *Karla-
magnús saga* and Danish *Karl Magnus Krønike.*
Legends in which Roland played a part
remained popular in England, generating a
series of Charlemagne romances in Middle
English, and in lowland Scotland, producing
the sixteenth-century *Taill of Rauf Colyear.* Two
versions of Roland's youthful deeds (*Enfances*)
were produced: *Aspremont*, probably composed
in the Norman kingdom of Sicily shortly before
1190 (it is a regular point of reference in
Ambroise's account of the Third Crusade), and
Girart de Vienne, composed by Bertrand de
Bar-sur-Aube for the court of Champagne
c. 1180, which makes Roland's companion-in-
arms at Roncevaux, Oliver, a member of the
Narbonnais clan, who were heroes of the most
fully developed cycle of Old French epics. The

legend of Roland's incestuous birth as son and nephew of Charlemagne is early associated with the legend of St Giles and also features in the now lost Castilian *Mocedades de Mainete* (Charlemagne's youthful exploits) and the German *Karl der Grosse*, by Der Stricker. As pseudo-history the legend of Roncevaux served crusading purposes in the *Historia Karoli Magni* ('Pseudo-Turpin Chronicle'), the oldest extant manuscript of which is the *Codex Calixtinus* (written *c.* 1170), preserved in Compostela. The reign of Charlemagne is largely reconstructed from epic poems in both the *Grandes Chroniques de France* (fourteenth century) and in the Burgundian *Croniques et Conquestes de Charlemaine* by David Aubert (fifteenth century). The lasting appeal of the legend is seen in the adaptations inspiring the Renaissance epics of Boiardo and Ariosto and in the still extant puppet theatres of Naples, Sicily and Liège. Via the *romancero* ballad, versions of the legend were taken from Spain and Portugal to the Americas and to Goa, where they are still productive. Artistic representations of the legend abound, from romanesque capitals in Estella and Fidenza, to the thirteenth-century 'Charlemagne Window' in Chartres cathedral, the Charlemagne reliquary in Aachen and the fifteenth-century statue of Roland in Dubrovnik. Now lost is a twelfth-century mosaic representing the Battle of Roncevaux in the cathedral in Bari.

P.E. Bennett

Troubadours: centres of creativity and travels of the poets

Some 400 troubadours working between *c.* 1100 and *c.* 1300 are known at least by name, including a dozen or so female poets or *trobairitz*. Originating in Aquitaine, Auvergne and the Limousin they spread in the later twelfth century into the Rhône valley, northern Italy and the Christian kingdoms of Iberia. The earliest whose poems survive is William IX, duke of Aquitaine (1071–1127), writing in Poitiers, Bordeaux and doubtless elsewhere, on travels that took him to the Holy Land (1100) and Spain. Bernart de Ventadorn, the 'classic' troubadour (*fl.* 1150–1200), was probably the son of Count Ebles II, 'The Singer', of Ventadorn, with whom William maintained a poetic correspondence, as he possibly did with the count of Anjou. Bernart wrote for the count of Toulouse and the viscountess of Narbonne, as well as for Eleanor of Aquitaine, William's grand-daughter, with whom he may have travelled to Normandy and England: he seems to have written at least one poem north of the Channel. Marcabru, a Gascon clerk at the court of William X of Aquitaine, wrote moral poems satirizing the 'noble love' (*fin'amor*) promoted by fellow troubadours. He also worked at the courts of Castile and Aragon and was in contact with Jaufré Rudel, prince of Blaye, himself a poet, whose death during the second crusade blended with his evocations of *amor de lonh* (distant love) gave rise to the romantic legend of his love for the countess of Tripoli. Most troubadours seem to have been peripatetic: great aristocrats and kings like William IX, Richard I of England and Alfonso II of Aragon for reasons of state; lesser men, like Bertran de Born (*c.* 1159–1215), to follow their lords. Peire Vidal (*fl.* 1183–1204) worked at the courts of Toulouse and Aragón, and travelled widely with the marquis of Montferrat, an avid patron of troubadours, probably accompanying him to Cyprus and Constantinople. The routes taking Gausbert de Poicibot from the Limousin to Spain are less well charted. The itinerant nature of these poets who maintained extensive networks of contacts among themselves is encapsulated in the professional name of Cercamon (Search-the-World: *fl.* 1137–49). Others,

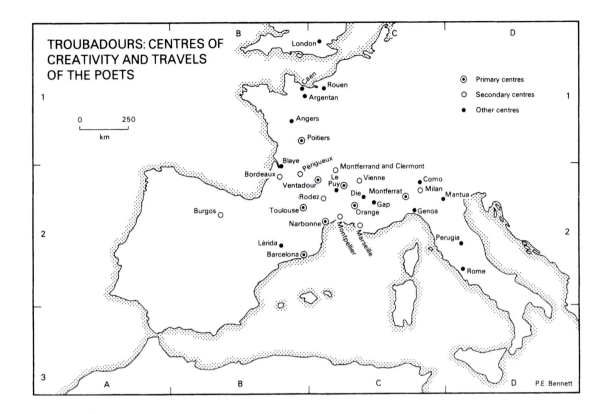

TROUBADOURS: CENTRES OF
CREATIVITY AND TRAVELS
OF THE POETS

particularly *trobairitz* like Maria of Ventadorn and the countess of Die but also Raimbaut d'Aurenga (count of Orange) and poor knights like Berenger de Palazol (*fl.* before 1164), remained in the service of local lords. Peire d'Alvernhe, from Clermont, is one of several poets reputed to have abandoned the cloister for an itinerant life in Occitania, northern Italy and Spain. Others took the contrary route: Folquet de Marseille, born into a merchant family possibly of Genoese origins, became bishop of Toulouse and Gui Folqueis became Pope Clement IV. Major centres like Vienne, home of the Dauphin, Orange, Le Puy (which gave its name to northern French poetic societies in the fourteenth century) and Toulouse, home of the *Jocs Floris* (Floral Games) of the fourteenth-century troubadour revival, proved magnets for many troubadours. Not all were Provençal: Lanfranc Cigala (*fl.* 1235–57) was from Genoa, Sordello (*fl.* 1220–69) from Mantua; Viscount Guillem de Bergedá (*fl.* 1138–92), Guillem de

Cabestany (writing in the second decade of the thirteenth century) and Guillem de Cervera (who wrote under the name of Cerveri de Girona: *fl.* 1259–85) were all Catalan. The constant and wide travels of people in the twelfth and thirteenth centuries, and the even wider travels of their books, which have only recently come to be properly recognized, meant that troubadour poetry had a lasting influence on poets in Sicily (Folquet de Romans worked for Frederick II), northern Italy (their impression on Dante and Petrarch has indelibly marked western culture), Spain, France and Germany (both *Minnesinger* and *Meistersinger*). Much of this cultural diffusion stemmed from the vast and interconnected politico-geographical influence of the houses of Anjou, Aragon-Toulouse and Provence, which, together with transalpine houses like Montferrat, provided a continuing tradition of poetic patronage as well as producing poets among their own members.

P.E. Bennett

Romanesque Europe

'Romanesque' was a term first used by Charles de Gerville, a Norman archaeologist, to describe western architecture from the fifth to the thirteenth centuries. It is now applied to a more restricted type of architecture and decorative arts which evolved in western Europe in the eleventh and twelfth centuries. Technically, Romanesque architecture amounts to a complete building system executed by highly skilled workers. Developments included the replacement of timber roofing, which was vulnerable to fire, with stone groin and barrel vaults. At first only small spaces were vaulted. Gradually, however, elongated naves were also vaulted, made possible only by strengthening the structure of the building. What is known as 'the first international Romanesque style' began in Lombardy where one bay of a church, such as San Ambrogio in Milan, was vaulted between the apse and the nave. The next step occurred in Catalonia where entire churches,

such as San Vicente de Castillo at Cardona and St-Martin-du-Canigou, were built with barrel vaulting. The culmination of Romanesque architecture is, however, to be seen at Durham Cathedral, in England, with its ribbed vaulting throughout supported by cylindrical and compound piers.

The dissemination of the style owed much to travelling ateliers of Lombard masons, recruited by abbots and bishops either to rebuild churches damaged during the upheavals and invasions of the tenth century or to build new churches for reformed religious orders. They moved along the Rhine and as far north as Sweden, training local craftsmen who were, in turn, recruited elsewhere. This explains the diffusion of regional trends throughout much of Europe. The Cluniac and Cistercian Orders played an important role in the network of patronage. The pilgrimage roads to Rome, Jerusalem and particularly Santiago de Compostela were also

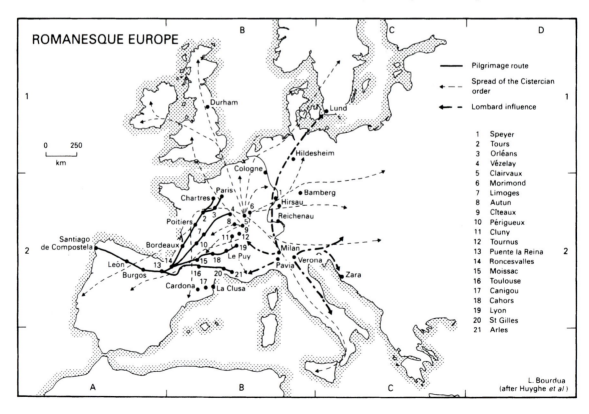

ROMANESQUE EUROPE

— Pilgrimage route
-◄- - Spread of the Cistercian order
◄— Lombard influence

1 Speyer
2 Tours
3 Orléans
4 Vézelay
5 Clairvaux
6 Morimond
7 Limoges
8 Autun
9 Cîteaux
10 Périgueux
11 Cluny
12 Tournus
13 Puente la Reina
14 Roncesvalles
15 Moissac
16 Toulouse
17 Canigou
18 Cahors
19 Lyon
20 St Gilles
21 Arles

L. Bourdua
(after Huyghe *et al*)

an important factor in the dissemination of style. Notable examples of Romanesque pilgrimage churches include Ste Foy at Conques, St Martial at Limoges, St Sernin at Toulouse and Santiago de Compostela.

L. Bourdua

Gothic Europe

The term 'Gothic' was coined in Italy as an expression of contempt to describe medieval architecture. It was particularly applied to a style of architecture that had evolved between the twelfth and sixteenth centuries and which required more sophisticated building methods than its Romanesque predecessor. Developments included greater use of cross-ribbed vaulting to roof larger areas; a system of supports including exterior flying buttresses; the substitution of large windows of multi-coloured glass for walls; and more complex façades with portals and programmes of sculpture. The greatest technical developments occurred in the Ile-de-France, where builders refused to use rib vaulting with heavy Norman walls and instead developed more adventurous vaulting techniques. Their solution was to reinforce piers by creating more projections on walls, either by grouping clusters of engaged columns internally or using bigger buttresses externally. Vault cells assumed a pointed shape, as did arches, and vaults were also made lighter through the use of well-cut stones of thin ashlar, instead of the rubble previously employed. Exterior flying buttresses reduced the thrust of the vaults and, despite their structural purpose, they became objects of beauty. The rebuilding

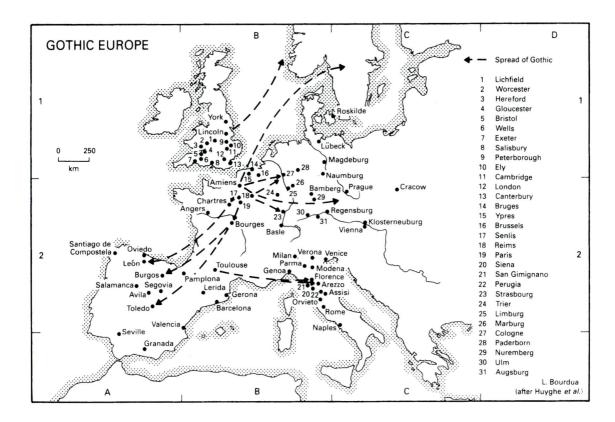

189

of the abbey church of St Denis, north of Paris, marked a turning point in the development of the style. The wide Gothic *chevet* (a double ambulatory) was created, an open structure with no walls between chapels, articulated by two rows of slender columns; stained glass was also used on an unprecedented scale. A parallel development occurred during rebuilding of Sens Cathedral, where from the start it was intended to cover the nave and choir with a cross-ribbed vault.

Most French cathedrals were designed on such an ambitious scale that few were finished as intended. (The desire for verticality was so great that Beauvais Cathedral remained unfinished.) English Gothic churches were lower than French examples, with more complex rib-vaulting designs (e.g. St Hugh's Choir at Lincoln Cathedral) and differing façades. In Germany, Gothic influence dates from the thirteenth century (e.g. Cologne Cathedral), as in Spain (e.g. the cathedrals of Burgos and Toledo). In Italy, apart from Cistercian abbeys such as Fossanova, many Romanesque features were retained.

L. Bourdua

The travels of Villard de Honnecourt

The architectural style now known as the Gothic had its origins in northern France during the second quarter of the twelfth century. The twelfth and thirteenth centuries saw a vast amount of building in western Europe and French architecture was the increasingly fashionable model. This can be observed in the geographical spread of the Gothic style and can

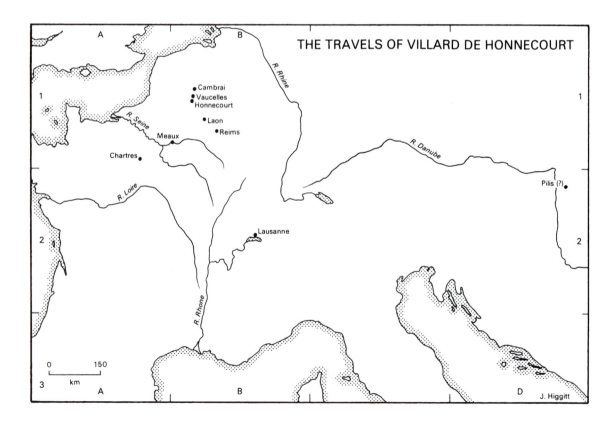

occasionally be documented, as in the hiring of William of Sens to rebuild Canterbury Cathedral in 1174 or in the presence of a mason from Paris in Wimpfen, who, it was noted in the late thirteenth century, built in the French style.

In the years around 1230 a French traveller, keenly interested in architecture, made a series of drawings, which are now in the *Bibliothèque Nationale* in Paris (ms. fr. 19,093). At some stage he wrote (or perhaps dictated) a series of captions in the French of Picardy. (Two hands added further texts later in the century.) The name he gives is usually modernized as Villard de Honnecourt. The varied contents include architectural details, plans, carpentry, mechanical devices, figure subjects (several after sculpture, both contemporary and antique) and animals (some copied from bestiaries and some perhaps from life). There are also diagrammatic representations of ideas deriving from the practice of masons and carpenters and figurative drawings based on geometric schemata. In both

the latter and in his 'preface' he lays self-conscious emphasis on geometry.

Villard has generally been thought of as a master mason who prepared a set of annotated drawings for the edification of his workshop. Recently his architectural competence has been questioned. Other suggestions are that he was a sculptor, or a metalworker, or a clerk with architectural, artistic and mechanical interests.

Whatever his trade, he tells us that he travelled to many lands, including Hungary. His sketches show that he visited modern buildings and building sites at Cambrai (near Honnecourt), Laon, Lausanne, Meaux, Reims and Vaucelles. Recent excavations at the site of the Cistercian abbey of Pilis in Hungary revealed tiles similar to those he sketched in Hungary. Whether artisan or clerk or some combination of the two, Villard was alert and well-travelled and his book shows one way in which (mainly French) visual and technical ideas were collected and, perhaps, diffused.

J. Higgitt

Westminster Palace, London

From the mid-twelfth century Westminster developed as a royal capital and governmental centre. Westminster Palace was a royal residence housing governmental offices, law courts and, often, parliament. For post-Conquest kings of England Westminster Abbey was the coronation church, the shrine church of the saint-king Edward the Confessor (canonized 1161) and, from the thirteenth century, a royal mausoleum. The multiple functions of the palace and the abbey made Westminster the centre of the English monarchy's temporal authority, the source of its spiritual and dynastic legitimacy and the setting for key royal ceremonies.

Westminster Abbey was re-founded as a Benedictine community under King Edgar (*c.* 960). Royal patronage, which was centuries older, continued with both Edward the Confessor (1042–66) and Henry III (1216–72)

rebuilding the abbey. There is, however, no firm evidence for a royal palace at Westminster until the Confessor's reign. The Conqueror's son, William Rufus, built Westminster Great Hall which at over 1500m², and spanned by Richard II's angel-lined hammerbeam roof, is still awe-inspiring. Coronation acclamations and feasts took place here and Henry III built a white marble throne on the dais. By the fourteenth century the Common Bench, King's Bench (KB) and court of Chancery (C) sat in the hall, although the law courts' enclosures, along with shops which lined the hall, were removed for key feasts. The Exchequer and Treasury were based in Westminster by 1216. Parliament too used Westminster, the Lords sitting in the Queen's Chamber and the Commons in the Abbey's chapterhouse or refectory. The primarily residential Privy Palace was expanded

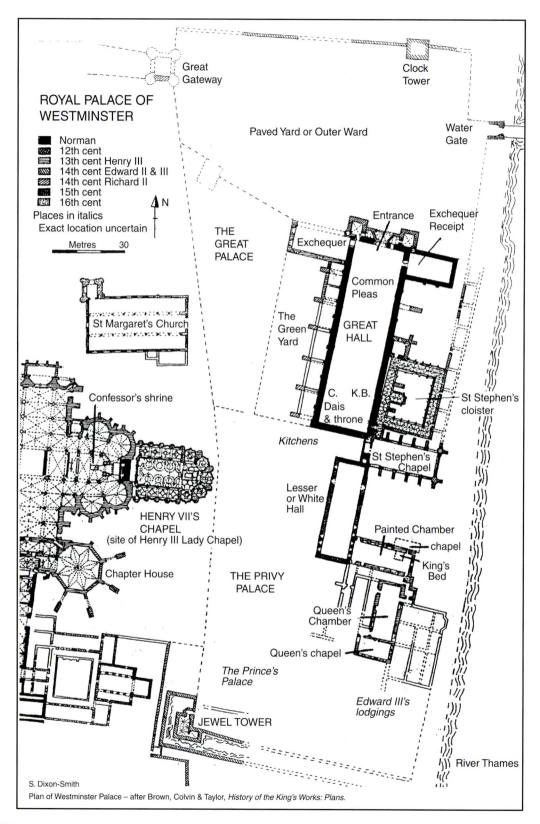

ROYAL PALACE OF
WESTMINSTER

■ Norman
▨ 12th cent
▤ 13th cent Henry III
▧ 14th cent Edward II & III
▨ 14th cent Richard II
▥ 15th cent
▩ 16th cent

Places in italics
Exact location uncertain

↑N

Metres   30

Great
Gateway

Clock
Tower

Paved Yard or Outer Ward

Water
Gate

THE
GREAT
PALACE

Entrance

Exchequer
Receipt

Exchequer

St Margaret's Church

The
Green
Yard

Common
Pleas

GREAT
HALL

St Stephen's
cloister

Confessor's shrine

C.   K.B.
Dais
& throne

Kitchens

St Stephen's
Chapel

HENRY VII'S
CHAPEL
(site of Henry III Lady Chapel)

Lesser
or White
Hall

Painted Chamber

chapel

Chapter House

THE PRIVY
PALACE

King's
Bed

Queen's
Chamber

Queen's chapel

The Prince's
Palace

Edward III's
lodgings

JEWEL TOWER

River Thames

S. Dixon-Smith

Plan of Westminster Palace – after Brown, Colvin & Taylor, *History of the King's Works: Plans.*

192

over the years but abandoned in favour of Whitehall Palace under Henry VIII. The palace's splendour is evident from the known thirteenth-century decoration of the Painted Chamber, including biblical scenes and personified Virtues trampling Vices. The present Houses of Parliament were built on the site after fire gutted the palace in 1834.

S. Dixon-Smith

La Sainte Chapelle, Paris

The Sainte Chapelle – a private chapel, built *c.* 1242–8 by Louis IX to house passion relics acquired from Baldwin II of Constantinople – is a masterpiece of gothic art and architecture. The envy of European princes, it was a model for palatine chapels in France and beyond. The perceived power and political importance of relics cannot be underestimated. Louis' acquisition of the Crown of Thorns, the ultimate symbol of Christ's royalty, was hailed by contemporaries as Christ identifying the French as the new 'chosen people' and crowning their king with Christ's own crown.

The Sainte Chapelle resembled a giant reliquary. The upper chapel, which housed the passion relics in a golden reliquary on a raised platform at the east end, resembles a great glass box, the *capella vitrea* of Arthurian legend. Every surface is encrusted with polychrome decoration, powdered with the heraldry of Louis and his mother, Blanche of Castile. The scenes depicted in the stunning $615m^2$ of stained glass run from the creation (A) to the end of time (Rose). The sequence of Old Testament history (A–E, K–N) is interrupted in the apse where the Passion is flanked by scenes from the lives and writings of New and Old Testament prophets of the Messiah. Louis' own actions (O) follow on from the actions of biblical kings (N). The first coming of Christ (H) faces the second coming (Rose). The king sat beneath Numbers (C), the scenes above dotted with apocryphal coronations, and the queen, appropriately, beneath Esther (H). Statues of apostles stand on corbels (1–12), notionally surrounding Christ represented by his relics or the king himself if he ascended the reliquary platform. Along the dado are roundels of the saints whose relics were processed out from local churches to greet the arrival of the Crown of Thorns.

Damaged by fire, flood and neglect, the chapel was extensively restored in the nineteenth century. The vast majority of the fabric and glass is original and stands as a monument to medieval craftsmanship and royal propaganda.

S. Dixon-Smith

Vernacular languages, *c.* 1200

The linguistic situation of medieval Europe is intrinsically difficult to map. This is principally because it cannot be assumed that language speakers were monolingual but also because the factors that governed language choice are social and not always recoverable today.

A useful initial distinction to make is between High-function and Low-function uses of language. High-function use covers religion, education, law and state administration: it requires codified and elaborated language. Low-function applies to conversation with family, neighbours, friends and local traders. To an extent this distinction overlaps with writing (High) and speaking (Low); but it is not the same since High-function language can be

LA SAINTE CHAPELLE, PARIS

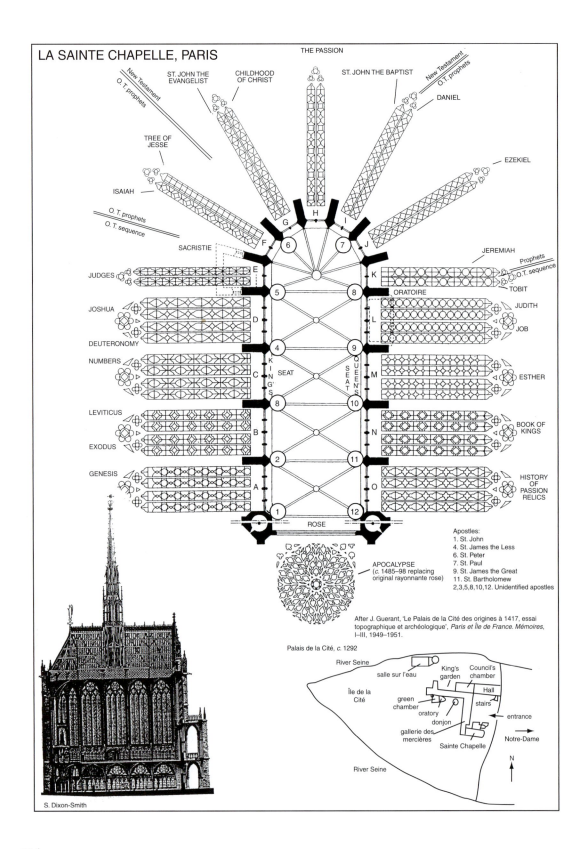

THE PASSION

ST. JOHN THE EVANGELIST

CHILDHOOD OF CHRIST

ST. JOHN THE BAPTIST

New Testament
O.T. prophets

New Testament
O.T. prophets

DANIEL

TREE OF JESSE

EZEKIEL

ISAIAH

O.T. prophets
O.T. sequence

SACRISTIE

JEREMIAH

Prophets
O.T. sequence

JUDGES

TOBIT

JUDITH

JOSHUA

ORATOIRE

JOB

DEUTERONOMY

NUMBERS

KING'S SEAT

QUEEN'S SEAT

ESTHER

LEVITICUS

BOOK OF KINGS

EXODUS

GENESIS

HISTORY OF PASSION RELICS

ROSE

APOCALYPSE
(c. 1485–98 replacing
original rayonnante rose)

Apostles:
1. St. John
4. St. James the Less
6. St. Peter
7. St. Paul
9. St. James the Great
11. St. Bartholomew
2,3,5,8,10,12. Unidentified apostles

After J. Guerant, 'Le Palais de la Cité des origines à 1417, essai
topographique et archéologique', *Paris et Île de France. Mémoires,*
I–III, 1949–1951.

Palais de la Cité, *c.* 1292

River Seine

salle sur l'eau

King's garden

Council's chamber

Île de la Cité

green chamber

oratory

Hall

stairs

entrance

donjon

Notre-Dame

gallerie des mercières

Sainte Chapelle

River Seine

N

S. Dixon-Smith

194

spoken and, for family letters and business purposes, Low-function use is in principle writable though no doubt ephemeral.

After the restriction of the Roman Empire to Byzantium, Latin was replaced by Greek as the High-function language in the East. Latin survived as the West's High-function language through the Catholic Church and through its acceptance by the rulers of the successor states. The new language of power in the West was, however, Germanic. This had an effect on the choice of Low-function language or vernacular, the languages of peoples conquered by the Romans now dying out, their speakers, with the exception of Basque and the insular Celtic, shifting to Latin or Germanic. In eastern Europe from the late sixth century Slav-speaking ethnic groups extended their influence from the Black Sea north of the Danube northwards, southwards and westwards, until their expansion was limited by Byzantium and the Franks. Latin initially survived as a Danube-frontier vernacular beyond the Daco-Romance area shown, as can be seen from the present islets of Arumanian and Megleno-Rumanian in Albania, ex-Yugoslav Macedonia and Greece. It may have been reinforced by eastwards migration from Dalmatia and Pannonia when the Slavs moved west, as the existence of Dalmatian (extinct in the 1880s) and Istro-Rumanian in Slovenia and Croatia suggest. Latin as a High-function language spread through the conversion of pagans well beyond the areas of Roman rule, reaching Ireland, Scandinavia and the Baltic, while the expansion of the Moors and Vikings and arrival of the Hungarians brought new languages of power.

Over time dialect continua, which still survive, established themselves for Latin (now Romance), Germanic and Slavonic, though the boundaries between these languages were initially fluid with, for example, islets of Romance speech surviving in the Germanic Meuse and Moselle valleys into the twelfth century and some evidence of an earlier, more easterly boundary of *franco-provençal* in the west of the canton of Fribourg. Geography and cultural differences ensured the division of Germanic initially into Norse and Germanic, while the southern Slavs were separated from other Slav-speakers by the Hungarians.

The map is intended primarily to reflect the distribution *c.* 1200 of vernaculars which had at least the social support to survive as distinct languages (Basque, Franco-Provençal, Rhaeto-Romance, Sardinian, Hungarian, Albanian, Daco-Romance) and of the remaining vernaculars which had already secured the political support allowing them to compete for High-function status. That political support could take the direct form of one political unit per vernacular, as in the case of the five Christian kingdoms of the Iberian peninsula from the earliest phases of the Reconquest. Alternatively, competing political entities sometimes had more than one language available to them, as in the British Isles. It was also possible that in larger states one language variety would in the long run be preferred, as in the selection of *langue d'oil* in France and High German in the Holy Roman Empire, reflecting the power base of the dominant rulers of these states. Finally, Norse, Italo-Romance and Slavonic were undergoing the process of fragmentation which would give rise to separate Nordic languages in Scandinavia; the emergence of first Venetian and in the fourteenth century of Tuscan in Italy; and after the Mongol invasions of the thirteenth century and the ongoing *Ostsiedlung* in the Baltic, the emergence of Russian among the eastern Slavs as a dominant variety to match Polish among the western Slavs. It was the prestige of the medieval elites and the fate of the political entities in which they exercised influence that paved the way to modern national languages.

C. Sneddon

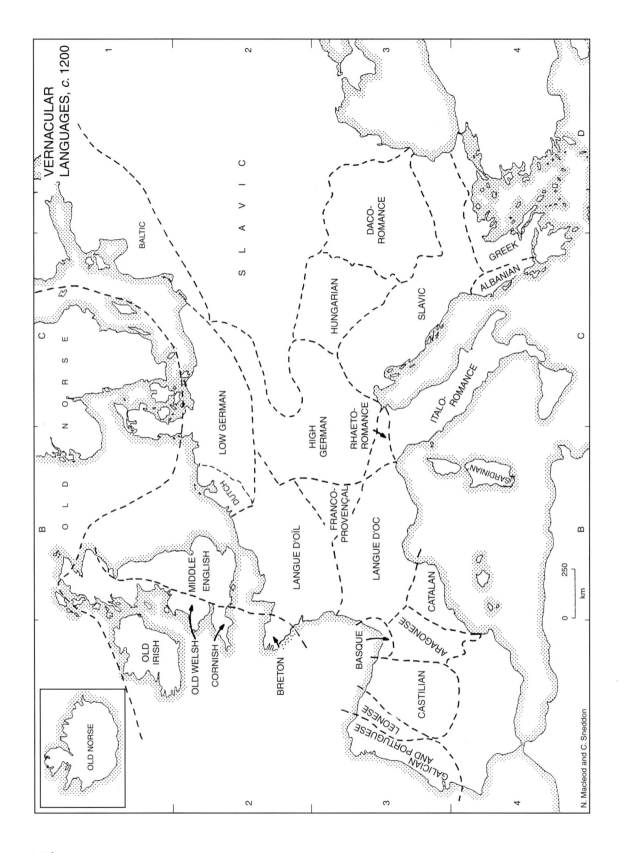

VERNACULAR LANGUAGES, c. 1200

BALTIC

S L A V I C

OLD NORSE

LOW GERMAN

HIGH GERMAN

HUNGARIAN

DACO-ROMANCE

SLAVIC

GREEK

ALBANIAN

RHAETO-ROMANCE

ITALO-ROMANCE

SARDINIAN

DUTCH

MIDDLE ENGLISH

OLD IRISH

OLD WELSH

CORNISH

BRETON

LANGUE D'OÏL

FRANCO-PROVENÇAL

LANGUE D'OC

CATALAN

ARAGONESE

BASQUE

CASTILIAN

LEONESE

GALICIAN AND PORTUGUESE

OLD NORSE

0   250
km

N. Macleod and C. Sneddon

196

Western travellers in the Far East in the 13th century

Most western European travellers to central and eastern Asia were merchants, prisoners or slaves. Apart from Marco Polo's account, dictated to Rustichello of Pisa and which swiftly captured the imagination of western Europeans, no other written report of their journeys survives. It was instead the diplomatic envoys and missionaries who left the fullest descriptions of their travels.

Before the first Council of Lyon (1245) Pope Alexander IV despatched four delegations of mendicants to the farthest known eastern regions and the court of the famed Mongol khan. Only one mission, led by Friar John de Plano Carpini, reached Güyüg Khan's court. Nevertheless, three delegations left reports of their expeditions. Andrew of Longjumeau's second journey to the East, on behalf of King Louis IX of France, inspired the missionary Friar William of Rubruck's journey in 1253.

The inclusion of works by John de Plano Carpini and Simon de St Quentin in Vincent of Beauvais' *Speculum Maius* (c. 1250), Roger Bacon's citation in *Opus Maius* (c. 1265) of William of Rubruck and John de Plano Carpini and Matthew Paris's use of Andrew of Longjumeau's text (c. 1254) demonstrate the immediate interest in travellers' stories. From these reports, especially that by William of Rubruck, western Europeans learnt about Nestorian Christians at the Mongol court, Buddhism, the landlocked Caspian Sea and Alexander's Gate, holding in the feared Gog and Magog, which had been broken.

The fourteenth and fifteenth centuries saw growing numbers of travellers to, and descriptions of, the East. Odoric of Pordenone's detailed and somewhat fantastical account of an extensive journey and the spurious, yet spiritual, *Travels of Sir John Mandeville* proved especially popular. The lasting legacy of these travellers would be the inspiration they provided Christopher Columbus and others in their search for the routes to China via the west.

S. David

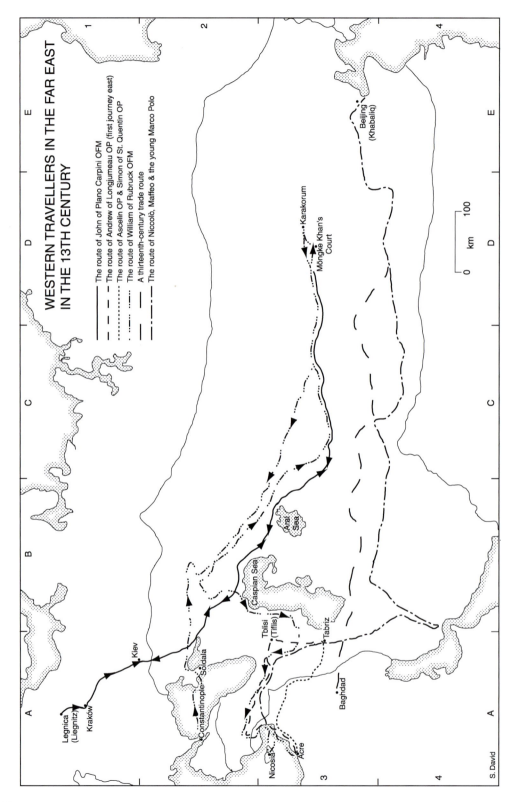

WESTERN TRAVELLERS IN THE FAR EAST
IN THE 13TH CENTURY

---- The route of John of Plano Carpini OFM
--- The route of Andrew of Longjumeau OP (first journey east)
····· The route of Ascelin OP & Simon of St. Quentin OP
-··-· The route of William of Rubruck OFM
—— A thirteenth-century trade route
-···- The route of Niccolò, Maffeo & the young Marco Polo

0   km   100

Legnica
(Liegnitz)
Krakόw
Kiev
Sόldaia
Constantinople
Nicosia
Acre
Tbilisi
(Tiflis)
Baghdad
Tabriz
Caspian Sea
Aral Sea
Karakorum
Mōngke Khan's
Court
Beijing
(Khanbaliq)

S. David

198

THE LATE MIDDLE AGES
c. 1300–*c.* 1500

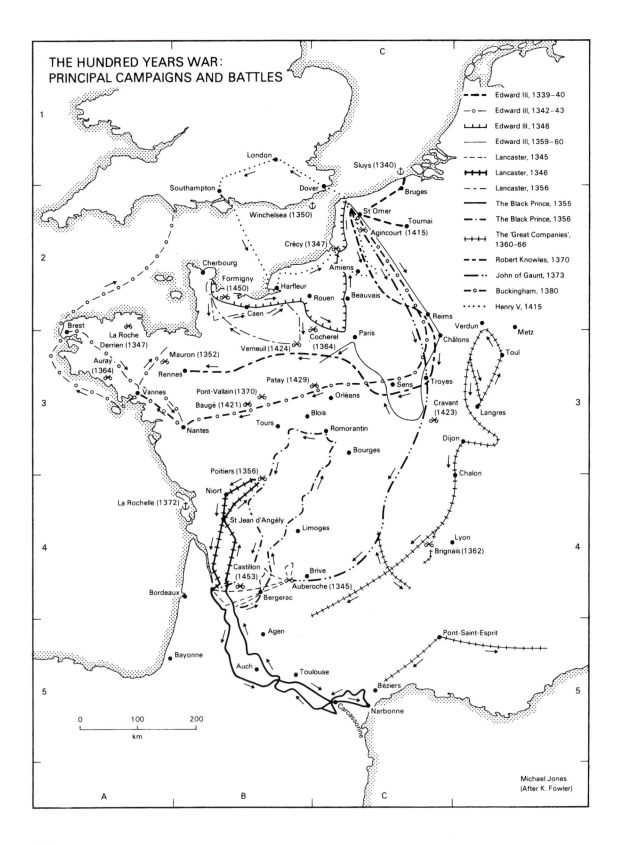

THE HUNDRED YEARS WAR:
PRINCIPAL CAMPAIGNS AND BATTLES

Edward III, 1339–40	
Edward III, 1342–43	
Edward III, 1346	
Edward III, 1359–60	
Lancaster, 1345	
Lancaster, 1346	
Lancaster, 1356	
The Black Prince, 1355	
The Black Prince, 1356	
The 'Great Companies', 1360–66	
Robert Knowles, 1370	
John of Gaunt, 1373	
Buckingham, 1380	
Henry V, 1415	

London
Southampton
Dover
Winchelsea (1350)
Sluys (1340)
Bruges
St Omer
Tournai
Agincourt (1415)
Crécy (1347)
Amiens
Cherbourg
Formigny (1450)
Harfleur
Rouen
Beauvais
Caen
Reims
Verdun
Metz
Brest
La Roche
Derrien (1347)
Cocherel (1364)
Paris
Châlons
Toul
Mauron (1352)
Verneuil (1424)
Auray (1364)
Rennes
Patay (1429)
Sens
Troyes
Langres
Vannes
Pont-Vallain (1370)
Orléans
Cravant (1423)
Baugé (1421)
Nantes
Tours
Blois
Romorantin
Dijon
Bourges
Chalon
Poitiers (1356)
Niort
La Rochelle (1372)
St Jean d'Angély
Limoges
Lyon
Brignais (1362)
Castillon (1453)
Brive
Bordeaux
Auberoche (1345)
Bergerac
Agen
Pont-Saint-Esprit
Bayonne
Auch
Toulouse
Béziers
Carcassonne
Narbonne

0   100   200
km

Michael Jones
(After K. Fowler)

WAR AND POLITICS

The Hundred Years War

The long-term causes of 'the Hundred Years War' (a description for the conflicts traditionally covering the years 1337–1453) lay in the claims of the king of France, following the treaty of Paris (1259), to sovereignty over the duchy of Guyenne (or Aquitaine), then held by his liege vassal, the king of England. Difficulties in implementing this complex treaty and subsidiary agreements (Amiens, 1279; Paris, 1303), allied to a more precise definition of sovereign rights, provoked conflict. In 1294 Philip IV declared Guyenne forfeit and invaded the duchy. Although peace was soon restored and diplomats tried to resolve the long-standing problems, these efforts failed as both sides became entrenched in their positions. In 1324 Guyenne was again confiscated and, although peace was agreed in 1327, the French handed back a diminished duchy (holding on to the Agenais) and demanded reparations. Nor was tension subsequently eased by the Process of Agen (1332). By now other causes intensified ill-feeling. The French alliance with Scotland, first formed in 1295, was renewed and resulted in French intervention in support of King David II and a series of English invasions of Scotland between 1332 and 1337. There was rivalry for allies in the Netherlands, where economic factors were important because of the Anglo-Flemish wool trade. At sea, piracy and naval activities, connected with French crusading plans, exacerbated bad relations.

The extinction of the Capetian dynasty in the direct line (1328) was a turning point because it allowed Edward III to claim the crown of France. At the time Philip of Valois, the nearest adult male claimant, was preferred as king. Edward, under the tutelage of Isabella and Mortimer, performed homage for his French lands. But after further efforts to resolve arguments over Guyenne, Edward undermined the basis on which Anglo-French relations had been predicated by claiming the crown of France. This he did tentatively and momentarily in 1337, then more permanently from January 1340. This may have been pure expediency but it has been pointed out that Edward's strategy up to 1360 suggests that he increasingly believed in his claim, even that the crown was almost within his grasp following spectacular victories at Crécy (1346) and Poitiers (1356). In any event, once adopted, the title 'king of France' was incorporated into the royal style until George III renounced it in 1801, apart from 1360–9 when an attempt was made to implement the treaty of Brétigny (1360) which ended the first major phase of the war.

If completed, this treaty would have given the English an enlarged and sovereign Guyenne, including Poitou, Saintonge, Périgord, Quercy and the Rouergue, vindicating Edward's resort to force. After a false start that had brought little advantage from campaigns in the Low Countries and which indeed led to bankruptcy, the opening of the Breton succession war (1341–64) and campaigns in Normandy and Guyenne saw the fame of English arms and chivalry spread throughout Europe. In 1359 Edward even prepared for his coronation at Reims but the failure of this campaign led to renewed negotiations with John II, captured at Poitiers, and to the partition of France in the treaty of Brétigny.

Failure to implement this treaty led to a renewal of war in 1369. Charles V quickly won most of the lands his father had lost, leaving English Guyenne reduced to a rump around Bordeaux and Bayonne. The effort to drive the

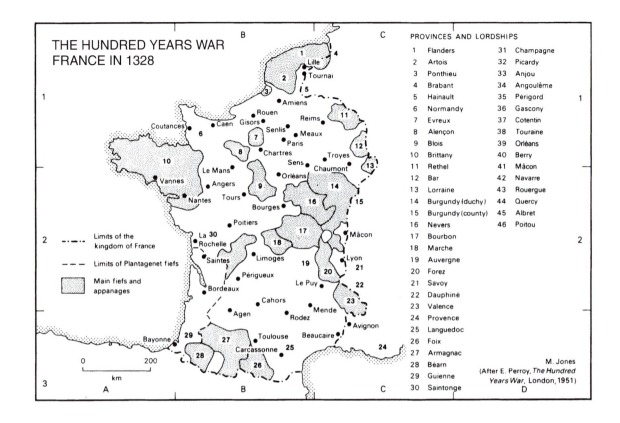

THE HUNDRED YEARS WAR
FRANCE IN 1328

	PROVINCES AND LORDSHIPS		
1	Flanders	31	Champagne
2	Artois	32	Picardy
3	Ponthieu	33	Anjou
4	Brabant	34	Angoulême
5	Hainault	35	Périgord
6	Normandy	36	Gascony
7	Evreux	37	Cotentin
8	Alençon	38	Touraine
9	Blois	39	Orléans
10	Brittany	40	Berry
11	Rethel	41	Mâcon
12	Bar	42	Navarre
13	Lorraine	43	Rouergue
14	Burgundy (duchy)	44	Quercy
15	Burgundy (county)	45	Albret
16	Nevers	46	Poitou
17	Bourbon		
18	Marche		
19	Auvergne		
20	Forez		
21	Savoy		
22	Dauphiné		
23	Valence		
24	Provence		
25	Languedoc		
26	Foix		
27	Armagnac		
28	Béarn		
29	Guienne		
30	Saintonge		

Limits of the kingdom of France

Limits of Plantagenet fiefs

Main fiefs and appanages

0   200
km

M. Jones
(After E. Perroy, *The Hundred Years War*, London, 1951)

English out completely proved, however, to be beyond the means of a war-torn country. With bases at Calais, Cherbourg and Brest, and the alliance, uncertain though it often was, of French princes like the count of Flanders, duke of Brittany or king of Navarre (who held extensive lands in northern France), the English continued to maintain a presence. Moreover, from the start both sides had involved their neighbours and war flared up elsewhere, notably after 1365 in the Iberian Peninsula.

The war developed a momentum of its own. Many participated for profit or excitement. From the 1340s both kings found it hard to control troops who recognized their distant authority. Parts of northern, central and south-western France especially, although no area was entirely spared, suffered from a lawless soldiery. For a period in the 1350s and 1360s bands of English, Breton, Gascon, Navarrese, German and other mercenaries (or *routiers*) pursued private gain and formed the Great Companies

which even tyrannized the pope at Avignon and defeated the duke of Bourbon at Brignais (1362). Civil wars in Flanders and Brittany or conflicts between powerful nobles added to the violence. Independent captains set up garrisons in districts between zones of English or French allegiance and cruelly exploited the population. Uprisings like the Jacquerie (1358) and the Tuchinat (from the 1360s) were fuelled by the distress caused by the *routiers*. The same phenomenon affected widespread regions from the 1420s when the freebooters earned the name of 'flayers' (*écorcheurs*). It was in this form that many people experienced the reality of war; others were victims of the great *chevauchées* launched by the English; others suffered in the long sieges of which those of Calais (1346–7), Rennes (1356–7), St-Sauveur (1374–5), Rouen (1418–19) and Orléans (1428–9) are the best known.

The pattern of short campaigns or longer sieges interspersed with truces and negoti-

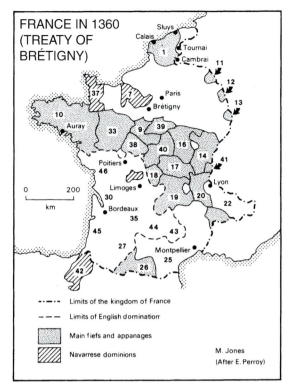

FRANCE IN 1360
(TREATY OF
BRÉTIGNY)

- ·—·—·—· Limits of the kingdom of France
- —— —— —— Limits of English domination
- [grey] Main fiefs and appanages
- [hatched] Navarrese dominions

M. Jones
(After E. Perroy)

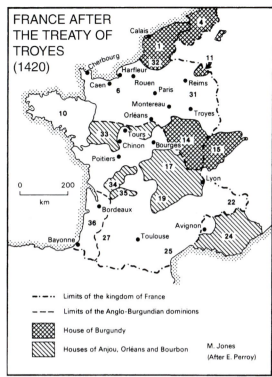

FRANCE AFTER
THE TREATY OF
TROYES
(1420)

- ·—·—·—· Limits of the kingdom of France
- —— —— —— Limits of the Anglo-Burgundian dominions
- [crosshatched] House of Burgundy
- [hatched] Houses of Anjou, Orléans and Bourbon

M. Jones
(After E. Perroy)

ations, established from the first years of the war, most obviously shaped events from 1369 to 1415. Richard II did not pursue with conviction the conflict he inherited but looked for peace. A twenty-eight-year truce came into force in 1398. Henry IV was largely prevented from reopening the war by revolts and illness but Henry V had few qualms about the justice of his cause. After his request that the terms of Brétigny be fulfilled was rejected, he launched the *chevauchée* that culminated in victory at Agincourt (1415). Thereafter, taking advantage of French divisions, he determined on a systematic conquest beginning with Normandy (1417–19). In 1419 the murder of John the Fearless, duke of Burgundy, drove his successor, Philip the Good, into an English alliance, delivered Paris to Henry and enabled him to attempt a novel solution to the war.

If it can be argued that up to 1419 Henry worked within the Brétigny tradition of trying to obtain extensive territories in full sovereignty (for which the claim to the French crown might

be seen as a cloak), in 1420 he adopted a new approach. In the treaty of Troyes Henry agreed with Queen Isabella and the Burgundians to disinherit the dauphin – the future Charles VII – and to marry Catherine, daughter of Charles VI, thus settling the crown on them and their issue and forming the double monarchy of England and France. Henry's premature death, two months before that of Charles VI (1422), leaving the infant Henry VI, ruined the chances of this audacious plan, though Henry VI was later crowned king at Paris (1431). The revival of the fortunes of Charles VII, 'the king of Bourges', slowly wore down English resistance. Too much significance should not be attached to Joan of Arc's exploits, such as the relief of Orléans (May 1429), but the French monarchy's renewed confidence, seen in the coronation which followed, was buoyed up by the defection of the Burgundians from their English allegiance in the treaty of Arras (1435). In 1436 Paris was recaptured by Constable Richemont, whilst from 1439 financial reforms also prepared the way for the restoration of royal authority. In England support for the war was at a low ebb. In 1444 a new truce was agreed at Tours. Henry VI undertook to marry Charles VII's niece and to return Maine. By 1449 Charles was ready to launch his reformed army. A brilliant campaign saw the reconquests of Normandy (1449–50). In 1451 Guyenne capitulated and, although it reverted to the English in 1452, resources dispatched for its defence proved inadequate. In 1453 the veteran commander John Talbot, earl of Shrewsbury, who with a handful of other outstanding captains had propped up the occupation of Normandy since 1422, was defeated and killed at Castillon in the last major battle of the war. Bordeaux yielded in October; no peace was sealed but the war was over. Beginning as a quarrel between lord and vassal, it had long since become a conflict between 'autonomous and self-contained kingdoms . . . and Frenchmen and Englishmen began to hate one another as Englishmen and Frenchmen' (Le Patourel).

M. Jones

The growth of the Burgundian state

The rise and fall of this state under its Valois dukes – Philip the Bold (1363–1404), John the Fearless (1404–19), Philip the Good (1419–67) and Charles the Bold (1467–77) – was a spectacular development. When the last Capetian duke of Burgundy died (1361), his lands escheated to the French crown and John II conferred the duchy on his youngest son, Philip (1363). His fortunes were further enhanced when he married the late duke's widow (1369) because she was heiress to the counties of Flanders, Artois, Rethel, Nevers and Burgundy. After almost fifty years of scheming and indirect influence in Brabant, this duchy together with that of Limbourg fell into Philip the Good's hands (1430). In 1421 he had purchased the county of Namur and between 1428 and 1433 he inherited the counties of Hainault, Holland and Zeeland. In 1443 he made good claims to the duchy of Luxembourg. In the south, in addition to the duchy and county of Burgundy, the county of Charolais was bought (1390) and John the Fearless acquired those of Tonnerre and Mâcon. Burgundian influence was also felt in many of the enclaves and prince-bishoprics along the border between France and the Empire, especially when ducal bastards were appointed as bishops. Thus, partly by dynastic accident and partly through deliberate policy, the dukes controlled a large complex of territories. These extended some 500 miles from north to south and between 150 and 250 miles from east to west at their maximum, though the two main blocs centring on Flanders and the Low Countries and on the two Burgundies were usually separated by a gap of c. 150 miles. Charles the Bold in particular tried to bridge this by acquiring intervening lands – bringing him into conflict with his neighbours, especially in Bar, Lorraine and Alsace.

Held together largely by personal ties between the duke (or his family) and the separate territories, including the highly urbanized Low Countries and the rich agricultural and human resources of Burgundy, the state remained primarily a dynastic creation though it developed certain institutions enabling the duke to exercise rule more effectively throughout his lands. A common currency was created (1433). Estates General were held. Representatives from every quarter could be found at court or in the duke's council and administration. The chivalric order of the Golden Fleece (1430) focused the loyalty of the high nobility of blood and service from all over the duke's dominions. For contemporaries Philip the Good or Charles the Bold was 'the great duke of the west' (*le grand duc du Ponant*). With more than three million subjects, the dukes had enormous resources of wealth and manpower. Their

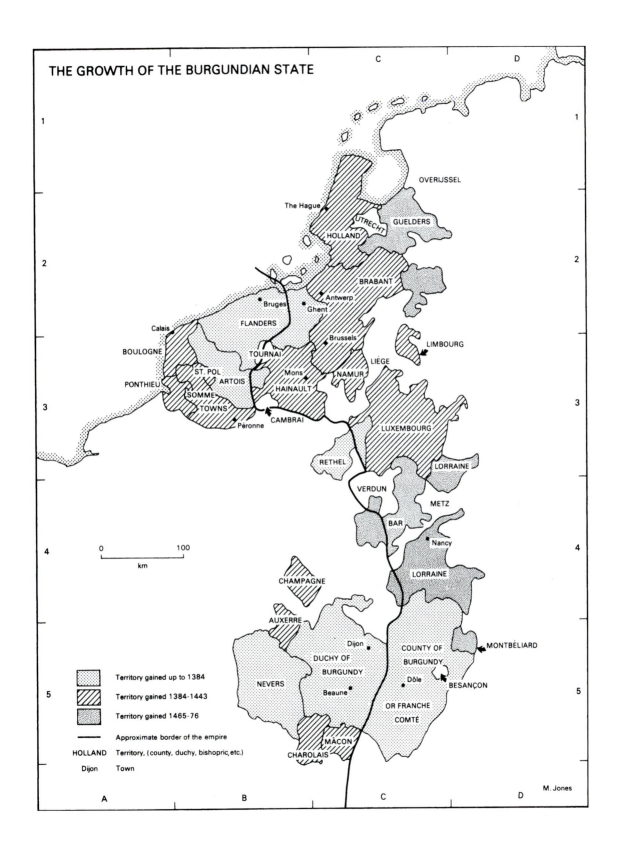

THE GROWTH OF THE BURGUNDIAN STATE

OVERIJSSEL

The Hague

UTRECHT

GUELDERS

HOLLAND

BRABANT

Antwerp

Bruges

Ghent

FLANDERS

Calais

Brussels

BOULOGNE

LIMBOURG

TOURNAI

LIÈGE

ST. POL

Mons

ARTOIS

NAMUR

PONTHIEU

HAINAULT

SOMME

TOWNS

Péronne

CAMBRAI

LUXEMBOURG

RETHEL

VERDUN

LORRAINE

METZ

BAR

Nancy

0   100

km

CHAMPAGNE

LORRAINE

AUXERRE

MONTBÉLIARD

Dijon

COUNTY OF

BURGUNDY

DUCHY OF

BURGUNDY

Dôle

BESANÇON

NEVERS

Beaune

OR FRANCHE

COMTÉ

Territory gained up to 1384

Territory gained 1384-1443

Territory gained 1465-76

Approximate border of the empire

HOLLAND   Territory, (county, duchy, bishopric, etc.)

Dijon   Town

MÂCON

CHAROLAIS

M. Jones

205

prestige equalled that of ancient kingdoms and aspirations for a crown first clearly emerged with Philip the Good in the 1440s. Under Charles it seemed that a new Middle Kingdom would appear. In 1473 Charles even had his coronation robes made in preparation for an interview at Trier with Emperor Frederick III, who was expected to decree his elevation. Sadly deceived when Frederick secretly left without a formal declaration, Charles redoubled his efforts to capture the duchy of Lorraine. Defeated by the Swiss (at Morat and Granson, 1476) and the Lorrainers (at Nancy, 1477), who were urged on by Louis XI of France and assisted by Charles's many enemies in the Rhineland and elsewhere, Charles's death before Nancy (5 January 1477) signalled the end of the Valois duchy. The main beneficiaries were the French king, who repossessed all the duke's French fiefs except Flanders, and the house of Habsburg. Charles's only heiress, Mary, desperate for protection against French aggression, married Maximilian, son of Frederick III (August 1477). Despite internal disputes in the Low Countries and Mary's premature death (1482), Maximilian managed to preserve the imperial fiefs of Burgundy, together with Flanders. Ephemeral and personal, the Valois duchy of Burgundy yet left an important heritage to successor states. Belgian and Dutch historians, in particular, have seen the period of Valois rule as decisive in the development of their nations.

M. Jones

The Scottish Wars of Independence

Edward I of England's efforts to take over Scotland in the 1290s sparked a long sequence of cross-border invasions and raids punctuated by some devastating battles; but neither side could force the other to give in. The main war zone stretched across middle Britain, roughly from the Tyne north to the Forth. But the regions beyond that zone were perhaps more significant: Scottish raids could never get far enough south to put unbearable pressure on the English Crown (nor, though it was tried in 1315, could that be done via Ireland); conversely, it was beyond English power permanently to dominate Scotland north of the Forth, yet without that Scotland could never be conquered. This was understood by Edward I, whose northern campaigns of 1296 and 1303 (map A) produced massive (but temporary) Scottish submissions; and by Robert I (Robert Bruce), whose great achievements in the south – including victory at Bannockburn (1314), and English recognition of Scottish independence (1328) – were only possible after he had won northern Scotland from his English and Scottish enemies (1307–13) (map A). And when the war reopened in 1332 after Robert I's death, Edward III soon accepted the impossibility of conquering the north; instead, he overran and annexed about half of southern Scotland (map B). By the later fourteenth century, the main issue in Anglo–Scottish warfare (border raiding apart) was the Scottish recapture of this English-held territory. It was mostly achieved by 1384, and thereafter the warfare gradually petered out. But some places stayed in English hands until well into the fifteenth century; the last to be regained by the Scots was Berwick, in 1461 – which was lost again, permanently, in 1482 (map B).

A. Grant

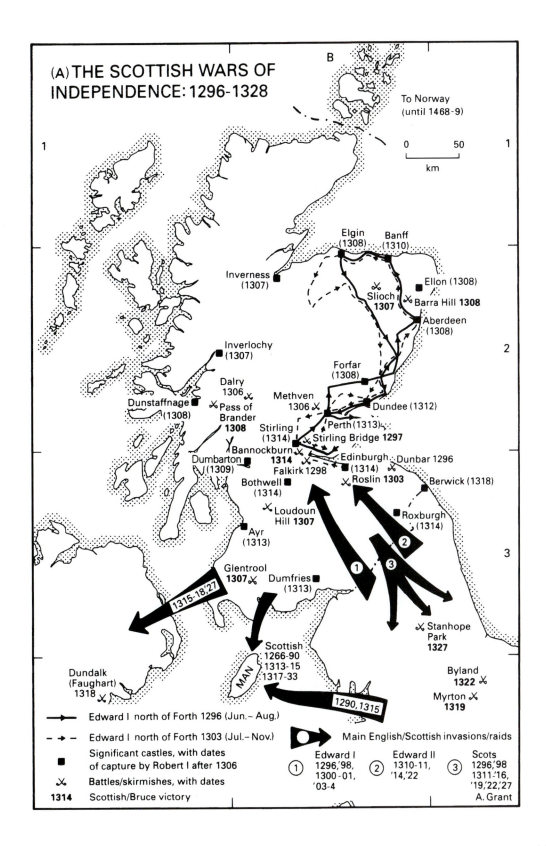

(A) THE SCOTTISH WARS OF INDEPENDENCE: 1296-1328

B

To Norway
(until 1468-9)

0   50
km

Elgin (1308)
Banff (1310)
Inverness (1307)
Ellon (1308)
Slioch 1307
Barra Hill 1308
Aberdeen (1308)
Inverlochy (1307)
Forfar (1308)
Dalry 1306
Methven 1306
Dundee (1312)
Dunstaffnage (1308)
Pass of Brander 1308
Perth (1313)
Stirling (1314)
Stirling Bridge 1297
Bannockburn 1314
Edinburgh (1314)
Dunbar 1296
Dumbarton (1309)
Falkirk 1298
Roslin 1303
Berwick (1318)
Bothwell (1314)
Roxburgh (1314)
Loudoun Hill 1307
Ayr (1313)
Glentrool 1307
Dumfries (1313)
1315-18,'27
Stanhope Park 1327
Dundalk (Faughart) 1318
Scottish 1266-90 1313-15 1317-33
MAN
Byland 1322
Myrton 1319
1290, 1315

➤——— Edward I north of Forth 1296 (Jun.–Aug.)

–➤– – Edward I north of Forth 1303 (Jul.–Nov.)

■   Significant castles, with dates
    of capture by Robert I after 1306

✗   Battles/skirmishes, with dates

1314   Scottish/Bruce victory

▶   Main English/Scottish invasions/raids

① Edward I
1296,'98,
1300-01,
'03-4

② Edward II
1310-11,
'14,'22

③ Scots
1296,'98
1311-'16,
'19,'22,'27

A. Grant

207

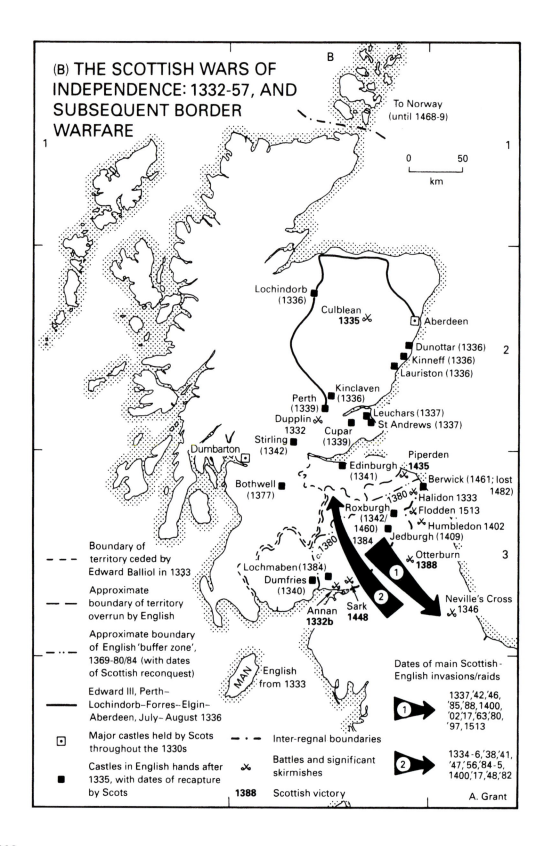

(B) THE SCOTTISH WARS OF INDEPENDENCE: 1332-57, AND SUBSEQUENT BORDER WARFARE

B

To Norway
(until 1468-9)

0   50
km

Lochindorb
(1336)

Culblean
1335

Aberdeen

Dunottar (1336)
Kinneff (1336)
Lauriston (1336)

Kinclaven
(1336)

Perth
(1339)

Dupplin
1332

Cupar
(1339)

Leuchars (1337)
St Andrews (1337)

Stirling
(1342)

Piperden
1435

Dumbarton

Edinburgh
(1341)

Berwick (1461; lost
1482)

Bothwell
(1377)

1380

Halidon 1333

Roxburgh
(1342/
1460)
1384

Flodden 1513

Humbledon 1402

Jedburgh (1409)

c.1380

Otterburn
1388

Lochmaben (1384)
Dumfries
(1340)

1

2

Neville's Cross
1346

Annan
1332b

Sark
1448

MAN

English
from 1333

Dates of main Scottish-
English invasions/raids

1

1337,'42,'46,
'85,'88, 1400,
'02,'17,'63,'80,
'97, 1513

Boundary of
territory ceded by
Edward Balliol in 1333

Approximate
boundary of territory
overrun by English

Approximate boundary
of English 'buffer zone',
1369-80/84 (with dates
of Scottish reconquest)

Edward III, Perth–
Lochindorb–Forres--Elgin–
Aberdeen, July–August 1336

2

1334-6,'38,'41,
'47,'56,'84-5,
1400,'17,'48,'82

Major castles held by Scots
throughout the 1330s

Inter-regnal boundaries

Castles in English hands after
1335, with dates of recapture
by Scots

Battles and significant
skirmishes

1388   Scottish victory

A. Grant

208

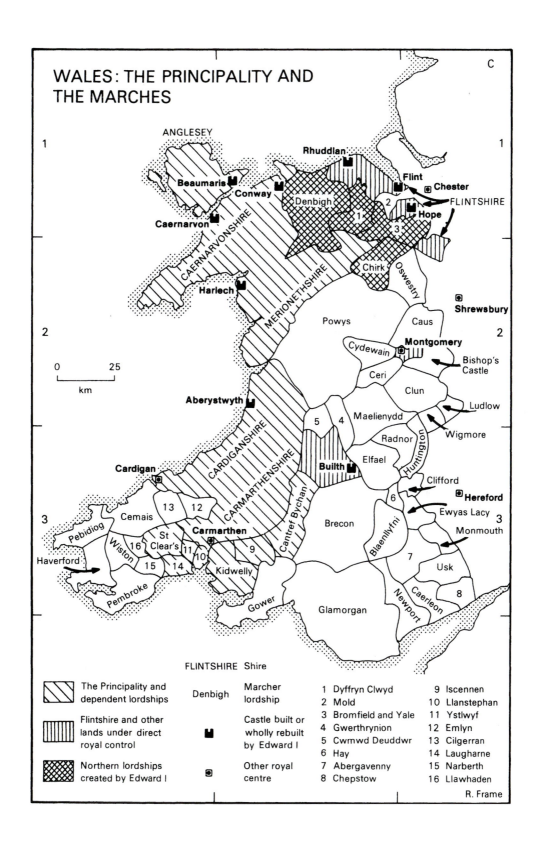

WALES: THE PRINCIPALITY AND
THE MARCHES

ANGLESEY

Rhuddlan

Beaumaris
Conway
Flint
Chester
FLINTSHIRE
Caernarvon
Denbigh
1
2
Hope
3

CAERNARVONSHIRE

Harlech

MERIONETHSHIRE

Chirk
Oswestry

Powys
Caus
Shrewsbury

Cydewain
Montgomery

Ceri
Bishop's
Castle

Clun
Aberystwyth

5   4   Maelienydd
Ludlow
Wigmore

Radnor

CARDIGANSHIRE

Builth
Elfael

Clifford
Hereford
Cardigan
Huntington

6
Ewyas Lacy
Monmouth
Cemais
13   12
Brecon
Blaenllyfni

Pebidiog
St
Clear's
Carmarthen
7
Usk

CARMARTHENSHIRE

Cantref Bychan

16   11
Wiston
9
Haverford
15   14
Kidwelly
8

Pembroke
Caerleon

Gower
Newport

Glamorgan

FLINTSHIRE Shire

		1 Dyffryn Clwyd	9 Iscennen
The Principality and dependent lordships	Denbigh Marcher lordship	2 Mold	10 Llanstephan
Flintshire and other lands under direct royal control	Castle built or wholly rebuilt by Edward I	3 Bromfield and Yale	11 Ystlwyf
		4 Gwerthrynion	12 Emlyn
		5 Cwmwd Deuddwr	13 Cilgerran
Northern lordships created by Edward I	Other royal centre	6 Hay	14 Laugharne
		7 Abergavenny	15 Narberth
		8 Chepstow	16 Llawhaden

R. Frame

Wales: the Principality and the Marches

During most of the thirteenth century the balance of territorial advantage between the Welsh rulers, the Marcher lords and the Crown had constantly shifted. But two broad tendencies were apparent: the growing assertiveness of royal government and the emergence of the princes of Gwynedd as effective overlords of native Wales. These developments helped to make the Welsh war of 1282–3 far more radical in its effects than its many predecessors. Edward I evicted Llywelyn ap Gruffydd from north Wales and seized his principality for the Crown; the takeover was aided by the firmer structure that Gwynedd had recently developed and by the defection of members of its ministerial class.

Edward's victory saw the former heartland of Llywelyn's power organized into the shires of Anglesey, Caernarvon and Merioneth, now controlled from Caernarvon by an English justiciar and chamberlain. Royal castles, often accompanied by boroughs where English settlement was promoted, were built at strategic points. This new area of Crown authority, with Edward's conquests in west Wales and the old royal lordships of Cardigan and Carmarthen, formed the Principality, which from 1301 was usually bestowed upon the king's eldest son. In the north-east, apart from the county of Flint which was ruled from Chester, most of the gains were distributed to English aristocrats, who also built castles, established boroughs and displaced native populations. This added to the mosaic of jurisdictionally privileged Marcher lordships which already occupied most of south Wales and the borders. In the Late Middle Ages there were some Welsh risings but only that of Owain Glyn Dŵr in the reign of Henry IV was other than localized and transient. In the more stable political conditions the Principality and the Marches were available for economic exploitation by the English Crown and nobility, with whom the Welsh squirearchy – displaying an intriguing mixture of careerism and resentment – took service.

R. Frame

Ireland: English and Gaelic lordship, *c.* 1350

Whereas in the Late Middle Ages the Welsh political map tended towards greater neatness and stability, that of Ireland remained fluid. In the mid-thirteenth century Ireland had probably seemed more firmly within English control than Wales: English lords dominated about three-quarters of the country and there was no single centre of native rule to match Gwynedd. In the age of Edward I, when royal administration was growing at the expense of baronial jurisdictions and the Dublin government was raising men, money and provisions for the Welsh and Scottish wars, the situation might still have been regarded with some satisfaction from Westminster.

The fourteenth century saw English Ireland weakened by famine, plague, emigration, the division of lordships among absentee heiresses, Scottish invasion and the growth of Gaelic military capacity close to Dublin. The retreat was slow and patchy. Even at the height of English power not just the unshired north and the western fringes but also enclaves of upland and bog in southern and eastern Ireland had remained Irish in culture and subject only to superficial influence. In the Late Middle Ages the areas of Gaelic custom and lordship expanded. But it should not be imagined that English rule was restricted to the hinterland of Dublin and a few coastal towns; even in the late fifteenth century – the era of the 'Pale' – the contraction was never so drastic. Royal authority penetrated,

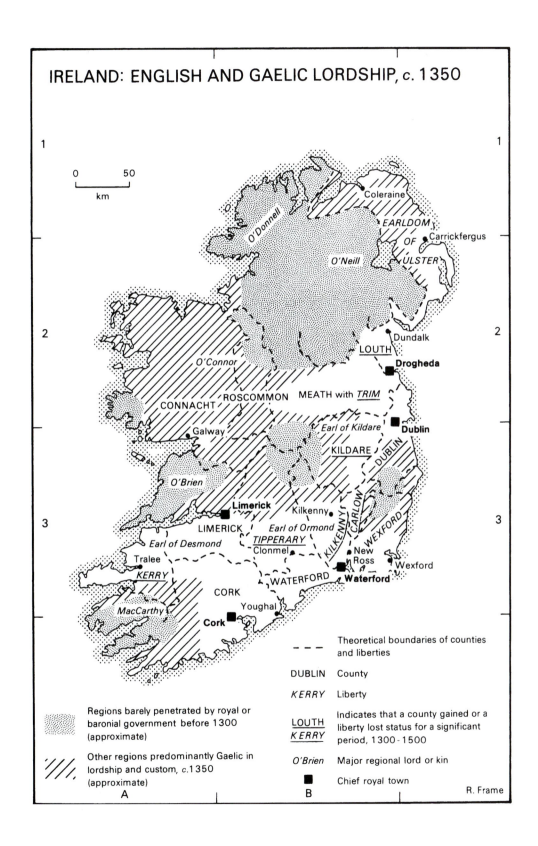

IRELAND: ENGLISH AND GAELIC LORDSHIP, c. 1350

0   50
km

O'Donnell

Coleraine

EARLDOM

OF

Carrickfergus

O'Neill   *ULSTER*

Dundalk

LOUTH

Drogheda

O'Connor

ROSCOMMON   MEATH with *TRIM*

CONNACHT

Galway

Earl of Kildare   **Dublin**

KILDARE

DUBLIN

O'Brien

Limerick

Kilkenny

CARLOW

WEXFORD

LIMERICK   *Earl of Ormond*

Earl of Desmond   *TIPPERARY*

Clonmel

New Ross   Wexford

Tralee

KERRY

WATERFORD   **Waterford**

CORK

Youghal

MacCarthy

Cork

– – –   Theoretical boundaries of counties and liberties

DUBLIN   County

KERRY   Liberty

<u>LOUTH</u>
<u>*KERRY*</u>   Indicates that a county gained or a liberty lost status for a significant period, 1300 - 1500

O'Brien   Major regional lord or kin

■   Chief royal town

Regions barely penetrated by royal or baronial government before 1300 (approximate)

Other regions predominantly Gaelic in lordship and custom, *c*.1350 (approximate)

A   B   R. Frame

however unevenly and indirectly, into a sizeable world where gentry communities, urban elites, Anglo-Irish magnates, and Gaelic lords co-existed in complex local balances and where English and Irish custom interacted. Across the official administrative divisions lay other boundaries and zones of command whose

informal and shifting character makes them impossible to depict precisely. The map pro-vides a – necessarily impressionistic – view of the gulf between the theoretical extent of royal administration and the regions actually subject to English law and government.

R. Frame

The emergence of Switzerland

The 1291 pact between the cantons of Uri, Schwyz and Nidwalden, later joined by Ob-walden, traditionally marks the birth of Switz-erland. Motivated by the desire to constrain Habsburg overlordship, this was probably the revival of an older alliance. After 1291 the cantons successfully played the Habsburgs off against other imperial families and in 1315 they defeated the Habsburgs at Morgarten. To further secure their quasi-autonomous status,

allies were sought and Lucerne, a town closely connected economically and ecclesiastically, joined in 1332. Temporary alliances with Zurich, Zug and Glarus, all wary of Habsburg intentions, were made permanent shortly after-wards. Bern, a less obvious ally, joined in 1352. For the next century and a half the eight cantons (sometimes together, sometimes on their own) were embroiled in wars, some defensive, some expansionist. Habsburg power

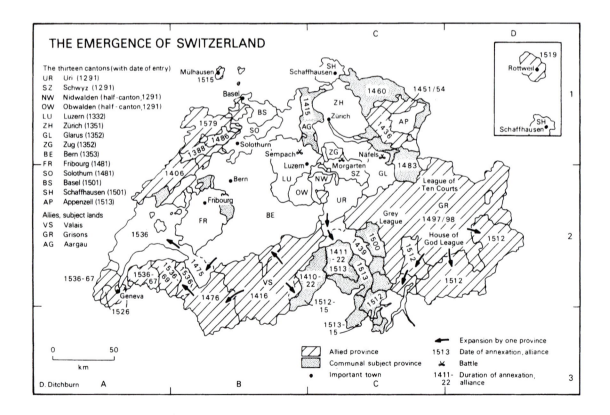

was further limited by victories at Sempach (1386) and Näfels (1388), and the joint cantonal occupation of Aargau in 1415. Victory in the Swabian War of 1499 confirmed Switzerland's *de facto* independence from the Empire. Bern's chief preoccupation was in the west, where it clashed with Burgundy. Not until Duke Charles the Bold's defeat and death at Nancy, in 1477, was this threat removed. Uri spearheaded southern expansion. Swiss participation in the Holy League secured the acquisition of the Ticinese provinces from Milan in 1512–13. Swiss influence also grew through a series of alliances with neighbouring provinces. There was reluctance, however, to admit new cantons. Fribourg and Solothurn joined in 1481, following their support in the Burgundian wars, while Basel and Schaffhausen, allies in the Swabian War, joined in 1501. Appenzell was only admitted in 1513. Unity was, however, originally based only on the desire to maintain cantonal independence. Initially there were no central institutions and cantonal interests frequently clashed. Yet, because of military success, the fragile unity of the unusual alliance between towns and rural communities was preserved.

D. Ditchburn

Late medieval Scandinavia

In 1360–1 the Danish king Valdemar Atterdag conquered Scania from Sweden and then Öland and Gotland. This provoked war with the Hanse, which perceived a threat to its commercial interests. Although Valdemar was supported by his son-in-law, Hakon VI of Norway, the Hanse

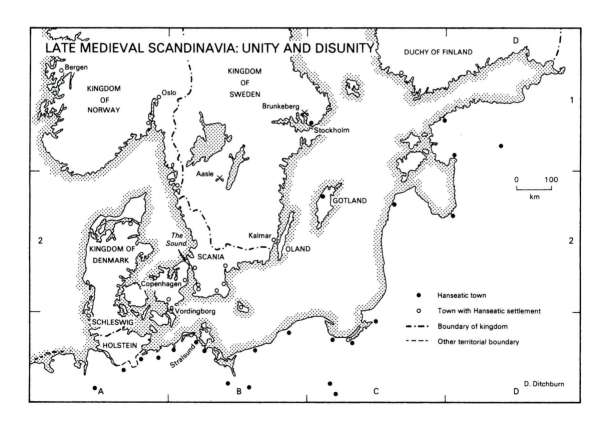

213

triumphed. Its domination of Scandinavia was confirmed by the peace of Stralsund (1370). Following further conflict with Denmark over the imposition of shipping tolls at the Sound, the peace of Vordingborg (1435) reaffirmed Hanseatic commercial privileges. Thereafter, faced with growing Dutch competition and renewed Danish hostility, the Hanse maintained its commercial domination of Scandinavia with difficulty. In 1387 Valdemar's formidable daughter Margaret had become regent of Denmark and Norway. At the invitation of discontented magnates, she invaded Sweden, defeating the Swedish king Albrecht at Aasle in 1389. Stockholm submitted in 1395 and the Scandinavian kingdoms were formally united by the Union of Kalmar in 1397. Gotland was conquered in 1409 while in 1460 King Christian I was also elected duke of Schleswig and Holstein. Nevertheless, the growth of royal power had its limitations.

Orkney and Shetland were ceded to Scotland in 1468–9. In Denmark and Sweden the monarchy remained elective. Powerful magnates, in particular, resented the imposition of heavier taxation and the appointment of foreign and non-noble officials. Discontent was greatest in Sweden. Revolts there were led by Engelbrecht Engelbrechtson and Karl Knutson, who was elected King Charles VIII of Sweden in 1448. The revolts were suppressed in 1457 but resumed in 1464. After the Swedish regent Sten Sture defeated the Danes at Brunkeberg in 1471, the Danish kings Christian I and John struggled to maintain their authority in Sweden. They received support from their kinsman, James IV of Scotland, and took advantage of divisions among the Swedish nobility. The Swedish resistance was generally backed by the Hanse. It was not, however, until 1523 that the Union of Kalmar was finally dissolved.

D. Ditchburn

Later medieval Germany: emperors and princes

German settlement respected few natural or political frontiers in the Middle Ages. In the Tirol it had spread south of the Alps and in the east beyond the frontiers of the German kingdom. By contrast the Valois rulers of the Low Countries were Frenchmen who sought ultimately to establish their own kingdom while Bohemia was the heartland of both the Luxembourg dynasty of German kings and the Czech national movement led by Jan Hus and his followers. Limited geographical and ethnic unity was matched by monarchical weakness. The German kingdom was part of the Holy Roman Empire and, following coronation by the pope, German kings were styled emperor. Yet little of the Empire, and even less of imperial pretensions to political leadership of the entire West, remained intact following the Hohenstaufen dynasty's clash with the papacy and the ensuing interregnum between 1250 and

1273. Thereafter imperial authority was in practice confined largely to Germany. The increasingly Germanic nature of the imperial monarchy was confirmed by the formal exclusion of the papacy from imperial elections in 1338. The rules for imperial elections were further clarified in the Golden Bull of 1356 with the designation of seven (German) electors. Even within Germany, however, the elective nature of kingship constrained monarchical power. Despite an almost unbroken succession of emperors from the Luxembourg family between 1346 and 1437, and then from the Habsburg family after 1438, no king could be certain that his heir would inherit the title. Moreover, the resources of German kings were scant. Most of the imperial lands had been usurped during the conflicts of the thirteenth century. Little, other than the imperial towns, remained and these were frequently mortgaged.

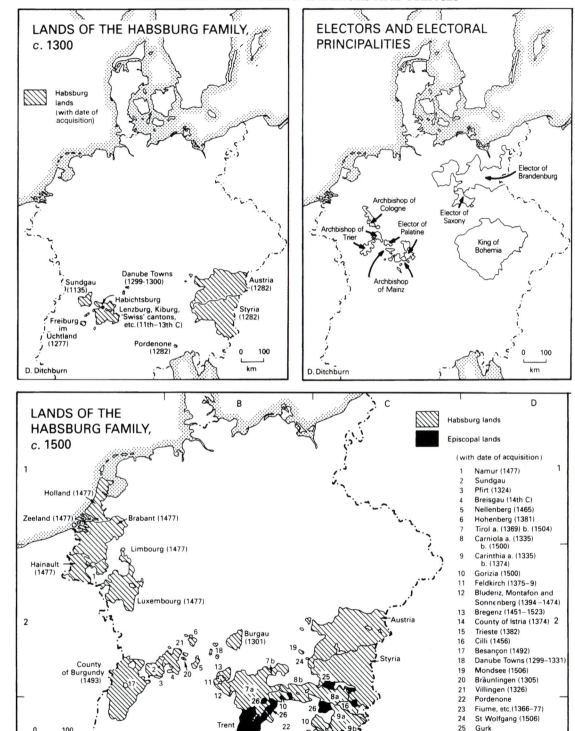

LANDS OF THE HABSBURG FAMILY, c. 1300

Habsburg lands (with date of acquisition)

Sundgau (1135)

Danube Towns (1299-1300)

Austria (1282)

Habichtsburg

Lenzburg, Kiburg, 'Swiss' cantons, etc. (11th–13th C)

Styria (1282)

Freiburg im Üchtland (1277)

Pordenone (1282)

0   100
km

D. Ditchburn

ELECTORS AND ELECTORAL PRINCIPALITIES

Elector of Brandenburg

Archbishop of Cologne

Elector of Saxony

Archbishop of Trier

Elector of Palatine

King of Bohemia

Archbishop of Mainz

0   100
km

D. Ditchburn

LANDS OF THE HABSBURG FAMILY, c. 1500

Habsburg lands

Episcopal lands

(with date of acquisition)

1   Namur (1477)
2   Sundgau
3   Pfirt (1324)
4   Breisgau (14th C)
5   Nellenberg (1465)
6   Hohenberg (1381)
7   Tirol a. (1369) b. (1504)
8   Carniola a. (1335) b. (1500)
9   Carinthia a. (1335) b. (1374)
10   Gorizia (1500)
11   Feldkirch (1375–9)
12   Bludenz, Montafon and Sonnenberg (1394–1474)
13   Bregenz (1451–1523)
14   County of Istria (1374)
15   Trieste (1382)
16   Cilli (1456)
17   Besançon (1492)
18   Danube Towns (1299–1331)
19   Mondsee (1506)
20   Bräunlingen (1305)
21   Villingen (1326)
22   Pordenone
23   Fiume, etc. (1366–77)
24   St Wolfgang (1506)
25   Gurk
26   Brixen

Note : excludes imperial lands

Holland (1477)

Zeeland (1477)

Brabant (1477)

Limbourg (1477)

Hainault (1477)

Luxembourg (1477)

Austria

Burgau (1301)

Styria

County of Burgundy (1493)

Trent

0   100
km

D. Ditchburn

215

Royal rights over the fragmentary morass of ecclesiastical and secular principalities had also diminished, partly through immunities granted in return for political support and partly through neglect. In the Golden Bull Charles IV (1347–78) recognized the impossibility of retrieving the situation by formally granting the electors extensive rights and freedoms from royal interference. These were privileges to which other princes also aspired. With limited resources and rights kings lacked the need and ability to develop strong institutions of central government. Beset by such difficulties the monarchy failed to emerge as a focus for political unity and, instead, German kings invested their energies in the augmentation of family lands (*Hausgut*) rather than imperial possessions (*Reichsgut*). In this the Habsburgs were strikingly successful. By 1300 they possessed Austria, Styria and various lands and jurisdictions around their ancestral castle of Habichtsburg. Other lands were acquired before 1500 by imperial grant, marriage, inheritance, purchase and conquest, while Habsburg influence was also exerted on ecclesiastical principalities such as Trent, Brixen and Gurk. While the territorial ambitions and achievements of the Habsburgs were unusual in extent rather than in essence, the growth of princely power, even that of the Habsburgs, was neither swift, unchallenged nor without setbacks. Penury forced many princes to mortgage or sell their lands while the custom of partible inheritance led to the division of many principalities between heirs. There were often aggressive neighbours to contend with: the Habsburgs lost the Swiss cantons and the Hungarians occupied part of their eastern territories in the 1480s. Within many principalities the estates (gatherings of lesser nobles, clergymen, townsmen and occasionally, as in Tirol, of peasants) exploited princely weakness and often acquired considerable influence in return for settling magnate disputes or granting taxation. Only as the Middle Ages came to a close did princes overcome such problems. Lordship gradually became more territorial: the Electors Palatine, for instance, exchanged other princes' serfs in the Palatinate for their own serfs elsewhere. The gradual introduction of regular taxation, primogeniture (which ended the fragmentation of lands) and notions of Roman law (which exalted the prince's position) further bolstered princely authority. Viewed from the perspective of an accretion of princely power, German developments slowly but more closely parallel growing royal power elsewhere in Europe.

D. Ditchburn

Northern Italy from the rise of the *signori* to the peace of Lodi

From the later thirteenth century control of many north Italian city-states passed from oligarchic communal governments to dynastic *signorie*. This was particularly the case in the Trevisan March, Lombardy, Emilia and the Marches where many *signori* came to control more than one town. The nineteenth-century characterization of these rulers as 'despots' reflects their contemporary designation as 'tyrants', but underestimates the elements of continuity between the communal and signorial regimes: both were very violent, neither was democratic. Indeed, the change of regime did not generally lead to radical transformations in the conduct of government. The *signori* gained the ascendant gradually, often holding office in the commune and using their wealth and political skills to extend their control over the communal bureaucracy and to suppress opposition. Smaller towns in their control were generally allowed a considerable degree of self-government and the administrative structures

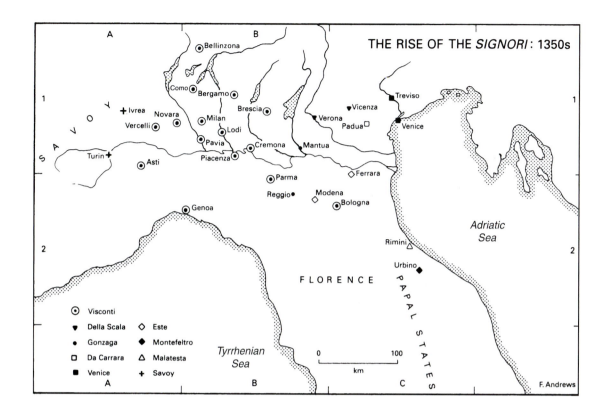

THE RISE OF THE *SIGNORI*: 1350s

Visconti
Della Scala
Gonzaga
Da Carrara
Venice
Este
Montefeltro
Malatesta
Savoy

of the communes frequently survived. Once in power the *signori* sought to legitimize their position and establish a hereditary right to govern, cultivating prestige through marriage alliances, artistic patronage, honours and titles, such as papal vicar or imperial duke, the latter a title acquired from the emperor by Giangaleazzo Visconti of Milan in 1395. In the search for political ascendancy, violence was ever-present. Factionalism within towns frequently led to plots and assassinations, such as that of Bartolomeo della Scala in 1381 at the instigation of his brother, Antonio, who sought to ensure his own control of the *signorie* of Verona and Vicenza. At the same time the struggle for supremacy between city-states led to almost constant warfare. The growing use of mercenary companies (often composed of foreign troops) led by *condottieri* (often lords of smaller centres such as the Malatesta in Rimini) increased the general political instability. The first map shows the situation in the 1350s when the lands

of the Visconti of Milan had extended to absorb several neighbouring cities. The situation was, however, fluid and smaller centres frequently changed hands: in 1336 the della Scala had controlled Brescia, Padua, Treviso, Feltre, Belluno, Parma and even Lucca but their defeat in 1339 at the hands of Florence and Venice (the only two major cities to remain ostensibly republican in form though the differences were often little more than a matter of diplomatic rhetoric) restricted the della Scala to Verona and Vicenza. The second map shows the situation at the peace of Lodi in 1454. In the intervening years the Milan-based *signorie* of the Visconti had expanded under Giangaleazzo and then partly fragmented following his sudden death in 1402. It was substantially restored once his son, Filippo Maria, came of age but in the 1420s war broke out between the long-standing enemies, Milan and Florence. Over the following decades most of the Italian peninsula became involved. Venice, increasingly concerned about

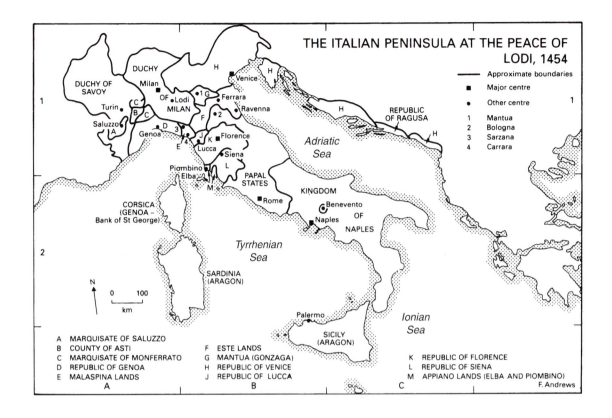

THE ITALIAN PENINSULA AT THE PEACE OF LODI, 1454

—— Approximate boundaries
■ Major centre
● Other centre
1 Mantua
2 Bologna
3 Sarzana
4 Carrara

A MARQUISATE OF SALUZZO
B COUNTY OF ASTI
C MARQUISATE OF MONFERRATO
D REPUBLIC OF GENOA
E MALASPINA LANDS
F ESTE LANDS
G MANTUA (GONZAGA)
H REPUBLIC OF VENICE
J REPUBLIC OF LUCCA
K REPUBLIC OF FLORENCE
L REPUBLIC OF SIENA
M APPIANO LANDS (ELBA AND PIOMBINO)

F. Andrews

the security of its hinterland and now intent upon a policy of expansion on the mainland (*terraferma*), joined an intermittent alliance with Florence against Milan. Later both Alfonso of Naples and papal forces were drawn into the conflict. Filippo Maria's death without legitimate male heirs in 1447 transformed the situation. The Visconti regime in Milan was replaced by the short-lived 'Ambrosian Republic' (1447–50). After the failure of the republic, named after the patron saint of the city, Milan fell under the control of Francesco Sforza, a *condottiere* who had fought for both Milan and Florence and who in 1441 had married Filippo Maria's daughter, Bianca. On 9 April 1454

Milan and Venice agreed to the peace of Lodi. The other major powers, Florence, the papacy and Naples, eventually also adhered to the peace. Together these five principal powers of Italy founded the Italian (or Italic) League. This sought, with limited success, to promote political stability in the peninsula by recognizing the territorial status quo, regulating military resources and establishing ground rules for the pursuit of war. Remarkably, it was to last for forty years.

F. Andrews

The expansion of the Crown of Aragon

James I (1213–76) conquered Mallorca (1229), Menorca (1232), Ibiza (1235) and Valencia

(1238). Subsequently Corsica and Sardinia were added to the Mediterranean possessions of the

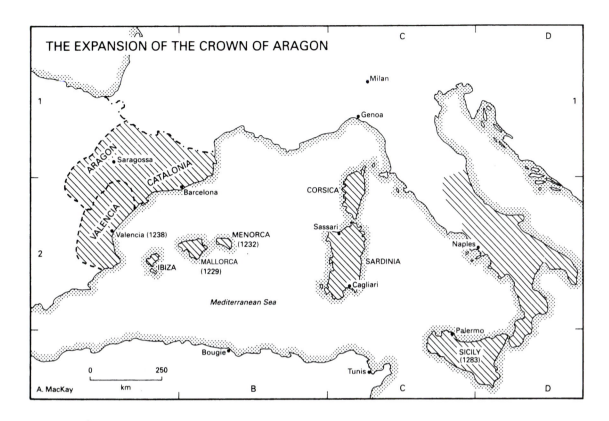

THE EXPANSION OF THE CROWN OF ARAGON

Crown of Aragon while an uprising against the Angevins in Sicily in 1282 led to its acquisition. Alfonso V (1416–58) devoted his reign to southern Italy, which he conquered, despite papal and Angevin opposition, after the death of Joanna II of Naples (1435).

The importance attached to Mediterranean possessions by Aragonese kings entailed serious repercussions for their realms in Spain. Peter III (1276–85) might have curbed the Aragonese nobility but for his preoccupation with Sicily. Succeeding kings had to accept constitutional limitations.

Institutional innovations were linked to the problem of 'absentee monarchy'. Kings had to delegate powers to *procuradores* and from the late fourteenth century lieutenants-general or viceroys appeared in Sardinia, Sicily and Mallorca, a pattern repeated in Aragon, Catalonia and Valencia as a result of Alfonso V's absence in Italy.

The powers of monarchs and their officials were severely curtailed by the various *cortes* of the federation. Consent was necessary for all laws and grievances had to be redressed before financial aid was granted. Between meetings of the *cortes*, royal officials were controlled by standing committees. The origins of the Catalan *Diputació* or *Generalitat* date from the thirteenth century when delegates were appointed to deal with problems once the representatives had dispersed, their main task being to control the raising and spending of money. By 1359 the *Generalitat* was a permanent body. Similar institutions were set up in Aragon and Valencia in 1412 and 1419. Controlling royal authority, the *cortes* were not democratic; they represented the privileged, defending the interests of the oligarchs who dominated the towns and the countryside.

A. MacKay

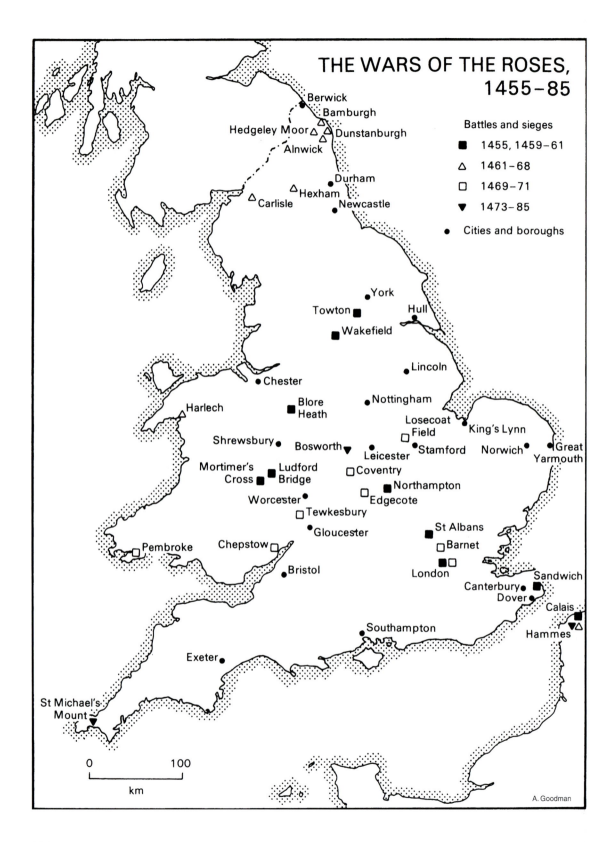

THE WARS OF THE ROSES,
1455–85

Battles and sieges

■ 1455, 1459–61
△ 1461–68
□ 1469–71
▼ 1473–85

● Cities and boroughs

Berwick
Bamburgh
Hedgeley Moor △ △ Dunstanburgh
Alnwick
Durham
Hexham
Carlisle
Newcastle
York
Towton ■
Hull
Wakefield ■
Lincoln
Chester
Blore
Heath ■
Nottingham
Harlech △
Losecoat
Field □
King's Lynn
Shrewsbury
Bosworth ▼
Leicester
Stamford
Norwich
Great
Yarmouth
Mortimer's
Cross ■
Ludford
Bridge ■
Coventry □
Northampton ■
Worcester
Edgecote □
Tewkesbury □
St Albans ■
Gloucester
Chepstow □
Barnet □
Pembroke □
London ■ □
Bristol
Sandwich ■
Canterbury
Dover
Calais ■
Southampton
Hammes ▼ △
Exeter
St Michael's
Mount ▼

0   100

km

A. Goodman

The Wars of the Roses

This name, symbolizing the dynastic conflict of the Houses of Lancaster and York, was apparently coined by Sir Walter Scott to describe the civil wars fought mainly in England and Wales between 1455 and 1485. They started with risings by Richard, duke of York, aimed at ousting the favourites of Henry VI (1452, 1455, 1459). But in 1460, after victory in another rising, York claimed the throne, a claim implemented by his son, who was proclaimed Edward IV in 1461. His rule was challenged in 1469–70 by some of his own supporters, who restored Henry VI: in 1471 the exiled Edward invaded England and regained the Crown. In 1483 Edward's brother Richard, duke of Gloucester, seized it from his young son, Edward V. Richard III defeated a revolt that autumn but in 1485 he was killed fighting Henry Tudor, representing the Lancastrian interest, at Bosworth. Plots and attempted risings on behalf of Yorkist pretenders recurred over the next twelve years but were speedily crushed by Henry VII.

The Wars of the Roses were mostly highly mobile campaigns, with few prolonged sieges: protagonists aimed to catch opponents un-prepared and to secure cities and boroughs, above all London and York, with minimal disruption, so as not to alienate support. The sometimes lengthy struggles to control geographically marginal castles in Northumberland (1461–4) and Wales (1461–8) formed an exceptional phase. Urban and rural communities in most parts of England and Wales were involved at different times in arraying for campaigns, manning local defences and victualling armies. But such involvement tended to be patchily regional, reflecting the rivalries and ambitions of particular magnates and their local clientage networks: many campaigns, lasting only a few weeks, were too short for widespread damage. Only in the crisis years of 1459–61 and 1469–71 did the conflicts acquire fuller dimensions. Occasionally foreign princes and foreign mercenaries were drawn into the Wars: exiles launched invasions from Calais and Ireland (possessions of the English crown) and from Scotland, Zeeland, Brittany and Normandy.

A. Goodman

Scotland: Crown and magnates, *c.* 1400 and *c.* 1460

At the end of the fourteenth century (map A), Scotland's old territorial pattern of 'provincial' earldoms and lordships was essentially intact, but two new 'scattered' earldoms, Douglas and Crawford, had been created. The Douglases – major recipients of royal rewards after the Wars of Independence – had gained vast estates throughout the country, especially in the borders and south-west. Meanwhile, many of the other earldoms – and indeed the Crown – had come to the Stewarts. Collectively they were the greatest kindred of all, but in *c.* 1400 they were riven by quarrels between Robert III, his son and his brothers, and the Crown's effect-ive power-base had contracted into the south-west. By *c.* 1460, however, Scotland's territorial structure had been transformed (map B). Most 'provincial' earldoms and lordships were in Crown hands – chiefly as a result of forfeitures following confrontations between James I (1406–37) and his Stewart kinsmen and between James II (1437–60) and the eighth earl of Douglas. Now – outside the Highlands – sheriffdoms, not earldoms and lordships, provided the geo-political framework, while the Crown's main power-base had been relocated centrally, in Lothian (around Edinburgh) and in Fife, Stirlingshire and Perthshire. And now the

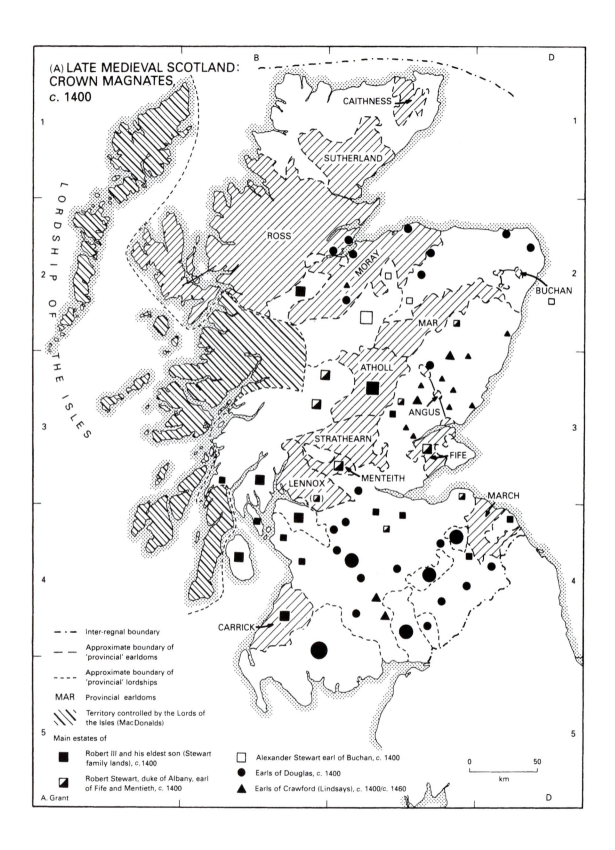

(A) LATE MEDIEVAL SCOTLAND:
CROWN MAGNATES,
c. 1400

B   D

1   1

CAITHNESS

SUTHERLAND

LORDSHIP OF THE ISLES

ROSS

MORAY

2   2

BUCHAN

MAR

ATHOLL   ANGUS

3   3

STRATHEARN

LENNOX   MENTEITH   FIFE

MARCH

4   4

CARRICK

—·—·— Inter-regnal boundary

— — — Approximate boundary of
'provincial' earldoms

- - - - - Approximate boundary of
'provincial' lordships

MAR   Provincial earldoms

Territory controlled by the Lords of
the Isles (MacDonalds)

5   5

Main estates of

■   Robert III and his eldest son (Stewart
family lands), *c.*1400

◪   Robert Stewart, duke of Albany, earl
of Fife and Mentieth, *c.*1400

□   Alexander Stewart earl of Buchan, *c.* 1400

●   Earls of Douglas, *c.* 1400

▲   Earls of Crawford (Lindsays), *c.* 1400/*c.* 1460

0   50
km

A. Grant   D

222

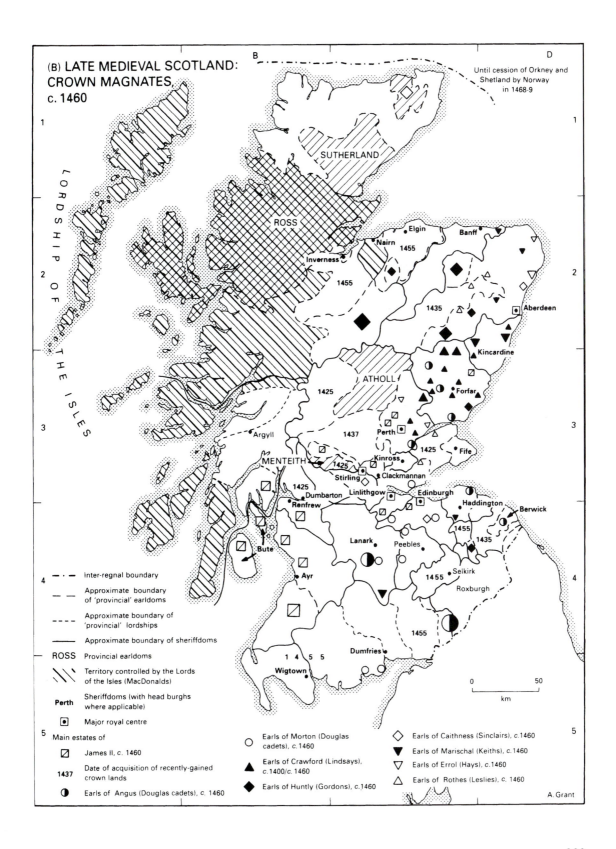

(B) LATE MEDIEVAL SCOTLAND: CROWN MAGNATES, c. 1460

Until cession of Orkney and Shetland by Norway in 1468-9

SUTHERLAND

ROSS

LORDSHIP OF THE ISLES

Elgin
Banff
Nairn
1455
Inverness
1455
1435
Aberdeen
1425
Kincardine
ATHOLL
Forfar
1437
Perth
Argyll
1425
Fife
Kinross
MENTEITH
1425
Stirling
Clackmannan
1425
Linlithgow
Dumbarton
Edinburgh
Renfrew
Haddington
Berwick
1455
1435
Lanark
Peebles
Bute
Selkirk
1455
Ayr
Roxburgh
1455
Dumfries
1 4 5 5
Wigtown

0   50
km

Legend:

- · — Inter-regnal boundary
- – – Approximate boundary of 'provincial' earldoms
- - - - Approximate boundary of 'provincial' lordships
- ——— Approximate boundary of sheriffdoms
- ROSS Provincial earldoms
- ⧄ Territory controlled by the Lords of the Isles (MacDonalds)
- **Perth** Sheriffdoms (with head burghs where applicable)
- ⊙ Major royal centre

Main estates of
- ⬚ James II, c. 1460
- **1437** Date of acquisition of recently-gained crown lands
- ◗ Earls of Angus (Douglas cadets), c. 1460

- ○ Earls of Morton (Douglas cadets), c. 1460
- ▲ Earls of Crawford (Lindsays), c. 1400/c. 1460
- ◆ Earls of Huntly (Gordons), c. 1460

- ◇ Earls of Caithness (Sinclairs), c. 1460
- ▼ Earls of Marischal (Keiths), c. 1460
- ▽ Earls of Errol (Hays), c. 1460
- △ Earls of Rothes (Leslies), c. 1460

A. Grant

223

magnates had scattered estates and local spheres of influence rather than provinces. That applied to the new earldoms created by James II for his supporters, except for the new 'provincial' earldoms of Argyll (Campbells) and Huntly (Gordons). These were bulwarks on the frontiers of the Highlands against the MacDonald Lordship of the Isles – the vast Gaelic power-block built up by the heads of Clan Donald (earls of Ross, 1437–75), which dominated most of the Highlands from the 1410s to the 1490s.

A. Grant

Late Medieval Iberia: Castile and Portugal

From 1350 to 1389 a long struggle was waged for control of Castile. It began primarily as a civil war between Peter (Pedro) I (1350–69) and a coalition of nobles led by his illegitimate half-brother, Henry (Enrique), count of Trastámara but both sides sought foreign support, particularly from France and England (which were already opposed in the Hundred Years War). In 1365, the exiled count of Trastámara invaded Castile, aided by French and English mercenaries, and proclaimed himself Henry II (1366). Peter fled to Bayonne and, helped by the English, mounted a counter-invasion defeating the Trastámarans at Nájera (1367). His triumph was brief. Charles V of France supported another invasion by Henry II (1369–79). Peter was finally defeated and murdered by his brother at Montiel (1369) but the threat to the Trastámaran dynasty continued.

In 1371 John of Gaunt, duke of Lancaster, married Peter I's eldest daughter and claimed the Castilian throne. When John (Juan) I of Castile (1379–90) invaded Portugal, João (John) I (1385–1433), assisted by English archers, inflicted a crushing defeat on the Castilians at Aljubarrota (1385). The treaty of Windsor, sealed in May 1386, cemented the alliance between England and Portugal and when Lancaster invaded Galicia and conquered La Coruña (1386) several months later, he was aided by a Portuguese army. Although Lancaster's attempt to win the Castilian throne failed, he was placated by the promise of a large cash settlement and by prestigious family alliances, which saw his daughters, Catherine and Philippa, married respectively to the future Henry III (1390–1406) of Castile and to João I of Portugal.

Peninsular conflict continued in the fifteenth century. During the minority of John II (1406–54), one of his regents, Henry III's brother, Fernando, won fame by conquering Antequera from the Moors (1410). 'Elected' to the Crown of Aragon at the Compromise of Caspe (1412), his short reign lasting until 1416 was marked by his continued interest in Castilian politics and the promotion of his family's interests. Interference in Castilian affairs by his sons, Alfonso V (1416–58), John II (1458–79) and Henry, Master of the Order of Santiago, led to the emergence of an 'Aragonese party' in Castile that was later challenged and defeated by John II's favourite, Alvaro de Luna, at the battle of Olmedo (1445).

After an auspicious start the reign of Henry IV of Castile (1454–74) degenerated into anarchy, the most serious crisis arising from an attempted deposition-in-effigy of the king at Avila in 1465 and the 'election' of his half-brother, Alfonso, as a rival king. After Alfonso's death in 1468 the political factions prepared for a crisis in the succession that pitted Henry's alleged daughter, the Princess of the Asturias, Juana 'la Beltraneja' (a name deriving from her putative father, the king's favourite, Beltrán de Cueva) against the king's half-sister, Isabella. The succession of Isabella I (1474–1504), who had married Fernando, heir apparent to the crown of Aragon in 1469, worried other kingdoms, which feared the birth of a new

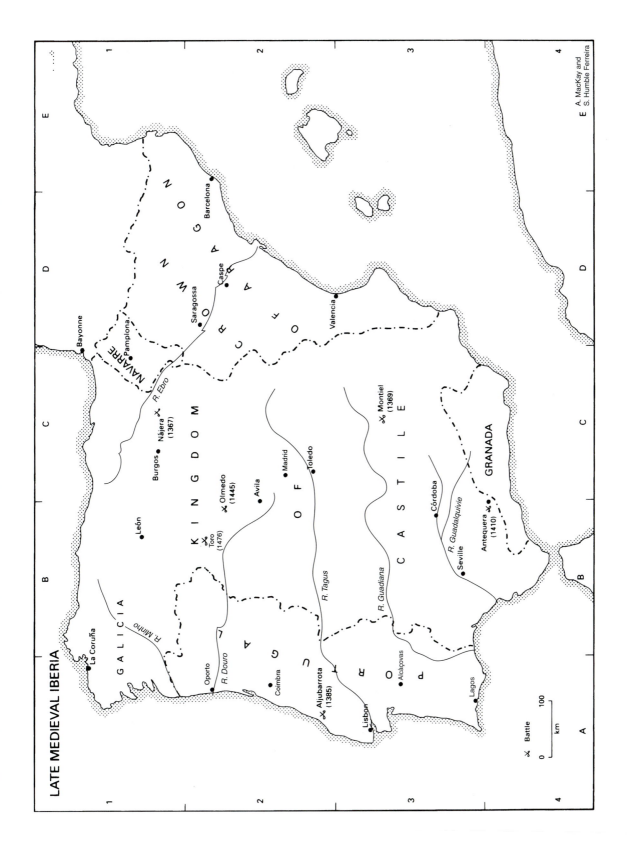

LATE MEDIEVAL IBERIA

Battle

0 100
km

A. MacKay and
S. Humble Ferreira

225

superpower. When Isabella succeeded to the throne in 1474, Afonso V of Portugal (1438–81) rallied troops to uphold the claims of the Princess of Asturias, his niece. After decisive defeats by Castilian forces at Toro (1476), Afonso V attempted unsuccessfully to enlist the support of Louis XI of France and Charles the Bold of Burgundy. The victory of Isabella and Fernando II of Aragon (1479–1516) over their rivals in Castile brought about a truce with Portugal, ratified in the treaty of Alcaçovas-Toledo (1479–80). This acknowledged Isabella as queen of Castile. The death of John II of Aragon in 1479 unified the kingdoms of Castile and Aragon, although their respective realms continued to retain widely differing institutions. While Portugal maintained independence, Muslim Granada was conquered in 1492 and the kingdom of Navarre was incorporated into Castile in 1512.

S. Humble Ferreira & A. MacKay

The rise of the Turks and the crusade

In the early fourteenth century the Byzantines lost western Anatolia to the Turks, the most successful of whom, the Ottomans, established themselves opposite Constantinople. This blocked further expansion until 1354, when involvement in the Byzantine civil wars allowed the Ottomans to establish a bridgehead at Gallipoli. This became their base for the conquest and settlement of Thrace, completed with their victory in 1371 over the Serbs at the battle of the Maritsa. Turkish expansion has been attributed to the *ghazi*-ethos, i.e. the Turks were warriors for the faith bent on extending the frontiers of Islam. They were also pastoralists seeking new lands for their flocks. They fed on the weakness of their opponents. In 1387 Thessalonica, the second city of the Byzantine Empire, voluntarily submitted to the Ottomans. In 1389 the Serbs were defeated at Kossovo and became their tributaries. In 1393 the Ottomans entered Trnovo and annexed Bulgaria. They were also taking over the Turkish emirates in Anatolia, including in 1397 Karaman. Constantinople only survived because of Tamburlane who invaded Anatolia and in 1402 defeated the Ottomans at Ankara. They needed nearly twenty years to recover from this defeat but under Murad II (1421–51) almost all the losses in the Balkans and in Anatolia, Karaman excepted, were made good. Murad put Ottoman power on a sounder basis by regulating recruitment into the janissaries, the slave troops who formed the core of the Ottoman army. It was left to his son, Mehmed the Conqueror (1451–81), to take Constantinople in 1453, thus endowing the Ottomans with a worthy capital, capable of holding their territories together and of enhancing the authority of the sultan. Mehmed rounded off his territories by annexing the remnants of the Byzantine Empire in the Peloponnese (1460), Trebizond (1461) and Karaman (1468). Already a major power, the Ottomans were poised for the mastery of the Mediterranean.

The threat from the Turks gave a new lease of life to the crusade which had lost its purpose after the fall of Acre in 1291. The Knights Hospitallers led the way. In 1308 they seized Rhodes from the Byzantines and used it as a base against Turkish piracy in the Aegean. Their success encouraged crusading activity which suited Venetian commercial interest and pandered to nostalgia for the glories of the crusade. There was a fashion for the creation of chivalric orders dedicated to the promotion of the crusade. The main success came with the crusade of 1344, which conquered Smyrna, handing it over to the Knights Hospitallers. The initiative thus wrested from the Turks in the Aegean, the focus of the crusade now

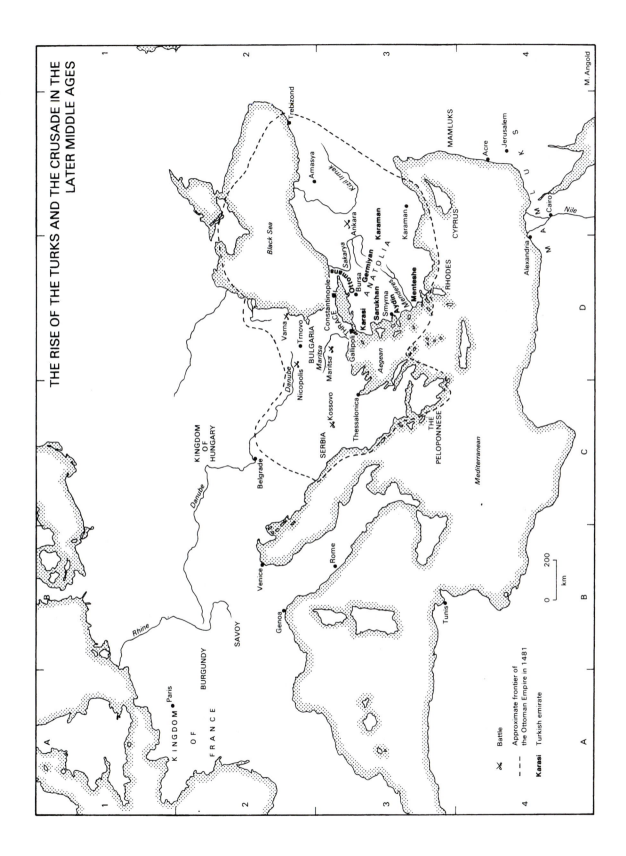

THE RISE OF THE TURKS AND THE CRUSADE IN THE
LATER MIDDLE AGES

M. Angold

Battle

Approximate frontier of
the Ottoman Empire in 1481

Karasi Turkish emirate

227

became Cyprus, where Peter I was preparing a crusade against the Mamluks of Egypt. Alexandria was stormed in 1365, but further progress was dampened by the Venetians who feared for their trade with Egypt.

The Ottoman advance into the Balkans shifted crusading interest to Byzantium. In 1366 Amadeus of Savoy went to the rescue of his cousin, the Emperor John V Palaiologos. The survival of Constantinople was a matter of urgency for the Hungarian King Sigismund, if only to divert the Ottomans from his frontiers. He was able to tap the crusading idealism of the French courts, already exploited in 1390 by the Genoese with Louis of Bourbon's crusade against Tunis. The new crusade was led by John the Fearless, the son and heir of the duke of Burgundy. The French met the Ottomans at Nicopolis in 1396 and were hopelessly defeated. This disaster effectively ended French participation in the crusade, though the Burgundian court continued to pay enthusiastic lip-service to the ideal. The crusade against the Ottomans became very much a Hungarian preserve. It came to grief in 1444 at Varna where a Hungarian crusade marching to the relief of Constantinople was defeated in a desperate two-day battle. Thereafter the crusade was relegated to the realms of wishful thinking. The Ottomans had proved too strong.

M. Angold

Dynastic union: Poland and Lithuania, 1386–1569

The Polish-Lithuanian Union was instituted in 1386 when the pagan Grand Duke Jogaila of Lithuania, fulfilling promises made at Krewo in 1385, adopted the name Władysław Jagiełło, converted to Catholicism and married Jadwiga, the young queen of Poland. In 1386 the Grand Duchy stretched from the Baltic almost to the Black Sea, having swept up the western lands of Kievan Rus', shattered by the Mongols; thus its population largely comprised Orthodox eastern Slavs. Krewo opened the way to the conversion of the pagan Lithuanians to Catholicism and to a dazzling career for the new Jagiellonian dynasty. Lithuania fiercely defended its separate political status after 1386. The Jagiellonians ruled the two states as a dynastic condominium. Jagiełło's cousin, Vytautas, was the *de facto* ruler of Lithuania from 1392 until his death in 1430. Thereafter, until the election of King Sigismund I in 1506, Poland and Lithuania only twice shared the same ruler: Casimir IV (1447–92) and Alexander (1501–6). Jagiellonians were, however, also kings of Hungary (1440–4, 1490–1526) and Bohemia (1471–1526). For all the looseness of the bonds, Poland and Lithuania grew ever closer. Polish military support enabled Lithuania to resist Muscovite attacks (though substantial territories were lost by 1537) and the Union enabled the defeat of the Teutonic Knights, the consequent incorporation of Royal Prussia into the Polish Crown (1454/66) and the creation of Ducal Prussia as a Polish fief (1525). The attractions of the Polish political system, with its extensive privileges for nobles, stimulated the transformation of Lithuanian institutions and political culture; enabling the last Jagiellonian king, Sigismund August, to drive through the Union of Lublin (1569). This united the diets of the two states and ensured that the Union would survive the dynasty's extinction in the male line in 1572.

R.I. Frost

DYNASTIC UNION:
POLAND AND LITHUANIA,
1386–1569

KNIGHTS OF THE SWORD

ROYAL
PRUSSIA

Danzig

TEUTONIC KNIGHTS

Trakai • Vilnius

MUSCOVY

Sholensk

GRAND

DUCHY OF

LITHUANIA

Vistula

MAZOVIA

Poznań

Warsaw

KINGDOM OF POLAND

Dnieper

Kraków

Lwów
(Luiu)

Kiev

HUNGARY

THE WILD PLAINS

0   km   500

CRIMEAN KHANATE

R.I. Frost

The rise of Muscovy

Kiev fell to the Mongols in 1240. The principality of Kiev along with the other south Russian principalities was swept away. In the north a number of principalities survived as tributaries of the khan of the Golden Horde. Leaving aside the city-state of Novgorod, the most important was the principality of Vladimir-Suzdal, the ruler of which was recognized as Grand Prince by the khan. From the turn of the thirteenth century it lost its ascendancy to the principalities of Tver' and Moscow. Both were situated close to the headwaters of the major Russian rivers, which ensured that they had good communications and avenues of expansion. Moscow was perhaps less exposed, being protected by marshes to the west and thick forest to the east, but the decisive factor in its favour was the combination of the approval

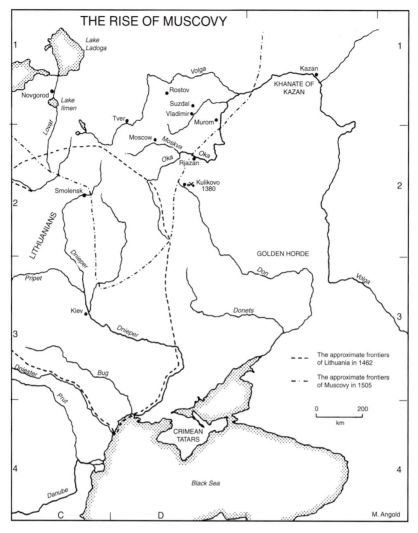

THE RISE OF MUSCOVY

Lake Ladoga
Volga
Kazan
KHANATE OF KAZAN
Novgorod
Lake Ilmen
Rostov
Suzdal
Vladimir
Murom
Tver
Moscow
Moskva
Oka
Oka
Rjazan
Kulikovo 1380
Smolensk
LITHUANIANS
Dnieper
Pripet
Dnieper
Kiev
Donets
GOLDEN HORDE
Don
Volga
Dniester
Bug
Prut
CRIMEAN TATARS
Danube
Black Sea

The approximate frontiers of Lithuania in 1462

The approximate frontiers of Muscovy in 1505

0   200
km

M. Angold

of the Mongols and the backing of the Ortho-dox Church. The princes of Moscow preferred to co-operate with the Mongols rather than oppose their rule. From the reign of Prince Ivan Kalita (1328–41) the khans consistently bestowed the title of Grand Prince on the princes of Moscow and with it seniority over the other Russian princes. Ivan also ensured that Moscow would become the permanent residence of the metro-politan of Kiev and all Russia, the head of the Russian Church, who was appointed from Con-stantinople. The metropolitan acted as arbiter between the Russian princes and normally used his influence to further Moscow's political interests. By 1380 the strength of Moscow was such that its prince, Dimitri Donskoj, was able to challenge the Mongols and win a great vic-tory over them at Kulikovo. Though obliged two years later to submit once again to Mongol overlordship, he preserved the title of Grand Prince and his pre-eminence among the Russian princes. A succession struggle later slowed down the momentum of Muscovite expansion. It was left to Ivan III (1462–1505) to complete the 'Gathering in of the Russian Lands' around Moscow. The culmination was the annexation of Novgorod in 1478 and of Tver' in 1485. Ivan had already thrown off the Mongol yoke once and for all in 1480.

M. Angold

GOVERNMENT, SOCIETY AND ECONOMY

The growth of royal fiscality in France

Until the thirteenth century French kings derived most of their income not from taxation but rather from their estates (*domaine*), like other great landholders. Under Philip IV (1285–1314) this ordinary income was augmented by careful exploitation of sovereign rights and boosted by windfalls from attacks on privileged groups like the Lombards, Jews and Templars; but it still failed to cover royal needs. Further revenue from taxation, usually termed 'extraordinary' taxation, was required. A crusading tithe levied on the clergy in 1147 and 1188 provided a model. In the thirteenth century the king raised similar tenths (*décimes*) from ecclesiastics at frequent intervals, with or without papal approval, and this remained a valuable source of income. But Philip IV, justifying his demands by pleas of evident necessity and defence of the realm in an emergency, now sought war subsidies directly from his lay subjects, though he normally also had to summon the feudal host (*arrière-ban*) beforehand. He also experimented with indirect taxes (*impôts*) on the sale of basic foodstuffs, drink and manufactured goods, together with customs dues like the *maltôte* (1295). The rudimentary financial administration was transformed, though it was the mid-fourteenth century before a proper system for collecting revenue derived from sources other than the royal *domaine* was devised. The Templars, royal bankers since the mid-twelfth century, were relieved of their duties in the 1290s and a royal *trésor* was set up. Accounting took place before an enlarged *curia de compotis* (1289) or *chambre des comptes*, which functioned fully as a court by the 1320s, even if it was 1381 before its first *président* appeared. Control of *impôts*, now termed *aides*, passed after 1390 to the *cour des aides* and a *cour du trésor* took over supervision of domainal revenues.

That extraordinary revenues should constitute a regular and permanent source of the Crown's peacetime income was long resisted. Some great duchies and counties, like Brittany, Burgundy, Flanders and Gascony, managed to preserve their fiscal autonomy. There was a failure to devise standard national means either for authorizing taxation or for levying and collecting it. Much was left to local endeavours, with the Crown simply grateful to receive a proportion of what it demanded. Philip IV called an assembly (or Estates General) and his successors occasionally found it expedient to summon them or meetings of regional Estates for northern and southern France (Languedoil and Languedoc) to consider the imposition of a particular tax – but it was to obtain their counsel not their consent. After 1439 the Estates General did not meet until 1484. In contrast, between 1330 and 1430 other provincial Estates were formed. Some, like those of Normandy, claimed the right to consent to taxes and were indeed consulted according to circumstance or tradition. Some modification of the form or burden of taxation could thus be negotiated. But from an early point the Crown was frustrated by the delays such consultation often entailed – decisions taken by Estates General had to be ratified by local Estates, and taxes granted in the larger bodies were seldom collected. It began to decide in advance the sum required and simply ordered provincial assemblies to authorize its levy. This they normally did by sharing out their quota amongst those liable to taxation in their area, the division (*répartition*) based on information derived from great inquiries, like that of 1328, into the number of hearths or households (*feux*) in regions under royal control. Hence the hearth tax (*fouage*) was the main form of direct taxation.

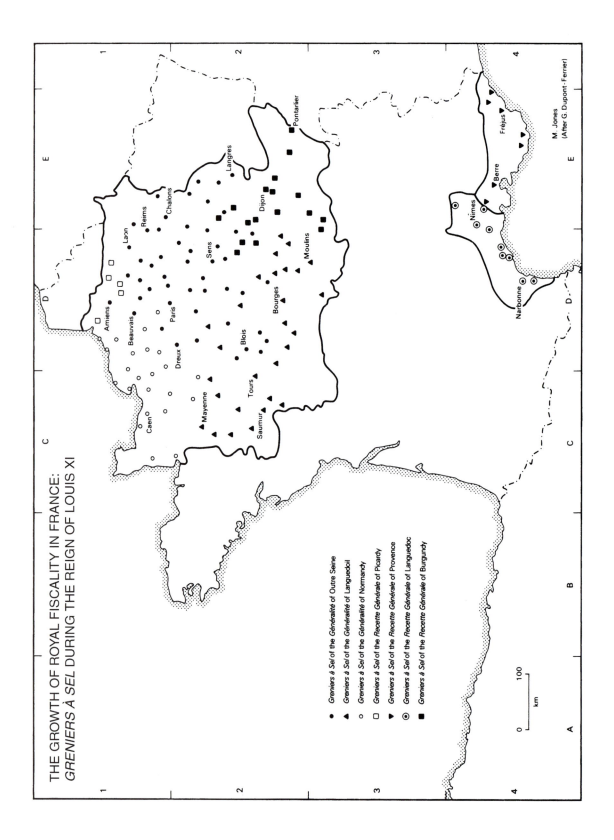

THE GROWTH OF ROYAL FISCALITY IN FRANCE:
GRENIERS À SEL DURING THE REIGN OF LOUIS XI

M. Jones
(After G. Dupont-Ferrier)

Legend:

- • *Greniers à Sel* of the *Généralité* of Outre Seine
- ▲ *Greniers à Sel* of the *Généralité* of Languedoil
- ○ *Greniers à Sel* of the *Généralité* of Normandy
- □ *Greniers à Sel* of the *Recette Générale* of Picardy
- ▼ *Greniers à Sel* of the *Recette Générale* of Provence
- ⊙ *Greniers à Sel* of the *Recette Générale* of Languedoc
- ■ *Greniers à Sel* of the *Recette Générale* of Burgundy

Place names: Pontarlier, Langres, Chalons, Reims, Laon, Dijon, Moulins, Sens, Bourges, Amiens, Beauvais, Paris, Dreux, Blois, Tours, Mayenne, Caen, Saumur, Fréjus, Berre, Nîmes, Narbonne

0   100   km

232

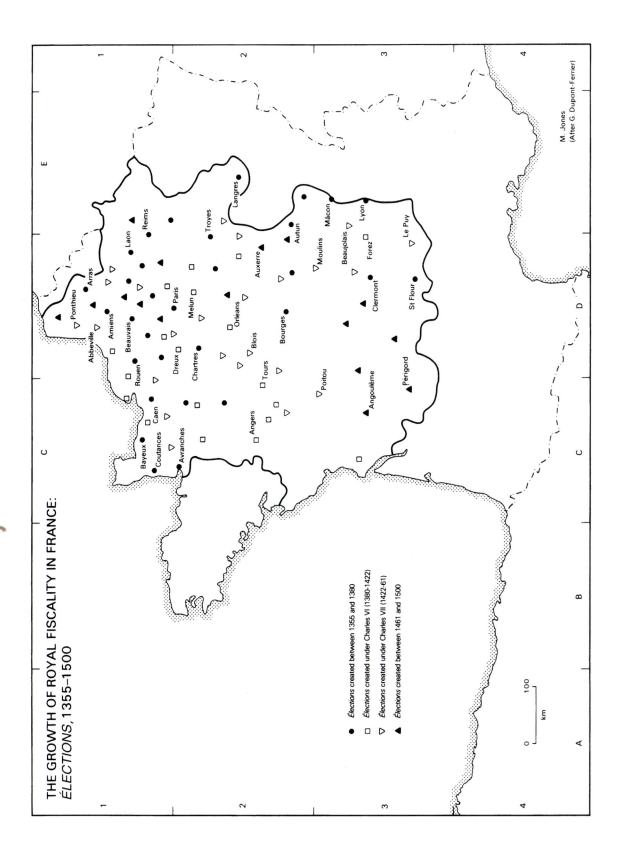

THE GROWTH OF ROYAL FISCALITY IN FRANCE:
ÉLECTIONS, 1355–1500

Langres

Reims

Laon

Troyes

Arras

Auxerre

Autun

Mâcon

Moulins

Lyon

Beaujolais

Forez

Le Puy

Ponthieu

Paris

Melun

Orléans

Clermont

St Flour

Amiens

Beauvais

Bourges

Abbeville

Dreux

Blois

Poitou

Angoulême

Périgord

Rouen

Chartres

Tours

Caen

Coutances

Angers

Bayeux

Avranches

Élections created between 1355 and 1380 ●
Élections created under Charles VI (1380–1422) □
Élections created under Charles VII (1422–61) ▷
Élections created between 1461 and 1500 ▲

0   100
km

M. Jones
(After G. Dupont-Ferrier)

233

Established during Philip IV's reign in the Midi, after 1355 it was applied in Languedoil also, where from the 1380s it was normally termed the *taille*. With demographic changes, especially after the Black Death, revision of the number of *feux* was necessary. The concept of the fiscal household, made up of varying numbers of real households, emerged. From the start, exemption from the *fouage* and *taille* was claimed by the nobility, clergy and other privileged groups (such as royal officials) – though they did not always enjoy it, especially during the permanent state of war which afflicted France after 1337.

It was this war with England that revealed the inadequacy of Crown income from war subsidies. After recourse to traditional means of raising extra income, especially currency manipulation, a series of taxes, already tried in limited form, were generalized. In 1341 a sales tax on salt, the *gabelle*, was imposed. Dropped in 1346, it was revived between 1356 and 1380. From 1383 it became permanent. In the fifteenth century it was raised from about one-third of the kingdom, at royal warehouses (*greniers*) where salt was deposited before sale. But the really critical period for the establishment of both direct and indirect taxes was 1355–70. An already serious political crisis in 1355 deepened in 1356 when John II was captured at Poitiers. To meet the enormous ransom of 3 million *écus* (£500,000) forced loans were levied and the traditional feudal aid was granted – but this was levied as a *fouage*. The sales tax (*aides*) was also extended, accustoming subjects to paying taxes on an annual basis, not only because of evident necessity but also for the common benefit. To collect this money royal France was divided into new administrative districts. The Estates of 1355–6 nominated collectors known as *élus* (hence *élections* for their circumscriptions). The *élections* were usually based on dioceses and were eventually grouped into regional *recettes générales* supervised by general councillors. From 1436 there were four main *recettes* under four *trésoriers* and four *généraux*. The addition of new territories to the royal *domaine* meant that by Louis XII's reign (1498–1514) there were ten or eleven *recettes* and some eighty-five *élections*. From 1360 the Crown took over the nomination and payment of the *élus* and their subordinates.

By this means a large proportion of John II's ransom was paid and the Crown came to depend on the regular levy of taxes. On his deathbed Charles V (1364–80), conscious of the tradition that such taxation was still considered exceptional, abolished the *fouage*. Military and political crises allowed his successor to re-establish both the *fouage* and the *aides*, which had been collected regularly until the Crown's position was again weakened after 1412. Charles VII (1422–61) was forced to consult extensively with various representative assemblies early in his reign. The *taille* was not levied from 1412 to 1423 nor *aides* between 1418 and 1428. After 1428 the king began to take taxes without consent and the Estates at Orléans in 1439 were the last to give general approval to raising the *taille*. In 1443 Languedoc and Dauphiné bought off the *aides* by conceding an annual lump sum, the *équivalent*. By this time the distinction between the *pays d'états* (regions with representative institutions) and those lacking them (*pays d'élections*) had emerged although it apparently made little difference to their relative burden of taxation. Normandy, a *pays d'états*, for example, produced between a sixth and third of royal revenue after its reconquest (1450). By then Charles VII was raising annually about 1.2 million *livres* from the *taille*. Under Louis XI (1461–83) the annual income of the Crown rose to about 4.7 million *livres*. Of this only about 100,000 came from the *domaine*, 650,000 from *aides* and no less than 3.9 million from the *taille*. By far the largest cost to the Crown was its expenditure on the army, established on a permanent basis in the 1440s and enormously expanded by Louis XI. During the minority of Charles VII (1483–90) there was a reaction against royal fiscality. The Estates General of 1484 reduced both the level of taxation and the size of the army but the beginning of French intervention in Italy soon raised the burden of taxation in the 1490s to 4 million *livres*.

M. Jones

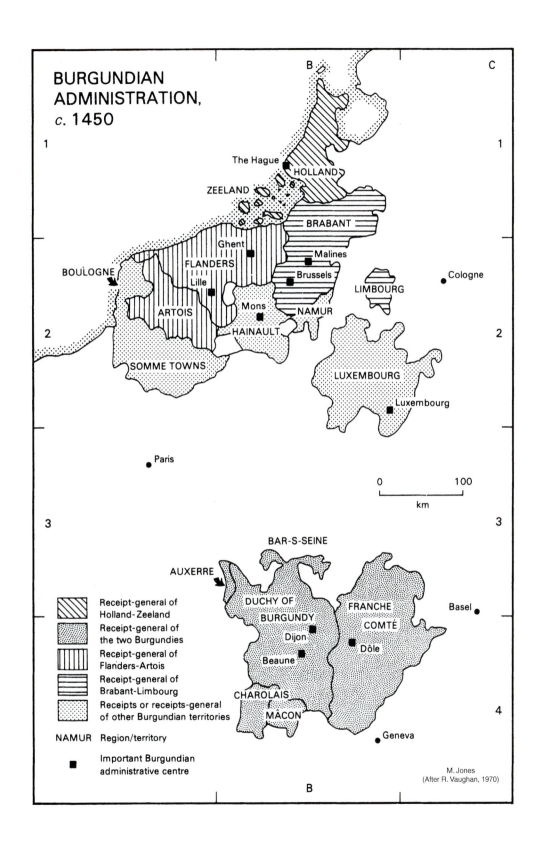

BURGUNDIAN
ADMINISTRATION,
c. 1450

B   C

1   1

The Hague
HOLLAND
ZEELAND
BRABANT
Ghent
Malines
FLANDERS
BOULOGNE   Brussels   Cologne
Lille   LIMBOURG
Mons   NAMUR
ARTOIS   HAINAULT

2   SOMME TOWNS   LUXEMBOURG   2

LUXEMBOURG

Paris

0   100

km

3   3

BAR-S-SEINE

AUXERRE

DUCHY OF   FRANCHE
BURGUNDY   COMTÉ   Basel
Dijon
Beaune   Dôle

Receipt-general of
Holland-Zeeland

Receipt-general of   CHAROLAIS
the two Burgundies
MÂCON
Receipt-general of
Flanders-Artois   4
Geneva
Receipt-general of
Brabant-Limbourg

Receipts or receipts-general
of other Burgundian territories

NAMUR   Region/territory

■   Important Burgundian
         administrative centre

M. Jones
(After R. Vaughan, 1970)

B

235

Burgundian administration, *c.* 1450

Recognizing local privileges, ducal government had a federal quality. Central institutions emerged gradually. A chancellor headed an omnicompetent ducal council. Finances were under a treasurer while a receiver-general, though not controlling all local receipts, handled revenues from all the duke's lands. Regional receivers were accountable before *chambres des comptes* at Lille (founded by the count of Flanders, 1382) and Dijon (reorganized, 1386). Subsequently *chambres* also emerged at Brussels and The Hague. From *c.* 1430–68 the duke disposed of important funds through a *trésor de l'épargne*. Charles also appointed a treasurer of wars. In both cases French or Breton practice was imitated. From the 1440s *commis sur le fait des finances*, chief financial officers, supervised their administration and advised the council. Locally, efforts were made to rationalize institutions in neighbouring territories. The two Burgundies and some adjacent territories – Flanders and Artois, Brabant and Limbourg, Holland and Zeeland – were often administratively combined. Northern predominance (in

Charles's reign the Netherlands produced five times more revenue than the two Burgundies) was marked early in Philip the Good's reign by the removal of responsibility for auditing the accounts of the ducal household, together with those of the receiver-general, from Dijon to Lille. From 1473 Charles attempted to establish alongside the newly created sovereign *parlement* for his Netherlandish territories at Malines a new *chambre des comptes* to replace those of Lille and Brussels. Other sovereign courts existed in Hainault (Mons) and the Franche Comté (Dôle), though the *parlement* at Beaune remained subject to that at Paris, which also heard appeals from Artois and Flanders. Most territories had representative institutions, like the Estates of Artois or Four Members of Flanders. Dukes consulted them, especially about taxes (*aides*). From 1425 Estates in adjacent territories tended to hold joint meetings; one such in 1464 is usually regarded as the first Estates General of the Low Countries which had an important future role, especially after Charles's death (1477).

M. Jones

The government of late medieval Germany

The limited powers of the German monarchy were reflected in the rudimentary nature of Germany's institutions of central government. The chancery was responsible for issuing royal charters and letters though it was small compared to that in other countries. Germany's representative assembly, the *Reichstag*, had developed by the Late Middle Ages from an advisory into a legislative body. Its membership, still somewhat fluid in the fifteenth century, comprised the electors, prelates, princes, some lesser lords and representatives of the imperial towns. The electors, constituted as the *Kurverein*, and urban envoys, constituted from

the 1470s as the Urban Diet, sometimes met independently of the *Reichstag* in order to articulate their respective interests. The *Reichstag* itself met frequently in the Late Middle Ages, though absenteeism, especially among northern members, was rife and the acceptance and implementation of its decisions only partial. Neither the *Reichstag* nor the emperor provided an effective remedy for Germany's pressing need for public peace and justice. Repeated attempts to outlaw feuding were ineffective and the provision of royal courts inadequate. The emergence of a chamber court (*Kammergericht*) – but with limited competence and resources – was

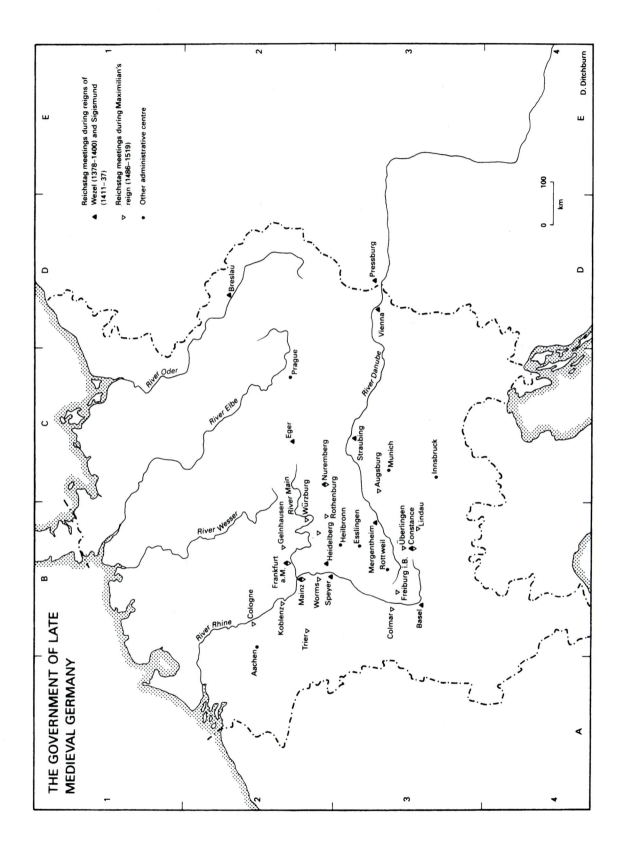

THE GOVERNMENT OF LATE
MEDIEVAL GERMANY

Reichstag meetings during reigns of
Wezel (1378–1400) and Sigismund
(1411–37)

Reichstag meetings during Maximilian's
reign (1486–1519)

Other administrative centre

100

km

0

D. Ditchburn

Aachen

Cologne

River Rhine

Koblenz

Trier

Frankfurt
a.M.

Mainz

Worms

Speyer

Gelnhausen

River Main

Würzburg

River Wesser

River Elbe

River Oder

Breslau

Prague

Eger

Nuremberg

Rothenburg

Heidelberg

Heilbronn

Esslingen

Mergentheim

Rottweil

Überlingen

Freiburg i.B.

Constance

Lindau

Colmar

Basel

Straubing

Augsburg

Munich

Innsbruck

River Danube

Vienna

Pressburg

paralleled by the demise of the royal court of justice (*Reichshofgericht*) in the mid-fifteenth century, following widespread grants of immunity from its jurisdiction. Royal taxation, meanwhile, remained largely *ad hoc* and meagre compared to that elsewhere. Several plans for reinvigorating imperial government were advanced in the fifteenth century though it was only after the deliberations of the Emperor-elect Maximilian (1493–1519) and the *Reichstag* held at Worms in 1495 that reforms were actually implemented. Following the declaration of a perpetual public peace and the prohibition of feuding, the *Kammergericht* was transformed into the *Reichskammergericht*, a supreme appellate court with a staff of salaried professional judges. The costs of this court and an imperial army were to be met from a new imperial property tax, the 'common penny' (*Gemeiner Pfennig*). Inability to enforce payment of the tax undermined the other reforms and the *Gemeiner Pfennig* was soon abandoned. Instead the government resorted for finance to *Kammerzieler*, a small biennial tax to support the *Reichskammergericht*, and other traditional but irregular levies including 'Roman money' (*Römermonate*), an aid originally intended to finance imperial coronations in Rome which evolved into a levy for military purposes. Maximilian was less enthusiastic about other reforms discussed at Worms, including the proposal associated with Berthold von Henneberg, archbishop of Mainz, to establish a permanent executive council. This body (the *Reichsregiment*) was, however, appointed in 1500. Presided over by the king or his deputy, its twenty members included repre-sentatives of the electors, other *Reichstag* estates and six newly established constituencies or 'circles' (*Kreise*), who together were entrusted with extensive powers over royal justice, finance and foreign policy. Ill-resourced, without means of asserting its authority and regarded with suspicion by Maximilian, the *Reichsregiment* floundered within two years though it was revived later in the sixteenth century. In consequence of political particularism and the limited success of the attempted governmental reforms, Germany lacked an equivalent to London, Paris or Edinburgh, which were emerging as national administrative centres. The *Reichstag* assembled in a variety of locations though usually, and increasingly under Maximilian, in central or southern Germany. The Urban Diet convened at Frankfurt, Speyer, Heilbronn and Esslingen and the *Kurverein* in yet other towns. The *Kammergericht* frequently sat at Rottweil. The *Reichskammergericht* was assigned to Frankfurt, where imperial elections were usually held, though royal coronations took place at Aachen. The royal insignia was lodged at Munich, then Karlstein, near Prague, and from 1424 at Nuremberg, where the *Reichsregiment* too was based. But in other respects, just as Prague may be regarded as the centre of Charles IV's (1347–78) empire, so Innsbruck was the centre of Maximilian's kingdom. It was in the administrative centre of his Tirolean lands that Maximilian first based his imperial chancery and court and here too that he established the imperial archive.

D. Ditchburn

Royal itineraries in Portugal

Portuguese kings, like their counterparts else-where, were continually on the move. Economic necessity, diplomacy, weather and pestilence determined an itinerary including most frequently the towns of Lisbon, Coimbra, Santarém and Évora. Visits were restricted to no more than two months in each location. By the later fifteenth century the expansion of the royal household altered this pattern, as the practical dilemma of accommodating growing numbers of courtiers increased. During Manuel I's reign (1495–1521) Coimbra lost importance and the royal itinerary focused more on new palaces in Lisbon, Évora and Almerim, near Santarém. As the Crown augmented its investment in its new palaces and as more nobles acquired private apartments in their proximity, the duration of royal visits at each centre increased significantly. Although the construction of the *Casa da India e Guiné* (1501) encouraged Lisbon's emergence as the administrative capital of Portugal, the Portuguese court remained itinerant.

S.C. Humble Ferreira

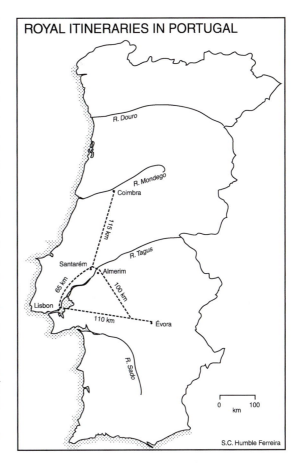

ROYAL ITINERARIES IN PORTUGAL

S.C. Humble Ferreira

Castilian *corregidores*, 1390–1474

Although officials known as *corregidores* existed by the early fourteenth century, the Castilian monarchy only made extensive use of them from Henry III's reign (1390–1406). Initially, they were the ideal agents to represent the Crown in dealing with problems in royal towns and they disposed of important powers over the political and economic life of the towns to which they were sent. Theoretically they were dispatched at the invitation of towns but in practice the king often appointed them without consultation. The salaries of *corregidores*, who were not usually natives of the areas in which they operated, were paid by the towns where they resided. This fact, coupled with their powers of intervention, aroused the hostility of urban oligarchies.

Most *corregidores* were either minor nobles or men with legal training (*letrados*). The main problems that they faced were internal urban disorders arising from clan-like feuds amongst regional elites, abuses in the administration of justice, corrupt levying and auditing of municipal finances and the usurpation of royal and municipal rights by the Church and the nobility.

The Catholic Monarchs extended appointments so considerably that by 1494 fifty-four *corregidores* existed. Although their increasing use generally enhanced royal power considerably, abuses by individual *corregidores* were frequent. Moreover, during the reign of Henry IV, the appointment of some *corregidores* fell into the

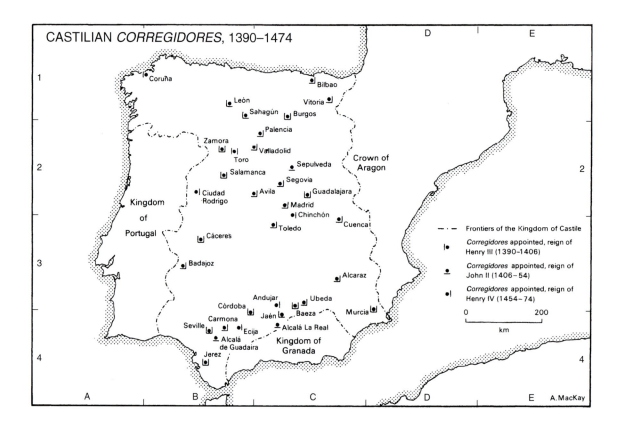

CASTILIAN *CORREGIDORES*, 1390–1474

Frontiers of the Kingdom of Castile

Corregidores appointed, reign of Henry III (1390–1406)

Corregidores appointed, reign of John II (1406–54)

Corregidores appointed, reign of Henry IV (1454–74)

0   200
km

A. MacKay

hands of great nobles and from John II's reign the Crown generally failed to support attempts by *corregidores* to prevent the aristocracy from usurping urban territories. When many Castilian towns rebelled in 1520 in the Revolt of the *Comuneros*, informed contemporaries agreed that abuses in the royal control of the system of *corregidores* had constituted a major cause of urban unrest.

A. MacKay

Representation at the Castilian *cortes*, 1445–74

During the fifteenth century the influence of the Castilian *cortes* declined sharply. This was paralleled by its increasingly unrepresentative nature. Attendance of the first and second estates was irregular since the king only summoned those whom he wanted to attend. Meeting irregularly and only when summoned by the king, the *cortes* mainly comprised representatives of the third estate (*procuradores*) and royal officials. Its main functions were to vote taxation and to present petitions, often evasively answered, to the king.

Forty-nine towns were represented in the *cortes* of 1391. By the mid-fifteenth century this decreased to a maximum of seventeen towns. These were all royal towns, the inhabitants of noble and ecclesiastical lordships being theoretically represented by the first and second estates. In practice, therefore, complete regions, such as Galicia, the Basque provinces,

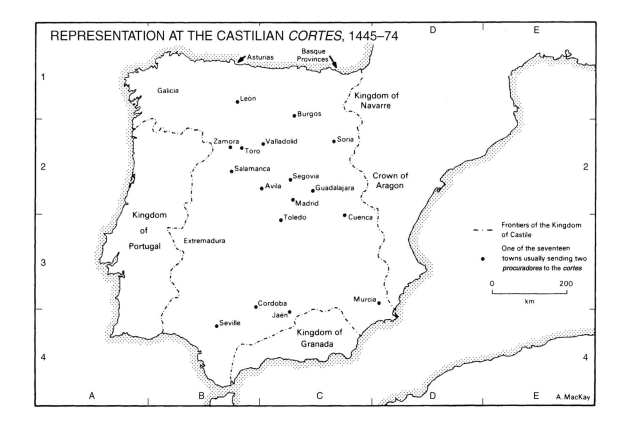

REPRESENTATION AT THE CASTILIAN *CORTES*, 1445–74

Asturias · Basque Provices · Galicia · León · Burgos · Kingdom of Navarre · Zamora · Valladolid · Soria · Toro · Salamanca · Segovia · Crown of Aragon · Avila · Guadalajara · Madrid · Kingdom of Portugal · Toledo · Cuenca · Extremadura · Cordoba · Murcia · Jaén · Seville · Kingdom of Granada · A. MacKay

--- Frontiers of the Kingdom of Castile

• One of the seventeen towns usually sending two *procuradores* to the *cortes*

0 ——— 200 km

Asturias and Extremadura were not represented.

The selection of *procuradores* was controlled by urban oligarchies, although the king occasionally intervened to nominate individuals. In 1432 the *cortes* of Zamora reaffirmed the old practice that non-nobles could not be *procuradores*. By then the Crown paid *procuradores'* expenses. In general, therefore, these *procuradores* were not necessarily more representative of the urban population than bishops were of those living in their lordships. They could readily agree to taxes which they themselves did not pay. The oligarchies they represented, proud of their participation in the *cortes*, could even expect to derive benefit from agreeing to royal requests to spend other people's money.

A. MacKay

Parliamentary representation in late medieval England

Representatives of shires, cities and boroughs were summoned to some parliaments in the reign of Edward I (1272–1307) and were customarily summoned from the reign of his son, Edward II (1307–27). Writs were sent from chancery to sheriffs ordering them to cause elections of two shire knights each to be held in thirty-seven shires. Cheshire and County Durham, where respectively the earls of Chester and bishops of Durham exercised regal

241

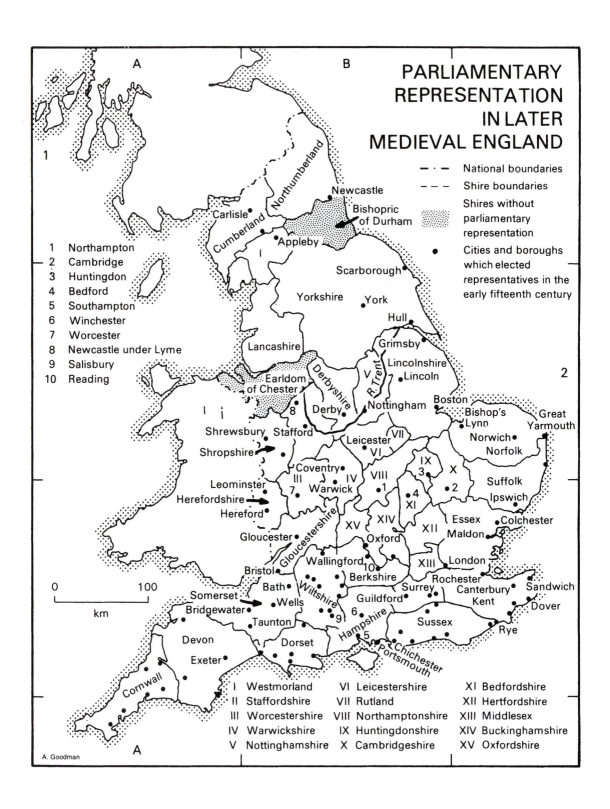

PARLIAMENTARY REPRESENTATION IN LATER MEDIEVAL ENGLAND

- – · – National boundaries
- – – – Shire boundaries
- Shires without parliamentary representation
- • Cities and boroughs which elected representatives in the early fifteenth century

1 Northampton
2 Cambridge
3 Huntingdon
4 Bedford
5 Southampton
6 Winchester
7 Worcester
8 Newcastle under Lyme
9 Salisbury
10 Reading

I Westmorland
II Staffordshire
III Worcestershire
IV Warwickshire
V Nottinghamshire
VI Leicestershire
VII Rutland
VIII Northamptonshire
IX Huntingdonshire
X Cambridgeshire
XI Bedfordshire
XII Hertfordshire
XIII Middlesex
XIV Buckinghamshire
XV Oxfordshire

A. Goodman

242

authority, were unrepresented. Only occasionally were those elected actually knights; more commonly they were gentlefolk, often lawyers and stewards of estates busy in local administration. Under the Lancastrian kings in the fifteenth century legislation ensured that elections in the shire court reflected truly the will of better-off, resident freeholders.

The number of boroughs which were ordered to elect two burgesses (London was unique in electing four citizens) and which sent them fluctuated. According to Professor McKisack, an average of seventy cities and boroughs were represented in Edward II's parliaments, and an average of eighty-three in the parliaments of Richard II (1377–99). The map shows cities and boroughs which returned in the early decades of the fifteenth century. Northern England was poorly represented compared with England south of the River Trent, with two unenfranchised shires and few cities and boroughs. Many enfranchised boroughs were dwindling into insignificance in terms of population and wealth by the fifteenth century, when there was a tendency for such boroughs to return members of aristocratic rather than bourgeois status, often non-resident. Gentlefolk had come to consider it prestigious and useful to sit in the Commons House, even as burgesses: the outnumbered shire knights apparently controlled the business of the House. By the time the 'Good Parliament' met in 1376, shire knights and burgesses were in the habit of sitting and debating together: then, under the leadership of the first known Commons Speaker, they demonstrated a remarkable ability to press reform of government on the Crown.

A. Goodman

The Great Famine, 1315–22

Northern Europe was devastated by a prolonged famine which began in 1315 and continued until at least 1318 and in many areas until 1322. Both chronicle and dendroclimatological (tree-ring) evidence attest that it was ostensibly caused by a series of cool summers and harsh winters combined with abnormal rainfall. The effect on the harvest was catastrophic. By modern standards medieval grain yields were in any case low – for wheat most scholars agree on a return of at best 3:1 or 4:1. In 1315–16 wheat returns declined by almost 80 per cent on some of Bolton Priory's demesnes in Yorkshire. Other regions and other grains were generally hit less severely although the harvest shortfall was exacerbated by several factors. Famine in England and Germany was felt in Norway as the northern European grain trade collapsed. Transport limitations made delivery of alternative supplies from unaffected areas difficult, though some arrived from Iberia and southern France. The grain shortage nonetheless significantly inflated prices. Meanwhile, sheep perished in a murrain affecting the British Isles and other livestock perished to disease from c.1317. In parts of Scandinavia, Germany, Ireland and on the Franco-Flemish and Anglo-Scottish frontiers famine coincided with war. Mortality rates are difficult to assess but 2,794 deaths were recorded at Ypres in six months of 1316 alone – perhaps 10 per cent of the population, a similar proportion to that in Tournai though perhaps double the proportion of fatalities in Bruges. While contemporaries saw God's hand at work, some historians have seen overpopulation as key to these developments. For many the 'crisis of the early fourteenth century', rather than the Black Death, was the turning point in the medieval economy and society – but debate continues.

D. Ditchburn

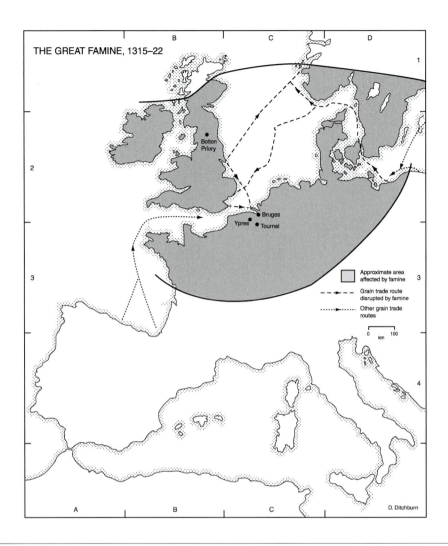

THE GREAT FAMINE, 1315–22

Bolton Priory

Bruges
Ypres • Tournai

Approximate area affected by famine

Grain trade route disrupted by famine

Other grain trade routes

0   100
    km

D. Ditchburn

The spread of the Black Death

The appearance and rapid spread of the Black Death or plague in Europe were facilitated by the *pax mongolica* and by those widespread trade routes which medieval merchants had established between Europe and Central Asia. The Black Death spread across Central Asia from China during the 1340s and, infecting Genoese merchants at the Crimean port of Caffa in 1347, it almost immediately reached Constantinople and was then rapidly disseminated along the trade routes to the Mediterranean and western Europe. By the end of 1348 it had affected most of southern and western Europe, appearing in England at Melcombe Regis during the summer, and in the course of the next two years it spread over the rest of the British Isles, Germany and Scandinavia.

Traditionally historians believed that the Black Death was bubonic plague (a disease of black rats which affected humans when the bacillus was spread by fleas) or its pneumonic variant. This longstanding orthodoxy was,

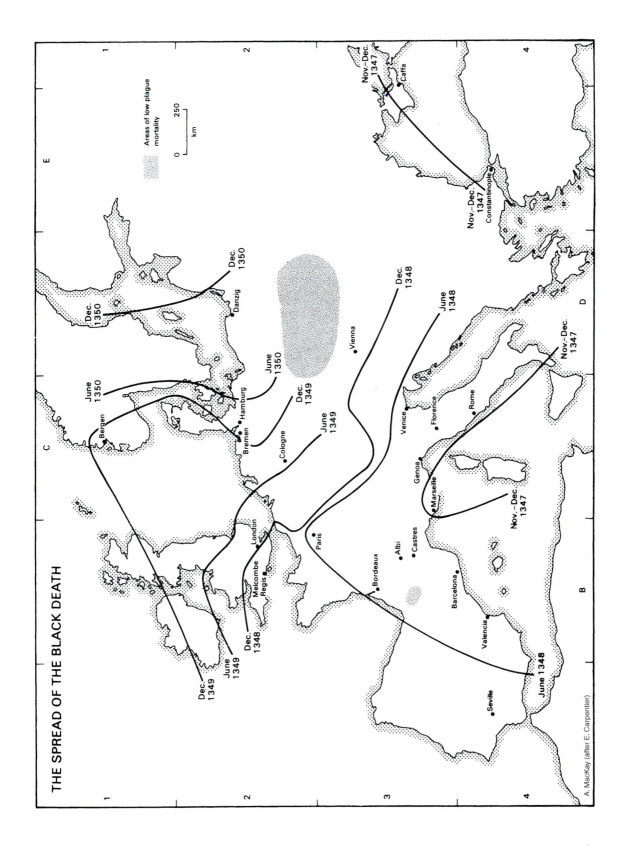

THE SPREAD OF THE BLACK DEATH

A. MacKay (after E. Carpentier)

Areas of low plague mortality

0   250
km

Caffa

Nov.–Dec. 1347

Nov.–Dec. 1347
Constantinople

Dec. 1350

Dec. 1350

Danzig

Dec. 1348

June 1348

June 1350

Bergen

June 1350

Hamburg

Bremen

June 1350

Cologne

Dec. 1349

Vienna

Nov.–Dec. 1347

June 1349

Dec. 1349

Venice

Florence

Rome

Genoa

Paris

Marseille

June 1349

London

Melcombe Regis

Dec. 1348

Castres

Albi

Nov.–Dec. 1347

Bordeaux

Dec. 1349

June 1349

Barcelona

Valencia

June 1348

Seville

245

however, challenged by Samuel K. Cohn who, noting the absence of rats from contemporary reports of the Black Death, argued in 2002 that, whatever else it was, the Black Death was not the rat-based bubonic plague. While the exact scientific nature of the Black Death remains uncertain, it is agreed that its impact was devastating even though, given the absence of adequate statistical data and variation in the incidence of the phenomenon, it is impossible to be precise about the number of people wiped out. Shaken by the calamity, contemporaries might understandably have exaggerated the results. The chronicler Froissart, for example, claimed that 'at least a third of all the people in the world died then'. Yet perhaps Froissart was not too wide of the mark and it may be suggested, with all due caution, that between one-quarter and one-third of the population of western Europe died as a result of the plague. This estimate must, however, also be considered within the context of the significant variations in the incidence of mortality. Some towns, and especially ports, suffered huge losses. Albi, Castres and Florence, for example, probably lost over half their populations, Genoa and Hamburg two-thirds, and Bremen up to three-quarters. On the other hand Bohemia, Poland, Hungary and perhaps the central plateaus of Castile seem to have been less affected by the plague.

Horrendous though the Black Death was, it was not an isolated phenomenon and it is important to bear in mind the periods both before and after the pandemic. The Black Death had been preceded by years of famine, particularly the great famine of 1315–18 in north-western Europe, and it is probable that population growth in general had already been checked before the pandemic. Malthusian analysis would suggest that the demographic increase of the twelfth and thirteenth centuries created a situation where population growth outstripped food resources, with the result that crises of subsistence became more serious and facilitated the 'collapse' of the fourteenth century. By the same token, the distinctive land:population ratios of central and eastern Europe and some areas of the Iberian Peninsula meant that these regions were relatively better endowed with land than they were with colonists and settlers. This, in turn, may help to explain why they were less affected by the Black Death.

After the Black Death the deadly disease became endemic for the remainder of the Middle Ages (and beyond), with sporadic outbreaks occurring at different times and in different places. These outbreaks, which were more pronouncedly urban in character, not only helped to check the recovery of the population but also seem to have hit hardest at those who lacked immunity – hence, for example, the 'Pestilences of the Children' in England in 1361 and in Catalonia in 1362–3 ('*mortalidad de los infantes*').

A. MacKay

Deserted English villages, *c.* 1100– *c.* 1500

According to the Maurice Beresford, 'there was probably never a decade in the Middle Ages which did not see the death of one or more villages'. Beresford's outline of the spatial and temporal incidence of village desertions has been modified little by subsequent research, except perhaps to indicate a higher casualty rate before the Black Death. The absence of tax assessments before 1297 and the imperfections of later sources and archaeological dating methods inhibit accurate dating of many desertions. Most disappearances can, however,

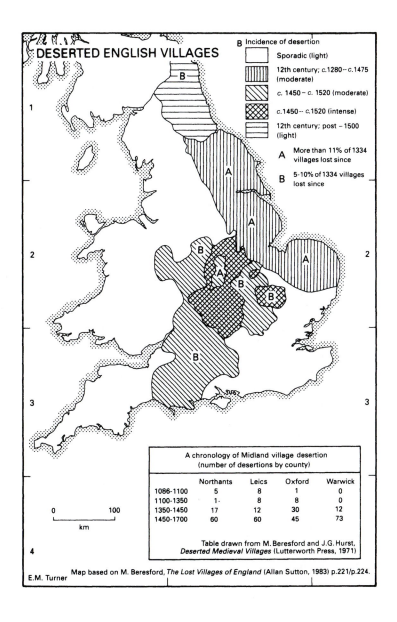

DESERTED ENGLISH VILLAGES

B Incidence of desertion

- ☐ Sporadic (light)
- ║ 12th century; c.1280– c.1475 (moderate)
- ╱ c. 1450 – c. 1520 (moderate)
- ▧ c.1450 – c.1520 (intense)
- ═ 12th century; post – 1500 (light)

A More than 11% of 1334 villages lost since

B 5-10% of 1334 villages lost since

A chronology of Midland village desertion (number of desertions by county)				
	Northants	Leics	Oxford	Warwick
1086-1100	5	8	1	0
1100-1350	1·	8	8	0
1350-1450	17	12	30	12
1450-1700	60	60	45	73

Table drawn from M. Beresford and J.G. Hurst, *Deserted Medieval Villages* (Lutterworth Press, 1971).

E.M. Turner

Map based on M. Beresford, *The Lost Villages of England* (Allan Sutton, 1983) p.221/p.224.

0 — 100 km

---

be located within broad periods. With the notable exception of the central Midlands, John Hales' observation in 1549 that 'the chief destruction of villages was before the reign of King Henry the Seventh' (i.e. 1485) holds true.

The incidence and causes of desertions varied regionally and over time. Nevertheless, a universal feature, especially before the late fourteenth century, was the greater vulnerability of smaller villages. Soil type and proximity to neighbours may have restricted growth and predisposed smaller villages to loss of economic viability when the agricultural terms of trade shifted unfavourably and certain demographic conditions prevailed.

Twelfth-century desertions were largely due to the sheep farming activities of Cistercians and local factors, such as coastal erosion and border raids. Desertions between the late thirteenth and mid-fourteenth centuries can

247

be attributed to the retreat from marginal land, colonized during the population expansion of the Central Middle Ages, where soils were perhaps exhausted and which, with later demographic contraction, was no longer required. Recurrent epidemics thereafter rarely caused the demise of villages directly. Rather, the casualties of the next 150 years seem associated with the continued abandonment of marginal arable land and the emergent comparative advantage of pastoral production occurring in the context of demographic stagnation and demand shifts. Particularly at risk were places, many in the Midland counties, where the relative advantage of pastoral or arable production was not strong.

Enclosures, so villainized by contemporary commentators, were clearly, then, a symptom rather than a cause of village desertion before 1500.

E.M. Turner

Late medieval transhumance in western Europe

Transhumance is the seasonal movement of livestock (notably sheep) in April/May and September/October between winter and summer pastures, allowing the avoidance of variations in climate. In Europe the displacement is of altitude. Transhumance differs from nomadism in that there is a permanent dwelling for part of the year. In 'normal' transhumance the permanent (winter) home is in the lowlands, while in 'inverse' transhumance the permanent (summer) home is in the mountains. Since large sheep flocks were moved great distances, late medieval transhumance involved considerable organization, as the fixed routes on the map help to illustrate. These tracks varied between 10m and 20m in width. Each had a strip of pasture on one or both sides, increasing the width by an average of 100m.

Transhumance was practised in the Balkans by Vlach shepherds, the summer settlement being the *katun*. It was particularly important to the economy of Dubrovnik. Inverse transhumance occurred in some places. So did 'oscillating' transhumance in which permanent homes lie on the migration route and accommodate flocks in spring and autumn. In Italy transhumance between the Abruzzi mountains and the Apulian Tavoliere was based on routes known as *tratturi delle pecore*. In the fifteenth century, as a result of intervention by Alfonso I of Aragon, sales of wool and sheep were centred on Foggia and transhumance was regulated by an institution known as the *Dogana*. The *tratturi*, therefore, linked the *Dogana* of Foggia with the highland areas of the Abruzzi. In Castile transhumance was catered for by numerous tributary tracks (*cañadas*) which fed three main north–south routes (*cañadas reales*). All were marked by stone pillars 1.5m high at 100m intervals. In the thirteenth century royal recognition of the *Mesta*, an association of stockmen, strengthened existing rights of way and the Crown derived income from the *servicio* and *montazgo* taxes levied on sheep movements. Southern France was characterized by both normal and inverse transhumance. *Carraïrés*, dating from the thirteenth century and formalized by *Statuts de la Transhumance* in the sixteenth century, were routes fed by narrower *drailles*. In Alpine transhumance, typified by Switzerland, pastures at different altitudes were emphasized more than the tracks. The pastures all fell within the mountain area and were grazed successively as the season advanced: *Hofweiden* at 1,000m, *Vorweiden* up to 1,500m, and *Alpweiden* up to over 2,000m.

It is difficult to reconstruct routes for northern Europe and none are shown on the map. There was oscillating transhumance in Iceland, with sheep wintered away and only moved to higher

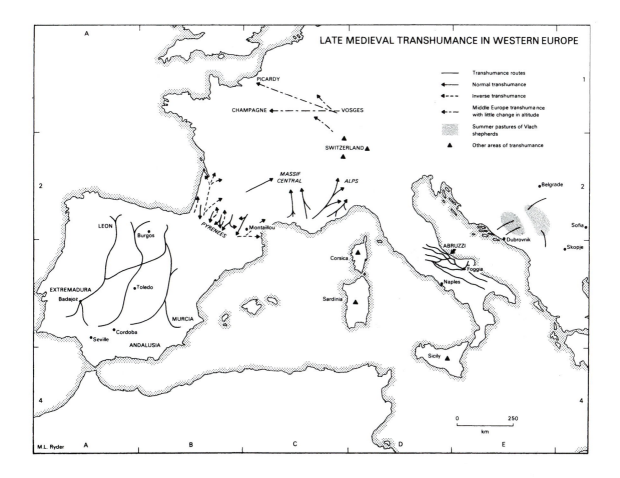

LATE MEDIEVAL TRANSHUMANCE IN WESTERN EUROPE

——	Transhumance routes
◄——	Normal transhumance
◄- - -	Inverse transhumance
◄- - -	Middle Europe transhumance with little change in altitude
(shaded)	Summer pastures of Vlach shepherds
▲	Other areas of transhumance

M.L. Ryder

ground during July and August. In Norway movements were eastwards, from western coast and valleys into the mountains, while in Sweden movements were westwards, the summer settlement being the *seter*. Evidence for transhumance in the British Isles also lies more in summer settlements than in migration routes, which probably became green drove roads and even ordinary roads, just as the summer settlements became permanent hill farms. In Wales the summer settlement was the *hafod* (in contrast to the lowland *hendre*). In the Pennines and Cumbria inverse transhumance persists, with the wintering on low ground of sheep in their first year. Pennine place names ending in 'sett'

derive from *seter*, indicating transhumance and Scandinavian influence. In Cumbria the Norse ending for *seter* is 'erg', an Irish loan word for summer settlement, which itself indicates that transhumance took place in Ireland. There was transhumance in all the mountainous areas of Scotland, the summer settlement being the shieling.

Fascinating insights into the lives of shepherds of the Pyrenean village of Montaillou is afforded by the early fourteenth-century Inquisition Register of Jacques Fournier, bishop of Pamiers.

M.L. Ryder

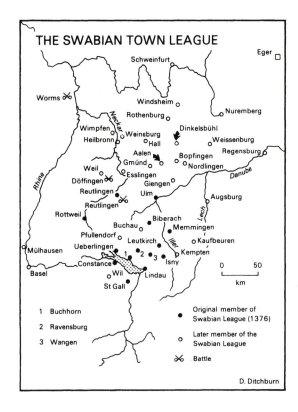

The Swabian Town League

Later medieval German urban leagues were temporary alliances between neighbouring towns. They were usually directed against knights and princes who threatened urban trading monopolies and jurisdictions. Despite their prohibition in the Golden Bull (1356), leagues flourished because weak kings failed to defend urban interests. When Charles IV and Wenzel imposed high taxation on some towns, and mortgaged others to their princely enemies in order to fund their dynastic ambitions, fourteen towns under Ulm's leadership formed the Swabian Town League in 1376. The League defeated its main local enemy, the count of Wurtemberg, at Reutlingen (1377), encouraging other towns, notably Regensburg (1381) and Nuremberg (1384) to join. Alliances were made with the Rhenish League (1381) and Swiss Confederation (1385) and the League received implicit imperial recognition in 1384. Nevertheless, in 1388 the princes defeated the Swabian League at Döffingen and its Rhenish allies at Worms. The leagues gradually fell apart thereafter and were again proscribed by the Pacification of Eger (1389).

D. Ditchburn

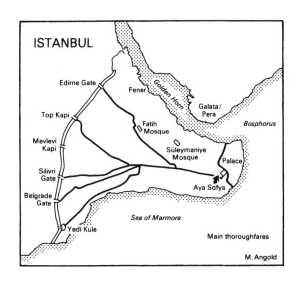

Istanbul

The city which the Ottoman Turks conquered from the Byzantines in 1453 was nigh derelict. Its restoration was among the most urgent tasks facing Mehmed the Conqueror. He drafted in settlers from all parts of his empire. His success is revealed by a census of the city made in 1477. There were at least 16,234 households, representing a total population of perhaps 100,000. Muslims formed about three-fifths of the population; Greeks just under a quarter, already concentrated in Fener, where the patriarchate found a resting place. The next largest community were the Jews – about a tenth of the population. Though always cosmopolitan, Istanbul was a thoroughly Muslim city. St Sophia was turned into the chief mosque. Mehmed had the Fatih mosque constructed on the site of the Church of the Holy Apostles. Attached to these were religious, charitable and educational institutions and, by way of endowment, markets, shops and workshops. The foundation of such complexes – or *imârets* – was typical of the growth of the city. The Conqueror's example was followed by his viziers and his successors. Among the most impressive is the Süleymaniye built by Süleyman the Magnificent (1520–66). By his reign the population of Istanbul was approaching the half million mark.

M. Angold

Novgorod

Novgorod, in existence by the ninth century, was the seat of a bishopric and from 1165 an archbishopric. It was also by the Late Middle Ages the centre of a large city-state with far-flung trading interests. The town was divided by the River Volkov but linked by a bridge. The St Sophia side was dominated by the cathedral and its surrounding fortress, the Kremlin. The market place, close to the wharfs on the commercial side, was surrounded by mercantile churches (such as St John's Church of the Russian merchants and the Good Friday Church of the Russian long-distance merchants) and by trading depots (such as the Gotenhof of the Gotland merchants and the Hanse's St Petershof). Politically, until its conquest by Ivan III of Russia in 1478, Novgorod was dominated by its archbishop and a group of urban-dwelling nobility. For administrative purposes the city was divided into fifths and these in turn into smaller units, the smallest of which was the street.

D. Ditchburn

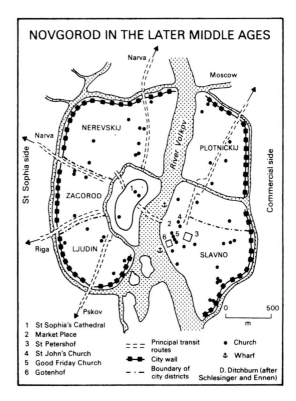

NOVGOROD IN THE LATER MIDDLE AGES

1 St Sophia's Cathedral
2 Market Place
3 St Petershof
4 St John's Church
5 Good Friday Church
6 Gotenhof

- - - Principal transit routes
●■● City wall
- · - Boundary of city districts

● Church
⚓ Wharf

D. Ditchburn (after Schlesinger and Ennen)

251

Dunfermline

Dunfermline's town plan was largely determined by geography and geology. Glacial drifts in prehistoric times established a surface pattern of a series of low ridges. It was along one of these ridges that the High Street, or Causagait, was laid out. Geography also determined that the town had no large open space where a market could be sited. Dunfermline's market, as a result, ran the length of Causagait and, by about 1500, even beyond the East Port. The market cross stood, unusually, at some distance from the tron (weighing machine) and the tolbooth, where market tolls were gathered. The townscape was dominated by the sheer mass of the abbey precincts, which gave rise to a periphery of surrounding roadways. There was much in the central core, however, that reflected other small medieval towns – a single street, flanked by back lanes; and the important market area protected by gates, or ports.

E.P. Dennison

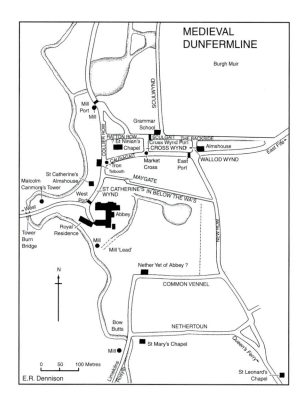

Seville

Within its walls the great trading city of Seville covered an area of 682 acres and to this must be added the extra-mural districts such as Triana. The original nucleus, characterized by small blocks of buildings and irregular streets, was in the south-east. Towards the north the blocks of buildings were larger and the streets rectilinear, above all in the north-west part which came into existence later. The large blocks of areas taken up by the monasteries and convents were prominent (there were nineteen by 1500), above all, those established in the thirteenth century and situated along the western front.

Administratively the city was divided into twenty-eight parishes and five districts and its population rose from approximately 5,000 *vecinos* (heads of households) in the 1430s to 7,000 *vecinos* in the 1480s, excluding temporary residents and the exiguous minorities of Jews and Muslims. This population was unevenly distributed, with the highest densities being in the southern part of the city. Here were to be found the centres of civil power, such as the *alcázar* or royal palace, the city council, the admiralty and the customs headquarters; the cathedral; the most important markets; the *alcaicería* or silk exchange; the area where international trade was transacted; the *lonjas* or commercial centres of merchants from different nations; and all those associated with these activities, such as money-changers, bankers and notaries. The urban configuration here had for the most part been inherited from the Muslims.

To the north of the city gates of Osario and Goles there was a lesser density of population, a predominance of occupations relating to agriculture, fishing and seamanship and a large number of labourers. Moreover, this was an area

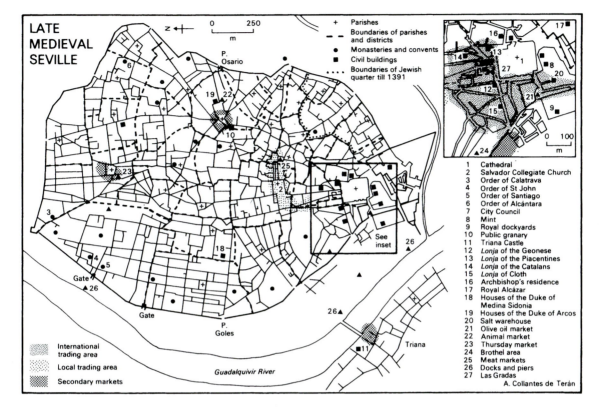

LATE MEDIEVAL SEVILLE

+ Parishes
- - Boundaries of parishes and districts
• Monasteries and convents
■ Civil buildings
.... Boundaries of Jewish quarter till 1391

1   Cathedral
2   Salvador Collegiate Church
3   Order of Calatrava
4   Order of St John
5   Order of Santiago
6   Order of Alcántara
7   City Council
8   Mint
9   Royal dockyards
10 Public granary
11 Triana Castle
12 *Lonja* of the Geonese
13 *Lonja* of the Piacentines
14 *Lonja* of the Catalans
15 *Lonja* of Cloth
16 Archbishop's residence
17 Royal Alcázar
18 Houses of the Duke of Medina Sidonia
19 Houses of the Duke of Arcos
20 Salt warehouse
21 Olive oil market
22 Animal market
23 Thursday market
24 Brothel area
25 Meat markets
26 Docks and piers
27 Las Gradas

A. Collantes de Terán

International trading area
Local trading area
Secondary markets

almost totally lacking in a co-ordinating infra-structure, apart from a market to supply the locality with provisions and another weekly market, for probably the same purpose, held every Thursday.

The houses of great nobles and patrician oligarchs were not in one particular district but dispersed throughout the city.

A. Collantes de Terán

Financial centres in western Europe

The Late Middle Ages witnessed several significant monetary and financial developments. With the exploitation of the Hungarian gold mines at Kremnica, gold coins became more common from the fourteenth century. Gold was used especially for international transactions. Silver, by contrast, became increasingly scarce from the later fourteenth century as its supply from mines in Sardinia, Bosnia and especially Kutná Hora, in Bohemia, declined. The shortage, exacerbated by wear and by hoarding, caused mints in most of northern Europe

(except London) to close between the 1440s and 1460s. The production of 'white silver' coins (made from silver alloy) and even of 'black money' (which included only tiny amounts of silver) was also affected – making for a shortage in the coins used by poorer people too. The situation was only resolved with the opening of new silver mines at Schneeberg in Saxony and Schwaz in the Tirol from the 1470s.

The bullion famine was to have profound effects on the economy since the religious, political and economic life of late medieval

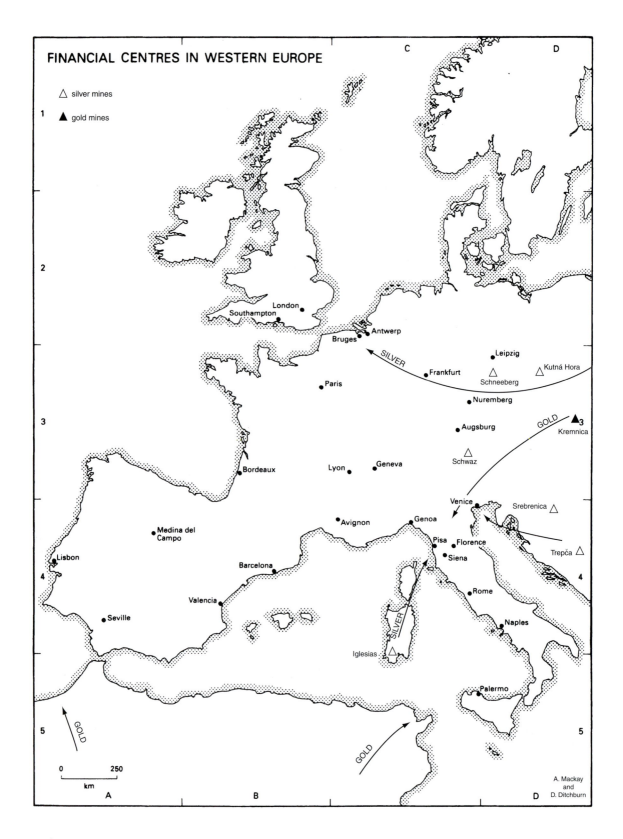

FINANCIAL CENTRES IN WESTERN EUROPE

△ silver mines

▲ gold mines

London
Southampton
Antwerp
Bruges
SILVER
Leipzig
Frankfurt
△ Schneeberg
△ Kutná Hora
Paris
Nuremberg
Augsburg
GOLD
▲3 Kremnica
△ Schwaz
Bordeaux
Lyon
Geneva
Venice
Srebrenica △
Avignon
Genoa
Pisa
Florence
Siena
Trepča △
Lisbon
Medina del Campo
Barcelona
Rome
Valencia
Naples
Seville
SILVER
Iglesias △
Palermo
GOLD
GOLD

0   250
km

A. Mackay
and
D. Ditchburn

Europe had become highly monetized. The revenues remitted to the curia at Avignon during the pontificate of John XXII (1316–34), for example, almost averaged 230,000 Florentine gold florins per year. Litigants and pilgrims also brought considerable sums of money to the papacy. Crusading activities likewise involved enormous expenditure, as did the Hundred Years War whether on ransoms, protection money (*appatissements*) or wages paid to mercenaries, of whom the most famous fought in the Great Companies operating in France and Spain during the fourteenth century. A memorable description of the profits made by freebooters in the Great Companies was given by the Bascot de Mauléon to the chronicler Jean Froissart in an interview in 1388.

The most prominent entrepreneurs in the financial markets of western Europe were the Italians, particularly the Florentines and Genoese. German families, such as the Fuggers of Augsburg who financed Charles V, emerged only later. The Italians were usually both merchants and bankers and their success owed much to advanced commercial techniques. These allowed them to organize their affairs from a home base and use 'partnerships' or 'correspondents' abroad. Insurance and accounting became specialized activities. Double-entry book-keeping was increasingly used as were different kinds of account books, for example to keep track of an individual's investments (including everything from trade to marriage contracts and dowries) or to maintain balances between a home company and branches abroad.

Permanent banking centres were scattered throughout western Europe but international banking was also catered for at the great international fairs, those of Champagne in the thirteenth century, and of Geneva, Medina del Campo and Lyon later on. Payments were normally made by bills of exchange, using the services of Italian or south German bankers. They involved the advance of funds at one financial or banking centre and the paying out of the amount involved at another centre, almost invariably in another currency. Exchange rates fluctuated. In theory, therefore, it was possible for a bill to be dishonoured at its destination and then to be rechanged back to its place of origin at a different exchange rate and at a profit. This gave rise to the practice of dry exchange, that is using bills of exchange as a pretext or cover for usury.

Frequently great financial and banking dynasties eventually reneged on their entrepreneurial background. This may have been partly due to a guilt complex about an incompatibility between their activities and religious values. The Peruzzi of Florence even opened up an account in their books on behalf of '*Messer Dommeneddio*' ('Mr God'), the profits being given to the poor, and the account being the only one to show a credit balance when their company failed. More generally it was a drive for political power and respectability. The Medici ruled Florence, became popes (Leo X and Clement VII), and even married royalty (Catherine de Medici, queen of France).

D. Ditchburn & A. MacKay

The German Hanse

The term 'Hanse', usually referring to a group of merchants or towns, was widely known in medieval Europe. The most important Hanse was the German Hanse, or Hanseatic League, formed by the merchants and towns of northern and central Germany, though there were also two non-urban members, the peasant community of Ditmarschen in Holstein and the grand master of the Teutonic Order. The lifeblood of the German Hanse was trade. Its members, active in northern Europe from the twelfth century until the League's demise in the seventeenth century, dominated Baltic trade during the thirteenth and fourteenth centuries.

The origins of the German control of Baltic trade lay in the German colonization of Slav lands east of the Elbe. Lübeck, the League's unofficial capital, was founded in 1143 and other new towns, frequently based on existing Slav settlements, followed. Germans, then, dominated the towns of northern Europe and from the twelfth century German merchants visited the traditional entrepots of northern Europe, such as Visby. Nonetheless the Baltic was ill-equipped to meet all their demands. Germans therefore travelled further afield: to Russia, Norway, the British Isles, the Low Countries, France and, by the fifteenth century, the Mediterranean.

They sold all the products of their home regions, but their grain, above all, was vital to both the urbanized Low Countries and those areas unable to produce sufficient corn themselves. Indeed, the control of grain supplies allowed Germans to win privileges for themselves, especially in Norway, where other foreign merchants were increasingly excluded. This, coupled with their development of ships, such as the 'cog' and 'hulk', suited to the transportation of bulk produce, and also the adoption of Flemish and Italian trading techniques, precipitated the German domination of Baltic trade.

Yet it was among the communities of German merchants abroad that the Hanse emerged. Frequently accommodated in self-contained settlements, merchants co-operated to defend and extend their privileges. Such a community emerged at Visby by *c.* 1160. Others followed, notably at the four Hanseatic staple towns ('*Kontors*') of Novgorod, Bergen, London and Bruges. Co-operation gradually developed between the German towns too. The catalyst to this was the desire to co-ordinate a response to common enemies, in the absence of a protective imperial authority. Initially co-operation developed on a regional basis, against pirates and local princes. By the late thirteenth century threats to Hanseatic merchants in Novgorod, Flanders and Norway prompted more ambitious policies, in the shape of trade embargoes and blockades. The zenith of urban co-operation was reached in 1367–70. In the face of Danish and Norwegian threats of political hegemony over the Baltic, the towns pursued a successful military response. Yet even at this high point, the Hanse was more concerned to protect its commercial interests than to pursue territorial aggrandisement.

In the fifteenth century the Hanse faced growing challenges to its commercial domination. English, Dutch, Scottish, Italian and south German merchants all attempted to intervene in the Baltic's lucrative trade while, within the towns, the ruling mercantile elites faced increasing discontent from middling merchants and craftsmen. The response to these threats was mixed. The Dutch, in particular, significantly developed their share of Baltic trade. This setback occurred partly because of the Hanse's increasing inability to maintain a united stance. Its institutions had only limited powers, and different regions, with different commercial interests, increasingly followed conflicting policies. These differences became even starker in the sixteenth and seventeenth centuries. Faced with the resurgence of the Scandinavian and Slav kingdoms, and their territorial ambitions, the Hanse became increasingly impotent. Though individual Hanseatic towns continued to prosper, the last Hanseatic Diet met in 1669, hoping for better times. They were not to come.

D. Ditchburn

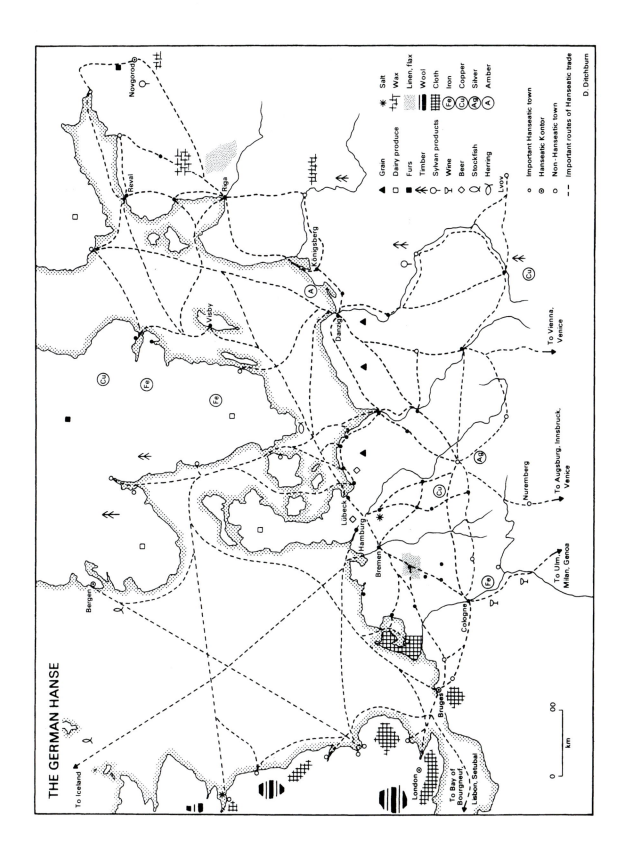

THE GERMAN HANSE

Grain			Salt	
Dairy produce			Wax	
Furs			Linen, flax	
Timber			Wool	
Sylvan products			Cloth	
Wine			Iron	Fe
Beer			Copper	Cu
Stockfish			Silver	Ag
Herring			Amber	A

Important Hanseatic town
Hanseatic Kontor
Non-Hanseatic town
Important routes of Hanseatic trade

D. Ditchburn

Novgorod

Reval

Riga

Königsberg

Visby

Danzig

Lübeck

Hamburg

Bremen

Cologne

Bergen

Bruges

London

Lvov

Nuremberg

To Vienna, Venice

To Augsburg, Innsbruck, Venice

To Ulm, Milan, Genoa

To Bay of Bourgneuf, Lisbon, Setubal

To Iceland

km

0   100

The herring trade

Salted herring was one of the earliest bulk goods to be produced and traded in northern Europe. Its commercial significance derived from the importance of fish in the medieval diet. This, in turn, was a consequence of ecclesiastical prohibitions on the consumption of meat, which applied on Wednesdays, Fridays and Saturdays and also at other times of the year, such as Lent. For a large part of the Middle Ages the main fishing areas were situated in or near the Sound. Local fishing colonies were transformed into international herring markets on Rügen (in the thirteenth century), in Scania and in the Bohuslen region (between the late thirteenth and late sixteenth centuries) and around the Limfjord in Denmark (from the fourteenth to sixteenth centuries). To these markets merchants brought the salt and barrels essential for the production of salted herring. Soon other products were traded there as well. The Scanian herring markets, in particular, were one of the most important European fairs. They were visited by merchants from all over northern Europe although in the thirteenth and fourteenth centuries Danish kings granted particular privileges to those from Lübeck and neighbouring Hanseatic towns. These towns tried to exclude other merchants from the Scanian fairs. Although they had succeeded by the early fifteenth century, the English and Dutch increasingly sought to exploit other fishing resources, in the North Sea and in Iceland. The Scanian fairs, meanwhile, lost their role as international centres of trade. Indeed, prolonged conflict between Lübeck and its allies and Denmark ensued, leading to the demise of the Scanian markets in the later fifteenth and sixteenth centuries. By then North Sea ports, especially in Holland and Zeeland, had come to dominate the international fish trade.

E. Frankot

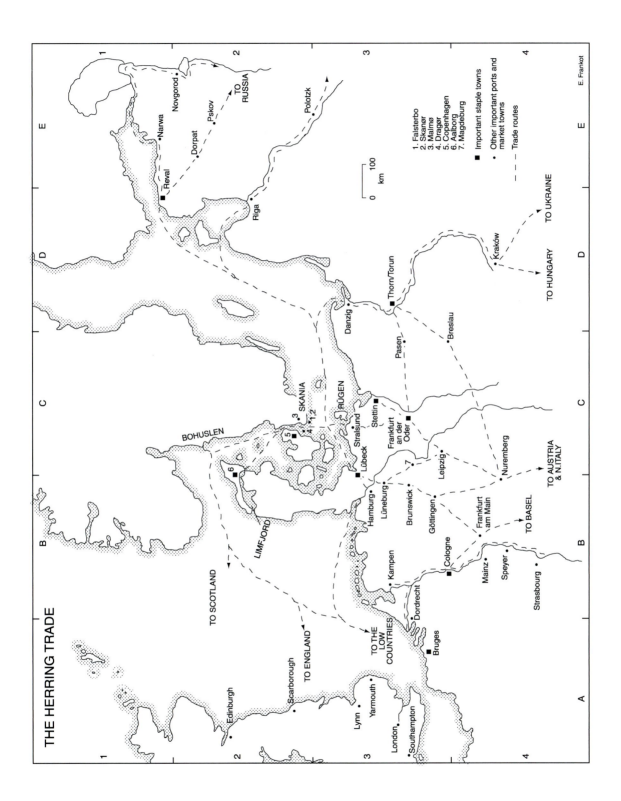

THE HERRING TRADE

1. Falsterbo
2. Skanor
3. Malmø
4. Dragør
5. Copenhagen
6. Aalborg
7. Magdeburg

■ Important staple towns

● Other important ports and
   market towns

--- Trade routes

E. Frankot

0   100
|————|
     km

TO RUSSIA

TO UKRAINE

TO HUNGARY

TO AUSTRIA
& N.ITALY

TO BASEL

TO THE
LOW
COUNTRIES

TO ENGLAND

TO SCOTLAND

Novgorod
Narwa
Reval
Dorpat
Pskov
Polotzk
Riga

Danzig
Thorn/Torun
Pasen
Breslau
Kraków

SKANIA
BOHUSLEN
RÜGEN
LIMFJORD

Stralsund
Stettin
Frankfurt
an der
Oder
Lübeck
Hamburg
Lüneburg
Brunswick
Leipzig
Göttingen
Nuremberg
Frankfurt
am Main
Cologne
Mainz
Speyer
Strasbourg
Kampen
Dordrecht
Bruges

Edinburgh
Scarborough
Lynn
Yarmouth
London
Southampton

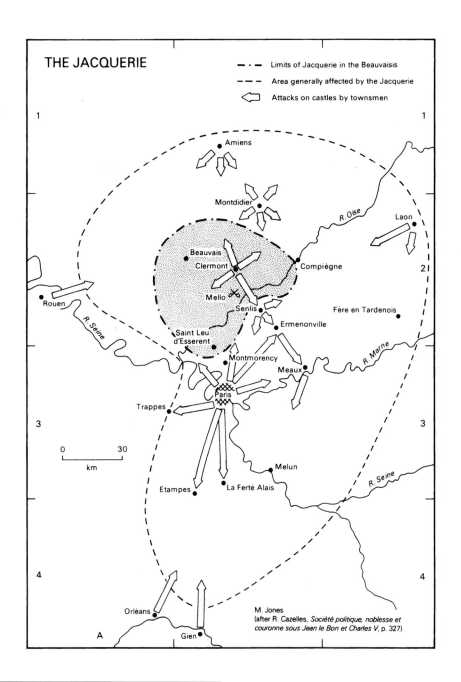

THE JACQUERIE

— · — Limits of Jacquerie in the Beauvaisis

— — — Area generally affected by the Jacquerie

◁ Attacks on castles by townsmen

M. Jones
(after R. Cazelles, *Société politique, noblesse et couronne sous Jean le Bon et Charles V*, p. 327)

The Jacquerie

This brief and violent uprising against the nobility broke out on 28 May 1358. Centred on the Beauvaisis, disturbances affected areas from Picardy to Orléans, especially after Etienne Marcel, leader of the Parisian merchants in dis-

pute with the government, joined the rebels and encouraged towns to attack seigneurial castles. Normally described as a peasants' revolt, most known rebels were rural artisans, such as coopers and stone-cutters, together with some minor clergy, petty royal officials and a few more well-to-do men. Led by Guillaume Cale and Jean Vaillant, rebel bands sustained an orgiastic destruction of noble property for a fortnight. By 8 June, however, urban interests, with Marcel the key figure, predominated.

Possible long-term causes included a painful readjustment following the Black Death, the difficulties of an unpopular government, led by the dauphin, in the war with the English and criticism of a nobility failing in its role as protectors of the peasantry. The immediate causes lay in the struggle between the dauphin and Marcel. An order promulgated on 14 May, calling for the strengthening or destruction of seigneurial strongholds, probably sparked off the revolt. Intended to improve security when the Paris region was threatened by soldiers temporarily unemployed because of the Anglo-French truce, some interpreted the measure as a tightening of hated seigneurial authority, whilst Marcel saw it as the dauphin's attempt to exert further pressure on Paris. Marcel sent forces against his noble adversaries in alliance with the rebels. But in doing so he alienated an ally, Charles II, king of Navarre, who ambushed and executed Cale before dispersing his forces at Mello, whilst Gaston, count of Foix, relieved Meaux. The nobles exacted a terrible revenge on a defenceless peasantry, whilst Marcel fell to a Parisian plot. By 10 August the dauphin, who had been on the point of fleeing, felt secure enough to issue letters of pardon to all involved and some semblance of a peace was re-established. The Jacquerie left a legacy of class hatred and fear, symbolized by the way its name was subsequently attached to other rebellions.

M. Jones

The Peasants' Revolt of 1381

The Revolt broke out in late May and early June 1381, first in Essex villages on the Thames estuary, then on the opposite bank in Kent. Rebel armies formed in both shires and met up after being admitted to London. There the youthful Richard II had to concede the abolition of serfdom, a low level of land rents and voluntary terms of employment. The rebels executed 'traitors', including royal officials whom they blamed for a recently imposed poll tax. But on 15 June the rebel captain, Wat Tyler, whilst making more radical demands, was mortally injured by the king's entourage: his demoralized supporters were rounded up and allowed to leave London.

The Essex and Kent risings were signals for widespread riots, attacks on property and coercion of landlords and officials. Big rebel bands formed in Hertfordshire, the East Midlands and East Anglia, some coercing a particular landowner or elite group, others roaming around to victimize and extort. But the Revolt in south-east England was generally stamped out in the second half of June and in July by Bishop Despenser of Norwich and by royal forces. The king revoked his pardons: a few hundred of the rebels died in battle or by execution.

The extent of participation in the Revolt is hard to determine. In the areas mainly affected many communities did not rise: evidence accumulates of action by manorial tenants against their lords elsewhere in England. In Essex, Kent, Suffolk and Hertfordshire well-to-do peasants, holders of local office, were well represented among the rebels. A few East Anglian gentlefolk joined in. Urban participation was widespread and crucial to many rebel successes. In Yorkshire risings were against unpopular urban regimes. At St Albans and Bury St Edmunds risings led or encouraged by urban elites were directed against the abbeys which controlled them: attacks on ecclesiastical landlords, especially abbots and monks, were conspicuous in the Revolt. Though enjoying only brief successes, the Revolt helped make the

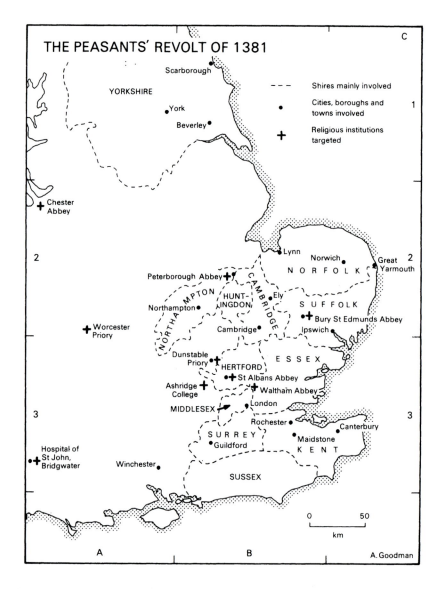

THE PEASANTS' REVOLT OF 1381

- - - Shires mainly involved

• Cities, boroughs and towns involved

✝ Religious institutions targeted

YORKSHIRE

Scarborough

York

Beverley

Chester Abbey

Lynn

Norwich

Great Yarmouth

NORFOLK

Peterborough Abbey

NORTHAMPTON

Northampton

HUNT-INGDON

CAMBRIDGE

Ely

SUFFOLK

Bury St Edmunds Abbey

Ipswich

Worcester Priory

Cambridge

Dunstable Priory

HERTFORD

ESSEX

Ashridge College

St Albans Abbey

Waltham Abbey

MIDDLESEX

London

Rochester

Canterbury

Maidstone

KENT

SURREY

Guildford

Hospital of St John, Bridgwater

Winchester

SUSSEX

0   50
km

A. Goodman

governing elites more cautious about the imposition of taxes on the commons and about resisting the trends to rent out demesne lands, commute servile works and grant higher wages.

A. Goodman

Aliens in late medieval England

The mobility of medieval society is illustrated by a poll tax imposed periodically on aliens in fifteenth-century England. In 1440 over 15,000 foreigners were identified. The total alien population was undoubtedly greater. Several foreigners – including children, regular clergy but latterly also students, Irish and Channel Islanders – were exempt. Others

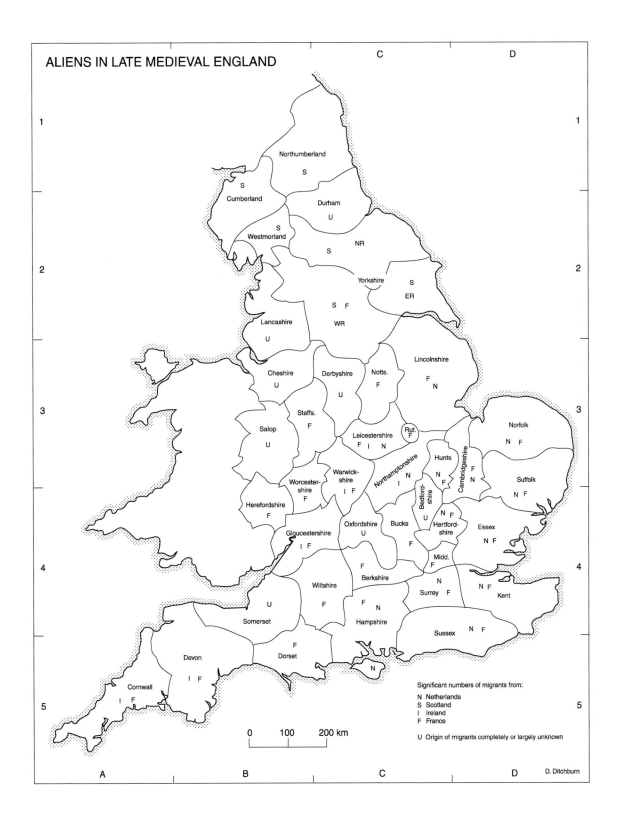

ALIENS IN LATE MEDIEVAL ENGLAND

Northumberland
S

Cumberland
S

Durham
U

Westmorland
S

Yorkshire
NR
S

Yorkshire
S
ER

Lancashire
U

Yorkshire
S F
WR

Lincolnshire
F N

Cheshire
U

Derbyshire
U

Notts.
F

Salop
U

Staffs.
F

Leicestershire
F I N

Rut.
F

Norfolk
N F

Worcester-
shire
F

Warwick-
shire
I F

Northamptonshire
I N

Hunts
N F

Cambridgeshire
F N

Suffolk
N F

Herefordshire
F

Bedford-
shire
U

Hertford-
shire
N F

Essex
N F

Gloucestershire
I F

Oxfordshire
U

Bucks
F

Midd.
F

Wiltshire
F

Berkshire
F

Surrey
N
F

Kent
N F

Somerset
U

Hampshire
F N

Sussex
N F

Devon
I F

Dorset
F

N

Cornwall
I F

Significant numbers of migrants from:

N Netherlands
S Scotland
I Ireland
F France

U Origin of migrants completely or largely unknown

0   100   200 km

D. Ditchburn

probably evaded assessment. This means that the tax returns are not a reliable census of England's immigrants. Certain migratory trends are, nonetheless, evident. In 1440 the Irish (of whom there were perhaps one thousand) tended to congregate from Cornwall to Northamptonshire, with only a few to the east or north and remarkably few in London too. Scots (of whom there were perhaps between two and three thousand) dominated the north, with some as far south as Kent. French migrants were found throughout the south, east and west, while those from the Netherlands, though also settled throughout the country, were most numerous in the south-east. There were, in addition, a few Icelandic, Manx and Orcadian incomers, mainly along the eastern seaboard. Those from the Channel Islands and Iberia were mostly in southern and western districts. Significant numbers of immigrants were located in towns and ports, such as London, Bristol and Hull, but also in rural areas. In the north, where a significant number of migrants were women, many aliens were identified as servants or labourers. Those described as 'vagabonds' were probably itinerant harvest workers. Elsewhere many migrants were either relatively well-to-do husbandmen or skilled craftsmen taking advantage of lucrative opportunities after the population declines caused by the Black Death. There was also a significant scattering of alien clergymen, who were to attract parliamentary complaint. Indeed, aliens generally were often the object of vociferous xenophobic agitation.

D. Ditchburn

RELIGION AND CULTURE

The Avignon papacy and papal fiscality

From 1305 to 1378 the papacy was removed from Rome and for nearly all of this period was resident at Avignon, a city situated on the river Rhône in Provence, then part of the Empire. Petrarch (d. 1374) likened life at the papal court in Avignon to the legendary vice, corruption and greed of Babylon, a literary device used to criticize worldly tendencies in the Church by Joachim of Fiore in the twelfth century and latterly by the Spiritual Franciscans too. 'Babylonian Captivity' has since gained currency as a term to describe this period of papal history but the Avignon popes were more exiles than captives. The rivalries of great Roman families had played a significant part in the ignominious end of Boniface VIII (1294–1303), and dissensions between Guelphs and Ghibellines in northern Italy led to the endemic wars that kept the popes across the Alps, even though they themselves took an active part in these conflicts. The plans of Clement V (1305–14) and John XXII (1316–34) to return to Italy gave way to their successors' complacency over absence from Rome. Nevertheless, there was a general, although unjustifiable, opinion that the papacy was in the French king's pocket and a feeling that the ills of the Church would be rectified by the pope's return to Rome. After Urban V (1362–70) made what amounted to a visit in 1369–70, Gregory XI's (1370–8) resettlement in Rome in 1377 proved permanent but after his death the Church was beset by the Great Schism, with the establishment of a rival line of popes at Avignon.

Beyond all else contemporaries condemned the grasping nature of the Avignon popes, who found themselves requiring additional funds to support a burgeoning bureaucracy and to finance the Italian wars. This need was exacerbated by falling revenues from the papacy's territorial possessions in Italy, due to the political upheaval there. Like any bishop, the pope derived his income from both temporal and spiritual sources, the latter of which were to become increasingly important. These originally consisted of nominal payments in recognition of papal authority, such as the census paid by a number of monasteries and Peter's pence paid by certain countries. In the thirteenth and early fourteenth centuries popes levied occasional tenths of the assessed value of benefices to finance crusades but most of the money collected went to lay rulers and was not used for its intended purpose. More lucrative were the exactions made in connection with the increasing practice of papal provision, or the pope's direct appointment to dignities and benefices: common services paid by archbishops, bishops and abbots; and annates paid by other provisors. The former amounted notionally to one-third and the latter to the whole of the assessed annual income, which was lower than the true value. In theory, the pope's right to provide to any church was well worked out by now but under John XXII the fiscal benefits of the practice were better realized. His constitution *Execrabilis* (1317) was enacted to end the abuse of pluralism but he also reserved to himself the disposal of benefices thus left vacant, enabling him to collect annates, then still a novelty in most of Europe. During his pontificate the provision of bishops and abbots began to become commonplace. The map, based on records of payment to the Apostolic Camera, shows how common services came to be exploited as a source of income, by comparing

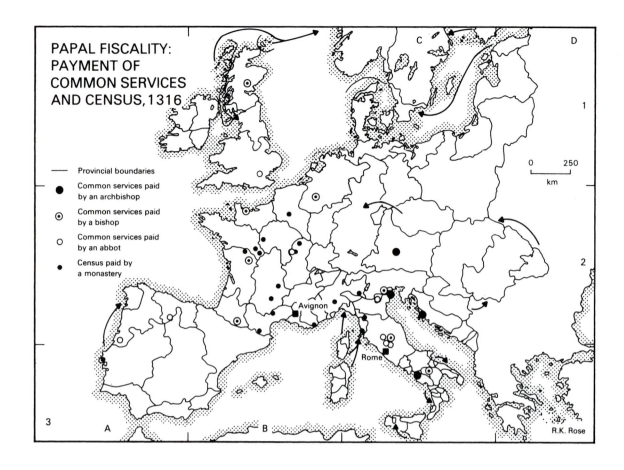

PAPAL FISCALITY: PAYMENT OF COMMON SERVICES AND CENSUS, 1316

— Provincial boundaries
● Common services paid by an archbishop
◉ Common services paid by a bishop
○ Common services paid by an abbot
· Census paid by a monastery

the first and the last full years of John XXII's pontificate. In both years the total census collected was near 100 florins. In contrast, common services were becoming the Holy See's principal source of income. In 1316–17 twenty-one prelates paid 9,343 florins, but in 1332–3 nearly one hundred churchmen paid about 38,370 florins, or more than a four-fold increase.

R.K. Rose

The Great Schism and the councils

Following the death in March 1378 of Gregory XI, who the previous year had returned the papacy to Rome, sixteen cardinals met in conclave. On 8 April they elected Bartolomeo Prignano, archbishop of Bari, as Urban VI (1378–89), amidst raucous demands from the populace for a Roman pope. Although the regularity of his election might be doubted because of the disturbances, in its aftermath it is clear that the cardinals did in fact recognize and treat Urban as the legitimate pope. Only after four months did thirteen of the electors, weary of their master's violent outbursts, desert him and declare his election invalid. In a second conclave at Fondi, in the kingdom of Naples, they elected the French king's cousin,

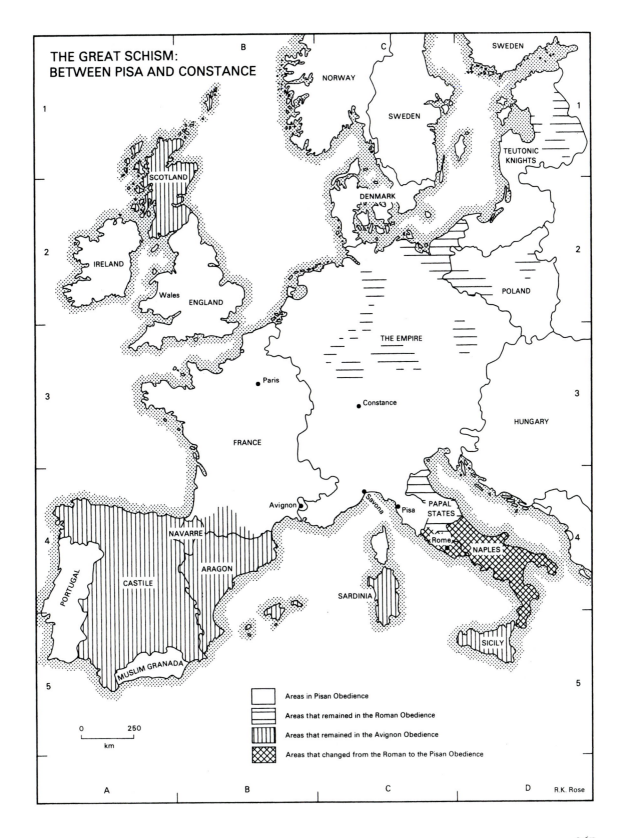

THE GREAT SCHISM:
BETWEEN PISA AND CONSTANCE

NORWAY

SWEDEN

SWEDEN

DENMARK

TEUTONIC
KNIGHTS

SCOTLAND

IRELAND

Wales ENGLAND

POLAND

THE EMPIRE

Paris

Constance

HUNGARY

FRANCE

Avignon

Savona

Pisa

PAPAL
STATES

Rome

NAPLES

NAVARRE

ARAGON

CASTILE

PORTUGAL

SARDINIA

SICILY

MUSLIM GRANADA

	Areas in Pisan Obedience
	Areas that remained in the Roman Obedience
	Areas that remained in the Avignon Obedience
	Areas that changed from the Roman to the Pisan Obedience

0   250
km

A   B   C   D   R.K. Rose

267

Robert of Geneva, as Clement VII (1379–94). Unable to dislodge Urban from Rome, Clement quite naturally chose to establish his court at Avignon, where five of Gregory XI's cardinals had obstinately remained in residence.

Allegiance to the rival popes largely reflected the national political alignments of Europe. Charles V of France had from the start encouraged the cardinals in their rebellion and prompted Joanna of Naples to follow his lead. It was natural, therefore, that England should remain loyal to Urban, while Scotland, France's ally, accepted the French pope. Within France itself, the clergy of Flanders and the English enclaves of Calais and Gascony rejected Clement. The Emperor Charles VI, along with other rulers of central Europe and Scandinavia, recognized Urban VI but parts of the German kingdom, especially those bordering France, followed the opposite course. Urban engineered the downfall of Joanna of Naples but his own creature also turned against him. Naples did not become officially Urbanist until 1400, though the Roman pope had until then enjoyed support in the kingdom. Portugal wavered between Rome and Avignon until 1385, when it finally embraced the former. The kings of Castile, Aragon and Navarre deferred their decisions until 1381, 1386 and 1390, respectively, when each in turn recognized Clement.

While military action proved futile, the delicate question of how to heal the schism was debated in the universities. Jurists and theologians were in universal agreement that a pope could only be deposed for heresy but neither pontiff was alleged to be a heretic. As early as 1379 Henry of Langenstein and Conrad of Gelnhausen, both of the University of Paris, advocated the calling of a general council, as superior to the pope, to examine the criminal misconduct of Urban VI and the illegal election of Clement VII. But it was generally accepted that only a pope could summon a general council. The scandal of the schism deepened when the Roman cardinals elected Boniface IX (1389–1404) after Urban's death. Despite exhortations from the French Crown not to proceed with an election after Clement died, his cardinals proclaimed Benedict XIII (1394–1423) pope. Afterwards the resignation of both popes, greatly promoted by Parisian scholars Pierre d'Ailly and Jean Gerson, was the most widely favoured means of ending the schism. In 1407 a meeting at Savona was arranged between Benedict and the Roman pontiff, Gregory XII (1406–15), but Gregory could not bring himself to make the final leg of the journey. Frustrated by inaction, cardinals from both camps joined together and summoned a general council to meet at Pisa in March 1409. Without universal support and of doubtful legitimacy, it was a sham, and the end result was not one pope but three. It was still generally acknowledged that only a council could solve the problem. The deadlock was broken by the Emperor-elect Sigismund, who summoned the Council of Constance, which met between 1414 and 1417. The Pisan pope, John XXIII, and Gregory XII resigned but Benedict XIII kept up the pretence until his death. The council was careful not to elect the one, new pope, Martin V (1417–31), until all 'nations' were represented, in November 1417.

R.K. Rose

The papal states

The papal states were the basis for the papacy's temporal power. Founded in 754 (when Pepin, king of the Franks, granted Pope Stephen II (752–7) the exarchate of Ravenna and the Pentapolis) they were directly governed by the pope as secular ruler and acquired political autonomy from neighbouring powers in the thirteenth century. Despite an extensive network of roads, largely based on ancient Roman routes, the diverse terrain of the states presented

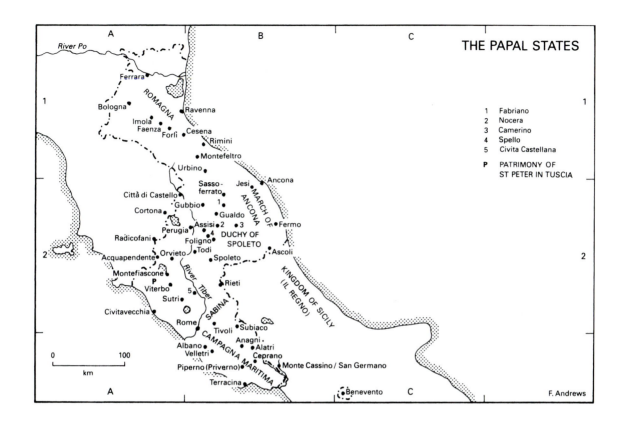

The map shows:

THE PAPAL STATES

River Po

A   B   C

ROMAGNA

Ferrara
Bologna • Ravenna
Imola • Faenza • Forlì • Cesena
• Rimini
• Montefeltro
Urbino •
Sasso-ferrato • Jesi • Ancona
Città di Castello • Gubbio • 1
Cortona • Gualdo
MARCH OF ANCONA
Assisi • 2 • 3 • Fermo
Perugia • 4
Radicofani • Foligno • DUCHY OF SPOLETO
Orvieto • Todi
Acquapendente • Spoleto • Ascoli
Montefiascone
P Viterbo River Tiber Rieti
Sutri • 5 SABINA
Civitavecchia KINGDOM OF SICILY (IL REGNO)
Rome • Tivoli • Subiaco
Albano • Anagni • Alatri
Velletri • Ceprano
Piperno (Priverno) • Monte Cassino / San Germano
CAMPAGNA MARITIMA
Terracina

• Benevento

1 Fabriano
2 Nocera
3 Camerino
4 Spello
5 Civita Castellana

P PATRIMONY OF
   ST PETER IN TUSCIA

0   100
km

F. Andrews

formidable administrative problems. The key cities of Rome, surrounded by an infertile coastal plain, and Bologna, in the productive region of Romagna, were separated by the Apennine passes and the wealthy march of Ancona, a hilly region of varied economic activity and numerous small *signori*. The whole area was ruled by papal governors or rectors based in Perugia, Orvieto, the Patrimony of St Peter in Tuscia, Romagna and elsewhere. During the papal absence in Avignon (1309–77) *de facto* authority was usurped by numerous communes and latterly by signorial dynasties, such as the Malatesta of Rimini and the Montefeltro of Urbino. The Roman hinterland was likewise dominated by families, such as the Orsini, Caetani, Colonna, da Vico and Anguillara, while Rome itself remained faction-ridden despite Cola di Rienzo's attempt to reorganize

city government in 1347. Bologna, meanwhile, had rebelled in 1334. For decades the region was beset by warfare. In 1353–67 Cardinal Egidio (Gil) de Albornoz was charged by Innocent VI (1352–62) to restore papal fortunes. Through military and diplomatic means some recognition of papal authority was achieved and the legitimacy of some *signori* was recognized by their appointment as papal vicars. After the papal return to Rome the papal states shared in the crisis of papal power provoked by the Great Schism and the conciliar movement: Ladislao of Naples, for example, seized Rome in 1408 and 1413. Papal authority was precariously re-established by Eugenius IV (1431–47). Thereafter income from the papal states did much to bolster financially a now spiritually weakened papacy.

F. Andrews

269

Illegitimacy and the papal Penitentiary

It has been estimated that nearly one-third of the children born during the Middle Ages were of illegitimate standing. Illegitimate children were discriminated against by the legal systems of church and state. If in receipt of a papal dispensation, they could, however, embark on an ecclesiastical career. These dispensations were granted by papal legates, nuncios and other authorized prelates, as well as by various offices at the papal court, of which the Penitentiary was the most significant. The surviving registers of the Penitentiary, dating from 1409, contain requests from throughout Latin Christendom for dispensation from various 'defects' including disability and illegitimacy. Between 1449 and 1533 the Penitentiary granted dispensation to 39,716 illegitimate supplicants. Of these, 36 per cent lived in the Empire, while 24 per cent came from the Iberian Peninsula, 17 per cent from France and 10 per cent from the British Isles. Italians accounted for only 9 per cent of the supplicants, with the remainder coming from eastern Europe and Scandinavia.

J. McDonald

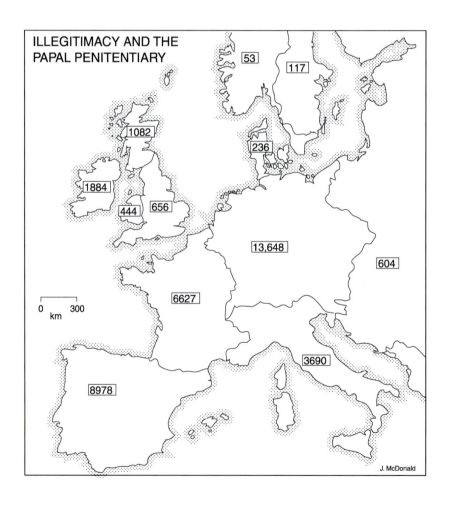

Byzantine cultural and monastic centres

The loss of Egypt and Syria to the Arabs in the seventh century deprived the Byzantine Empire of many of its major cultural centres. These included Alexandria, along with Athens, the major university, and Beirut, the main centre of legal studies. Constantinople was left with a virtual monopoly of higher education, scholarship and letters. Even here the university established in 425 disappeared. Education was a matter of private tutors and private schools. State supervision was limited to the provision of funds to selected masters and schools. There was no institution of higher education approaching the model of the western university. Byzantium inherited the Hellenistic educational curriculum with its emphasis on rhetoric. Speculative thought, whether philosophical or theological, remained a private concern. This remained true in the twelfth century when the supervision of education came under the patriarchs of Constantinople. The disintegration of the Byzantine Empire after the Latin conquest of 1204 meant that Constantinople lost its cultural monopoly. Byzantine scholars found refuge at Nicaea and at Trebizond. After the recovery of Constantinople in 1261 the Emperor Michael VIII

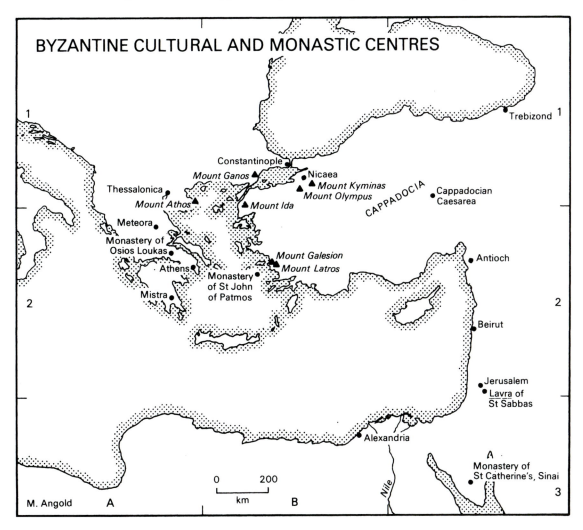

BYZANTINE CULTURAL AND MONASTIC CENTRES

Trebizond

Constantinople
Mount Ganos
Nicaea
Mount Kyminas
Mount Olympus
CAPPADOCIA
Cappadocian Caesarea
Thessalonica
Mount Athos
Mount Ida
Meteora
Monastery of Osios Loukas
Mount Galesion
Mount Latros
Athens
Monastery of St John of Patmos
Antioch
Mistra
Beirut
Jerusalem
Lavra of St Sabbas
Alexandria
Nile
A
Monastery of St Catherine's, Sinai

0   200
km

M. Angold   A   B

Palaiologos took steps to revive education and scholarship but Constantinople never regained its cultural monopoly, being challenged by Thessalonica in the fourteenth century. In the final phase Mistra became the most prestigious centre of Byzantine scholarship thanks to the activities of the Platonist George Gemistos Plethon and his circle.

While education and scholarship were the preserve of a tiny elite, monasticism involved the whole of Byzantine society. Constantinople was always the major centre of Byzantine monasticism. From its foundation in the mid-fifth century the monastery of St John Stoudios at Constantinople was among the most prestigious. Its rule served as a model for many other monastic foundations though Byzantium had no monastic orders as such. Instead, there were Holy Mountains. The most famous and enduring example is Mount Athos, which is a confederation of monasteries under the presidency of a *protos*. Other examples were Olympus, Latros, Ida, Kyminas, Galesion and Ganos. The Meteora in Thessaly became an important monastic centre from the mid-fourteenth century. The rock-monasteries of Cappadocia indicate the hold that monasticism enjoyed in the provinces. Contact was maintained with distant orthodox monastic centres, such as St Catherine's on Mount Sinai, while the *lavra* of St Sabbas outside Jerusalem exerted a deep influence on Byzantine monasticism with its combination of the coenobitic and eremitical life.

M. Angold

The Bohemian Lands and the Hussite Wars, 1415–37

In the fourteenth century the Bohemian Lands (Bohemia and Moravia) became the administrative centre of the Holy Roman Empire. Charles IV, king of Bohemia and emperor (1347/55–78), transformed Prague into a splendid imperial capital in the late gothic style. His most important achievements included the foundation of the oldest central European university at Prague in 1347. The university rapidly became a hotbed of heresy, producing important preachers and reformers, such as Jan Hus and his principal follower, Jakoubek of Stríbro. This climate of dissent was aggravated by the weak government of Wenceslas IV (1378–1419) and lack of ecclesiastical direction after the Schism of 1378. The deposition of Wenceslas from the imperial throne (1400) and the Decree of Kutná Hora (1409), whereby the Czechs gained a controlling majority in the administration of the university, meant that the international significance of Bohemia and the Prague university diminished. Bohemia became isolated and shunned abroad as the home of heresy.

Following the burning of Hus in 1415 and his followers' condemnation by the Council of Constance, the Hussites enshrined certain demands for reform in the Four Articles of Prague (1420): the free preaching of the Word of God, communion in both kinds, the confiscation of the secular property of the clergy and the punishment of public sin. But the new movement soon splintered into several factions: the Utraquists who demanded no more than the right to receive communion in both kinds (*sub utraque specie*); a moderate party led by Jakoubek of Stríbro; the Taborites, adherents of chiliasm or Millenarianism; and the Adamites, a sect which went naked and denied the doctrine of the Real Presence.

The areas of greatest Hussite activity were Prague, where Hus and his followers preached at the Bethlehem Chapel, north-west, west and south Bohemia; Moravia and Slovakia remained

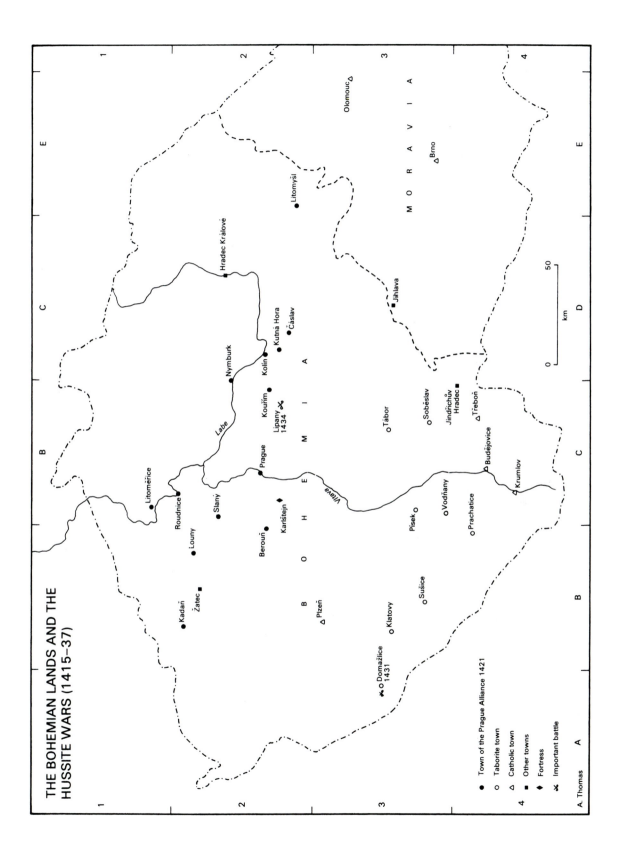

THE BOHEMIAN LANDS AND THE
HUSSITE WARS (1415-37)

MORAVIA

BOHEMIA

Olomouc △

△ Brno

Litomyšl ●

Hradec Králové ■

Jihlava ■

Nymburk ●
Kutná Hora ●
Kolín ●
Čáslav ●

Kouřím ●
Lipany
1434 ⚔

Tábor ○

Soběslav ○
Jindřichův
Hradec ■
△ Třeboň

Litoměřice ○

Roudnice ◆

Slaný ○

Prague ■

Karlštejn ◆

Budějovice ■

Krumlov ◆

Vodňany ○

Prachatice ○

Písek ○

Louny ●

Beroun ●

Sušice ○

Kadaň ●
Žatec ■

△ Plzeň

Klatovy ○

Domažlice ○
1431 ⚔

Labe

Vltava

0   50

km

● Town of the Prague Alliance 1421
○ Taborite town
△ Catholic town
■ Other towns
◆ Fortress
⚔ Important battle

A. Thomas

273

Catholic throughout the Hussite Wars. The Taborites, consisting mainly of peasants and gentry, founded the town of Tábor (1420) and established a municipal form of government which abolished the feudal system. The movement soon spread to the so-called Five Towns – Plzeň, Slaný, Žatec, Louny and Klatovy – which were regarded by the radical preachers as the final refuge of the elect against the Anti-Christ.

In 1420 an anti-Hussite crusade under Sigismund, king of Hungary and emperor (1411–37), marched into Bohemia and captured Prague where Sigismund was crowned. The Taborites, led by the dynamic Jan Žižka, drove the crusaders out of Prague. A second Catholic assault met with disaster. Following a third victory over the crusaders in 1421, the Bohemian diet met at Čáslav where it accepted the Four Articles of Prague and rejected Sigismund's claim to the throne.

The Hussites undertook their own religious crusades abroad, into Poland and Germany, led by Žižka's successor, Prokop Holý. Internecine strife among the heretics enabled further Catholic invasions in 1427 and 1431 when Sigismund's forces were decisively defeated at the battle of Domažlice. By the 1430s the moderate wing of the Hussites sought a peaceful solution to the Bohemian question. Its initiative resulted in an agreement between the Utraquist nobility and the Catholics (the Compactata of Basel). The two forces allied to crush the extremists at the battle of Lipany in May 1434. The destruction of the Taborite cause cleared the way for further negotiations. The Utraquists abandoned their insistence on the obligatory use of the chalice throughout Bohemia but demanded that the new archbishop should be of the Utraquist persuasion. In 1436 the Compactata of Basel was ratified at Jihlava and Sigismund returned to Prague as king in August 1436. This event marked the beginning of a new *modus vivendi* between Hussites and Catholics which was to last until the loss of Czech independence in 1620.

A. Thomas

Christians, Jews and *conversos* in late medieval Iberia

The tensions between Christians and Jews that were a feature of European life were also present in the Iberian Peninsula. They were, however, tempered by a measure of *convivencia* in a land where Christian, Muslim and Jew dwelt side by side. Thus, there were no anti-Jewish riots in Castile during the Black Death, although such riots did occur in the Crown of Aragon, which was more open to the currents of mainstream European anti-semitism.

From the mid-fourteenth century *convivencia* began to break down in the face of an increasing exclusivity. In the late 1370s Ferrant Martínez, the archdeacon of Ecija, began a campaign against the Jews which culminated in a wave of massacres throughout Castile and the Crown of Aragon during the summer of 1391. Many Jews were killed; many submitted to baptism to save their lives. Although forced conversion was in theory frowned upon by the Church, *conversos* were nevertheless considered to be technically Christians and were prohibited from returning to Judaism. Thus *converso* communities sprang up alongside decimated Jewish ones or, as in the case of Barcelona, supplanted the Jewish community altogether. Henceforth Jewish life would tend to shift from the large towns to smaller rural centres.

If forced conversion was meant to solve 'the Jewish problem', it only compounded it in Christian eyes. The sincerity of *converso* faith was questioned – and all the more fiercely by 'Old Christians' who saw former Jews successfully scaling the social, economic and political barriers which, as Jews, they had previously found insurmountable. Accordingly, in the

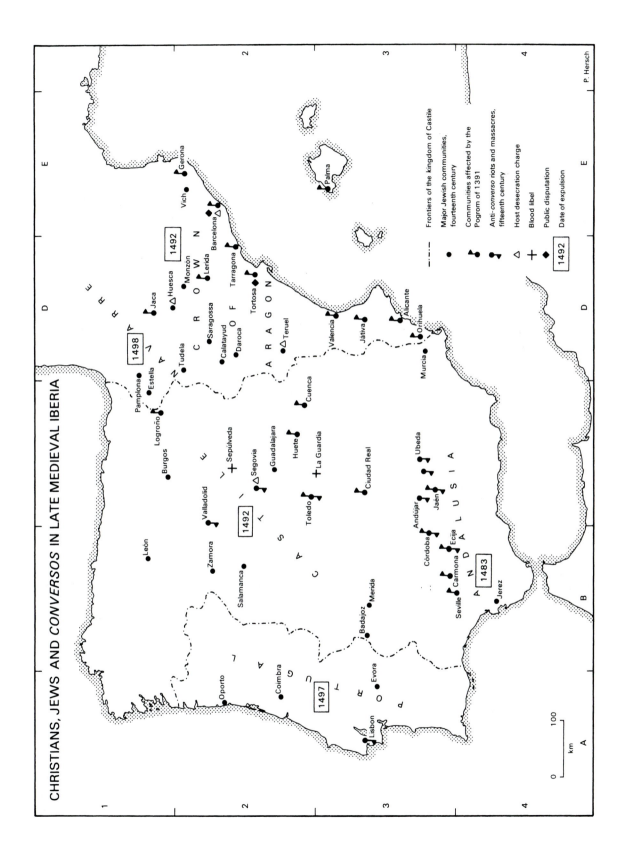

CHRISTIANS, JEWS AND *CONVERSOS* IN LATE MEDIEVAL IBERIA

Frontiers of the kingdom of Castile

Major Jewish communities, fourteenth century

Communities affected by the Pogrom of 1391

Anti-*converso* riots and massacres, fifteenth century

Host desecration charge

Blood libel

Public disputation

Date of expulsion

P. Hersch

275

anti-*converso* uprising in Toledo in 1449, the Toledan Old Christians drafted statutes which prohibited *conversos* from holding all offices and benefices. Anti-*converso* violence, which surfaced again in Toledo in 1467, was particularly acute in the massacres which were perpetrated in many Andalusian towns in 1473.

The existence of the *converso* communities led to greater pressure on the Jews, for they were perceived as the cause of continuing crypto-Judaism amongst *conversos*. To combat this, segregatory laws were promulgated in 1412, designed 'to seek the best method . . . so that Christian believers . . . shall not be brought into any errors as a result of close contact with the infidels'. In 1415, after the Disputation at Tortosa, similar decrees were enacted in Aragon.

Christian zealots were not, however, satisfied with segregation and the limiting of Jewish rights. Two courses of action, it was argued, were required. First, crypto-Judaism could only be overcome by the introduction of an Inquisition; second, Jewish influence over the *conversos* could only be overcome by their expulsion. These ideas, adumbrated in works such as Alonso de Espina's *Fortalitium Fidei*, continued to gain ground, and on 27 September 1480 the Catholic Monarchs appointed Inquisitors in Castile who began their work in Seville in 1481.

Conversos, often subjected to torture, were discovered to be crypto-Jews and received varying punishments, ranging from pilgrimage to death by burning. During the first decade of the Inquisition's operations over 10,000 *conversos* were condemned. The expulsion of the Jews was authorized on 31 March 1492; in May those Jews who refused to convert left for Portugal, North Africa and Turkey. Those who fled to Portugal only found temporary refuge, for five years later they again faced forcible conversion. As in Spain, this led to the rise of crypto-Judaism and on 23 May 1536 an Inquisition was set up in Portugal on the Spanish model.

With the expulsion of the Jews anti-semitism took on a more racial tone. Anti-Jewish libels had already reappeared in an anti-*converso* form, as in the famous blood libel trial of the case of 'the holy child of La Guardia' (1490–1). Similarly *conversos*, like Jews, kept hosts for evil purposes. But now purity of blood (*limpieza de sangre*) became an obsession and, although many *conversos* managed to hide their 'defect', those who were known not to possess 'pure' blood increasingly found themselves barred from entering many offices in Church and state.

P. Hersch

Pogroms in Germany

Germany's Jewish communities resided mainly in towns and often in particular districts of towns. On several occasions, notably in the wake of the first and second crusades, these religiously and physically distinctive communities were persecuted. The Black Death unleashed further persecutions, some spontaneous, some planned, in over eighty towns between November 1348 and August 1350. The means by which the disease spread were not understood, prompting accusations that 'outsiders' had poisoned drinking water. In some areas foreign pilgrims were blamed: in

Germany, among other places, suspicion fell on Jews. Yet fear of the onset of disease, rather than the search for scapegoats after its outbreak, accounts for the German massacres, which occurred in communities not yet affected by disease. Likewise, pogroms frequently occurred *before* the arrival of Flagellants who have often been accused of whipping up anti-Jewish sentiments. These feelings were perhaps instead encouraged (consciously or unconsciously) by local preachers. Many pogroms occurred on Sundays or feast days. Traditionally the pogroms of the 1340s have also been seen as an

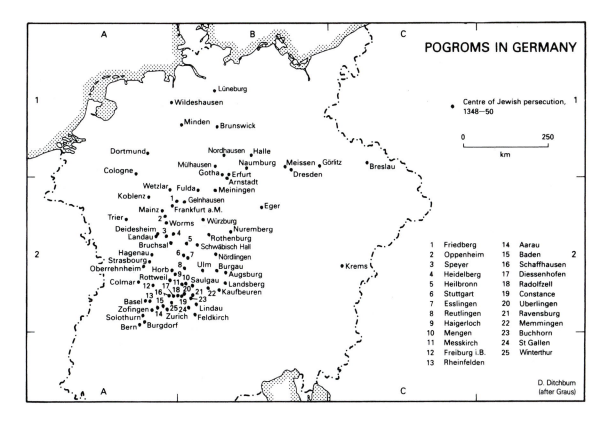

Centre of Jewish persecution, 1
1348—50

0   250
km

1	Friedberg	14	Aarau
2	Oppenheim	15	Baden
3	Speyer	16	Schaffhausen
4	Heidelberg	17	Diessenhofen
5	Heilbronn	18	Radolfzell
6	Stuttgart	19	Constance
7	Esslingen	20	Uberlingen
8	Reutlingen	21	Ravensburg
9	Haigerloch	22	Memmingen
10	Mengen	23	Buchhorn
11	Messkirch	24	St Gallen
12	Freiburg i.B.	25	Winterthur
13	Rheinfelden		

D. Ditchburn
(after Graus)

expression of social tension between the unrepresented crafts (seen as hostile to Jews) and the governing patriciate (seen as protective of Jews or prepared to acquiesce in their massacre in order to appease the craftsmen). Of late this interpretation has been dismissed; the cancellation of debts owed to murdered Jews benefited debtors of diverse social standing. The political background to the pogroms is also significant. As rival contenders asserted claims to the Crown, none was in a position to exercise the traditionally protective role assumed by emperors towards Jewish communities. The cluster of pogroms in Meissen and Thuringia reflected the anti-Jewish sentiments of the local lord. By contrast only one pogrom, at Krems, occurred in lands firmly controlled by the more sympathetic Habsburgs.

D. Ditchburn

Margery Kempe

Margery Kempe was born *c.* 1373, the daughter of John Brunham, perhaps the most eminent merchant of his generation in the leading English port of King's (then Bishop's) Lynn. When aged about twenty, she married John Kempe, son of a prosperous skinner there. They had fourteen children. Her conventional way of life was punctuated by deeply felt spasms of religious remorse and longing. In 1413, when the couple were on a tour of Yorkshire shrines, she at last persuaded a reluctant John to agree that they take vows of chastity. By then she had the sensation that Christ spoke to her soul. She was to develop a rich interior spiritual life of

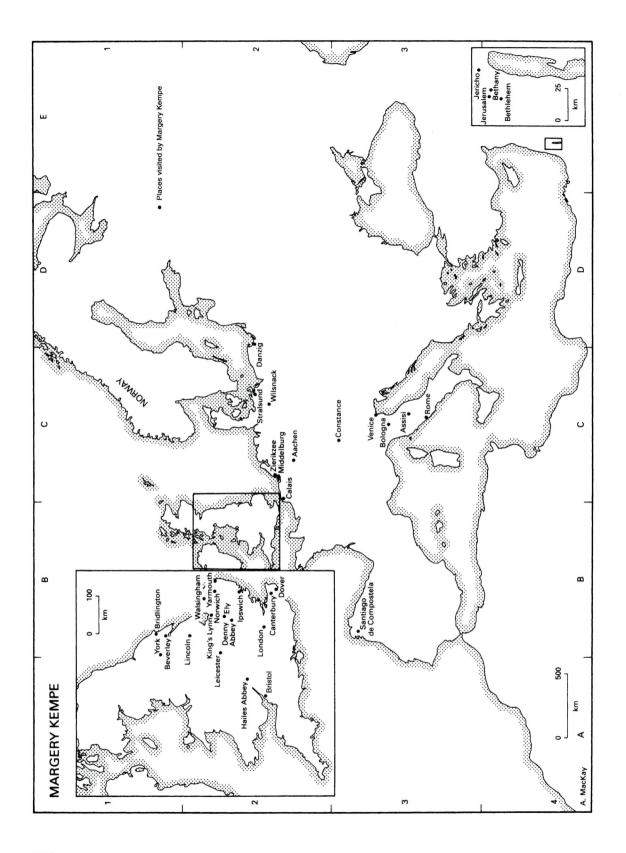

MARGERY KEMPE

Places visited by Margery Kempe

NORWAY

Danzig
Stralsund
Wilsnack
Zierikzee
Middelburg
Aachen
Calais
Constance

Venice
Bologna
Assisi
Rome

Santiago
de Compostela

York • Bridlington
Beverley
Lincoln
Walsingham
King's Lynn • Yarmouth
Leicester • Norwich
Denny • Ely
Abbey • Ipswich
London • Canterbury
Dover
Hailes Abbey •
Bristol

100
km

Jericho •
Jerusalem •
Bethany
Bethlehem

0   25
km

500
km

A. MacKay

dialogues with Him and the Blessed Virgin Mary, of visions of their temporal sufferings and of insights into the nature of the Godhead, the Trinity and Heaven. This amalgam was heavily derived from deep study of the works of contemplative writers, notably Richard Rolle, Walter Hinton and Margery's supreme exemplar, St Bridget of Sweden.

Our knowledge about Margery is derived from the book which she dictated in 1436–8. This emphasizes that her visions, her violent ecstatic trances, her well-informed homilies and defiance of confessors often heaped sufferings on her, inflicted by the hostile and sceptical. She bore them for Christ's sake. The book's testimony suggests that, in addition to the quest for indulgences, contemplative devotion, with its intensely human Christocentric and Marian focuses, fuelled international pilgrimage. The robust Margery was certainly not seeking physical cures but redemption and the avoidance of the pains of Purgatory. In 1413–18, she tells us, she visited Jerusalem, the Holy Land, Assisi, Rome and Santiago de Compostela as a pilgrim. In 1438, after accompanying her German daughter-in-law to Danzig, she followed the suggestion that she visit the popular Eucharistic shrine at Wilsnack in Brandenburg.

Margery's book gives information about the conventions and incidental experiences of pilgrimage. To finance her international journeys she relied initially on money received from those she would pray for at shrines. In England, along main routes and in towns, accompanied by her husband or a male fellow pilgrim or servant, she found travel comfortable and generally safe. A woman travelling abroad could join a pilgrim company but was expected to observe its rigid rules of conduct. The mass shipping of English pilgrims to Santiago was big business. For northern Europeans going to Rome or, via Venice, to the Holy Land, the pilgrimage trade was well organized too. In Mediterranean regions Christians and the Muslims of the Holy Land were tolerant of northerners, so long as they behaved according to stipulated conventions. However, when Margery returned from Wilsnack to England, reliant on the wavering protection of a hired male companion and not sticking to well-trodden pilgrimage routes, she sometimes encountered hostility and danger, fuelled by anti-English sentiment.

Though the book shows Muslims being kind to Margery, and Romans tolerating her as a beggar, it does not testify strongly that international travels promoted acculturation. Margery remains patriotically the burgess's daughter from Lynn, with a preformed vision of sacred landscapes. Though her spirituality was reinforced by her religious experiences in Jerusalem and Rome, it was formed by books expounded to her in her native town and by the regional pieties she absorbed in Norfolk and Yorkshire. However, since her first amanuensis, a layman from Lynn, wrote in a mixture of English and German, the original draft of the book did illustrate how close historic trading links across the North Sea could develop acculturation. It also testifies to the high profile of Englishmen and women of various ranks on the pilgrim ways to some of the great shrines of Christendom.

A. *Goodman*

Penitential pilgrimages from Antwerp, 1398–1513

As indicated in the previous entry, pilgrimages were undertaken for many different reasons. The traditional link between pilgrimage and penance also remained strong in the Late Middle Ages, reinvigorated by both ecclesiastical and secular authorities. Many bishops imposed pilgrimage as a penance and Inquisitors too dispatched the heretics of southern

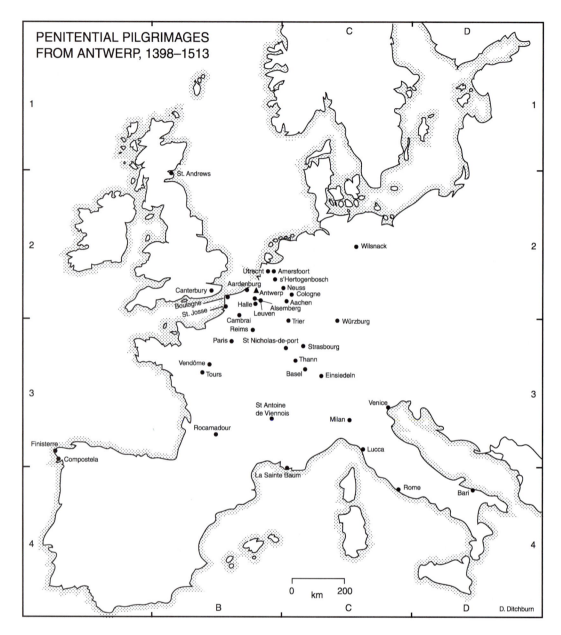

PENITENTIAL PILGRIMAGES
FROM ANTWERP, 1398–1513

St. Andrews

Wilsnack

Utrecht • • Amersfoort
Aardenburg • s'Hertogenbosch
Canterbury • • Neuss
Boulogne • Antwerp • Cologne
St. Josse • Halle • Aachen
Leuven Alsemberg
Cambrai • • Trier
Reims • • Würzburg
Paris • St Nicholas-de-port
Strasbourg
Vendôme • • Thann
• Tours Basel • • Einsiedeln

St Antoine
de Viennois
Milan •
Rocamadour •
Venice •
Finisterre
Compostela •
La Sainte Baum
Rome •
Lucca •
Bari •

0   km   200

D. Ditchburn

France to prominent shrines. From the fourteenth century the practice was also adopted by secular courts, notably in northern France, the Low Countries and Germany. The graver the crime, the more remote the pilgrimage imposed. Particularly serious offences resulted in an instruction to visit several distant shrines or not to return within a stipulated period. These, in effect, were sentences of exile. Most sentences specifed closer locations. The map indicates forty destinations (excluding Cyprus) most frequently imposed by the magistrates of Antwerp between 1398 and 1513. Cologne featured on 293 occasions, followed by Trier (203), s'Hertogenbosch (198) and Wilsnack (196). It is possible that several sentences were commuted, as each shrine was equated with a price. The tariff compiled at Oudenarde rated

Bari at 20 Parisian pounds, Compostela at 12 pounds, St Andrews at 8 pounds and Aardenburg at 12 shillings. Commutation was not, however, the norm. At Lille, where 1,027 sentences of pilgrimage were delivered between 1407 and 1559 (most commonly to Halle (near Brussels), Cologne and Boulogne), only 16 per cent of sentences are known to have been commuted. At Douai (about 40km to the south) commutations reached 44 per cent of total sentences. Those who undertook pilgrimages of this sort were expected to obtain a certificate at their destination to prove that the sentence had been performed.

D. Ditchburn

Knightly journeys

Travel was part of a chivalric education. Young knights and squires accompanied leading figures at court on pilgrimage to the Holy Land or on the tournament circuit. They thus acquired experience of foreign lands and courts and an opportunity to make their mark. A good example is Bertrandon de la Broquière, a Gascon squire in Burgundian service. In 1432 he went as a young man on pilgrimage to the Holy Land with a party of Burgundian nobles but then decided that he would make his way home overland, because he was told that it was impossible. Disguising himself as best he could he joined a caravan on its way from Mecca to the Ottoman capital of Bursa. From there he made his way to Constantinople, where he met up with the Milanese ambassador in whose company he visited the Ottoman ruler Murad II at Adrianople before returning across the Balkans to western Europe. The report he provided for the duke of Burgundy provides an accurate and perceptive account of conditions in the Ottoman Empire shortly before the fall of Constantinople (1453), notable for its lack of prejudice against either Turks or Muslims.

Five years later a Castilian squire Pero Tafur went on pilgrimage to the Holy Land but on his way home he stopped in Cyprus, where he joined an embassy to Mamluk Cairo, which allowed him to visit Egypt and Mount Sinai. Further introductions took him to Constantinople, where he passed himself off as a long lost relative of the Emperor John VIII Palaiologos, who was preparing to leave for Venice to attend a church council. Tafur preceded him to Venice and then explored Germany and eastern Europe before returning to Italy, where he caught up with the emperor at the Council of Florence (1439). He wrote up his experiences as a romance of travel. Dedicated to a grand commander of the order of Calatrava, it was designed as a textbook of chivalry.

Pero Tafur knew of the Castilian embassy to Tamburlane under Ruy Gonzalez de Clavijo, which set out in 1403 and reached Samarkand the next year. He recognized this as a journey even more remarkable than his own. Still more remarkable are the objectivity and clarity of Clavijo's reporting, whether describing Constantinople or the rebuilding of Samarkand, and his grasp of the recent history of the lands through which he travelled. The lack of prejudice is striking and underlines the quality of late medieval diplomats, exemplified by men such as the Burgundian Ghillebert de Lannoy. In old age he dictated an account of his travels to his chaplain, from which we learn of his pilgrimage as a young knight to the Holy Land, his participation in the Iberian tournament circuit, a journey through eastern Europe, where he visited Novgorod, and later a diplomatic mission to Scotland, which gave him the opportunity to cross over to Ireland and make a pilgrimage to St Patrick's Purgatory. His major diplomatic venture came in 1421, when Duke Philip II of Burgundy and Henry V of England sent him to the Byzantine emperor and the Mamluk sultan, as part of preparations for a

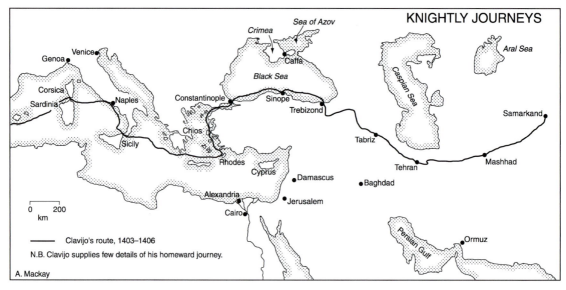

KNIGHTLY JOURNEYS

— Clavijo's route, 1403–1406

N.B. Clavijo supplies few details of his homeward journey.

A. Mackay

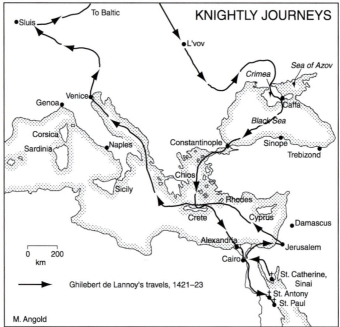

KNIGHTLY JOURNEYS

→ Ghilebert de Lannoy's travels, 1421–23

M. Angold

crusade. Lannoy travelled across central and eastern Europe to the Crimea, where he took ship to Constantinople and on to Egypt, which he explored extensively, even reaching the monasteries of St Antony and of St Paul close to the Red Sea. The fruit of his travels was a vastly detailed report on the resources and defences of Mamluk Egypt, which provided military intelligence of the highest order.

These accounts define the effective limits of western European geographical knowledge on the eve of the 'Great Discoveries'. Two things stand out. The first is a new familiarity with the lands of eastern Europe. The second is the work

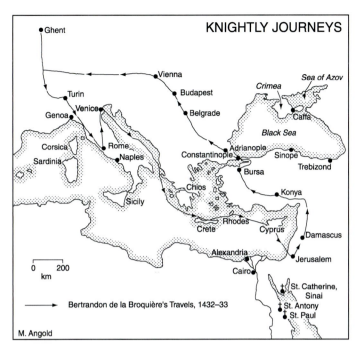

KNIGHTLY JOURNEYS

- Ghent
- Vienna
- Turin
- Budapest
- Venice
- Genoa
- Belgrade
- Corsica
- Rome
- Sardinia
- Naples
- Constantinople
- Adrianople
- Sinope
- Crimea
- Sea of Azov
- Caffa
- Black Sea
- Trebizond
- Bursa
- Chios
- Konya
- Sicily
- Rhodes
- Crete
- Cyprus
- Damascus
- Alexandria
- Jerusalem
- Cairo
- St. Catherine, Sinai
- St. Antony
- St. Paul

0   200
km

→ Bertrandon de la Broquière's Travels, 1432–33

M. Angold

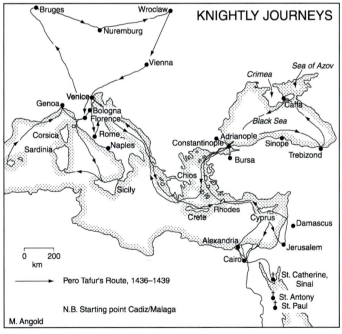

KNIGHTLY JOURNEYS

- Bruges
- Wroclaw
- Nuremburg
- Vienna
- Venice
- Genoa
- Bologna
- Florence
- Corsica
- Rome
- Sardinia
- Naples
- Constantinople
- Adrianople
- Sinope
- Crimea
- Sea of Azov
- Caffa
- Black Sea
- Trebizond
- Bursa
- Chios
- Sicily
- Rhodes
- Crete
- Cyprus
- Damascus
- Alexandria
- Jerusalem
- Cairo
- St. Catherine, Sinai
- St. Antony
- St. Paul

0   200
km

→ Pero Tafur's Route, 1436–1439

N.B. Starting point Cadiz/Malaga

M. Angold

of Catholic missionaries and Italian merchants: the former still maintained a presence in the Armenian lands, while the latter were permanently established in Damascus, Cairo, Tabriz and the ports of the Black Sea. Together they did much to facilitate the work of western diplomats and other travellers.

M. Angold

283

Froissart's world

The writer Jean Froissart created a vivid image of fourteenth-century society, especially in his *Chronicles*, a work that both entrances and infuriates historians. Unreliable in its details of date, place and person and featuring colourful but often quite fanciful anecdotes, the work nevertheless brilliantly captures the character of the times. The wide travels undertaken by Froissart, for instance to Scotland in 1365, a horse carrying his pack and a greyhound at his side, were vital in imbuing his writing with a sense of authority. Travel allowed him to be present at great events and to consort with important people. The writer was at Bordeaux for the birth of the future Richard II in 1367, attended the coronation of Charles V at Rheims in 1380 and stationed himself at Abbeville to observe Anglo-French diplomacy in 1393. Froissart also sought out informants on his travels who would describe distant places and prominent happenings. At Orthez in 1388–9 Froissart enjoyed the hospitality of the count of Foix and the conviviality of the Inn of the Moon hostelry, while gaining information on conflicts in the Iberian peninsula and elsewhere. In this way his work embraced areas far beyond his own personal experience. He had not been there, but Froissart felt able to depict the western isles of Scotland, 'the meeting place of Ireland and Norway'. He described events in regions even further afield, such as the crusading expedition against the Ottoman Turks in 1396 which reached its bloody conclusion at Nicopolis on the distant banks of the Lower Danube. Travel for Froissart was not without its perils – he was robbed in Avignon – but it provided him with one means to create a compelling and fascinating image of his times.

A.J. Macdonald

Journeys of major Italian artists, *c.* 1250 and *c.* 1400

The establishment of the actual presence of artists in specific centres of artistic activity at various times is important for our understanding of the way aspects of art, such as style, technique, iconography and prestige, might be assessed in their historical context. Very often tantalizing similarities exist between the work of two artists in, for example, style or iconography and the temptation has been to assume that there must have been some direct contact between them. However, with the development of more systematic art-historical scholarship, this tendency has been modified so that, unless firm documentation makes the connection quite clear, such spontaneous assumptions have been called into question. Emphasis has been placed on known chronological facts so that it might be seen at what period in an artist's develop-ment he may have affected, or been affected by, the work of another. Consequently, whatever knowledge we have of journeys or visits made by artists to other artistic centres is of distinct value.

In terms of influence, it is not always necessary to show an artist's presence in a particular place as panel paintings and also small sculptures may well have been transported from one place to another. However, with fresco painting and large-scale sculpture, the presence of the artist in a particular place must be assumed and it is, therefore, of great help to know the dates of such visits.

In the list as set out, the purpose is to record these visits when they are securely known, and also, where a question mark is added, to record fairly well-substantiated visits.

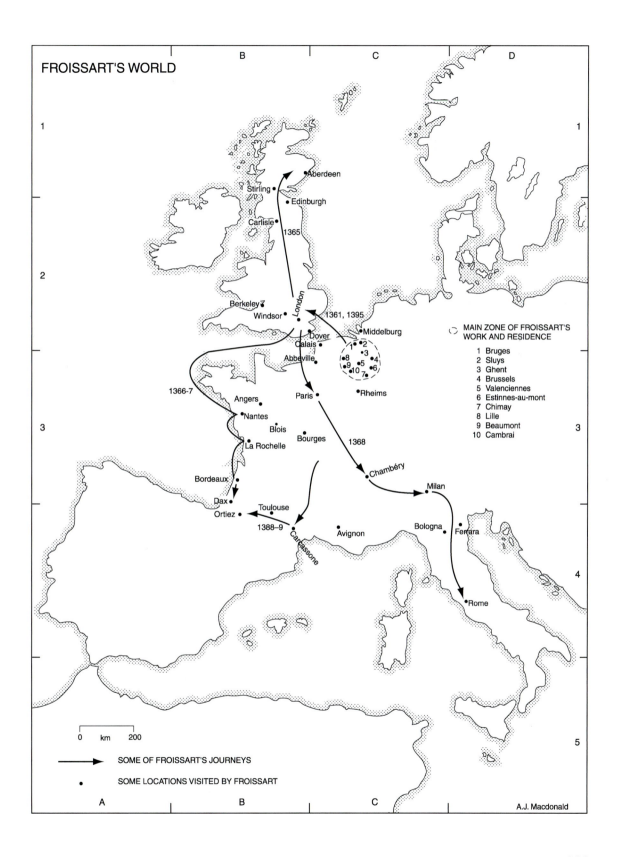

FROISSART'S WORLD

MAIN ZONE OF FROISSART'S
WORK AND RESIDENCE

1 Bruges
2 Sluys
3 Ghent
4 Brussels
5 Valenciennes
6 Estinnes-au-mont
7 Chimay
8 Lille
9 Beaumont
10 Cambrai

Aberdeen
Stirling
Edinburgh
Carlisle
1365

Berkeley
Windsor
London
Middelburg
1361, 1395
Dover
Calais
Abbeville
1366-7
Angers
Nantes
Paris
Rheims
Blois
Bourges
La Rochelle
1368
Bordeaux
Chambéry
Dax
Milan
Ortiez
Toulouse
1388-9
Avignon
Bologna
Ferrara
Carcassonne
Rome

0   km   200

⟶   SOME OF FROISSART'S JOURNEYS

•   SOME LOCATIONS VISITED BY FROISSART

A.J. Macdonald

285

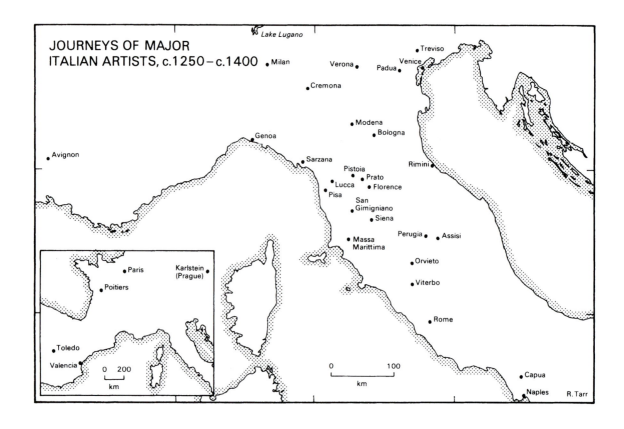

JOURNEYS OF MAJOR
ITALIAN ARTISTS, c.1250 – c.1400

Lake Lugano
Milan
Treviso
Verona
Padua
Venice
Cremona
Modena
Bologna
Genoa
Avignon
Sarzana
Rimini
Pistoia
Prato
Lucca
Florence
Pisa
San
Gimigniano
Siena
Perugia
Assisi
Massa
Marittima
Orvieto
Viterbo
Rome
Capua
Naples
R. Tarr

Paris
Karlstein
(Prague)
Poitiers
Toledo
Valencia
0   200
km

0   100
km

As might be expected, there is a great deal of movement between centres in the various regions of Italy. This is important to establish, as Italy was at that time an accumulation of different states with quite widely divergent cultural backgrounds, so that the interchange of artistic ideas between them is in itself significant. However, the most striking journeys were made to other parts of Europe, for example, that of the Florentine artist, Starnina, to Spain or that of the Sienese, Simone Martini, to Avignon. The natural barrier of the Alps may have restricted travel, but we have one reference to a Sienese architect, Ramo di Paganello, who returned from somewhere beyond the Alps to Siena in 1281, and the Sienese painter, Duccio, may well have been in Paris in 1296 and 1297. Indeed, we know that the Roman mosaicist Filippo Rusuti was working as a painter for the French king in Poitiers in 1308.

As the list shows, individual artists, perhaps for reasons of reputation, or possibly through lack of work, travelled more or less widely. Giotto, for example, travelled the length and breadth of Italy and may also have been as far afield as Provence. Others, however, seem to have stayed put, like his pupil, Taddeo Gaddi, who may never have moved from Tuscany. It is also possible to speculate on the itinerary of journeys like, for example, the one made by Tomaso da Modena who painted frescoes in Treviso which would have demanded his presence there, and who, around 1360, was commissioned to make some panels for Charles IV's palace at Karlstein, outside Prague. Although he could have sent these pictures, Treviso is on the way, as it were, from Modena to Prague, and so it is not impossible that he made what would have been at the time a quite adventurous journey.

Useful though the known evidence is, it must always be borne in mind that, like any historical evidence, it may not give the whole picture. No doubt there was much more interaction and contact than has come down to us and we must assume that artists made more journeys and travelled more often than the surviving records enable us to know for certain.

R. Tarr

DATES OF ARTISTS' BIRTH AND SOJOURNS

Sculptors and architects

Nicola Pisano (born *c. 1210, Apulia?*) Capua 1240s; Lucca 1258; Pisa 1260; Siena 1265–8; Pistoia 1273; Perugia 1277–84?

Giovanni Pisano (b. *c. 1250, Pisa*) Siena 1265–8; Perugia 1277–84?; Siena 1284–96; Massa Marittima? 1287; Pisa 1298; Pistoia 1300–1; Pisa 1302–10; Padua? *c.*1305–6; Prato *c.* 1312; Genoa? 1313; Siena 1314.

Arnolfo Di Cambio (b. *c. 1245, Florence*) Siena 1265–8; Rome 1276?–7; Viterbo? 1276; Perugia 1281; Orvieto? 1282?; Rome 1285, 1293, 1300; Florence 1296, 1300–2.

Tino Da Camaino (b. *c. 1280–5, Siena*) Pisa *c.* 1306–15; Siena 1319–20; Florence 1321–3; Naples 1323/4–37.

Lorenzo Maitani (b. *c. 1275, Siena*) Orvieto 1310–30; Perugia 1317, 1319–21; Siena 1322.

Andrea Pisano (b. *c. 1290, Pontedera, near Pisa*) Florence 1330–40; Pisa? 1343–7?; Orvieto 1347–8.

Nino Pisano (b. *c. 1315, Pisa?*) Pisa? 1342?; Orvieto 1349–53; Pisa 1357–8.

Andrea Orcagna (b. *c. 1308, Florence*) Florence 1343/4–57; Orvieto 1358–60; Florence 1364–8.

Giovanni Di Balduccio (b. *c. 1300, Pisa?*) Pisa 1317–18; Bologna 1320–5?; Sarzana? 1327–8; Milan *c.*1334–60.

Bonino Da Campione (b. *c. 1330, Campione, L. Lugano*) Cremona 1357; Milan 1363; Verona 1374.

Painters

Coppa Di Marcovaldo (b. *c. 1230, Florence*) Florence? 1261; Pistoia 1265–9, 1274; Orvieto? 1265–8?

Cimabue (b. *c. 1250, Florence?*) Rome 1272; Assisi 1270s–1280s; Pisa 1301–2.

Filippo Rusuti (b. *c. 1260, Rome*) Poitiers 1308.

Cavallini (b. *c. 1255, Rome*) Naples 1308.

Duccio (b. *c. 1255, Siena*) Florence? 1285; Paris? 1296–7.

Giotto (b. *1265/75, Florence*) Rome? 1300; Assisi 1309; Padua *c.* 1305–13? Naples 1328–32 (possible journeys to Rimini, Avignon).

Simone Martini (b. *c. 1290, Siena*) Naples 1317; Assisi 1330s?; Avignon 1340–4.

Matteo Giovannetti (b. *c. 1310, Viterbo*) Avignon 1344–5.

Pietro Lorenzetti (b. *c. 1295, Siena*) Assisi 1316–19?

Ambrogio Lorenzetti (b. *c. 1300, Siena*) Florence 1321–7.

Barna Da Siena (b. *c. 1320, Siena*) San Gimigniano 1350s?

Taddeo Gaddi (b. *c. 1310, Florence*) Pisa 1342; Pistoia? 1353.

Giovanni Da Milano (b. *c. 1330, Como?*) Florence *c.* 1350–66; Prato 1354; Rome 1369.

Tomaso Da Modena (b. *c. 1325, Modena*) Treviso 1350s; Karlstein (Prague) 1360?

Giusto De' Menabuoi (b. *c. 1350, Florence*) Padua 1370.

Altichiero (b. *c. 1350, Verona*) Padua 1379–84.

Agnolo Gaddi (b. *c. 1350, Florence*) Rome 1369; Prato 1392–5.

Spinello Aretino (b. *c. 1360, Arezzo*) Florence 1387; Pisa 1391–2; Siena 1408.

Starnina (b. *1354, Florence*) Toledo and Valencia 1398–1401.

R. Tarr

The travels of Guillaume Dufay

Guillaume Dufay (or Du Fay) (?1397–1474) was perhaps the most acclaimed musician of his generation. Born in the Netherlands, he spent much of his career at Cambrai Cathedral, serving in his youth as a choirboy and subsequently as a canon. He held several other clerical appointments too, often as an absentee. Like many musicians (and students) Dufay's career was effectively subsidized by the church. Between the 1420s and the 1450s he worked extensively in Italy, his illustrious patrons including the Malatesta of Rimini, the Este of Ferrara and the dukes of Savoy, as well as the papacy. He served two spells in the papal choir during the pontificates of Martin V (1417–31) and Eugenius IV (1431–47). Dufay's compositions of both religious and secular music were vast and varied. Those that survive include seven complete masses, twenty-eight individual mass movements, as well as numerous hymns, motets and chansons. His Italian works included *Nuper roarum flores*, a festive motet performed at the dedication of Brunnelleschi's dome of Florence Cathedral (1436), as well as other ceremonial pieces to mark the coronation of Eugenius IV (1431) and the peace of Viterbo (1433). Though highly productive and much in demand, Dufay's work was not strikingly innovative. His reputation rested on compositions of agreeable melody and the use of traditional isorythmic styles. He is especially associated with a distinctive technique for singing improvised polyphony, known as *fauxbourdon*. Often credited with helping to establish a base line that was consistently lower than the tenor, he also consolidated use of major and minor intervals which were to become the basis of harmony until the early twentieth century.

D. Ditchburn

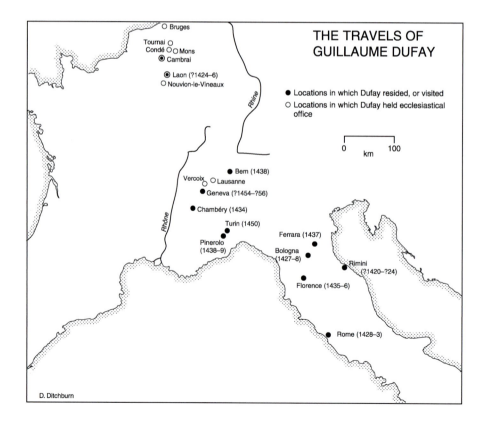

The rediscovery of classical texts

One factor that inaugurated the Renaissance was a more accurate knowledge of the ancient world. Petrarch (1304–74), pursuing the original texts of classical authors, was the first to feel the need for a precise picture of antiquity. When in Avignon, he profited from the riches of French libraries and from international contacts: in 1328 Landolfo Colonna brought from Chartres the rare Fourth Decade of Livy's *History of Rome*, enabling Petrarch to assemble the most complete and accurate text of Livy since antiquity; by 1354 other friends had obtained copies of Plato and Homer in Greek for him. In 1333 Petrarch himself discovered the lost *Pro Archia* of Cicero in a monastery in Liège. This was important, not least because the speech in defence of the poet Archias contained a famous encomium of the 'studia humanitatis'. The phrase became the slogan for disciplines which humanists championed: grammar, rhetoric, poetry, history and moral philosophy. In 1345 Petrarch made another discovery in the cathedral library of Verona – Cicero's *Letters to Atticus*. These personal letters allowed for a more accurate historical picture of Cicero and encouraged Petrarch and later humanists to publish their personal correspondence.

Boccaccio (1313–75), following Petrarch's example, inspected the library of the great abbey at Monte Cassino. There in 1355 he transcribed for Petrarch another speech of Cicero, Varro's *De Lingua Latina* and Apuleius' *The Golden Ass*, a text which not only influenced the author of the *Decameron* but also many other European novelists. The most important manuscript from Monte Cassino, containing Tacitus' *Annals* XI–XV and *Histories* I–V, also found its way to Florence, possibly by the agency of Boccaccio. Tacitus' condemnation of the Roman emperors shaped the republican 'Civic Humanism' of men like Leonardo Bruni (1370–1444). The century ended with Salutati discovering Cicero's *Ad Familiares* in a manuscript from Vercelli in 1391.

Enthusiasm for original texts expanded in the fifteenth century, leading to the recovery of most of the classical writings known today. Though only the most important can be mentioned, the map shows how the pace of discoveries increased and how, following Petrarch in the fourteenth century, the major figure of the new century was Poggio Bracciolini (1380–1459). When not on secretarial duty at the Council of Constance, Poggio combed the adjacent monasteries: he found two speeches of Cicero at Cluny (1415), the complete text of Quintilian's *Education of the Orator* in St Gall (1416), which stimulated the many Renaissance treatises on education, the poems of Lucretius, Manilius and Silius Italicus in other monasteries (1417), and in London (1420) and Cologne (1423) he came across what remains of Petronius' *Satyricon*. In Italy the complete texts of Cicero's *Orator* and *De Oratore* along with his unknown *Brutus* were discovered by Gherardo Landrianni at Lodi (1422). This manuscript provided the stimulus and terminology for Italian humanists to write the literary histories of their own time. In 1429 Nicholas Cusanus brought to Rome a manuscript containing twelve plays of Plautus, which, with the comedies of Terence, were influential in shaping Renaissance comedy in Europe. The two most significant texts after 1450 were Tacitus' *Minor Works*, brought from Fulda to Rome (1455), and Tacitus' *Annals* I–VI which reached Rome from Corvey (1508) and led to the printing of the first edition of Tacitus' *Complete Works* (1515).

Interest in Greek texts also began in the Trecento with Petrarch and Boccaccio reading Homer in Latin translation. But in 1397 Manuel Chrysoloras came to Florence and taught humanists like Bruni to read Greek and translate Plutarch and Plato into Latin. An idea of the enthusiasm for Greek can be gained from Giovanni Aurispa's return from Greece in 1423 with 238 manuscripts. In 1438 the Council of Ferrara-Florence encouraged a further influx of Greek scholars, as did the fall of Constantinople (1453). Amidst this popularity for Greek culture Marsilio Ficino (1433–99) translated the whole of Plato into Latin (1485)

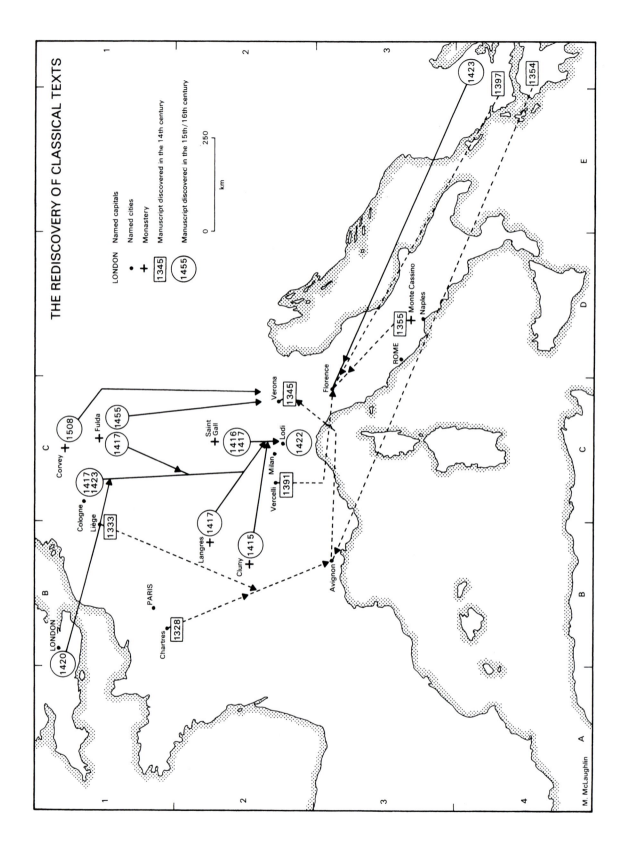

THE REDISCOVERY OF CLASSICAL TEXTS

LONDON Named capitals
•   Named cities
+   Monastery
1345   Manuscript discovered in the 14th century
1455   Manuscript discovered in the 15th/16th century

0   250
km

M. McLaughlin

and while Aristotle's *Poetics* shaped literary criticism in the sixteenth century, the vogue for Plato was to engulf Europe and challenge the medieval domination of Aristotle in the field of philosophy.

M.L. McLaughlin

The spread of printing

Johann Gutenberg, probably involved in printing experiments by the 1440s, is usually credited with producing the first printed book, using moveable type, at Mainz in 1454 or 1455.

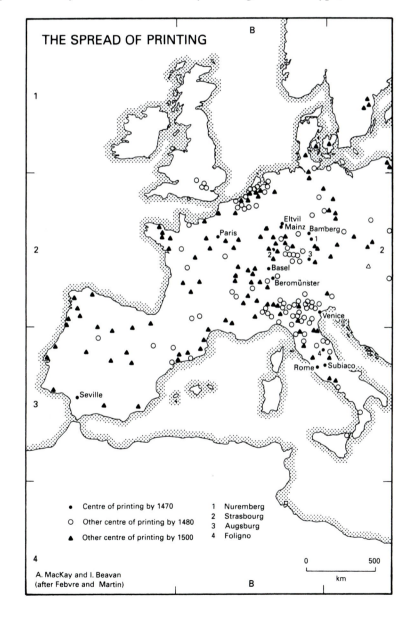

THE SPREAD OF PRINTING

- • Centre of printing by 1470
- ○ Other centre of printing by 1480
- ▲ Other centre of printing by 1500

1 Nuremberg
2 Strasbourg
3 Augsburg
4 Foligno

A. MacKay and I. Beavan
(after Febvre and Martin)

0   500
km

This was the 'Gutenberg' or 'Forty-two Line' Bible, consisting of 643 pages arranged in double columns of forty-two lines. Of perhaps 180 copies produced (some on vellum but most on paper) forty-eight have survived: the survival of printed texts is more likely than that of manuscripts.

Increased literacy and the slow production rate of manuscript copiers ensured that printing spread rapidly throughout Germany and (from 1464) Italy, and to Paris and Seville by 1470. Printing was introduced to the Low Countries by 1473, England from 1476 and most other European countries by 1500, though not until 1503 in Istanbul and 1507 in Scotland.

Being commercial enterprises, presses initially concentrated on printing 'best sellers', especially Bibles, popular religious works (such as the mystical treatise, the *Imitation of Christ*, by Thomas à Kempis) and school books (such as Donatus' *Grammar*). The availability of paper, increasing use of spectacles and printing of books (albeit in limited quantity) further stimulated a growth in that literacy which had partly provoked the initial spread of printing.

Indeed, the towns in which printing flourished (usually commercial rather than ecclesiastical centres) were often relatively well provided with schools.

Co-operation between humanists and printers stimulated the Bible-oriented concentration of reformers like Erasmus and Luther, an emphasis which was subsequently adopted by Catholic reformers too, the Complutensian Polyglot Bible published at Alcala under the patronage of Cardinal Cisneros being a celebrated example.

A professional copier of manuscripts working under pressure could produce some four hundred folios in six months. In comparison some six million books (representing thousands of different titles) had been printed by the start of the sixteenth century. Scholars could obtain a vast array of texts from one bookshop instead of tramping round many different manuscript shops or monastic libraries. Princes, too, succumbed to the attraction that influenced others: the Emperor Maximilian, for example, had himself portrayed in a printer's workshop.

A. MacKay and I. Beavan

Universities in the Late Middle Ages

If the earliest universities were international centres of learning that drew students from all over Europe, the universities of the Late Middle Ages were more dependent upon royal and municipal patronage and served more regional needs. Spurred by rising national interests, secular rulers in the first half of the fourteenth century founded new *studia* and asserted influence over the older universities in their territories. As part of his campaign against Pope Boniface VIII, Philip IV of France (1285–1314) worked to sever relations between the University of Paris and the papacy and to enforce the masters' allegiance to the French crown. In north-central Italy communes such as Padua, Perugia, Siena, and Florence attempted to erect their own *studia* to compete with Bologna. But

perhaps the most significant lay initiative came from the Emperor Charles IV: in founding the universities of Prague (1347), Kraków (1364), Vienna (1365) and the short-lived Pécs in Hungary (1367) Charles altered the map of medieval university education to include central Europe for the first time.

The crisis of the Great Schism, which began in 1378, profoundly affected Europe's *studia generalia*. Divided loyalties meant that whole universities aligned themselves with one pope or the other. Foreign students and masters were sometimes pressured to leave, thus compromising the international character of many *studia*. And because it was the universities that shaped the debate about how the Schism could be healed – many of the most influential

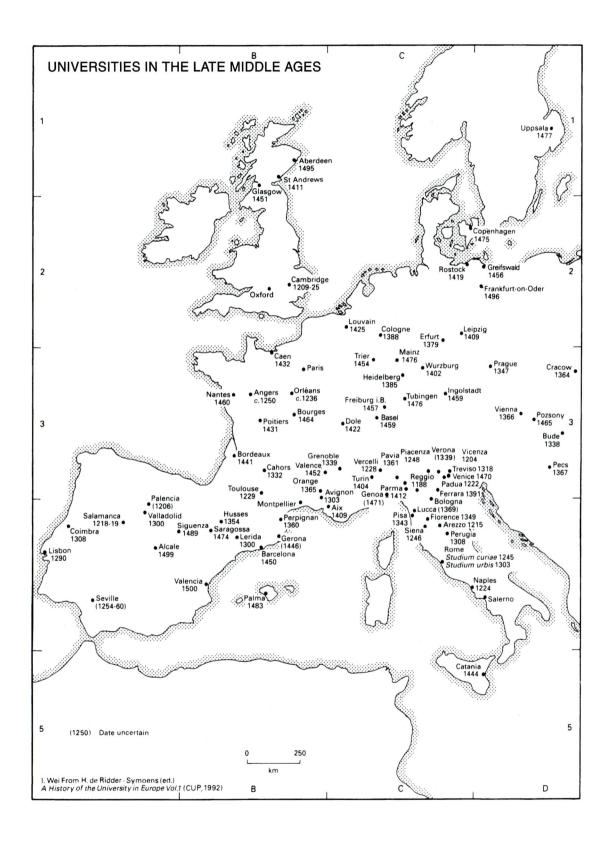

UNIVERSITIES IN THE LATE MIDDLE AGES

B

C

1   Uppsala
1477

Aberdeen
1495
St Andrews
1411
Glasgow
1451

Copenhagen
1475

2   Rostock   Greifswald
1419   1456

Cambridge
1209-25

Oxford

Frankfurt-on-Oder
1496

Louvain
1425
Cologne
1388
Erfurt
1379
Leipzig
1409

Caen
1432
Paris

Trier
1454
Mainz
1476
Wurzburg
1402
Prague
1347
Cracow
1364

Heidelberg
1385

Nantes
1460
Angers
c.1250
Orléans
c.1236
Freiburg i.B.
1457
Tubingen
1476
Ingolstadt
1459
Vienna
1366
Pozsony
1465

3   Poitiers
1431
Bourges
1464
Dole
1422
Basel
1459
Bude
1338

Bordeaux
1441
Grenoble
1339
Vercelli
1228
Pavia
1361
Piacenza
1248
Verona
(1339)
Vicenza
1204
Pecs
1367

Cahors
1332
Valence
1452
Treviso 1318

Orange
1365
Turin
1404
Reggio
1188
Venice 1470
Padua 1222

Toulouse
1229
Avignon
1303
Genoa 1412
Parma
Ferrara 1391
Bologna

Palencia
(1206)
Montpellier
Aix
1409
Lucca (1369)
Florence 1349

Salamanca
1218-19
Valladolid
1300
Husses
1354
Perpignan
1360
Pisa
1343
Arezzo 1215

Coimbra
1308
Siguenza
1489
Saragossa
1474
Lerida
1300
Gerona
(1446)
Siena
1246
Perugia
1308

Lisbon
1290
Alcale
1499
Barcelona
1450
Rome
Studium curiae 1245
Studium urbis 1303

Valencia
1500
Naples
1224

Seville
(1254-60)
Palma
1483
Salerno

Catania
1444

5   (1250)   Date uncertain

0   250

km

I. Wei From H. de Ridder - Symoens (ed.)
A History of the University in Europe Vol.1 (CUP, 1992)

conciliarist theories were developed at Paris – Roman and Avignonese popes alike began granting privileges to local secular or religious authorities willing to found new *studia* that would support their cause. Urban VI alone erected a faculty of theology at Vienna in 1378 and founded Heidelberg in 1385; and over the next four years he granted *studium generale* status to Cologne, Lucca, Kulm and Erfurt. Thus the popes themselves contributed both to the proliferation of *studia generalia* that had a questionable claim to 'general' status and also to the more national character of the late medieval universities.

M.M. Mulchahey

European expansion at the end of the Middle Ages

During the fourteenth century the trade of Genoese, Castilians and Portuguese expanded in North Africa. Factories were established on the Moroccan coast, traders accompanied caravans across the Sahara to the Niger towns and maritime expeditions visited the Atlantic Islands, raiding the Canaries for slaves who fetched a good price in Mediterranean Europe. The Genoese also invested extensively in sugar production in the southern parts of the Iberian Peninsula.

Early in the fifteenth century permanent settlements were made by French and Castilians in the Canary Islands and this prompted the Portuguese to occupy the Azores and Madeira where the Genoese soon introduced the cultivation of sugar cane. The Portuguese nobility also turned its attention to warfare in Morocco once the Hundred Years War in the Iberian Peninsula finally came to an end in 1411. The main object of the party led by the Infante Dom Henrique (Henry the Navigator) was to seize Moroccan territory and major assaults were launched on Ceuta, Tangier, Alcacer and Arzila which all fell into Portuguese hands by 1471. The Portuguese nobility also raided for slaves along the African coast and in the Canary Islands. During the regency of the Infante Dom Pedro (1440–9) the Portuguese, encouraged by the high price of slaves, sailed south of the Sahara to trade with the well-organized kingdoms of the Senegambia region, discovering that gold and ivory could also be obtained in exchange for salt, horses, wheat and cloth which came from the Mediterranean countries or the islands.

Trading was of less interest to the Portuguese nobility than obtaining territory or holding military commands. While willing to acquire seigneurial rights in the various islands that were discovered, the nobility were more interested in Moroccan and Spanish adventures and between 1469 and 1474, during the reign of Afonso V, the trade with Africa was leased to a Lisbon merchant, Fernão Gomes. Gomes' captains explored the Gulf of Guinea, discovering the lucrative opportunities for trade in gold. Trade was interrupted by war with Castile between 1474 and 1479. Europe's first colonial war took place in the Canaries and along the coast of Guinea and the threat posed by Castile encouraged the Portuguese Crown to give direct control of the African trade to the Infante João. Before he came to the throne in 1481, the treaty of Alcaçovas between Castile and Portugal had made the first partition of territory – Castile conceding the Atlantic Islands and the Guinea trade to Portugal, in return for being confirmed in the sovereignty of the Canary Islands.

After the fall of Granada in 1492, the Castilians began to exploit openings overseas. Expeditions were mounted against Morocco in imitation of the Portuguese and the Canary Islands were parcelled out among would-be conquerors. It was the desire to exploit the opportunities presented by the treaty that led

Isabella of Castile to grant a contract to the Genoese adventurer, Columbus, to undertake voyages and conquests to the west. The Portuguese, meanwhile, had continued to expand their trade under direct royal auspices. A castle was built at Elmina in 1482 to dominate the gold trade and an official royal factory was opened at the court of the king of the Congo to channel the slave trade of the region through royal hands. It was the Crown also which organized the exploratory voyages of Diogo Cão (1483–6) and Bartolomeu Dias (1487–9), and the overland journey of Pero de Covilhão who was dispatched to India, Africa and Arabia to spy out the opportunities of royal trade.

After Columbus' discoveries in 1492 not only the Caribbean islands but the whole of the New World threatened to pass out of the Castilian Crown's control since Columbus' contract had granted him the hereditary governorship of lands he discovered. In its anxiety to establish royal authority the Castilian crown hastened to organize voyages of its own and set in motion the struggle for the control of the New World between rival *conquistadores* and between the *conquistadores* and the Crown. The scramble for conquest between the Spaniards based in Santo Domingo, who set out to conquer Cuba and then Mexico and Honduras, and those based in Darien and Panama, who pushed north into Nicaragua and then organized the conquest of the Inca Empire, was mirrored in the competition between the Spaniards of Santa Marta and Cartagena and the Germans in Venezuela for the conquest of the Columbian plateau.

The individual rivalries of the *conquistadores* gave way to a struggle between the conquerors and the Crown, aided and abetted by the Church, for the control of the spoils. The struggle was not finally resolved until the 1550s when the Pizarro brothers were dead, the Welser control over Venezuela had ceased and the viceroyalties of Peru and Mexico were finally established.

The Portuguese, meanwhile, had established a maritime trading empire. In the Atlantic it was based initially on the gold trade of Elmina and the Brazilwood trade of the American coast. The expansion of the Genoese sugar production from one island group to another led, however, to the emergence, first in São Tomé and then in Brazil, of the classic triangular Atlantic commerce which linked the slave trade of mainland Africa with the sugar-growing regions and the sugar market in Europe. In the east the Portuguese tried to impose a royal trading monopoly on the spice trade of Malabar and the Moluccas and on the international trade in horses, ivory and gold. This monopoly was to be operated from a number of fortified ports which guarded access to the western Indian Ocean and which acted as customs posts for the regulation of all eastern commerce.

Since 1479 the Iberians had managed to avoid conflict. At Tordesillas in 1494 they agreed to divide the Atlantic world between them and when Magellan, a Portuguese sailing in Castilian service, found an alternative route to the Far East in 1519, the Iberian monarchs again avoided conflict, extending the partition to the eastern hemisphere by the treaty of Saragossa (1529). The peaceful settlement of the dispute was greatly assisted by the fact that the Spaniards had not found a way of sailing back across the Pacific. The separate development of the empires was, however, to end in 1545 when the Spaniards made the first of the great discoveries of silver mines in South America. The flow of silver to Europe was to provide the means to meet the huge deficit on trade which the Portuguese ran with the countries of the Indian Ocean and the Far East. Peruvian silver was to travel via Seville to India and China and for the first time weld the economies of the world together as one.

M. Newitt

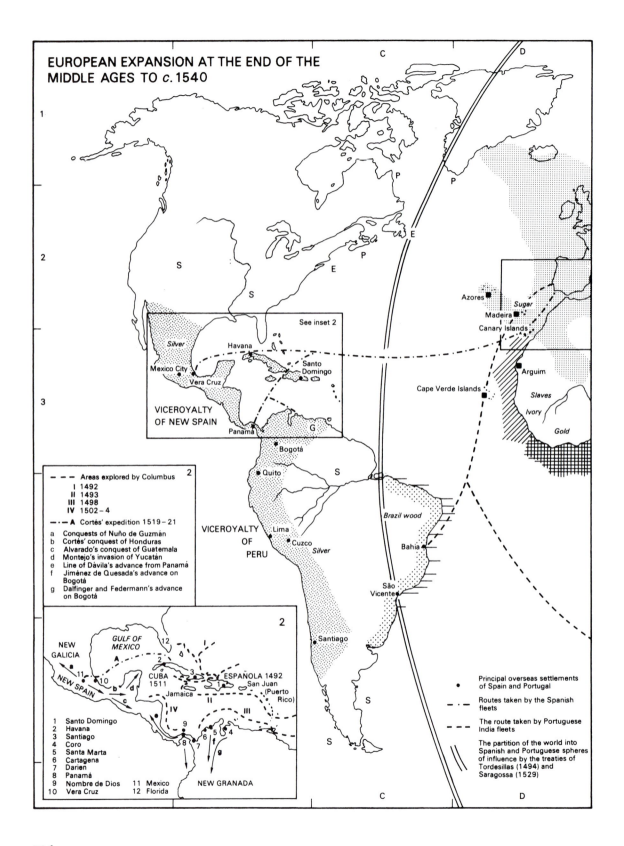

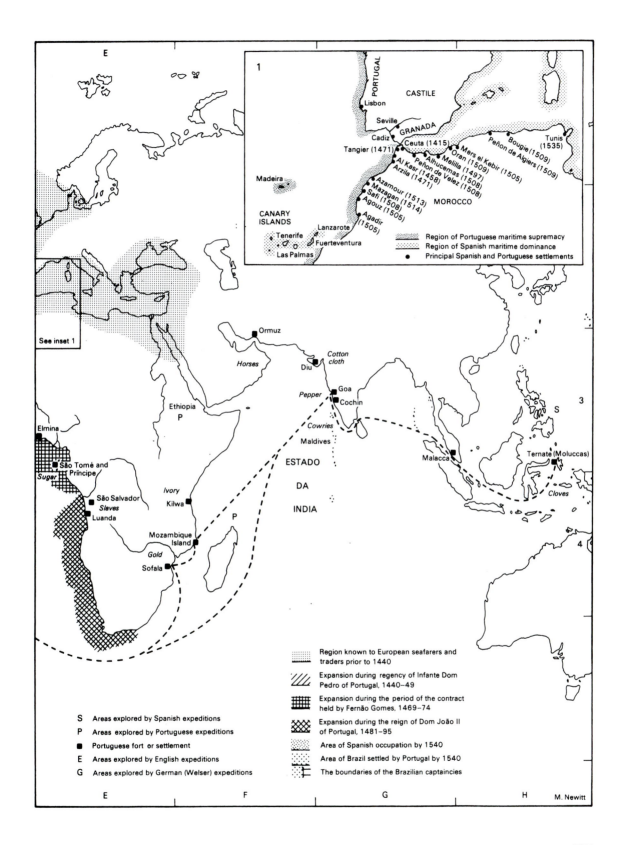

1

PORTUGAL
CASTILE
Lisbon
Seville
GRANADA
Cadiz
Ceuta (1415)
Tangier (1471)
Bougie (1509)
Tunis (1535)
Peñon de Algiers (1509)
Mers el Kebir (1505)
Oran (1509)
Melilla (1497)
Alhucemas (1508)
Peñon de Velez (1508)
Al Kasr
Arzila (1471)
Azamour (1513)
Mazagan (1514)
Safi (1508)
Agouz (1505)
Agadir (1505)
MOROCCO

Madeira

CANARY ISLANDS
Tenerife
Lanzarote
Fuerteventura
Las Palmas

░░░░░ Region of Portuguese maritime supremacy
▒▒▒▒▒ Region of Spanish maritime dominance
● Principal Spanish and Portuguese settlements

See inset 1

E

Ormuz
Horses
Cotton cloth
Diu
Pepper Goa
Cochin
Ethiopia
P
Elmina
São Tomé and Príncipe
Sugar
Cowries
Maldives
ESTADO
DA
INDIA
Malacca
Ternate (Moluccas)
S
Cloves
São Salvador
Slaves
Luanda
Ivory
Kilwa
P
Mozambique Island
Gold
Sofala

S   Areas explored by Spanish expeditions
P   Areas explored by Portuguese expeditions
■   Portuguese fort or settlement
E   Areas explored by English expeditions
G   Areas explored by German (Welser) expeditions

░░ Region known to European seafarers and
    traders prior to 1440
/// Expansion during regency of Infante Dom
    Pedro of Portugal, 1440–49
▦▦ Expansion during the period of the contract
    held by Fernão Gomes, 1469–74
▧▧ Expansion during the reign of Dom João II
    of Portugal, 1481–95
░░ Area of Spanish occupation by 1540
∴∴ Area of Brazil settled by Portugal by 1540
    The boundaries of the Brazilian captaincies

M. Newitt

E   F   G   H

SUGGESTIONS FOR FURTHER READING

The suggestions which follow are intended for the school or undergraduate student, or the general reader, who wishes to seek more information on particular topics. Quite deliberately, therefore, most references are to modern publications in English. The bibliography is arranged in order of the appearance of the corresponding map. In addition to material cited under specific headings, the following introductory works are of relevance to a variety of topics:

D. Abulafia *et al.* (eds), *The New Cambridge Medieval History*, 7 vols., Cambridge, 1995–2005.

M. Barber, *The Two Cities: Medieval Europe, 1050–1320*, 2nd edn, London, 2004.

M. Bull, *Thinking Medieval: An introduction to the study of the Middle Ages*, Basingstoke, 2005.

R. Collins, *Early Medieval Europe, 300–1000*, 2nd edn, Basingstoke, 1999.

C.W. Hollister and J. Bennett, *Medieval Europe: A short history*, 9th edn, Boston, MA, 2002.

G. Holmes (ed.), *The Oxford History of Medieval Europe*, Oxford, 1992.

B. Rosenwein, *A Short History of the Middle Ages*, Peterborough, Ont., 2nd edn, 2004.

D. Waley and P. Denley, *Late Medieval Europe, 1250–1520*, 3rd edn, Harlow, 2001.

The Roman Empire, AD 395

A. Cameron, *The Later Roman Empire*, London, 1993.

A. Cameron, *The Mediterranean World in Late Antiquity, AD 395–600*, London, 1993.

E. Gibbon, *The Decline and Fall of the Roman Empire*, revised by J.B. Bury, 3 vols, London, 1900.

D. Kagan (ed.), *The End of the Roman Empire: Decline or transformation?*, 2nd edn, Lexington, MA, 1978.

B. Ward-Perkins, *The Fall of Rome and the End of Civilization*, Oxford, 2005.

Barbarian migrations and kingdoms

E. Collins, *Early Medieval Spain: Unity in diversity, 400–1000*, 2nd edn, Basingstoke, 1995.

E. James, *The Franks*, Oxford, 1988.

G. Halsall, *Warfare and Society in the Barbarian West, 450–900*, London, 2003.

J. Moorhead, *Theoderic in Italy*, Oxford, 1993.

T.F.X. Noble (ed.), *From Roman Provinces to Medieval Kingdoms*, London, 2006.

J. Smith, *Europe after Rome*, Oxford, 2005.

C. Wickham, *Framing the Early Middle Ages: Europe and the Mediterranean, 400–800*, Oxford, 2005.

I.N. Wood, *The Merovingian Kingdoms, 450–751*, London, 1994.

The Empire of Justinian

R. Browning, *Justinian and Theodora*, revd edn, London, 1987.

O. Mazal, *Justinian I und seine Zeit*, Cologne, 2001.

J. Moorhead, *Theoderic in Italy*, Oxford, 1993.

J. Moorhead, *Justinian*, Harlow, 1994.

The expansion of Islam

F.N. Donner, *The Early Islamic Conquests*, Princeton, 1981.

J.F. Haldon, *Byzantium in the Seventh Century*, Cambridge, 1990.

W.E. Kaegi, *Byzantium and the Early Islamic Conquests*, Cambridge, 1992.

H. Kennedy, *The Prophet and the Age of the Caliphates: The Islamic near east from the sixth to the eleventh centuries*, 2nd edn, Harlow, 2004.

Italy, 8th century

T.S. Brown, *Gentlemen and Officers: Imperial administration and aristocratic power in Byzantine Italy, 554–800*, London, 1984.

N. Everett, *Literacy in Lombard Italy, c.569–774*, Cambridge, 2003.

T.F.X. Noble, *The Republic of Saint Peter*, Philadelphia, 1984.

G. Tabacco, *The Struggle for Power in Medieval Italy: Structures of political rule*, Cambridge, 1989.

C. Wickham, *Early Medieval Italy*, London, 1980.

The Carolingian Empire and its division

P. Godman and R. Collins (eds), *Charlemagne's Heir: New perspectives on the reign of Louis the Pious*, Oxford, 1990.

E. Goldberg, *Struggle for Empire: Kingship and conflict under Louis the German, 817–876*, Ithaca, 2006

M. Innes, *State and Society in the Early Middle Ages*, Cambridge, 2000.

R. McKitterick, *The Frankish Kingdoms under the Carolingians*, London, 1983.

S. MacLean, *Kingship and Politics in the Late Ninth Century: Charles the Fat and the end of the Carolingian Empire*, Cambridge, 2003.

J. Nelson, *Charles the Bald*, London, 1992.

T. Reuter, *Germany in the Early Middle Ages, 800–1056*, London, 1991.

P. Riché, *The Carolingians: A family who forged Europe*, Philadelphia, 1993.

J. Story (ed.), *Charlemagne: Empire and society*, Manchester, 2005.

The Moravian Empire

P. Barford, *The Early Slavs*, London, 2001.

C. Bowlus, *Franks, Moravians and Magyars: The struggle for the middle Danube, 788–907*, Philadelphia, 1995.

E. Goldberg, *Struggle for Empire: Kingship and conflict under Louis the German, 817–876*, Ithaca, 2006.

The Byzantine Empire under the Macedonian Dynasty

C. Holmes, *Basil II and the Governance of the Empire, 976–1025*, Oxford, 2005.

P. Magdalino (ed.), *Byzantium in the Year 1000*, Leiden, 2002.

G. Ostrogorsky, *History of the Byzantine State*, 2nd edn, Oxford, 1968.

P. Stephenson, *Byzantium's Balkan Frontier: A political study of the northern Balkans, 900–1204*, Cambridge, 2000.

W.T. Treadgold, *A Concise History of Byzantium*, Basingstoke, 2001.

M. Whittow, *The Making of Orthodox Byzantium, 600–1025*, Basingstoke, 1996.

Vikings

W. Davies (ed.), *From the Vikings to the Normans*, Oxford, 2003.

F.D. Logan, *The Vikings in History*, 3rd edn, London, 2005.

E. Roesdahl and D.M. Wilson (eds), *From Viking to Crusader: Scandinavia and Europe, 800–1200*, New York, 1992.

P.H. Sawyer, *Kings and Vikings: Scandinavia and Europe, AD 700–1100*, London, 1982.

P.H. Sawyer (ed.), *The Oxford Illustrated History of the Vikings*, Oxford, 1997.

Magyars

C. Bowlus, *Franks, Moravians and Magyars: The struggle for the middle Danube, 788–907*, Philadelphia, 1995.

P. Engel, *The Realm of St Stephen: A history of medieval Hungary, 895–1526*, London, 2001.

T. Reuter, *Germany in the Early Middle Ages, 800–1056*, London, 1991.

The East European states, c. 1000

P. Barford, *The Early Slavs*, London, 2001.

J.V.A. Fine, *The Early Medieval Balkans*, Ann Arbor, 1983.

P. Stephenson, *Byzantium's Balkan Frontier: A political study of the northern Balkans, 900–1204*, Cambridge, 2000.

A.P. Vlasto, *The Entry of the Slavs into Christendom*, Cambridge, 1970.

The Ottonian Empire

K.J. Leyser, *Rule and Conflict in an Early Medieval Society: Ottonian Saxony*, London, 1979.

K.J. Leyser, *Medieval Germany and Its Neighbours, 900–1250*, London, 1982.

T. Reuter, *Germany in the Early Middle Ages, 800–1056*, London, 1991.

Scandinavia, *c.* 1000

K. Helle (ed.), *The Cambridge History of Scandinavia*, vol. 1, Cambridge, 2003.

J. Jesch, *Women in the Viking Age*, Woodbridge, 1991/2003.

B. Sawyer and P. Sawyer, *Medieval Scandinavia*, Minneapolis, 1993.

Britain and Ireland, *c.* 1000

J. Campbell (ed.), *The Anglo-Saxons*, Oxford, 1982.

W. Davies (ed.), *From the Vikings to the Normans*, Oxford, 2003.

T.C. Edwards, *Early Christian Ireland*, Cambridge, 2000.

D. Ó Cróinín, *Early Medieval Ireland, 400–1200*, London, 1995.

D. Ó Cróinín (ed.), *A New History of Ireland*, Vol. I, Oxford, 2005.

P. Stafford, *Unification and Conquest: A political and social history of England in the tenth and eleventh centuries*, London, 1989.

B. Yorke, *Kings and Kingdoms of Early Anglo-Saxon England*, London, 1990.

France, *c.* 1000

M. Bull (ed.), *France in the Central Middle Ages, 900–1200*, Oxford, 2002.

J. Dunbabin, *France in the Making, 843–1180*, 2nd edn, Oxford, 2000.

E. Hallam and J. Everard, *Capetian France, 987–1328*, 2nd edn, Harlow, 2001.

S. Reynolds, *Fiefs and Vassals*, Oxford, 1994.

Italy, 11th century

B. Kreutz, *Before the Normans: Southern Italy in the ninth and tenth centuries*, Philadelphia, 1991.

C. La Rocca, *Italy in the Early Middle Ages, 476–1000*, Oxford, 2002.

G.A. Loud, *The Age of Robert Guiscard: Southern Italy and the Norman Conquest*, Harlow, 2000.

P. Skinner, *Family Power in Southern Italy: The duchy of Gaeta and its neighbours, 850–1139*, Cambridge, 1995.

Iberia, 8th–11th centuries

H. Kennedy, *Muslim Spain and Portugal: A political history of al-Andalus*, Harlow, 1996.

A. MacKay, *Spain in the Middle Ages: From frontier to empire, 1000–1500*, London, 1977.

B.F. Reilly, *The Contest of Christian and Muslim Spain, 1031–1157*, Cambridge MA and Oxford, 1992.

B.F. Reilly, *The Two Spains*, Cambridge, 1993.

Royal Carolingian residential villas

C. Cubitt (ed.), *Court Culture in the Early Middle Ages*, Turnhout, 2003.

R. Samson, 'Carolingian palaces and the poverty of ideology', in M. Locock (ed.), *Meaningful Architecture: Social interpretations of buildings*, Aldershot, 1994.

Continental coins and mints

P. Grierson and M. Blackburn, *Medieval European Coinage*. Vol. I: *The Early Middle Ages*, Cambridge, 1986.

Aristocratic landholding

M. Innes, *State and Society in the Early Middle Ages*, Cambridge, 2000.

J. Smith, *Europe After Rome*, Oxford, 2005.

C. Wickham, *Framing the Early Middle Ages: Europe and the Mediterranean, 400–800*, Oxford, 2005.

Anglo-Saxon burhs and mints

R. Abels, *Alfred the Great: War, kingship and culture in Anglo-Saxon England*, London, 1998.

J. Campbell (ed.), *The Anglo-Saxons*, Oxford, 1982.

R.H.M. Dolley (ed.), *Anglo-Saxon Coins*, London, 1961.

H.R. Lyon, *The Governance of Anglo-Saxon England*, London, 1984.

Royal itineraries: 11th-century France and Germany

J. Bernhardt, *Itinerant Kingship and Royal Monasteries in Early Medieval Germany, c.936–1075*, Cambridge, 1993.

England under William I

R. Bartlett, *England under the Norman and Angevin Kings, 1075–1225*, Oxford, 2000.

D. Crouch, *The Normans: The history of a dynasty*, London, 2002.

R. Fleming, *Kings and Lords in Conquest England*, Cambridge, 1991.

B. Golding, *Conquest and Colonisation: The Normans in Britain, 1066–1100*, revd edn, Basingstoke, 2001.

Scandinavian settlement

B.E. Crawford, *Scandinavian Settlement in Northern Britain*, London & New York, 1995.

Early medieval towns

G.P. Brogiolo, N. Gauthier and N. Christie (eds), *Towns and their Territories between Late Antiquity and the Early Middle Ages*, Leiden, 2000.

T.S. Brown, *Gentlemen and Officers: Imperial administration and aristocratic power in Byzantine Italy, 554–800*, London, 1984.

N. Christie and S. Loseby (eds), *Towns in Transition: Urban evolution in late antiquity and the early middle ages*, Aldershot, 1996.

R. Hodges, *The Anglo-Saxon Achievement*, London, 1989.

R. Hodges and D. Whitehouse, *Mohammed, Charlemagne and the Origins of Europe*, London, 1983.

R. Krautheimer, *Rome: Profile of a city, 312–1308*, Princeton, 1980.

P. Llewellyn, *Rome in the Dark Ages*, London, 1971.

P. Magdalino, *Constantinople médiévale: Études sur l'évolution des structures urbaines*, Paris, 1996.

C. Mango, *Le developpement urbain de Constantinople (IV–VIIe siècles)*, Paris, 1985.

P. Sherrard, *Constantinople: Iconography of a sacred city*, London, 1965.

Trade routes of the Carolingian Empire

R. Hodges and D. Whitehouse, *Mohammed, Charlemagne and the Origins of Europe*, London, 1983.

M. McCormick, *Origins of the European Economy: Communications and commerce, AD 300–900*, Cambridge, 2001.

H. Pirenne, *Mohammed and Charlemagne*, London, 1939.

A. Verhulst, *The Carolingian Economy*, Cambridge, 2002.

The economy of San Vincenzo

R. Hodges, *A Dark-Age Pompeii: San Vincenzo al Volturno*, London, 1990.

R. Hodges (ed.), *San Vincenzo al Volturno: The 1980–1986 excavations*, 2 vols, Rome, 1993–5.

C. Wickham, *La terra di San Vincenzo al Volturno e il problema dell' incastellamento di Italia centrale*, Florence, 1985.

Christianity and paganism

P. Brown, *The Rise of Western Christendom: Triumph and diversity, AD 200–1000*, 2nd edn, Oxford, 2003.

H. Chadwick, *The Church in Ancient Society: From Galilee to Gregory the Great*, Oxford, 2001.

J.N. Hilgarth, *Christianity and Paganism, 350–750*, Philadelphia, 1986.

R.A. Markus, *The End of Ancient Christianity*, Cambridge, 1990.

Early and northern monasticism

O. Chadwick, *John Cassian*, Cambridge, 1950.

H.B. Clarke and M. Brennan (eds), *Columbanus and Merovingian Monasticism*, Oxford, 1981.

M. Dunn, *The Emergence of Monasticism: From the desert fathers to the early Middle Ages*, Oxford, 2000.

C. Etchingham, *Church Organisation in Ireland, AD 650 to 1000*, Maynooth, 1999.

C.H. Lawrence, *Medieval Monasticism*, 3rd edn, Harlow, 2001.

D. Parry and E. de Waal (eds), *The Rule of Saint Benedict*, Leominster, 1990.

Irish and Anglo-Saxon centres on the Continent

J.J.G. Alexander, *Insular Manuscripts: 6th to the 9th Century*, London, 1978.

L. Bieler, *Ireland: Harbinger of the Middle Ages*, London, 1963.

D.N. Dumville, *A Palaeographer's Review: The insular system of scripts in the early Middle Ages*, 2 vols, Kansai, 1999–2003.

W. Levison, *England and the Continent in the Eighth Century*, Oxford, 1946.

H. Lowe (ed.), *Die Iren und Europa im früheren Mittelalter*, 2 vols, Stuttgart, 1982.

T.F.X. Noble and T. Head (eds), *Soldiers of Christ: Saints and saints' lives from late antiquity and the early middle ages*, London, 1995.

M. Richter, *Ireland and her Neighbours in the Seventh Century*, Dublin, 1999.

Bede's world

P.H. Blair, *The World of Bede*, 2nd edn, Cambridge, 1990.

J. Campbell (ed), *The Anglo-Saxons*, Oxford, 1982.

L.A.J.R. Houwen and A.A. MacDonald (eds), *Beda Venerabilis: Historian, monk & Northumbrian*, Groningen, 1996.

H. Mayr-Harting, *The Coming of Christianity to Anglo-Saxon England*, London, 1972.

P. Riché, *Education and Culture in the Barbarian West, 6th–8th Centuries*, Columbia, 1975.

St Cuthbert

G. Bonner, D. Rollason and C. Stancliffe (eds), *St Cuthbert, his Cult and his Community to A.D. 1200*, Woodbridge, 1989.

D. Rollason, M. Harvey and M. Prestwich (eds), *Anglo-Norman Durham, 1093–1193*, Woodbridge, 1994.

Relics in Saxony

K. Bodarwé, 'Roman martyrs and their veneration in Ottonian Saxony', *Early Medieval Europe*, 9 (2000).

C. Carrol, 'The bishoprics of Saxony in the first century after Christianisation', *Early Medieval Europe*, 8 (1999).

W. Lammers (cd.), *Die Eingliederung der Sachsen in das Frankenreich*, Darmstadt, 1970.

The Carolingian Renaissance

J. Contreni, *Carolingian Learning, Masters and Manuscripts*, Aldershot, 1992.

R. McKitterick (ed.), *Carolingian Culture: Emulation and innovation*, Cambridge, 1994.

Centres of reform, 10th and 11th centuries

N. Hunt (ed.), *Cluniac Monasticism in the Central Middle Ages*, London, 1971.

D. Iogna-Prat, *Order and Exclusion: Cluny and Christendom face heresy, Judaism and Islam, 1000–1150*, Ithaca, 2002.

C.H. Lawrence, *Medieval Monasticism*, 3rd edn, Harlow, 2001.

J. Nightingale, *Monasteries and Patrons in the Gorze Reform: Lotharingia, c.850–1000*, Oxford, 2000.

Peace and truce of God

T. Head and R. Landes, *The Peace of God: Social violence and religious response around the year 1000*, Ithaca, 1992.

G. Tellenbach, *The Church in Western Europe from the Tenth to the Early Twelfth Century*, Cambridge, 1993.

Iconoclasm and the dualist heresies in Byzantium

L. Brubaker and J. Haldon, *Byzantium in the Iconoclast Era (c.680–850): The sources*, Aldershot, 2000.

A. Bryer and J. Herrin, *Iconoclasm*, Birmingham, 1977.

J. Haldon and L. Brubaker, *Byzantium in the Iconoclast Era (680–850): A history*, Cambridge, 2005.

J. Hamilton and B. Hamilton, *Christian Dualist Heresies in the Byzantine World, c.650–c.1405*, Manchester, 1998.

Byzantine missions among the Slavs

R. Browning, *Byzantium and Bulgaria*, London, 1975.

F. Dvornik, *Byzantine Missions among the Slavs*, New Brunswick, 1970.

D. Obolensky, *The Byzantine Commonwealth*, London, 1971.

A.P. Vlasto, *The Entry of the Slavs into Christendom*, Cambridge, 1970.

Papal authority and schism

H. Chadwick, *East and West: The making of a rift in the church*, Oxford, 2003.

H.E.J. Cowdrey, *Pope Gregory VII, 1073–1085*, Oxford, 1998.

C. Morris, *The Papal Monarchy: The western church from 1050 to 1250*, Oxford, 1989.

I.S. Robinson, *The Papacy, 1073–1198: Continuity and innovation*, Cambridge, 1990.

Episcopal sees in Europe at the end of the 10th century

R. Bartlett, *The Making of Europe: Conquest, colonization and cultural change, 950–1350*, London, 1993.

G. Tellenbach, *The Church in Western Europe from the Tenth to the Early Twelfth Century*, Cambridge, 1993.

Cartography

E. Edson, *Mapping Time and Space: How medieval mapmakers viewed their world*, London, 1997.

P.D.A. Harvey, *Medieval Maps*, London, 1991.

N.R. Kline, *Maps of Medieval Thought: The Hereford paradigm*, Woodbridge, 2001.

Scandinavia, 12th century

E. Christiansen, *The Northern Crusades: The Baltic and the Catholic frontier, 1100–1525*, London, 1980.

K. Helle (ed.), *The Cambridge History of Scandinavia*, vol. 1, Cambridge, 2003.

B. Sawyer and P. Sawyer, *Medieval Scandinavia*, Minneapolis and London, 1993.

The Hohenstaufen Empire

D. Abulafia, *Frederick II*, new edn, London, 2002.

B. Arnold, *Princes and Territories in Medieval Germany*, Cambridge, 1991.

B. Arnold, *Medieval Germany, 500–1300: A political interpretation*, Basingstoke, 1997.

H. Fuhrmann, *Germany in the High Middle Ages, c.1050–1200*, Cambridge, 1986.

A. Haverkamp, *Medieval Germany 1056–1273*, 2nd edn, Oxford, 1992.

J.K. Hyde, *Society and Politics in Medieval Italy*, London, 1973.

P. Munz, *Frederick Barbarossa: A study in medieval politics*, London, 1969.

G. Tabacco, *The Struggle for Power in Medieval Italy: Structures of political rule*, Cambridge, 1989.

D. Waley, *The Italian City Republics*, 3rd edn, London, 1988.

B. Weiler, *King Henry III and the Staufen Empire*, London, 2006.

Southern Italy and Sicily, 12th century

H. Houben, *Roger II of Sicily: A ruler between east and west*, Cambridge, 2002.

G.A. Loud, *The Age of Robert Guiscard: Southern Italy and the Norman conquest*, Harlow, 2000.

G.A. Loud and A. Metcalfe (eds), *The Society of Norman Italy*, Leiden, 2002.

D. Matthew, *The Norman Kingdom of Sicily*, Cambridge, 1992.

Wales, Ireland and Scotland

G.W.S. Barrow, *The Anglo-Norman Era in Scottish History*, Oxford, 1980.

G.W.S. Barrow, *Kingship and Unity: Scotland, 1000–1306*, 2nd edn, Edinburgh, 2003.

D. Carpenter, *The Struggle for Mastery: Britain, 1066–1284*, London, 2003.

R.R. Davies, *The First English Empire: Power and identities in the British Isles, 1093–1343*, Oxford, 2000.

S. Duffy, *Ireland in the Middle Ages*, Basingstoke, 1997.

M.T. Flanagan, *Irish Society, Anglo-Norman Settlement, Angevin Kingship*, Oxford, 1989.

R. Frame, *The Political Development of the British Isles, 1100–1400*, Oxford, 1990.

Angevins and Capetians

R. Bartlett, *England under the Norman and Angevin Kings, 1075–1225*, Oxford, 2000.

J. Gillingham, *Richard I*, New Haven, 1999.

J. Gillingham, *The Angevin Empire*, 2nd edn, London, 2001.

E. Hallam and J. Everard, *Capetian France, 987–1328*, 2nd edn, Harlow, 2001.

R.V. Turner, *King John*, Harlow, 1994.

W.L. Warren, *Henry II*, London, 1973.

Catalonia, 1080–1180

S.P. Bensch, *Barcelona and its Rulers, 1096–1291*, Cambridge, 1995.

T.N. Bisson, *The Medieval Crown of Aragon*, Oxford, 1986.

B.A. Catlos, *The Victors and the Vanquished: Christians and Muslims of Catalonia and Aragon, 1050–1300*, Cambridge, 2004.

The Empire of the Comneni, 1081–1185

M.J. Angold, *The Byzantine Empire, 1025–1204: A political history*, 2nd edn, New York, 1997.

M.J. Angold, *Church and Society in Byzantium under the Comneni, 1081–1261*, revd edn, Cambridge, 2000.

A. Harvey, *Economic Expansion in the Byzantine Empire, 900–1200*, London, 1990.

A.P. Kazhdan and A.W. Epstein, *Change in Byzantine Culture in the Eleventh and Twelfth Centuries*, Berkeley, Los Angeles and London, 1985.

P. Magdalino, *The Empire of Manuel I Komnenos, 1143–1180*, Cambridge, 1993.

Crusades and Templars

M.J. Angold, *The Fourth Crusade: Event and context*, Harlow, 2003.

M. Barber, *The New Knighthood: A history of the order of the Temple*, Cambridge, 1994.

M. Bull, *Knightly Piety and the Lay Response to the First Crusade*, Oxford, 1993.

M. Bull *et al.* (eds), *The Experience of Crusading*, 2 vols, Cambridge, 2003.

A. Forey, *The Military Orders from the Twelfth to the Early Fourteenth Centuries*, Basingstoke, 1992.

B. Hamilton, *The Leper King and his Heirs: Baldwin IV and the crusader kingdom of Jerusalem*, Cambridge, 2000.

J. Riley-Smith (ed.), *The Atlas to the Crusades*, London, 1990.

J. Riley-Smith, *The First Crusaders, 1095–1131*, Cambridge, 1997.

J. Riley-Smith, *What Were the Crusades?*, 3rd edn, Basingstoke, 2002.

J. Riley-Smith, *The Crusades: A History*, 2nd edn, London, 2005.

Byzantium in the 13th century

M.J. Angold, *The Fourth Crusade*, Harlow, 2003.

J. Dunbabin, *Charles I of Anjou*, Harlow, 1998.

S. Runciman, *The Sicilian Vespers*, Cambridge, 1958.

Italy in the second half of the 13th century

C. Backman, *The Decline and Fall of Medieval Sicily, 1296–1337*, Cambridge, 1995.

J. Dunbabin, *Charles I of Anjou*, Harlow, 1998.

J.K. Hyde, *Society and Politics in Medieval Italy*, Basingstoke, 1973.

P. Jones, *The Italian City-States: From commune to signoria*, Oxford, 1997.

J. Larner, *Italy in the Age of Dante and Petrarch*, Harlow, 1980.

S. Runciman, *The Sicilian Vespers*, Cambridge, 1958.

G. Tabacco, *The Struggle for Power in Medieval Italy: Structures of political rule*, Cambridge, 1989.

D. Waley, *The Papal State in the Thirteenth Century*, London, 1961.

The *Ostsiedlung*

R. Bartlett, *The Making of Europe: Conquest, colonization and cultural change, 950–1350*, London, 1993.

E. Christiansen, *The Northern Crusades: The Baltic and the Catholic frontier, 1100–1525*, London, 1980.

Poland in the Central Middle Ages

P. Górecki, *Economy, Society and Lordship in Medieval Poland, 1100–1250*, New York, 1992.

P. Górecki, *Parishes, Tithes and Society in Earlier Medieval Poland, c. 1100–c. 1250*, Philadelphia, 1993.

The Premyslide-Habsburg conflict
J. Bérenger, *A History of the Habsburg Empire, 1273–1700*, Harlow, 1994.

The Mongol-Tatar invasions
J. Fennell, *The Crisis of Medieval Russia, 1200–1304*, London, 1983.

D. Jackson, *The Mongols and the West, 1221–1410*, Harlow, 2005.

D. Morgan, *The Mongols*, Oxford, 1986.

P. Ratchnevsky, *Genghis Khan: His Life and Legacy*, ed. T.N. Haining, Oxford, 1991.

France in the reign of Philip the Fair
M. Barber, *The Angevin Legacy and the Hundred Years War, 1250–1340*, Oxford, 1990.

J. Favier, *Philippe le Bel*, Paris, 1978.

J.R. Strayer, *The Reign of Philip the Fair*, Princeton, 1980.

Iberia, 12th and 13th centuries
D. Lomax, *The Reconquest of Spain*, London, 1978.

A. MacKay, *Spain in the Middle Ages: From frontier to empire, 1000–1500*, London, 1977.

J.F. O'Callaghan, *A History of Medieval Spain*, Ithaca, 1975.

B.F. Reilly, *The Contest of Christian and Muslim Spain, 1031–1157*, Oxford, 1992.

Provisioning war in the 12th century
M.T. Clanchy, *From Memory to Written Record: England, 1066–1307*, 2nd edn, Oxford, 1993.

A.J. Otway-Ruthven, *A History of Medieval Ireland*, 2nd edn, 1980.

R.L. Poole, *The Exchequer in the Twelfth Century*, Oxford, 1912.

Castles
J.R. Kenyon, *Mediaeval Fortifications*, 2nd edn, London, 2005.

N.J.G. Pounds, *The Mediaeval Castle in England and Wales*, Cambridge, 1990.

Government in France, 1180–1226
J. Baldwin, *The Government of Philip Augustus: Foundations of French royal power in the Middle Ages*, Berkeley, 1986.

Settlement
T.F. Glick, *Irrigation and Society in Medieval Valencia*, Cambridge, MA, 1970.

M.G. Jiménez, *En torno a los orígenes de Andalucia*, 2nd edn, Seville, 1988.

M.G. Jiménez, 'Frontier and settlement in the kingdom of Castile (1085–1350)', in R. Bartlett and A. MacKay (eds), *Medieval Frontier Societies*, Oxford, 1989.

P. Toubert, *Les structures du Latium médiéval*, Rome, 1973.

C. Wickham, *Il problema dell' incastellamento nell' Italia centrale*, Florence, 1985.

C. Wickham, *The Mountains and the City*, Oxford, 1988.

Maritime and town laws
M. Bateson, 'The laws of Breteuil', *English Historical Review*, 15 (1900); 16 (1901).

W. Ebel, 'Lübisches Recht im Ostseeraum', in C. Haase (ed.), *Die Stadt des Mittelalters*, revd edn, 3 vols, Darmstadt, 1976–8.

E. Frankot, *Of Laws of Ships and Shipmen: Medieval maritime law and its practice in the towns of northern Europe*, forthcoming, 2007.

R. Urena y Smenjaud, *Fuero de Cuenca*, Madrid, 1935.

The Contado of Lucca
V. Tirelli, 'Lucca nella seconda metà del secola XII: società e instituzioni', in *I ceti dirigenti dell'età comunale nei secoli XII e XIII*, Pisa, 1982.

D. Waley, *The Italian City Republics*, 3rd edn, London, 1988.

Communal movements, Lombard League
A. MacKay, *Spain in the Middle Ages: From frontier to Empire, 1000–1500*, London, 1977.

G. Tabacco, *The Struggle for Power in Medieval Italy: Structures of political rule*, Cambridge, 1989.

B. Tate and M. Tate, *The Pilgrim Route to Santiago*, Oxford, 1987.

D. Waley, *The Italian City Republics*, 3rd edn, London, 1988.

Towns, fairs and passes
R.H. Britnell, *The Commercialization of English Society, 1000–1500*, Cambridge, 1993.

B.M.S. Campbell *et al.*, *A Medieval Capital and its Grain Supply*, London, 1993.

J.M. Murray, *Bruges, Cradle of Capitalism, 1280–1390*, Cambridge, 2005.

N. Ohler, *The Medieval Traveller*, Woodbridge, 1989.

H. Planitz, *Die Deutsche Stadt im Mittelalter*, Graz, 1954.

N.J.G. Pounds, *An Economic History of Medieval Europe*, 2nd edn, Harlow, 1994.

J.E. Tyler, *The Alpine Passes*, Oxford, 1930.

Environmental change
A.T. Grove and O. Rackham, *The Nature of Mediterranean Europe: An ecological history*, New Haven, 2001.

K. Kirby and C. Watkins, *The Ecological History of European Forests*, Wallingford, 1998.

P. Szabo, *Woodland and Forest in Medieval Hungary*, London, 2000.

J. Thirsk (ed.), *The English Rural Landscape*, Oxford, 2000.

Latin episcopal sees in the 13th century
R. Bartlett, *The Making of Europe: Conquest, colonization and cultural change, 950–1350*, London, 1993.

C. Morris, *The Papal Monarchy: The Western Church from 1050–1250*, Oxford, 1989.

Monks, mendicants, béguines, humiliati
F. Andrews, *The Early Humiliati*, Cambridge, 1999.

F. Andrews, *The Other Friars: Carmelites, Augustinians, Sack and Pied Friars*, Woodbridge, 2006.

B.M. Bolton, *The Medieval Reformation*, London, 1983.

L. Bourdua, *The Franciscans and Art Patronage in late medieval Italy*, Cambridge, 2004.

Maria Motta Broggi, 'Il catalogo del 1298', in M.P. Alberzoni *et al.* (eds), *Sulle Tracce degli Umiliati*, Milan, 1997, pp. 3–44.

R.B. Brooke, *The Coming of the Friars*, London, 1975.

J.R. Burton, *The Monastic and Religious Orders in Britain, 1000–1300*, Cambridge, 1994.

W.A. Hinnebusch, *The History of the Dominican Order*, 2 vols, New York, 1973.

C.H. Lawrence, *The Friars*, London, 1994.

C.H. Lawrence, *Medieval Monasticism*, 3rd edn, Harlow, 2001.

L.J. Lekai, *The White Monks*, Okauchee, 1953.

L.K. Little, *Religious Poverty and the Profit Economy*, London, 1978.

L.J.R. Milis, *Angelic Monks and Earthly Men: Monasticism and its meaning to medieval society*, Woodbridge, 1992.

J. Moorman, *A History of the Franciscan Order from its Origins to the Year 1517*, Oxford, 1968.

S. Murk-Jansen, *Brides in the Desert: The spirituality of the Beguines*, London, 1998.

W. Simons, *Beguine Communities in the medieval Low Countries, 1200–1565*, Philadelphia, 2001.

R.W. Southern, *Western Society and the Church in the Middle Ages*, Harmondsworth, 1973.

The Conciliar Fathers, 1215
B.M. Bolton, 'A show with a meaning: Innocent III's approach to the Fourth Lateran Council, 1215', *Medieval History*, 1 (1991).

J.C. Moore (ed.), *Pope Innocent III and His World*, Aldershot, 1999.

J.C. Moore, *Pope Innocent III, 1160/61–1216*, Leiden, 2003.

J. Sayers, *Innocent III: Leader of Europe, 1198–1216*, London, 1993.

Shrines and revivals, c. 1200–c. 1300
D. Birch, *Pilgrimage to Rome in the Middle Ages*, Woodbridge, 1998.

G. Dickson, *Religious Enthusiasm in the Medieval West: Revivals, crusades, saints*, Aldershot, 2000.

G. Dickson, *Imagining the Children's Crusade*, Basingstoke, 2006.

R.C. Finucane, *Miracles and Pilgrims: Popular beliefs in medieval England*, Basingstoke, 1995.

B. Ward, *Miracles and the Medieval Mind*, revd edn, Philadelphia, 1987.

Heresy, Albigensian crusade and the Inquisition

M. Barber, *The Cathars: Dualist heretics in Languedoc in the High Middle Ages*, Harlow, 2000.

A. Friedlander, *The Hammer of the Inquisitors*, Leiden, 2000.

M.D. Lambert, *Medieval Heresy: Popular movements from the Gregorian Reform to the Reformation*, 3rd edn, Oxford, 2002.

R.I. Moore, *The Formation of a Persecuting Society*, Oxford, 1987.

A.P. Roach, *The Devil's World: Heresy and society, 1100–1300*, Harlow, 2005.

S. Shahar, *Women in a Medieval Heretical Sect: Agnes and Huguette the Waldensians*, Woodbridge, 2001.

S.L. Waugh and P.D. Diehl (eds), *Christendom and its Discontents: Exclusion, persecution and rebellion, 1000–1500*, Cambridge, 1996.

Anti-semitism, 1096–1306

N. Berend, *At the Gate of Christendom: Jews, Muslims and 'pagans' in medieval Hungary, c.1000–c.1300*, Cambridge, 2001.

M.R. Cohen, *Under Crescent and Cross: The Jews in the Middle Ages*, Princeton, 1994.

R.I. Moore, *The Formation of a Persecuting Society*, Oxford, 1987.

K.R. Stow, *Alienated Minority: The Jews of medieval Latin Europe*, Cambridge, MA, 1992.

The 12th-century Renaissance

R.L. Benson and G. Constable (eds), *Renaissance and Renewal in the Twelfth Century*, Cambridge, MA, 1982.

C.H. Haskins, *The Renaissance of the Twelfth Century*, Cambridge, MA, 1927.

C. Morris, *The Discovery of the Individual, 1050–1200*, London, 1972.

R.N. Swanson, *The Twelfth-century Renaissance*, Manchester, 1999.

The emergence of universities

A.B. Cobban, *The Medieval Universities: Their development and organisation*, London, 1975.

A.B. Cobban, *English University Life in the Middle Ages*, London, 1999.

S.C. Ferruolo, *The Origins of the University: The schools of Paris and their critics, 1100–1215*, Stanford, 1985.

H. de Ridder-Symoens (ed.), *A History of the University of Europe*, vol. 1, Cambridge, 1992.

French epic

G. Burgess (ed.), *The Song of Roland*, Harmondsworth, 1990.

J.J. Duggan (ed.), *La Chanson de Roland/The Song of Roland: The French corpus*, 3 vols, Turnhout, 2005.

D.D.R. Owen, *The Legend of Roland: A pageant of the Middle Ages*, London, 1973.

K. Pratt, *Roland and Charlemagne in Europe: Essays on the reception and transformation of a legend*, London, 1996.

Troubadours

W.E. Burgwinkle Garland (ed.), *'Razos' and Troubadour Songs*, New York and London, 1990.

S. Gaunt and S. Kay (eds), *The Troubadours: An introduction*, Cambridge, 1999.

M. Egan (ed.), *Les vies des troubadours*, Paris, 1985.

L. Paterson, *The World of the Troubadours: Medieval Occitan society, c.1100–c.1300*, Cambridge, 1993.

Architecture

C.F. Barnes, *Villard de Honnecourt, the Artist and his Drawings: A critical bibliography*, Boston, MA, 1982.

J. Bony, *French Gothic Architecture of the 12th and 13th Centuries*, Berkeley and London, 1983.

T. Bowie, *The Sketchbook of Villard de Honnecourt*, Bloomington and London, 1959.

F. Bucher, *Architector: The lodge books and sketch-books of medieval architects*, New York, 1979.

K.J. Conant, *Carolingian and Romanesque Architecture 800–1200*, 3rd edn, Harmondsworth, 1973.

A. Erlande-Brandenburg, *The Cathedral Builders of the Middle Ages*, London, 1995.

L. Grodecki, *Gothic Architecture*, London, 1986.

H.R. Hahnloser, *Villard de Honnecourt*, 2nd edn, Graz, 1972.

Abbot Suger, *On the Abbey Church of St Denis and Its Art Treasures*, ed. E. Panofsky, Princeton, 1946.

G. Zarnecki, *Art of the Medieval World*, Englewood Cliffs and New York, 1975.

Le Carnet de Villard de Honnecourt: L'art et les techniques d'un constructeur gothique, Paris, 2001. [CD Rom]

Westminster Palace

P. Binski, *The Painted Chamber at Westminster*, London, 1986.

H.M. Colvin, R. Allen Brown and A.J. Taylor, *The History of the King's Works: The Middle Ages*, London, 1963.

C. Riding and J. Riding (eds), *The Houses of Parliament: History, art and architecture*, London, 2000.

La Sainte Chapelle

M. Aubert and J. Verrier (eds), *Les Vitraux de Notre Dame et de la Sainte-Chapelle de Paris*, Corpus Vitrearum Medii Aevi: France I, 1959.

B. Brenk, 'The Sainte Chapelle as a Capetian political program', in V.C. Raguin, K.L. Brush and P. Draper (eds), *Artistic Integration in Gothic Buildings*, Toronto, 1995, pp. 195–207.

Language

R. Wright, *Late Latin and Early Romance in Spain and Carolingian France*, Liverpool, 1982.

R. Wright (ed.), *Latin and the Romance Languages in the Early Middle Ages*, Philadelphia, 1996.

Western travellers

C. Dawson (ed.), *The Mongol Mission: Narratives and letters of the Franciscan missionaries in Mongolia and China*, London, 1955; reprinted as *Mission to Asia*, Toronto, 1980.

P. Jackson, *The Mongols and the West 1221–1410*, Harlow, 2005.

The Hundred Years War

C.T. Allmand, *The Hundred Years War*, revd edn, Cambridge, 2001.

M. Barber, *The Angevin Legacy and the Hundred Years War, 1250–1340*, Oxford, 1990.

P. Contamine, *War in the Middle Ages*, Oxford, 1984.

A. Curry, *The Hundred Years War*, revd edn, Basingstoke, 2003.

J. Sumption, *The Hundred Years War*, 2 vols, London, 1990–99.

Growth of the Burgundian state

D. Nicholas, *Medieval Flanders*, Harlow, 1992.

W. Prevenier and W. Blockmans, *The Promised Lands: The Low Countries under Burgundian rule, 1369–1530*, Philadelphia, 1999.

R. Vaughan, *Philip the Bold*, London, 1962/2002.

R. Vaughan, *John the Fearless*, London, 1966/2002.

R. Vaughan, *Philip the Good*, London, 1970/2002.

R. Vaughan, *Charles the Bold*, London, 1973/2002.

Scotland

G.W.S. Barrow, *Robert Bruce and the Community of the Realm of Scotland*, 4th edn, Edinburgh, 2005.

A. Grant, *Independence and Nationhood: Scotland, 1306–1469*, London, 1984.

B. Harris and A.R. MacDonald (eds), *Scotland: The making and unmaking of the nation, c.1100–1707. Vol. I: The Scottish Nation, origins to c.1500*, Dundee, 2006.

A.J. Macdonald, *Border Bloodshed: Scotland and England at war, 1369–1403*, East Linton, 2000.

R. Nicholson, *Scotland: The later Middle Ages*, Edinburgh, 1975.

Wales

A.D. Carr, *Medieval Wales*, Basingstoke, 1995.

R.R. Davies, *Conquest, Co-existence and Compromise: Wales, 1063–1415*, Oxford, 1987.

A.J. Taylor, *The Welsh Castles of Edward I*, London, 1986.

D. Walker, *Medieval Wales*, Cambridge, 1990.

Ireland

A. Cosgrove (ed.), *A New History of Ireland*, Vol. II, Oxford, 1987.

R. Frame, *Colonial Ireland, 1169–1369*, Dublin, 1981.

K. Nicholls, *Gaelic and Gaelicized Ireland in the Middle Ages*, 2nd edn, Dublin, 2003.

K. Simms, *From Kings to Warlords: The changing political structures of Gaelic Ireland in the later Middle Ages*, Woodbridge, 1987.

Switzerland

E. Bonjour, H.S. Offler and G.R. Potter, *A Short History of Switzerland*, Oxford, 1952.

A. Dado *et al.*, *Ticino medievale: Storia di una terra lombarda*, Locarno, 1990.

H. Heibling *et al.*, *Handbuch der Schweizer Geschichte*, 2 vols, Zurich, 1980.

Scandinavia

K. Helle (ed.), *The Cambridge History of Scandinavia*, vol. 1, Cambridge, 2003.

B. Sawyer and P. Sawyer, *Medieval Scandinavia: From conversion to Reformation, c.800–1500*, Minneapolis and London, 1993.

Emperors and princes: Germany

G. Benneke, *Maximilian I (1459–1519): An analytical biography*, London, 1982.

H. Cohn, *The Government of the Rhine Palatine in the Fifteenth Century*, London, 1965.

F.R.H. Du Boulay, *Germany in the Later Middle Ages*, London, 1983.

H.S. Offler, 'Aspects of government in the late medieval empire', in J.R. Hale *et al.* (eds), *Europe in the Later Middle Ages*, London, 1962.

Italy

D. Hay and J. Law, *Italy in the Age of the Renaissance, 1380–1530*, Harlow, 1989.

J. Larner, *Italy in the Age of Dante and Petrarch, 1216–1380*, Harlow, 1980.

Spain and Portugal

T.N. Bisson, *The Medieval Crown of Aragon*, Oxford, 1986.

R. Costa Gomes, *The Making of a Court Society: Kings and nobles in late medieval Portugal*, Cambridge, 2003.

J. Edwards, *The Spain of the Catholic Monarchs, 1474–1520*, Oxford, 2000.

S. Haliczer, *The Comuneros of Castile: The forging of a revolution, 1475–1521*, Wisconsin, 1981.

A. MacKay, *Spain in the Middle Ages: From frontier to empire*, London, 1977.

B.F. Reilly, *The Medieval Spains*, Cambridge, 1993.

The Wars of the Roses

C. Carpenter, *The Wars of the Roses: Politics and the constitution in England, c. 1437–1509*, Cambridge, 1997.

J. Gillingham, *The Wars of the Roses*, new edn, London, 2001.

A. Goodman, *The Wars of the Roses: Military activity and English society, 1452–97*, London, 1981.

A. Goodman, *The Wars of the Roses: The soldier's experience*, Stroud, 2005.

A.J. Pollard (ed.), *The Wars of the Roses*, 2nd edn, Basingstoke, 2001.

Turkey and the crusade

F. Babinger, *Mehmed the Conqueror and his Time*, Princeton, 1978.

J.V.A. Fine, *The Late Medieval Balkans*, Ann Arbor, 1987.

N. Housley, *The Later Crusades from Lyons to Alcazar, 1274–1580*, Oxford, 1992.

R.P. Lindner, *Nomads and Ottomans in Medieval Anatolia*, Bloomington, 1983.

E. Zachariadou, *Trade and Crusade*, Venice, 1983.

Lithuania and Poland

E. Christiansen, *The Northern Crusade*, London, 1988.

R.I. Frost, *The Oxford History of the Polish-Lithuanian Union*, forthcoming.

S.C. Rowell, *Lithuania Ascending: A pagan empire within east central Europe, 1295–1345*, Cambridge, 1994.

Muscovy
R.O. Crummey, *The Formation of Muscovy, 1304–1613*, London, 1987.

J. Fennell, *The Crisis of Medieval Russia, 1200–1304*, London, 1983.

J. Martin, *Medieval Russia, 980–1584*, Cambridge, 1995.

J. Meyendorff, *Byzantium and the Rise of Russia*, Cambridge, 1981.

Fiscality in France
J.B. Henneman, *Royal Taxation in Fourteenth Century France*, 2 vols, Princeton and Philadelphia, 1971–6.

J.R. Major, *Representative Government in Early Modern France*, New Haven and London, 1980.

M. Wolfe, *The Fiscal System of Renaissance France*, New Haven, 1972.

Burgundy, Germany, Portugal *see* The Growth of the Burgundian State; Emperors and Princes: Germany; Spain and Portugal, *above*.

Castilian *corregidores*
A. Bermúdez Aznar, *El corregidor en Castilla durante la baja edad media (1348–1474)*, Murcia, 1974.

S. Haliczer, *The Comuneros of Castile: The forging of a revolution, 1475–1521*, Wisconsin, 1981.

Representation at the Castilian *cortes*
W. Piskorski, *Las cortes de Castilla en el periodo de tránsito de la edad media a la edad moderna (1188–1520)*, Barcelona, 1930.

C.O. Serrano, *Las cortes de Castilla y León y la crisis del reino (1445–1474): El registro de cortes*, Burgos, 1986.

Parliamentary representation in England
G. Holmes, *The Good Parliament*, Oxford, 1975.

M. McKisack, *The Parliamentary Representation of the English Boroughs during the Middle Ages*, Oxford, 1932.

J.S. Roskell, *The Commons in the Parliament of 1422*, Manchester, 1954.

J.S. Roskell *et al.* (eds), *The History of Parliament: The House of Commons, 1386–1421*, Stroud, 1993.

The Great Famine
B.M.S. Campbell (ed.), *Before the Black Death: Studies in the 'crisis' of the early fourteenth century*, Manchester, 1991.

B.M.S. Campbell, *English Seigniorial Agriculture, 1250–1450*, Oxford, 2000.

W.C. Jordan, *The Great Famine: Northern Europe in the fourteenth century*, Princton, 1996.

The Black Death
S.K. Cohn, *The Black Death Transformed*, London, 2002.

R. Horrox, *The Black Death*, Manchester, 1994.

P. Ziegler, *The Black Death*, new edn, Stroud, 2003.

Deserted villages
M. Beresford, *The Lost Villages of England*, revd edn, Stroud, 1998.

Transhumance
C.J. Bishko, 'The Castilian as plainsman: the medieval ranching frontier in La Mancha and Extremadura', in A.R. Lewis and T.F. McGann (eds), *The New World Looks at its History*, Austin, 1963.

E.H. Carrier, *Water and Grass: A study in the pastoral economy of southern Europe*, London, 1932.

J. Klein, *The Mesta: A study of Spanish economic history, 1273–1836*, Cambridge, MA, 1920.

E. Le Roy Ladurie, *Montaillou: Cathars and Catholics in a French village, 1294–1324*, London, 1978.

M.L. Ryder, *Sheep and Man*, London, 1983.

C.D. Smith, *Western Mediterranean Europe: A historical geography of Italy, Spain and southern France since the Neolithic*, London, 1979.

Later medieval towns

N. Angermann and K. Friedland (eds), *Markt und Kontor der Hanse*, Cologne, 2002.

M. Brisbane and D. Gaimster (eds), *Novgorod: The archaeology of a Russian medieval city and its hinterland*, London, 2001.

H. Inalcik, 'The policy of Mehmed II toward the Greek population of Istanbul and the Byzantine buildings of the city', *Dumbarton Oaks Papers*, 23–4 (1969–70).

B. Lewis, *Istanbul and the Civilization of the Ottoman Empire*, Norman, 1963.

M. Lynch, M. Spearman and G. Stell (eds), *The Scottish Medieval Town*, Edinburgh, 1988.

D. Nicholas, *The Later Medieval City, 1300–1500*, London, 1997.

A. Collantes de Terán Sánchez, *Sevilla en la baja edad media: la ciudad y sus hombres*, 2nd edn, Seville, 1984.

W. Vischer, 'Geschichte des schwäbishen Städtebundes der Jahre 1376–1389', *Forschungen zur deutschen Geschichte*, 2 (1862).

Financial centres in western Europe

R. De Roover, *The Rise and Decline of the Medici Bank*, Cambridge, MA, 1963.

E.S. Hunt and J. Murray, *A History of Business in Medieval Europe, 1200–1500*, Cambridge, 1999.

A. MacKay, *Money and Prices in Fifteenth-century Castile*, London, 1981.

J. Murray, *Bruges, Cradle of Capitalism, 1280–1390*, Cambridge, 2005.

P. Spufford, *Money and its Uses in Medieval Europe*, Cambridge, 1988.

The German Hanse and herring

P. Dollinger, *The German Hansa*, London, 1970/1999.

K. Friedland, *Die Hanse*, Stuttgart, 1991.

C. Jahnke, *Das Silber des Meeres*, Cologne, 2000.

T.R. Lloyd, *England and the German Hanse, 1157–1611*, Cambridge, 1991.

Popular revolts

S.J. Cohn, *Popular Protest in Late Medieval Europe*, Manchester, 2004.

R.B. Dobson (ed.), *The Peasants' Revolt of 1381*, 2nd edn, London, 1983.

A. Dunn, *The Peasants' Revolt: England's failed revlution of 1381*, Stroud, 2004.

G. Fourquin, *The Anatomy of Popular Rebellion in the Middle Ages*, New York, 1978.

Aliens in England

J.L. Bolton, 'Irish migration to England in late medieval England', *Irish Historical Studies*, 32 (2000), pp. 1–21.

S. Thrupp, 'A survey of the alien population of England in 1440', *Speculum*, 32 (1957), pp. 262–73.

The Avignon papacy; the Schism and the Councils; the Papal states

E. Goeller (ed.), *Die Einnahmen der apostolischen Kammer unter Johan XXII*, Paderborn, 1910.

W.F. Lunt, *Papal Revenues in the Middle Ages*, 2 vols, New York, 1934.

G. Mollat, *The Popes at Avignon, 1305–1378*, Edinburgh, 1963.

J.B. Morrall, *Gerson and the Great Schism*, Manchester, 1960.

P. Partner, *The Papal State under Martin V*, London, 1958.

P. Partner, *The Lands of St Peter: The papal state in the Middle Ages and the early Renaissance*, London, 1972.

Y. Renouard, *The Avignon Papacy, 1305–1403*, London, 1970.

R.N. Swanson, *Universities, Academics and the Great Schism*, Cambridge, 1979.

W. Ullmann, *The Origins of the Great Schism*, London, 1948.

D. Waley, *The Papal State in the Thirteenth Century*, London, 1961.

The papal Penitentiary

K. Salonen, *The Penitentiary as a Well of Grace in the Late Middle Ages: The example of the province of Uppsala, 1448–1527*, Helsinki, 2001.

K. Salonen and C. Krötzl (eds), *The Roman Curia, The Apostolic Penitentiary and the Partes in the Later Middle Ages*, Rome, 2003.

Byzantine cultural and monastic centres

R. Browning, *The Byzantine Empire*, London, 1980.

J.M. Hussey, *The Orthodox Church in the Byzantine Empire*, Oxford, 1986.

D.M. Nicol, *Meteora: The Rock Monasteries of Thessaly*, London, 1963.

L. Rodley, *Cave Monasteries of Byzantine Cappadocia*, Cambridge, 1985.

S. Runciman, *Mistra*, London, 1980.

C.M. Woodhouse, *Gemistos Plethon: The last of the Hellenes*, Oxford, 1986.

Bohemia and Hussite Wars

F.M. Bartos, *The Hussite Revolution, 1424–37*, Boulder, 1986.

T.A. Fudge, *The Crusade Against Heretics in Bohemia, 1418–1437: Sources and documents*, Aldershot, 2002.

Jewish and *conversos* communities

M.R. Cohen, *Under Crescent and Cross: The Jews in the Middle Ages*, Princeton, 1994.

J. Edwards, *The Jews in Christian Europe*, London, 1991.

J. Edwards, *The Jews in Western Europe, 1400–1600*, Manchester, 1994.

A. Haverkamp (ed.), *Zur Geschichte der Juden im deutschland des Späten Mittelalters und der Frühen Neuzeit*, Stuttgart, 1981.

G.D Starr-le Beau, *In the Shadow of the Virgin: Inquisitors, friars and conversos in Guadalupe, Spain*, Princeton, 2003.

Margery Kempe and pilgrimage

A. Goodman, *Margery Kempe and her World*, Harlow, 2002.

J. van Herwaarden, *Between Saint James and Erasmus*, Leiden, 2003.

D. Webb, *Medieval European Pilgrimage, c.700–1500*, Basingstoke, 2002.

B.A. Windeatt (ed.), *The Book of Margery Kempe*, Harlow, 2000/Woodbridge, 2004.

Knightly journeys

J.R. Goodman, *Chivalry and Exploration, 1298–1630*, Woodbridge, 1998.

W. Paravicini (ed.), *Europäische Reiseberichte des späten Mittelalters: Eine analytische Bibliographie*, 3 vols, Frankfurt-am-Main, 1994–2000.

J.-P. Rubiés, *Travel and Ethnology in the Renaissance*, Cambridge, 2000.

Froissart's world

Jean Froissart, *Chronicles*, ed. G. Brereton, Harmondsworth, 1978.

J.J.N. Palmer (ed.), *Froissart: Historian*, Woodbridge, 1981.

Journeys of major Italian artists

J. Pope-Hennessey, *Italian Gothic Sculpture*, London, 1965.

A. Smart, *The Dawn of Italian Painting*, Oxford, 1978.

J. White, *Art and Architecture in Italy, 1250–1400*, Harmondsworth, 1966.

Guillaume Dufay

J.E. Cumming, *The Motet in the Age of Du Fay*, Cambridge, 1999.

D. Fallows, *Dufay*, London, 1982.

Rediscovery of classical texts

G. Billanovich, 'Petrarch and the textual tradition of Livy', *Journal of the Warburg and Courtauld Institutes*, 14 (1951), pp. 137–203.

L.D. Reynolds (ed.), *Texts and Transmissions: A survey of the Latin classics*, Oxford, 1983.

L.D. Reynolds and N.G. Wilson (eds), *Scribes and Scholars: A guide to the transmission of Greek and Latin literature*, Oxford, 1968.

R. Sabbadini, *Le scoperte dei codici latini e greci ne' secoli XIV e XV*, 2 vols, Florence, 1905–14.

Printing

E. Eisenstein, *The Printing Revolution in Early Modern Europe*, 2nd edn, Cambridge, 2005.

L. Febvre and H.-J. Martin, *The Coming of the Book: The impact of printing, 1450–1800*, London and New York, 1990.

L. Hellinga and J.B. Trapp, *The Cambridge History of the Book in Britain: Vol. III, 1400–1557*, Cambridge, 1999.

Universities

A.B. Cobban, *English University Life in the Middle Ages*, London, 1999.

W.J. Courtenay, *Parisian Scholars in the Early Fourteenth Century: A social portrait*, Cambridge, 1999.

H. de Ridder-Symoens (ed.), *A History of the University of Europe*, vol. 1, Cambridge, 1992.

European expansion

F. Fernandez-Armesto, *Before Columbus: Exploration and colonisation from the Mediterranean to the Atlantic, 1229–1492*, London, 1987.

F. Fernandez-Armesto, *Columbus*, Oxford, 1991.

M. Newitt, *A History of Portuguese Overseas Expansion, 1400–1668*, London, 2004.

J.S.R. Phillips, *The Medieval Expansion of Europe*, 2nd edn, Oxford, 1998.

P.E. Russell, *Prince Henry the Navigator: The rise and fall of a cultural hero*, Oxford, 1984.

Index: Atlas of Medieval Europe

Toledo, Spain 9, 14, 42, 44, 91, 133, 183, 190, 276
Tonnere, France 204
Tordesillas, treaty of (1494) 295
Torhout, Belgium 159
Toro, battle of (1476) 226
Torre, della, Milanese family 121
Tortosa, Disputation at (1415) 276
Tortosa, Spain 105
Totila, Gothic leader 10
Toulouse, France 9, 37, 164, 174, 176, 180, 183,
    186
Toulouse, Raymond, count of 110, 111
Touraine, France 103
Tournai/Doornik, Belgium 9, 288
Tours, France 70, 72, 77, 164, 204
Tours, France, battle of (732) 14
Tours, Gregory of, bishop 10–11
Tours, Martin of, monk 66, 68, 70
trade 57, 61–3, 107, 119, 121, 213–14, 252, 256,
    294; Alpine routes 159–60; maritime 147;
    routes 157–9
Trani, Italy 90, 167
transhumance 248–9
Transylvania, Romania 161
Trastámaran dynasty 224
travellers 159–60, 197, 281–8
Trebizond, Turkey 112, 119, 226, 271
Trent, Italy 216
Treviso, Italy 123, 216, 217, 286
Trier, Germany 6, 9, 79, 96, 206, 279, 280
Trnovo, Bulgaria 226
Trondheim, Norway 33, 163
troubadours 186–7
Troyes, France 159; Council of (129) 116; treaty of
    (1420) 203
Tuam, Ireland 164
Tuchinat uprising (1360s) 202
Tudellén, treaty of (1151) 105
Tunis, Tunisia 110, 113, 133
Turin/Torino, Italy 123, 288
Turkey, Turks 111, 226–8, 276
Tuscany, Italy 16, 141, 169, 286
Tuscia, Italy 269
Tver', Russia 229, 230
Tyler, Wat, peasant leader 261
Tyre, Lebanon 114

Ubeda, Spain 145

Uclés, Spain 133
Uí Néill, Irish dynasty 36
Ukraine 87
Ulfila, missionary 66
Ulm, Germany 250
Umbria, Italy 16
Ummayad caliphate 42
universities 182, 183–4, 271–2, 292–4
Uppsala, Sweden 33, 95, 163
Urban II, pope 109, 110
Urban V, pope 265
Urban VI, pope 266, 268, 294
Urbino, Italy 269
Uri, Switzerland 212
Utraquist, Hussite sect 272, 274

Vaclav/Wenceslas II, king of Bohemia and Poland
    127, 129
Vaillant, Jean, peasant leader 261
Valdemar IV (Atterdag), king of Denmark 213
Valencia, Spain 42, 44, 105, 133, 135, 144–5, 164,
    218, 219; battle of (1146) 105; battle of (1236)
    42
Valenciennes, France 131
Valens, Emperor 7
Valldaura, Spain 107
Vallombrosa, Italy 80
Valois, Charles of, brother of Philip IV 121, 131
Valois dynasty, dukes of Burgundy, 204–6, 214;
    see also Charles the Bold; John the Fearless; Philip
    the Bold; Philip the Good
Vandals, tribe 9, 10, 12, 59, 66
Värmland, Norway 33
Varna, battle of (1444) 228
Varro, Marcus Terentius, Roman scholar 289
Vaspurakan, Turkey 24
vassalage 39
Vastergarn, Gotland 63
Vättern, Lake 33
Vendôme, France 103
Veneto, Italy 160
Venezuela, America 295
Venice, Italy 16, 18, 80, 107, 110, 112, 119, 123,
    156, 160, 217, 218, 279, 281
Ventadorn, Bernard de, troubadour 186
Ventadorn, Maria de, troubadour 186
Vercelli, Italy 121, 289
Verdun, France 20; treaty of (843) 131